THE NEW
CAMBRIDGE MODERN HISTORY

ADVISORY COMMITTEE
SIR GEORGE CLARK   SIR JAMES BUTLER
J. P. T. BURY   E. A. BENIANS

XIII
COMPANION VOLUME

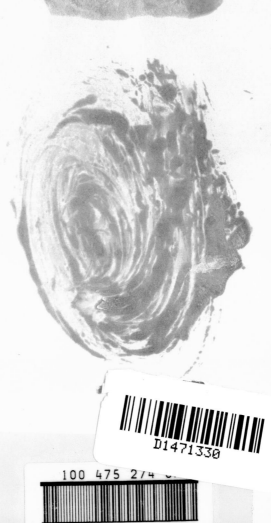

THE NEW
CAMBRIDGE MODERN
HISTORY

XIII
COMPANION VOLUME

EDITED BY
PETER BURKE

CAMBRIDGE UNIVERSITY PRESS

CAMBRIDGE

LONDON   NEW YORK   NEW ROCHELLE

MELBOURNE   SYDNEY

Published by the Press Syndicate of the University of Cambridge
The Pitt Building, Trumpington Street, Cambridge CB2 1RP
32 East 57th Street, New York, NY 10022, USA
296 Beaconsfield Parade, Middle Park, Melbourne 3206, Australia

First published 1979
First paperback edition 1980

Printed in Great Britain at the
University Press, Cambridge

British Library Cataloguing in Publication Data

The New Cambridge Modern History.
Vol. 13: Companion volume

1. History, Modern
I. Burke, Peter, *b. 1937*
909.08   D208   57-14935

ISBN 0 521 22128 5 hard covers
ISBN 0 521 28017 6 paperback

CONTENTS

CONTENTS

ILLUSTRATIONS

CHAPTER I

INTRODUCTION:
CONCEPTS OF CONTINUITY
AND CHANGE IN HISTORY

CONTINUITY and change: in a sense this is what all historians study all the time, and it is no surprise to find historical monographs on a wide variety of subjects appearing under this kind of title.[1] Historians are professionally concerned with change, and therefore with the absence of change (which is one of the ways of defining continuity). If volumes I–XII of the *New Cambridge Modern History* have already dealt with these themes, the reader may well be asking what is the point of a thirteenth volume, which covers the same period as all the rest, from the late fifteenth to the mid-twentieth century. The short answer to this question is that there is more than one way of being concerned with change, or more than one kind of change to be concerned with.

Historians have traditionally dealt with the narrative of events, especially political events; Thucydides, Tacitus, Guicciardini, Clarendon and Ranke are among the great masters of this genre in the West. This style of history involves a close study of changes over the short-term. The traditional historian may also be interested in changes over the long-term; he may choose his subject because he thinks it a 'turning-point' in history; but he is likely to assume rather than to argue that a break in continuity occurred at this point. Guicciardini began his *History of Italy* and Ranke began his *Latin and Teutonic Nations* with the turning-point of the 1490s, just like the old and the *New Cambridge Modern History*, but they did not justify their choice in any detail. The narrative mode does not allow it. In the twentieth century, however, we have seen a break with traditional narrative history which, like the break with the traditional novel or with representational art or with classical music, is one of the important cultural 'discontinuities' of our time. Economic, social and cultural historians have rebelled against the dominance of the short-term and the political. The critique of traditional history has been sharpest and most articulate in France, from the days of François Simiand to those of Fernand Braudel.[2]

---

[1] C. Hill, *Change and Continuity in Seventeenth-Century England* (London, 1974); M. Kolinsky, *Continuity and Change in European Society: Germany, France and Italy since 1870* (London, 1974); R. O'Day and F. Heal (eds.), *Continuity and Change: Personnel and Administration of the Church in England, 1500–1642* (London, 1976).

[2] F. Simiand, 'Méthode Historique et Science Sociale' (1903), repr. in *Annales E.S.C.*, 15, 1960, 83–119; F. Braudel, 'History and the Social Sciences' (1958), trans. in P. Burke (ed.), *Economy and Society in Early Modern Europe* (London, 1972), pp. 11–40. There had been a similar reaction against the history of events in the late eighteenth century.

The essential criticism of *histoire événementielle*, as the French call it, 'the history of events', is that it is superficial. Events are mere 'surface disturbances' says Braudel, 'crests of foam that the tides of history carry on their strong backs'. In place of the history of events – or rather, to supplement it – Braudel offers a history of the middle-term and the long-term (*la longue durée*). His great work on the Mediterranean world in the age of Philip II is divided into three parts to emphasise his favourite point that time moves at different speeds. Part I deals with geographical time, with the slowly changing relationship between man and his physical environment; mountains and plains, coasts and islands, climate and communications. In part II, Braudel changes gear to deal with 'social time', with the rather more rapid changes in economic, social and political systems. In part III he accelerates into 'individual time', time as contemporaries experienced it, and he writes in more or less traditional style about the conflict between the Spanish and the Ottoman empires in the reign of Philip II, about the Holy League and the battle of Lepanto.[1]

There is only one Braudel but the approach to history in terms of *structure* and *conjoncture* (structures and trends – not quite the same as continuity and change) has been followed by a number of historians of the so-called '*Annales* school', for example in Pierre Goubert's book on Beauvais and the countryside around it, and in Pierre Chaunu's mammoth study of the trade between Seville and the Americas in the sixteenth and seventeenth centuries.[2]

Marxists too have long been trying to go behind the history of events to that of the 'underlying' economic and social structures. Marx never wrote a work of pure history, although there are penetrating passages of historical analysis in a number of his books, and Engels' *Peasant War in Germany* was traditional in form, however revolutionary in its political sympathies, but later Marxists have produced a new kind of history not unlike that of the *Annales* school. Outstanding examples include Halvdan Koht's *Norwegian Peasant Revolts* (1926), Jan Romein's *The Lowlands by the Sea* (1934), and Emilio Sereni's *Capitalism in the Countryside* (1947), or more recently, Witold Kula's *Economic Theory of the Feudal System* (1962), Edward Thompson's *The Making of the English Working Class* (1963), and Maurice Agulhon's *The Republic in the Village* (1970).[3]

Another approach to change over the long-term was offered by Max Weber, who was a historian before he was a sociologist. His controversial

---

[1] F. Braudel, *The Mediterranean and the Mediterranean World in the Age of Philip II* (1949), Eng. trans., 2 vols, New York and London, 1972–3.

[2] P. Goubert, *Beauvais et le Beauvaisis de 1600 à 1730* (Paris, 1960); H. and P. Chaunu, *Séville et l'Atlantique, 1504–1650* (8 vols, Paris, 1955–9).

[3] H. Koht, *Norsk Bondereising* (Oslo, 1926); J. Romein, *De Lage Landen bij de Zee* (Utrecht, 1934); E. Sereni, *Il Capitalismo nelle Campagne* (Turin, 1947); W. Kula, *Teoria Ekonomiczna Ustroju Feudalnego* (Warsaw, 1962; Eng. trans., London, 1977); M. Agulhon, *La République au Village* (Paris, 1970).

essay on *The Protestant Ethic and the Spirit of Capitalism* (1904–5) gave a non-Marxist, if not an anti-Marxist, account of social trends, emphasising the importance of religious ideas as well as that of economic factors in the process of social change. He devoted much of his life to an exploration of the increasingly rational organisation of Western society and culture over the last few centuries; the 'rationalisation', as he called it, of law and government, business, religion, even music.[1]

Some practising historians have been influenced by Weber; more by the *Annales* school; still more by Marxism. As a result, continuity and change are ceasing to be taken for granted. They have become problematic, the subject of debate within the profession. Hence this pair of concepts need to be examined in some detail.

In this pair, 'continuity' is something of a residual category. Like most residual categories it is ambiguous. 'Continuity' may refer to the absence of change, but the term is also used to describe a particular kind of change, change which is even in rate and constant in direction. The ambiguity is understandable in that historians tend to dislike abstract models, while concrete examples of unchanging societies are impossible to find. In what circumstances can one expect to find continuity? There was a time when historians accepted an equivalent to the physicist's law of inertia. They wrote as if continuity, in one sense or the other, could be taken for granted, while change, especially violent or rapid change, required explanation. 'Why did the French Revolution occur?' was a normal historical question, but 'Why did the old regime last until 1789?' was not. However, in our age of rapid social change, continuity no longer seems self-explanatory, and historians, like other people, are beginning to revise their ideas.[2]

Why does an old regime persist? I am using the term in a deliberately wide sense which is not restricted to forms of political organisation – there are also economic old regimes, demographic old regimes, old regimes in religion, literature, science, architecture. How do all these systems resist change? One answer to this question may be given in terms of tradition. Values, techniques and forms persist because they are 'reproduced' in each successive generation, thanks to the training of the young by parents, teachers, priests, employers and other 'agents of socialisation', as sociologists call them. The family, the school, the church, the workshop and other institutions ensure the survival of the values; the values, internalised by the younger generation, ensure the survival of the institutions. There are two points to be emphasised here. The transmission of culture is, or can be, a self-perpetuating process; but this self-perpetuating process

[1] For introductions to his ideas, see D. G. MacRae, *Weber* (London, 1974), and R. Bendix, *Max Weber: an Intellectual Portrait* (New York, 1960).

[2] A. Gershenkron, *Continuity in History and Other Essays* (Cambridge, Mass., 1968), pp. 11–39; B. Moore, Jr, *Social Origins of Dictatorship and Democracy* (Boston, 1966), pp. 291, 485–7.

is the result of a great deal of hard work. It may seem like 'inertia' from the point of view of the would-be innovator, but not from that of the people involved in the process of handing down traditions.[1]

The classical tradition, for example, has often been described in terms of metaphors like 'survival' or 'inheritance' or 'legacy'; one needs to make an effort to remember that this inheritance was not automatic, that it depended on beating some knowledge of certain classical authors into generation after generation of schoolboys. As a result of this process, the classics could be taken as models by adult writers who produced new poems and plays according to the classical conventions. The history of science is not very different in this respect from the history of literature. We tend to think of science in terms of innovation, but in science as in literature there are models or 'paradigms' which the younger generation were and are trained to follow, so that one historian has been able to describe most scientific work as 'mopping-up operations', in the sense of new discoveries within the framework of a tradition.[2] The traditions themselves change, but only very slowly. In short, there is a cultural *histoire de longue durée* as well as a cultural *histoire événementielle*.

There are other kinds of continuity in history, for which the term 'tradition' does not seem appropriate. Demographic continuity, for example. The population of a given village may remain more or less stationary for centuries, while the individuals composing it make their entrances and their exits, because the birth rate and the death rate (or the relationship between them) remain constant. At this point it may be useful to introduce a mechanical metaphor and to describe the village population as being in a state of 'equilibrium'. In this context 'equilibrium' is a better term than 'continuity' because it draws attention to the fact that a given population often oscillates around a certain figure as if there were 'mechanisms' operating to restore the 'balance' every time it is disturbed. In the long-term, equilibrium may be equated with stability; in the short-term it cannot. In one year a plague may wipe out a third of the village population; after this blow the birthrate is likely to rise until the old population is restored. The birth rate may continue to rise, but if no more food is available, death or migration is likely to cancel out the gains and bring the population back to its old level, a state of 'ecological equilibrium' in which people make demands on their environment which the environment can sustain indefinitely.[3] We might use the biological

[1] P. Bourdieu and J-C. Passeron, *Reproduction in Education, Society and Culture* (Eng. trans., London and Beverly Hills, 1977).

[2] G. Highet, *The Classical Tradition* (Oxford, 1949); R. R. Bolgar, *The Classical Tradition and its Beneficiaries* (Cambridge, 1954); T. S. Kuhn, *The Structure of Scientific Revolutions* (Chicago, 1962), esp. pp. 10–34.

[3] H. J. Habakkuk, *Population Growth and Economic Development since 1750* (Leicester, 1971), pp. 7–24; on ecological equilibrium, R. G. Wilkinson, *Poverty and Progress* (London, 1973); cf. ch. IV below.

metaphor of 'homeostasis' as an alternative to 'equilibrium', or we might use the cybernetic metaphor of 'positive feedback'. The point is to suggest that a society does not change because it does not change, that the various factors inhibiting change may reinforce one another. Blacks in the USA, for example, have a low status because they have a low income, but they have low incomes because they have a low status. They are relatively poor and uneducated because white people are prejudiced against them, but white people are prejudiced against them partly because they are poor and uneducated.

But what about the individuals involved and their freedom of choice? Metaphors like 'equilibrium' are dangerous if they encourage us to forget that a population is composed of individuals who do not respond mechanically to changes in their environment. However, what was happening in the village with a stationary population cannot be understood simply in terms of individual goals. Individual villagers are not concerned to maintain the population at a certain level but to maintain a certain standard of living for themselves and their families. To achieve these goals certain strategies are open to them: to marry or to remain single, to leave the village or to remain in it, and so on. 'Equilibrium' is a name for what emerges from all these individual decisions interacting with natural events over which individuals have no control – notably death – and with cultural traditions (like the local farming and inheritance systems), which constitute the rules of the game which individuals play. As a corrective to human ethnocentrism, it should be added that animals and birds also adapt themselves to their environment by limiting their numbers; storks, for example, practice infanticide.[1]

That society as a whole could be analysed as a set of 'interlocking' or mutually reinforcing mechanisms for self-perpetuation was the central idea of the functionalists, sociologists and social anthropologists of the early twentieth century such as Émile Durkheim, Vilfredo Pareto and Bronislaw Malinowski. They saw not only law and custom but also myth, ritual and religion as ways of maintaining social cohesion, stability or equilibrium. It may not be coincidence that Pareto had been trained as an engineer and Malinowski as a physicist; but their approach, currently somewhat unfashionable in their own disciplines, should not be dismissed as nothing but a mistaken attempt to apply mechanical models to human affairs. Functionalism itself performs a useful intellectual function. To ask about any past belief, practice or institution, 'Did it contribute to social stability?' emancipates us from a tourist's view of the past as a repository of quaint old customs, for example, witchcraft. It has recently been suggested that in Tudor and Stuart England the belief in witches 'helped to uphold the traditional obligations of charity and neighbourliness at a

[1] V. C. Wynne-Edwards, *Animal Dispersion in Relation to Social Behaviour* (Edinburgh, 1962).

time when other social and economic forces were conspiring to weaken them'.[1]

Economic, social, political and even cultural historians can all profit – and some have profited – from the careful use of the concept of equilibrium. Given the growth of her economy from the late sixteenth century onwards, and her long record of technological innovations, it is paradoxical that China did not pass through an industrial revolution at about the same time as Europe. A recent hypothesis to explain this Chinese non-revolution is that the economy was caught in a 'high-level equilibrium trap'. Water transport was relatively cheap for a pre-industrial society, so that there was little encouragement for a transport revolution; agricultural yields were relatively high, diminishing the incentive for further improvements. The situation was not one of stagnation but it was one of equilibrium: 'quantitative growth, qualitative standstill'.[2]

For social historians too the concept of equilibrium may have its uses. From the point of view of an ambitious individual, upward social mobility is a conscious goal; but social mobility may also be seen as a (probably unintended) device or mechanism for preventing changes in the social structure. Movement within the system discourages attempts to change the system. The opportunities it afforded for social mobility may explain why the English old regime survived the eighteenth century while the French old regime did not. Again, Marc Bloch's classic study *Feudal Society* presents the feudal system as an adaptation to a particular milieu (a milieu of invasions, anxiety, 'monetary famine' and so on), a 'system' in the sense that different institutions reinforced one another or interlocked.[3]

Political historians have found concepts like equilibrium and stability useful on occasion. J. H. Plumb has suggested that Sir Robert Walpole created a political system which acquired 'immense inertia' and so persisted 'almost to our own day'.[4] At an international level the concept of the 'balance of power', formulated in the sixteenth century, still seems indispensable. Even cultural historians might benefit from a kind of equilibrium analysis, alien as the term is to their current vocabulary. Malinowski described myth as a story about the past which has the function of justifying the present and thus contributing to social stability. Magna Carta was used in this way by seventeenth-century English

[1] K. V. Thomas, *Religion and the Decline of Magic* (London, 1971), p. 564, a book which makes discriminating use of functional explanations. G. C. Homans, *English Villagers of the Thirteenth Century* (Cambridge, Mass., 1941) is a pioneering work of functionalist history, written by a Harvard sociologist. Cf. M. M. Postan, 'Function and Dialectic in Economic History', in his *Fact and Relevance* (Cambridge, 1971), ch. 4.

[2] M. Elvin, *The Pattern of the Chinese Past* (London, 1973), pp. 298–315.

[3] M. Bloch, *Feudal Society* (1939–40: Eng. trans., London, 1961). The influence of Durkheim may be seen in Bloch's emphasis on social cohesion.

[4] J. H. Plumb, *The Growth of Political Stability in England, 1675–1725* (London, 1967), esp. pp. 187–8.

lawyers in search of precedents.[1] Rituals too may be seen as mechanisms for maintaining society as it is. Coronations, for example, have the function of 'legitimating' the ruler. Even apparently subversive rituals like carnivals may make a contribution to social stability. To use yet another mechanical metaphor, they may act as a 'safety-valve', encouraging the discontented to blow off steam, in other words to play at revolt instead of rebelling in earnest.[2]

To sum up so far. Historians are professionally concerned with change; but to understand why change occurs it is necessary to study the obstacles to change, resistance to change, factors promoting stability or continuity. It was in this area that the functionalists were most successful. Indeed, one might say that they were too successful. They gave such a plausible account of the self-perpetuation process that they made it difficult to understand how major changes ever take place. Hence some sociologists and social anthropologists are now rejecting functionalism and are moving somewhat closer to history.

The second of our pair of concepts, 'change', is so obviously the historian's concern that definition may well appear superfluous; but it may be useful to draw a few distinctions. Change may be gradual or rapid, smooth or violent, and the people living through it may be more or less aware that it is going on. We experience events, and some people even try to control them. We live through trends, but do not experience them directly or totally, and may not be aware that they are occurring. In sixteenth-century Spain, for example, prices rose continually and at an unprecedented rate, owing – say some modern historians – to the import of silver from the New World, which meant that too much money was chasing too few goods. Of course the Spaniards themselves noticed that prices were going up; the prices of specific commodities in specific towns and villages. They accused the Genoese merchants of profiteering or advanced other local or temporary explanations.[3] Short-term fluctuations, in this case as in so many others, prevented contemporaries from seeing the long-term trend, let alone explaining it. The history of long-term trends, the pattern of millions of small events, is usually 'unconscious history', as Braudel calls it.[4] The historian cannot study it by trying to relive the past as it appeared to contemporaries.

What, then, can the historian do? One answer is that he can try to write 'serial history'. 'Serial history' is a new term, coined about 1960, but the

---

[1] F. Thompson, *Magna Carta: its Role in the Making of the English Constitution, 1300–1629* (Minneapolis, 1948).

[2] M. Gluckman, *Custom and Conflict in Africa* (Oxford, 1956), pp. 109–36; V. Turner, *The Ritual Process* (London, 1969), pp. 166–203; P. Burke, *Popular Culture in Early Modern Europe* (London, 1978), ch. 7.

[3] E. J. Hamilton, *American Treasure and the Price Revolution in Spain, 1501–1650* (Cambridge, Mass., 1934).

[4] Braudel, 'History', pp. 26–7.

procedures it describes are at least a generation older. Serial history is the systematic study of long-term trends as they are revealed by a series of relatively homogeneous data; price records, for example. Three famous early examples of serial history are the studies of prices undertaken by François Simiand, Ernest Labrousse and Earl Hamilton, all published between 1932 and 1934.[1] It was, of course, no accident that historians began to take prices seriously at a time of galloping inflation in Germany and the Great Crash in the USA. Simiand offered a historical explanation for the slump and distinguished four phases of economic expansion (A-phases) and four phases of contraction (B-phases) since 1500. Labrousse was concerned with the relative importance of long-term price movements and of seasonal and other short cycles. Hamilton was interested in the impact of American treasure on the Spanish economy between 1501 and 1650; he found that the records of charitable institutions gave him the long series of homogeneous data he needed. It should not be thought, incidentally, that there is no more to price history than writing down a long list of prices for a century or more. To reveal what contemporaries could not see, the general trend, it is necessary to average out the prices charged for different commodities and in different seasons of the year; to compute five-year or ten-year averages, in order to smooth out the short-term trends, and so on.

Whether or not they consciously followed the lead of the price historians, other scholars have also been adopting serial methods. In the late 1940s, the serious study of historical demography began; it was no accident that this was a time of growing concern with the world population explosion. Historical demography, as practised by Louis Henry, Pierre Goubert, E. A. Wrigley and so many others, is a form of serial history – the study of a series of births, marriages and deaths, based on sources, such as parish registers, which provide fairly homogeneous data.[2] At much the same time – a time when the clergy were becoming increasingly worried by the emptying of the churches – Gabriel Le Bras was creating a historical sociology of religion by studying another series of data; episcopal visitations, which revealed the frequency of attendance at Sunday mass and Easter communion in France and other parts of the Catholic world.[3]

This last example of serial history raises certain problems which historians of price and population trends do not have to worry about. They study prices to learn about prices, or birth rates to learn about birth

---

[1] F. Simiand, *Recherches Anciennes et Nouvelles sur le Mouvement Général des Prix* (Paris, 1932); C. E. Labrousse, *Esquisse du Mouvement des Prix et des Revenus en France au 18e Siècle* (Paris, 1933); Hamilton, *Treasure*; cf. P. Chaunu, 'L'Histoire Sérielle', in *Revue Historique*, 243, 1970, 297–320.

[2] For details, see ch. IV below.

[3] For a summary of findings on France and England, see ch. XI below; on the method, P. Chaunu, 'Une Histoire Religieuse Sérielle', in *Revue d'Histoire Moderne*, 12, 1965, 5–34.

rates; whereas Le Bras and his followers study attendance at mass and communion in order to learn about attitudes. They concern themselves with attendance figures as 'indicators' or 'indexes' of religious fervour. (An 'index' may be defined as a 'standardised, reliable, scalar and economical' indicator; an indicator is something measurable which varies with, and so may be used to study, something which is not.)[1] Can devotion be measured in this way? Is the concept 'devotion' precise or objective enough? Does attendance at communion have the same meaning for participants (whose attitudes we are, after all, concerned to discover), in 1970 (say), as in 1870 or 1770? A decline in attendance at mass or communion or a decline in vocations to the priesthood no doubt indicates a more general trend; but what it indicates is not obvious, and must be investigated by other means.

Given this very substantial qualification, there seems to be no limit to the long-term trends which can be investigated by the methods of serial history. Geneviève Bollême has studied changes in popular attitudes as they are revealed by changes in the language of French almanacs in the seventeenth and the eighteenth centuries. Michel Vovelle has studied attitudes to death in eighteenth-century Provence by looking at changes in the conventional formulae of wills; he has also studied a series of altarpieces representing Purgatory.[2] This last example is a reminder that there is a sense in which art historians and archaeologists have long practised serial history without using the term. The concepts 'Renaissance' and 'Baroque', for example, refer to trends over time established by arranging a large number of paintings, sculptures and buildings in chronological order, just as the archaeologist arranges his axe-heads, coins and potsherds. Like the serial historians of prices and populations, archaeologists and art historians are concerned with 'the shape of time'.[4]

In fact, time has several different shapes, of which it may be useful to distinguish three. In the first place, there is the pattern of oscillation round a fixed point, the 'equilibrium' already discussed. A second pattern is that of a gradual rise or decline. The growth in the numbers of soldiers and bureaucrats in Europe since 1500, relative to the total population, are obvious examples of rising trends which will be discussed in more detail in chapters VI and VII below. The decline of Spain in the seventeenth century can be treated, to some extent, in serial terms, since a decline in population and in output was part of the Spanish problem. A third pattern is that of abrupt change, for which the traditional metaphors of the historian's craft

[1] B. Barber, *Social Stratification* (New York and Burlingame, 1957), p. 169.

[2] For an enthusiastic appraisal of future possibilities, see F. Furet, 'Quantitative History', in *Daedalus*, Winter 1971, 151–66; G. Bollême, *Les Almanachs Populaires au 17e et 18e Siècles* (Paris–The Hague, 1969); M. Vovelle, *Piété Baroque et Déchristianisation en Provence* (Paris, 1973); G. and M. Vovelle, *Vision de la Mort et de l'au delà en Provence* (Paris, 1970).

[3] G. Kubler, *The Shape of Time* (New Haven, 1962). Kubler does not seem to know about the French serial historians, nor they about him.

are 'watershed' and 'turning-point'. From the point of view of the serial historian, this kind of change is a 'discontinuity'; from the point of view of the people experiencing the discontinuity, it may be a 'crisis' or a 'revolution'.

Why do all these sorts of change occur? Historians like to claim that they have no 'theory' of social change, that they let the 'facts' speak for themselves. In practice, however, they do have expectations, expectations which are not altogether unlike the more self-conscious 'models' of their colleagues in the social sciences. Self-consciousness has its advantages; to be aware of alternative models of social change helps us to avoid being dominated by any one of them.[1]

For example, there is the evolutionary model of Émile Durkheim and Talcott Parsons, in which change is seen as a process of 'structural differentiation', consequent on the increasing division of labour. Society gradually becomes more complex as individual roles become more specialised and social groups diverge more and more from one another – skilled workers from unskilled, townsmen from peasants, and so on. Some changes are seen as 'adjustments' or 'adaptations' to earlier changes; a process by which society slowly establishes a threatened equilibrium, not in the sense of returning to the old situation, but in that of achieving a new balance of forces within a new system. A small number of historical studies have been written in these terms.[2]

Marxists criticise this model for its built-in assumptions that 'society' acts as one and that social change is essentially a harmonious process. Their model, on the contrary, emphasises the coercion of the majority by a minority, social 'contradictions' and social conflicts, particularly class conflict. Marx also suggested that changes in the economic 'base' of a society occur first and lead to changes in its political and cultural 'superstructure'; and also that societies pass through 'stages', a sequence of different economic and social systems including feudalism, capitalism and socialism. There has been much debate among Marxists over the question whether every society must necessarily pass through all the stages, and the degree to which the superstructure can in turn affect the base.[3] It is necessary to make allowance for the possibility of 'cultural lag', as one American sociologist has called it; the fact that different sectors of society

[1] E. J. Hobsbawm, 'From Social History to the History of Society' in *Daedalus*, Winter 1971, 20–43, discusses the implicit models of working historians; a sociological essay which historians should find intelligible and useful is M. Ginsberg, 'Social Change', repr. in S. N. Eisenstadt (ed.), *Readings in Social Evolution and Development* (London, 1970), pp. 37–68.

[2] Examples of history written with the help of this model are N. Smelser, *Social Change in the Industrial Revolution* (London, 1959), and K. Hopkins, 'Structural Differentiation in Rome', in I. M. Lewis (ed.), *History and Social Anthropology* (London, 1968), pp. 63–79.

[3] K. Marx, *Selections*, ed. T. Bottomore and M. Rubel (Pelican ed., Harmondsworth, 1963), pp. 67–81; for a confrontation with the Talcott Parsons' model, see the critique of Smelser in the preface to E. P. Thompson, *The Making of the English Working Class* (London, 1963).

do not change at the same time. The provinces may lag behind the capital; the social structure is unlikely to change as quickly as political institutions or artistic styles.[1]

Most practising historians are both less dogmatic and less rigorous than either Durkheim or Marx, and tend to combine elements from different models. Braudel, for instance, suggests that the history of events is essentially determined by long-term economic trends, but he does not want to be 'trapped', as he puts it, in Marxism or any other complete theory. Lawrence Stone argues that a society is both 'a moral community held together by shared values' and also 'a system of control'; that 'all societies are in a condition of uneasy equilibrium', but that serious disequilibrium may develop, as it did in England from the Reformation onwards, and especially from the 1620s. The decline of the aristocracy and the 'crisis of confidence' in the government were among the 'preconditions' of a revolution which was 'precipitated' and finally 'triggered' by later events.[2]

In intellectual as in social history it seems useful to distinguish change within the system from change of the system; but intellectual revolutions may not follow quite the same pattern as political and social ones. The best-known attempt to devise a model in this field is that of Thomas Kuhn. Kuhn sees scientific change as essentially discontinuous or revolutionary, involving the replacement of one scientific 'paradigm' by another. In place of the sociologist's 'disequilibrium', he offers us 'anomaly'; that is, the awareness of discrepancies between current theories of nature and nature itself. The perception of a serious anomaly is followed by a period in which scientists try to adjust their old paradigm, but with ever-diminishing success. This 'crisis' is finally resolved by a breakthrough to a new paradigm. Kuhn's model, suitably modified, is proving useful in other fields of intellectual history, notably the history of political theory.[3]

In trying to understand the process of change over time, a few more concepts may have their uses. One is what the Dutch historian Jan Romein used to call 'the law of the retarding lead'. Whether or not it is a 'law' in the strict sense, there do seem to be recurrent situations in which the historian finds himself suggesting that a nation or other social group took the lead in a new development precisely because it had lagged behind in the one before. The Italian contribution to Gothic architecture was less outstanding than the French, the German, the English; but it was in Italy that the breakthrough to Renaissance architecture occurred, quite suddenly, in the early fifteenth century. During the Enlightenment,

---

[1] On cultural lag, W. F. Ogburn, *On Culture and Social Change* (Chicago and London, 1964), pp. 86–95. Ogburn coined the term in 1914.

[2] L. Stone, *The Causes of the English Revolution* (London, 1972); for criticisms, see H. G. Koenigsberger's review in *Journal of Modern History*, 46, 1974, 99–106.

[3] Kuhn, *Structure*, passim; J. Pocock, *Politics, Language and Time* (London, 1972), pp. 13–26.

German thinkers seemed to be lagging behind the French, the English, even the Dutch; but when Enlightenment values were called into question in the later eighteenth century, Germans suddenly took the lead. Metaphorically speaking, one might say that the Italians and the Germans had not invested so much in Gothic or the Enlightenment as others had, so that it was easier for them to make the break when it was needed; but it would not be easy to translate that verdict into more literal terms.

Another concept which helps us understand the process of change is that of cumulative causation, or the 'snowball effect'. This is the opposite of the concept of equilibrium. There are situations in which it makes sense (as we have seen) to say that a society does not change because it does not change; there are also situations where society changes because it changes, where one change reinforces another. To return to the Blacks in the USA. If White prejudice against the Blacks decreases, their standard of living will rise; and if their standard of living rises, prejudice against them will decrease.[1] It is as if there were a 'critical threshold' between stability and cumulative change; as if a society can 'absorb' shocks up to a certain point only. After this structural changes begin and the snowball starts to roll. A well-known type of economic change is what John Maynard Keynes called the 'multiplier effect'. A small increase in investment can have a disproportionate effect on the economy, because the investment creates jobs; the people with the new jobs have money to spend, thus increasing effective demand; the increased demand leads to the creation of more jobs, and so on. There are many such multiplier effects in history, even if they do not always lend themselves to precise calculations. Marx and Engels gave a famous description of the process by which change generates still more change; in the *Communist Manifesto* they compared modern bourgeois society to a sorcerer (presumably thinking of the sorcerer's apprentice), unable to control the forces he has conjured up. Within a cultural tradition it is not too difficult to find a multiplier effect of ever-increasing 'corruption', in the sense of distance from the original. Transmitters may misunderstand or misremember the tradition, and pass on these mistakes to their pupils, who add new mistakes of their own, and so on. For a vivid image of this process of corruption, one has only to look at a series of early British coins, each one step further from its Roman prototype.

An obvious but useful distinction to bear in mind when trying to explain the process of change in a given society is that between internal (or 'endogenous') and external (or 'exogenous') factors. Late nineteenth-century scholars tended to explain change externally in terms of the 'diffusion' of ideas, customs and techniques from one part of the world to another. In reaction against this view, functionalist sociologists and

[1] G. Myrdal, *Economic Theory and Underdeveloped Regions* (second ed., London, 1963), pp. 11–22.

anthropologists have stressed endogenous factors, like the division of labour or social conflict within a given society. However, to discuss change in internal or external terms alone is like trying to cut with half a pair of scissors, or discussing price trends in terms of supply (ignoring demand) or vice versa. It may be pointed out to the diffusionists that there are societies which successfully resist techniques and (still more) ideas from outside; the contrast between the traditional Chinese rejection of foreign ideas and the equally traditional Japanese enthusiasm for foreign ideas cannot be explained in diffusionist terms. To the functionalists one may raise the objection that major social changes have sometimes been imposed on a community from outside after that community has been conquered, as the Normans conquered England, the Turks conquered the Balkans, or the Spanish conquered Mexico and Peru.[1] The conquerors may deliberately try to change the old social structure, or they may change it by misunderstanding it, as in the notorious case of the British and the Bengali zamindar system.[2]

Yet even in these dramatic cases of social and cultural change following conquest, the break with the past is never complete. Even if the conquered are willing to accept the culture of their conquerors, they may misunderstand it, seeing it in terms of the categories of their own culture. The Spaniards, for example, introduced Catholicism to Mexico, including the cult of the Virgin Mary. The Mexicans adopted the cult of Mary with enthusiasm, but somehow in the process Mary was assimilated to the local mother goddess, Tonantzin.[3] To focus on continuity makes one aware of change, but to concentrate on change revives one's awareness of continuity.

There is a limit to the usefulness of discussing grand questions like these at a general level. What we need are case-studies of key topics, and a few such are provided in the following eleven chapters. It should be obvious that no attempt has been made to 'cover' European history. The chapters are no more uniform than the contributors, who include not only British scholars but also Americans, Frenchmen and Norwegians. One contributor would probably describe himself as a Marxist; another is a leading member of the *Annales* school; others are more difficult to characterise. However, each contributor was asked to bear in mind the following questions when preparing his essay. What factors assured continuity in this particular field? When were the major breaks in continuity? Why did these breaks occur? Contributors were also invited to comment on the common assumption that the major discontinuity in European history since 1500 came with the industrial revolution. Was this true in their field or

---

[1] For a critique of functionalists, A. D. Smith, *The Concept of Social Change* (London, 1973). On conquest, G. Foster, *Culture and Conquest* (Chicago, 1960) and the duplicated proceedings of the Past and Present Conference on this theme (1971).

[2] On zamindars, T. R. Metcalf, *The Aftermath of Revolt* (Princeton, 1965), pp. 37, 174–6.

[3] J. Lafaye, *Quetzalcoatl et Guadalupe* (Paris, 1974), part 3, ch. 1.

not? In other words, do economic and social and political and cultural history share a common chronology, or do they have chronologies of their own? Finally, I asked Professor Galtung and his colleagues to discuss the relation between the world and the West over a long time-span; for five hundred years is surely too short, and Europe too small, for a proper consideration of the problems of change and continuity in history.

CHAPTER II

THE ENVIRONMENT AND THE ECONOMY

> The central problem in tracing economic changes in what we would today call an 'under-developed' community, bears on the question of the sources of its food, so much so that in this field economic history may be considered an extension of human 'ecology', the relationship of men and men's communities with their habitat or environment.
>
> David Herlihy

I

EUROPE'S natural environment has interacted with the Continent's vigorous economic history over the last several hundred years largely in ways conducive to growth. Three attributes of the European environment – its particular location on the surface of the earth, its comparative freedom from natural disasters, and the variety of its resources – are discussed in this first section. The next section discusses influences of the environment on the location of industry, the section after that touches on the effect of industrial and other forms of pollution on the human habitat, and the final section deals with the way Europeans expanded their effective resource base by securing control over other continents.

In considering these matters it is worth emphasising the experience of the western part of Europe. That experience is not a close guide to what was happening simultaneously in the remainder of the Continent, but there are two reasons for thinking it exceptionally significant in the history of almost the whole world. The former is that from the fifteenth century western Europeans disrupted other ecosystems by plunder, trade and colonialism, and by introducing old world diseases among vulnerable populations, sufficiently to amount to a reshaping of the whole globe's demographic, economic and political life. The latter is that from the eighteenth century, with the industrialisation of Europe itself, these disturbances were raised to an entirely new order of magnitude.

The treatment here concentrates on western European history in the long-run and is in essence a saga of material success, although not without subplots concerning difficulties scarcely overcome and not without concern for some of the penalties of success. In stressing the long-run trend it should not be overlooked that this was compounded of many short-runs and that economic welfare was affected not only by a progressive extension of command over more and more resources but by interruptions such as harvest failures. Studies of the effects of long-term climatic change on the economy have for various reasons proved ambiguous, but T. S. Ashton was right to point out that for preponderantly agricultural economies (and even England remained one of these as late as the eighteenth century), 'what was happening at Westminster or in the City was of small account compared with what was happening in the heavens'. He was referring to innumerable disturbances caused by the weather which made the trend of growth flutter and which economic policies were powerless to steady. Minor waverings of this kind are painted out in the broad-brush history that follows, but it should not be forgotten how insistent they were.

Of the three overmastering characteristics of the European environment, first comes the indefeasible matter of its position. Sheer location helped western Europeans to have their cake and eat it too. They were shielded by mileage and cushioned by dense forests and intervening peoples against the furious attacks of the warrior nomads of central Asia. Most of the damage done by these invaders was inflicted in earlier periods than concern us here. The Magyars who reached the mouth of the Loire in the tenth century had reached both the end of the line and the end of their time. But for central Europeans the threat from Islam remained serious, with a deep wound as late as 1683 when Vienna was beseiged. Western Europe took quite long enough to make economic headway in the teeth of its own feudal and national conflicts without such assaults from outside. It is however probable that simple distance from the epicentres of Eurasian military upheaval gave the west a real advantage.

In a more positive sense, too, western Europe's location proved an advantage. Ideas could filter from China by land routes during the intervals when these were not politically blocked. Contiguity with Islam provided access to refined Indian and Chinese knowledge and a means of rediscovering the knowledge of the Ancient World. Further, once the conditions for maritime expansion were set in the fifteenth century, the Atlantic coastal nations were well placed for an infusion of specie, marine products, timber, and tropical and semi-tropical crops. Initial location does not of course account for the Discoveries. Neither Europe's new naval technology nor the restless bellicosity of the Europeans is explicable solely in environmental terms. The natural environment, though it can be altered by human action, is to all intents and purposes ever-present; the means and will to make use of it in given ways are not; environmental factors are necessary but not sufficient explanations of historical change. In the event western Europe was given an unprecedented and virtually unchallenged opportunity to begin annexing the resources of other spheres. The chance was grasped. Early in the process Spain acquired silver mines in Central America and thereby a purchasing power which astounded the European imagination. To writers of the seventeenth and eighteenth centuries Peru became the symbolic name for any new frontier, whether for scooping up codfish, felling timber, or tilling virgin land. Yet the 'real' resources that north-western Europeans secured on these prosaic frontiers, each a new 'Peru', proved immensely more fruitful in their economic and technological effects than silver ever had for Spain. We will return to these crucial extensions of the European resource base in section IV below.

Europe's second great asset lay in relative freedom from natural disasters. The severity and more particularly the frequency of floods, tidal waves, earthquakes, locust invasions and similar mishaps were greater in Asia and in many other parts of the non-European world. The elaborate economies founded in oriental river valleys on a basis of hydraulic agriculture were vulnerable to floods. It was always easier (though still a social achievement) to organise public works for the purpose of sharing out irrigation water than to build earthen dikes capable of withstanding raging floods. Similarly the monsoon agricultures of the East were at the mercy of a greater climatic variance than European farming. Their yield might be greater on an average of years, but they were made unstable by intermittent, ruinous failures of the monsoon. Europe was not of course immune from nature's buffets. The wreck of Lisbon by the earthquake of 1755, along with the Calabrian earthquakes of the 1780s, stands out. Locust invasions sometimes reached as far north and west as southern and eastern France. Occasional hailstorms wrought havoc among the standing crops: more than one thousand French communes were battered in 1788 and their harvest ruined on what proved to be the brink of the Revolution. And there were severe cattle plagues, crop diseases like the potato blight and the phylloxera, and epidemic diseases among the human population. These catastrophes shocked European economies off any notional equilibrium growth path. Their impact was however weaker than the jolts administered to Asia. Within Europe the north-western quadrant was especially sheltered.

A related suggestion may be added, which, if it holds, would be of some consequence for understanding Europe's long-run economic growth. It is that natural disasters may have produced not only lower absolute levels of damage in Europe than in Asia but different relative effects on the supplies of capital and labour. In Asia both capital and labour were repeatedly destroyed, the former (sometimes both) by the fury of the elements and the instability of the earth's crust, the latter by epidemics. Since both were affected there may have been no long-run tendency for the ratio of capital to labour to alter. In Europe, by contrast, damage to capital in the form of buildings and other structures, implements, and stocks of goods, may have been less severe relative to the destruction of the labour supply by epidemic disease. Such a bias against the destruction of capital in Europe could have been reinforced by two features of sixteenth- and seventeenth-century economic change, which in turn it would have influenced. Firstly, more durable building materials were being used for ordinary (i.e. non-military and non-religious) buildings, at a period when the rate of technological change was not fast enough for long-lived equipment to be a handicap. Until within at the most the last two hundred years there was no comparable improvement in public health or medical technology which might conserve the supply of labour. Secondly, there was a shift in the allocation of capital investment away from religious structures to materially productive ends, a move connected with the general secularisation of society.

An increasing ratio of capital to labour in European economies may have encouraged the substitution of the former for the latter. Initially this may have taken the form of shifts among hand-tool technologies (distaff-spinning wheel, sickle-scythe) rather than a dramatic invention and adoption of machines. This may have helped the European economy to overhaul Asia's initial advantage of higher average production in the agricultural sector. Certainly, in the long-term, the absolute supply of labour grew in both Europe and Asia: their populations went up. The supply of capital also increased in both zones, capital being to a large extent directly created by labour, for example when land was reclaimed for cultivation. The essential difference may have lain in an increasing ratio of capital to labour in use in the European but not the Asian economy. The mere speculation that global consequences flowed from a divergent impact of disasters is intriguing.

Thirdly, Europe had the advantage of what may be termed a diversified portfolio of resources. Europe's 'carrying capacity' in terms of population was surpassed by that of the flood plains of Middle Eastern and Asian rivers, where settled agriculture and dense populations had arisen well back in prehistoric times. Nevertheless the terrain of Europe was varied and so was the range of climates, soils, raw materials and sources of energy. The assortment of resources within a small compass was generally satisfactory. However differences in geology, physiography and climate across Europe from west to east and south to north ensured that regional and national portfolios differed. *L'Europe est multiple.* Diverse factor endowments gave rise to sets of areas which possessed comparative advantage in one product or another. This made it good sense to trade. The Continent's layout as a peninsula of peninsulas with many navigable waterways also made for vigorous intra-European trade. Commerce flourished whenever there was peace and order.

The intricacy of environmental differences within Europe makes it next to impossible in a brief space to provide a conventional inventory of resources. There are two more fundamental reasons why such an inventory would be misleading. First, whether or not the products of nature are resources in an economic sense depends on there being a technology to use them. Since European technology developed over time, haltingly at first, later with a shattering, perpetual rush, new sources of energy could constantly be harnessed and additional substances extracted and processed. Different inventories, therefore, would have to be provided for each successive short period, and since technological innovation was geographically staggered, for various groups of regions too. Second, besides the incremental expansion of Europe's own effective resource base as the result of technological change, there was a massive expansion beginning with the Discoveries. Thenceforth the European resource endowment was supplemented from farther and farther afield: an already varied portfolio became immensely more diverse.

II

As late in time as the nineteenth century a large proportion of all productive activity was located and carried on in small and non-urban units. Many productive processes remained uncluttered by complicated apparatus; methods were often subtle and equipment subtly wrought, but in palpably ancient rather than modern ways. Fishing, by way of illustration, which was of much greater weight in the economy than today, involved less elaborate procedures even than hunting would have done. It was more like a lucky dip. The equipment of the fisherman was quite extensive and varied and numerous crafts were needed to supply it, but there was no trace of advanced mechanisation and a high (though decreasing) percentage of fishing boats still put out from little fishing villages rather than harbour towns. In very many ways the economy was therefore Lilliputian, bearing always in mind that Lilliput and indeed Blefuscu, were not primitive, though both relied on handicrafts, like indeed the England and France of the 1720s that Dean Swift was satirising.

Much of industry merely involved processing raw materials supplied by farming, fishing, lumbering, quarrying, or relatively shallow mining. The small processing plants were distributed far and wide throughout essentially rural areas. Even manufacturing proper was chiefly rural and had actually become more rural in the late Middle Ages and again, perhaps, in the late seventeenth century. There were of course town workshops, but for a long time the urban market was quite small and there was no reason for all producers to locate in towns. While manufacturing was done largely by hand labour rather than by using inanimate power there was no special incentive for it to become highly concentrated. Rural industries continued to extend even when urban industries were also growing, specialising by product from place to place, sometimes from one village to the next, and decisively contracting only towards the end of the eighteenth century and in the nineteenth century when mechanisation brought more and more processes to mill sites, or to steam engines inside factory towns. Until then any increase in the demand for manufactures required the multiplication of existing units of production. In the physical sense these units were cottages, small farms, and some small village workshops, having within them the simplest equipment, at most a stocking frame or weaver's loom, and employing only part of the labour time of a small farmer or his family. Socially the system was tenacious in the extreme. The movement of labour into the factories, when these had been established, tended to be slow, mainly because of a stickiness unavoidable in cottage industry, where home and place of work were one and the same and not readily exchanged for the factory.

Pre-factory industry was at once simple and complicated. Domestic manufacturing for the purposes of the individual household was widespread through Europe. So was cottage industrial production for the market, but more patchily, and an underlying order may be discerned in the distribution of the patches. By and large they avoided and over time even retreated from areas where crops were grown to sell on the market. The plains and areas of better soil had been settled early. If these regions could manage to produce food in excess of their local needs, they exported it – at least to other regions, if not internationally – and in return bought manufactured wares. Areas where food-crop production was more costly tended to specialise in rural domestic manufacturing for the market, selling their wares to the agricultural plains and buying supplies of cereals. Because the plains were very much under the thumb of manorial lords and their counterparts it was difficult for people from districts which could not readily produce their own bread to relocate on them. There was a great deal of temporary or seasonal labour migration out of the areas poorer for cereal growing, but no very ready permanent emigration. The populace tended to stay put and make what shifts it could, which included taking up more and more cottage industry and disposing of the products to the farmers of the plains. Hence the cereal-deficient areas came to form the great patches of pre-factory industry. The environmental basis of this reciprocity lay in differential ability to raise bread grains cheaply.

There were two main sorts of area of high cost cereal production which harboured cottage industries producing goods for sale: sandy lowland heaths and steep, rocky uplands. The latter predominated, but the fact that the two topographic extremes were involved suggests that the key to their 'proto-industrialisation' lay more in a disadvantage in producing their own food competitively than in an advantage in producing manufactures. A case might be made out that many upland areas did possess an absolute advantage in manufacturing, thanks to the presence of forests for charcoal, deposits of iron ore, and fast streams which provided water-power, but no such endowments favoured lowland heaths like the Veluwe in the Netherlands or the Jutish Heaths in Denmark and rural industry flourished there too.

This outline of occupational distributions is necessarily shadowy. There were anomalies; there were shifts in distributions over the centuries; and there is a lack of data, region by region and period by period, on a comparable basis. There were varying degrees of participation in the market although by modern standards the involvement was often slight. Yet the two great groups of agricultural and cottage-industrial regions are recognisable and the trade between them was extensive and probably one of the great unsung modernising forces of European history. Each set of regions was adjusted to its comparative advantage. A distinct shift in comparative advantage seems to have taken place during the later seventeenth and early eighteenth centuries when food imports into western Europe were high and New World food crops were being inserted into the agricultural regime. The terms of trade presumably turned against agriculture, for populations were not growing fast and food was in general relatively cheap. This made it easier for regions of rural industry to secure a supply of food in exchange for a smaller volume of manufactured wares than before – or in practice to become quite prosperous, in a bucolic fashion, now that food (and drink) were cheap, through an increased export of manufactures. Trade in foodstuffs and light manufactures was not merely inter-regional but often international and apparently helped to raise incomes in pre-factory Europe to levels which, as far as they may be conjectured, compared favourably with the more prosperous countries in less-developed parts of the world today.

The economic advance of early modern Europe is evident both in the growing wealth of the landowners and farm operators of the plains and the progress of the peasant communities of many upland areas. The hired farmhands of the arable lowlands may not have prospered in the same degree since although environmental control was not strict there, social control by the agrarian lords was. Upland communities, prominent among those which came to concentrate on rural industry, had been deeply afflicted by the demographic pressures of the sixteenth century. With thin soils, steep slopes, high precipitation, short growing seasons and bad communications, they could not feed themselves adequately, not at any rate in all years. They were torn by revolts, banditry and wholesale witch-crazes. There was trade with the lowlands, but it was seemingly not enough or sufficiently general. But by the eighteenth century the uplands had diversified their economies, exporting more labour (such as mercenary soldiers), using the streams to power sawmills and iron works, and above all expanding handicraft industries. Their prosperity was dependent on the receipt of foodstuffs from the plains and in years of general harvest failures they could still suffer famine, but inter-regional specialisation and trade had made them and the whole European economy more resilient since the sixteenth century.

The economic welfare of communities dependent on rural domestic industry turned eventually on whether or not they overlay or had cheap access to deposits of coal. Growth had proceeded far in a Smithian fashion, by the extension of the market, by trade among diverse regions. Once the steam engine was attached to manufacturing machinery – a development that must be treated as exogenous to the present exposition – coal became a crucial input to a swelling number of industrial processes. It so happened that many areas of rural domestic industry lay above coal-bearing strata. This was not so much because the coal was valuable to the cottager for his manufacturing by-employment as because coal districts were prominent among those where cereal growing was unrewarding. Poor areas for farming were not highly regarded by powerful men and an independent peasantry had been able to retain a foothold in them. The cost of this was to engage in rural industry and other non-farming activities in order to produce the wherewithal to exchange for bread. When coal became the prime source of industrial energy those areas of rural industry that possessed it were set to blossom, but those that did not have coal were slowly strangled by the competition.

There were intermediate stages. When demand for manufactures first went up very rapidly there was a feverish expansion of output by cottagers using the old handicraft methods. Because hand weaving was often the subsidiary occupation of small farmers its products, according to Adam Smith, were for a time brought to market more cheaply than those of the factory. But once the boom passed the chill of factory competition was sharp and cottage units were winnowed, their place being taken as each economic upturn drew in investment capital by more and more powerful machines. The handloom weavers were trapped, and ultimately extinguished, in this frictional drag. Among the areas of cottage industry were some others which reached a half-way house of mechanisation: waterpower. The first applications of steam to manufacturing were to pump water back above mills on the streams. New processes were run by watermills from the late eighteenth century, and because the fastest streams were present in the kinds of upland district previously occupied by handicraft industry, that transition was made readily enough. It did not last, but proved an evolutionary dead-end, like the remarkable and at first sight anomalous increase of windmills in the early decades of the British 'Industrial Revolution'. Direct applications of steam power, based on coal, fairly soon won out.

Thus in upland areas without coal, industry shrivelled during the nineteenth century. The pockets which survived seemed to do so on the basis of recondite skills in the manufacture of curiosities. The production of most consumer goods was subjected to sterner factory and machine competition. The bulk of the populations of uplands without coal was pressed back into low-grade farming and despite a steady drain of young people into the cities these regions were not really abandoned until the rural exodus of the twentieth century, the *Höhenflucht*.

The great sprawls of cottage industry thus fell back on the coalfields, changing their technology and adapting their organisation to the imperatives of the machine and the factory. There were admittedly exceptions to this location pattern – Swedish iron, Swiss textiles, Vosges textiles – and it has been asserted that, 'the link between early industry and the occurrence of coal was no more than a tenuous relationship between areas of upland relief, poor soils, Paleozoic rocks and associated coal, water-power and either timber for charcoal or pasture for sheep' (C. T. Smith). There was a little more of a causal nexus than that. Coal did form a real bridge between cottage and factory industry. Where there was coal the former fused into the latter where it stood. Where the presence of coal was unknown or uncertain, entrepreneurs and even the state began urgently to scrape around for it. For all the official recognition the countries of mainland Europe could not however make very speedy use of coal. They were able to import from Britain the associated technology in its most effective embodiment: engineers. But each link in the technological chain had to be present and every part of the equipment had to be adapted to the new processes – furnaces, refineries, workshops. Her longer experience with the joint use of coal and iron gave Britain an edge over the Continent, which found imitation harder than was at first supposed. Significantly the lead was shortest over two other coal-bearing areas, in Belgium and the Rhineland, which similarly had ancient metallurgical traditions. Then, as other parts of the mainland strove and caught up, coal set the pattern of nineteenth-century industrialism throughout Europe. A divorce from the venerable locations represented by coalfields where earlier still there had been cottage industry came only in the twentieth century with hydro-electric power and oil.

The energy shift to coal was paralleled by a move from animate to inanimate raw materials. The situation as demand grew in the eighteenth century has been graphically expressed: 'there was not enough cheap meadowland or sour milk in all the British Isles to whiten the cloth of Lancashire once the water frame and the mule replaced the spinning-wheel; and it would have taken undreamed of quantities of human urine to cut the grease of the raw wool consumed by the mills of the West Riding' (David Landes). The solution was the emergence of a chemical industry. First England, then western Europe, was freed from the limitations of what could be grown on a finite land base by substituting inorganic chemicals for organic materials. Among the burgeoning industries of the classic 'Industrial Revolution' was cotton, the supposed leading sector, the type specimen of all new industries. Cotton was imported. The ability to import any raw material like that on a scale and with enough regularity to sustain an industry was in itself an historical novelty, deriving in this case from that earlier turning-point in Europe's history, the Discoveries. The new ocean trades must appear less fundamental than the scientific and technological advances of the late eighteenth century, if only because the latter eventually could be generalised to all forms of production whereas the economic potential of raw material importation was limited. Yet in the historical context whether the consequences of the Discoveries were really of less significance for Western economic growth may be doubted.

III

Since soot is a prime pollutant, coal-based industry left the mark of Cain on the living world. In general its effects, and those of other polluting substances, however, increased the scale rather than the kind of environmental damage associated with productive activities. There were deleterious consequences from economic activity, even farming, very much earlier, which some examples may illustrate. Archaeological sites have revealed that soil wash has persisted as the result of farming quite moderate slopes in southern England since 500 B.C., even under the gentle rainfall regime of that part of the world. At Codsall, Staffordshire, a field enclosed in the eighteenth century A.D. has subsequently lost topsoil at a rate of 0.1 cm per annum from windblow and mild sheetwash and because it has been carried off on rootcrops, wheels, hooves and labourers' boots. The process may seem slow but it is irreversible. Where soil was scarcer and the movement faster desperate efforts were made to reverse it; soil eroded down the steep slopes of the Alps was carted back up in buckets. The most damaged agricultural environment of all in Europe is along the Mediterranean, especially in Italy and Spain. There has been erosion down to bare rock in places and as a result a faster run-off which had led to a flood problem. Florence, for instance, lies in a countryside richly wooded in prehistoric times but relentlessly cut over, eroded and leached out during the historic period. Since at least the second century A.D. the city has suffered recurrent floods which have increased in intensity and frequency. Since 1500 there has been on average a major flood every eight years. The build-up of water on the plains has intensified the Italian problem with malaria.

Even symptoms of environmental disharmony like occupational diseases did not wait until the steam age or the factory age to manifest themselves. There is medical testimony from early modern times that industrial jobs involving chemicals, like varnishing and gilding, produced characteristic sicknesses. It is not surprising, at least on a second thought, that specialised or continuous contact with foreign substances, part and parcel of at least luxury goods production from very early times, was harmful to the artisans. A simple unmechanised task like digging out the whetstones for scythes is known to have condemned the men and women who toiled in the quarries to dust-choked, abraded lungs. In the English Potteries the dry-grinding of flintstones for the makers of earthenware caused silicosis in the workers, even though as early as 1726 Thomas Benson had taken out a patent for his method of grinding flints under water. The problems associated with the working environment were as much associated with poverty and an overcrowded labour market, and the absence of institutional measures to force manufacturers to internalise the relevant costs and not pass them on to the workforce or to consumers, as with the technological level of production. What industrialisation proper seems to have done is chiefly to have exposed a much higher proportion of the population to harmful substances, both at work and at home, but eventually, after agonizingly prolonged teething troubles, to have produced also the technology and wealth to clear up the mess. Indeed pre-industrial poverty is likely to have made workers more careless with their health, and more willing to put up with and even develop a taste for distressing conditions, than they have needed to do since the industrial world became rich and real wages rose.

There had been a real foretaste of the problems and environmental squalor of the manufacturing city in the emergence of large 'pre-industrial' cities in northern Europe. In those latitudes they were a novel habitat, offering short-term economic opportunities in return for longer-term health risks. Big commercial and administrative cities (they were of course dotted with workshops) already in early modern times placed a strain on services and generated unenviable pollution. By the early seventeenth century London required an aqueduct to convey water from thirty-eight miles away. In 1662 William Petty observed that London was growing westwards, to escape 'the fumes, steams and stinks of the whole easterly pile'. The rich were moving to the western suburbs, upwind, to avoid air pollution which was, however, not merely the product of the industrial combustion of coal as brick makers, dyers and maltsters turned over to it as a fuel in the sixteenth century but also, or even primarily, because of the replacement of wood by coal in domestic hearths. That change was drawn out over an immense period (a Londoner had been executed in 1306 for burning pit-coal) but it had already culminated before the age of coal-burning heavy industry. Both ways there were baleful consequences, from the hazard of cancer of the scrotum for chimney sweeps and climbing boys to wide-spread air pollution threatening the whole city population.

The point that severe pollution long preceded any conventional date for the 'Industrial Revolution' may be reinforced by considering the Netherlands. The trading and processing economy there was busily fouling its nest in the sixteenth century. As early as 1582 Dutch linen-bleachers who dumped lye and milk into the canals were ordered to use separate disposal systems called 'stinkerds'. This was less to protect the populace from noisome wastes than to ensure clean supplies of water for other industrialists, just as in eighteenth-century Lancashire the need for clean water on the part of the bleachers and dyers rather than considerations of public health led to the first attempts to use sand-bed filters for water purification.

Nevertheless there must have been a public gain were it not for the fact that Dutch cotton-printers continued to use the canals to dump ink and dye residues. The paper mills, breweries, distilleries, chandleries, soap works, brick ovens, madder ovens, and tanneries (which used whale oil and were called '*stinkmolens*' in Holland) characteristic of the most advanced parts of late pre-industrial Europe all polluted the air and water.

While settlements were still small, manufacturing works tiny, and the use of agricultural chemicals negligible, the wind could cleanse the air and the rain and streams could flush away wastes; wells could be relied on for drinking water and cesspits could cope with sewage. As settlements grew in size there was excessive competition for the quondam free goods, air and water. Rivers instead of wells became the chief source of potable water and almost the sole receptacle for wastes, as sewage was transferred to them from the richer suburbs by the innovation of waterborne carriage. The two tasks together placed more of a strain on the rivers than they could bear. Their self-cleansing properties and salubriousness vanished. The Fleet river in London had been an open sewer from as early as the fourteenth century. Nevertheless the connection between contaminated water and disease was not unequivocally demonstrated until the Soho cholera outbreaks of the 1850s, only after which (apart from a pioneering effort by Altona in 1843) were flushed sewers built to convey wastes right outside municipal bounds. There was a fairly rapid diffusion of this procedure in Europe during the second half of the nineteenth century, while in Paris under Napoleon III the pollution of the Seine forcibly drew attention to artesian sources of water.

But despite early instances of water pollution early industrial areas by themselves were seldom big enough to cause the total deoxygenation of rivers before the nineteenth century. In the heart of industrial Lancashire the Mersey and Irwell continued to provide water for drinking and washing clothes until 1780. At least the rivers still looked clean. By the early nineteenth century, however, they had lost all their fish and other aquatic life and scum was so thick on the Irwell that birds could walk on its surface. Casual illustrations of a similar deterioration are not hard to find, but it is difficult to discover a systematic survey of increasing river pollution. One indication of the trend is to be found in Netboy's study of the contracting distribution of the Atlantic salmon, a species of fish which moves from the sea up the rivers to spawn. The chronology of the effect of pollution on the salmon accords in general terms with that of other aspects of pollution, with records of severe but localised damage back in the Middle Ages and widespread severe harm occurring during nineteenth-century industrialisation. Once shoals had been vast and salmon were cheap enough sometimes to be fed to pigs. Long after the earliest conservation enactment, in 1446, when the corporation of Dublin ordered all tanners and glovers to cease and desist from ejecting wastes into the Liffey to the detriment of the salmon, it was not uncommon along the western edge of Europe for indentures of apprenticeship to restrict the number of meals at which the apprentices might be served salmon. *Autres temps, autres mœurs*. Nineteenth-century industry solved that quixotic problem in France and Britain. More and more mills were built for textiles, flour, paper, timber, and tanning. High weirs to raise the head of water for milling purposes were put up. The salmon were cut off from their spawning grounds and in one river basin after another they were extinguished.

Thus, although the 'Industrial Revolution' may by no means be blamed for initiating environmental deterioration, it altogether exploded the scale. Factory wastes began to run together into whole detritus landscapes. It was no longer possible for mining slag to be discreetly, even attractively, screened by a few acres of trees, as it had been about the old Roman iron mines in the Forest of Dean. The scarred and scabbed tracts grew too large. Air pollution became ever more difficult for the urban rich to escape. Atmospheric pollution engulfed great tracts out in the countryside. At Huy, in the industrial valley of Meuse in Belgium, in the 1890s the peasants were obliged to breathe through handkerchiefs as they went about their holdings. They devised cloth nosebags for their cattle but even so the animals were afflicted by 'fog asthmas' in 1902 and 1911, and sixty people died there in a smog disaster in 1930, the tip of an iceberg of bronchial complaints. In London several hundreds of people had been killed by a 'smoke-fog' (smog) in 1872 and as late as 1952, 4,000 died there in the worst air pollution disaster known.

Men could not evade the consequences of spending a lifetime in urban-industrial habitats so large, by the nineteenth century, that it was no longer possible to walk out into the fields of an evening. The workforce in the industrial slums of the nineteenth and twentieth centuries became pasty-faced, affected by environmental diseases like tuberculosis and rickets as the sunlight was shrouded from deep, dark, dank courts, maimed by the unguarded teeth of iron machines, and subjected to new occupational diseases – like 'fossy jaw' among the London match girls when 'free' phosphorus was produced and used for the first time ever. Increasing reliance on processed and adulterated food, on watered milk like 'London blue', reinforced the ravages wrought on health and physique by a lifetime spent inside bigger and more unequivocally industrial cities than had ever existed before.

That industrialisation produced eventual social benefit is hardly to be contradicted. The evidence is there in national figures of rising per capita real income. The evidence of the tables of life expectancy is even more persuasive. The actuary necessarily takes into account those disamenities associated with economic growth which G.N.P. calculations either exclude or actually count as services produced, such as expenditures on cleaning up pollutants. The wealth, technology, and cheaper produced goods which industrialisation poured forth could cure many of the unfortunate side-effects of an increasing material output. But for a long, long time producers cultivated their private affairs without regard for the social costs imposed by the spillover of wastes. Profit inured a minority of men, and necessity inured the majority, to aesthetic deprivation, sensory affront and hazard to health and life.

Technology itself is neutral. It may be used so as to impair man's ecological niche. Over a lengthy period of Western economic growth little attention was paid to damage to the environment. Controls waited on institutional innovation, on a generalising of particular laws and sterner enforcement of them, and these things waited on the crossing by sizeable and influential groups of some threshold of material welfare beyond which they might start to seek different, less tangible, improvements in the common lot. European economies, as they cracked the eggshell of feudalism and stepped out via absolutism and mercantilism to the greatest degree of *laissez-faire* the world has known, did not possess the will for self-regulation. A considered balance between the production of material goods and the production of environmental disamenities was not struck. The social costs of pollution were freely passed on to the populace at large. Few penalties attached to the producers of disamenities, either factory owners or even for most of the twentieth century the managers of state factories. Without penalties the social conscience remained thread-bare. A mass of regulations originating in the protection of old sectional interests did offer some means of obliging manufacturers to internalise these costs, but a concerted effort to use them waited on the post-Keynes generations who, having experienced nothing except full employment and rising incomes, felt they could afford to urge their political representatives to improve the quality of life. Until then, that is until the second half or even the start of the last third of the twentieth century, the richest econo-mies concentrated on material output. Incomes were low for many people still and the primary goal was to raise them; the Commonweal must fare as best it might. Until then the negative externalities of increased produc-tion were inescapable and had to be borne.

IV

Early modern Europe held significant reserves of land and raw materials within its bounds. There persisted north of the Alps enclaves which could be and were brought into cultivation, or at least used more intensively, for the benefit of the metropolitan heart which lay about the Amsterdam–London axis. These reserves were of five main kinds, listed here in what was approximately an ascending order of importance. First, there were heathlands of infertile soils which could be taken in and out of cultivation according to the movement of grain prices. The poorer expanses would not sustain cropping for long even under the best existing practice (sheepfold and root crops) but they were available as land of last resort. Second, there were extensive wetlands. This marshland was made to give good crops in place of a thin yield of fish, fowl, and rough pasturage. Dutch engineers began to drain marshes all over Europe – in Poland, Germany, England, France and Italy – in the sixteenth century, while Frederick the Great exulted on the completion of a big drainage project in Prussia in 1753 that he had, 'conquered a province in peacetime'. Third, there were forests into which cultivation could be pushed, supplying timber as a joint product with cleared farmland. Woodland clearance also created an externality for agriculture by destroying the redoubts of predators like wolves. Fourth, unlike the densely-occupied crop lands of the Mediterranean, there was north of the Alps under-used capacity in the shape of fallow fields. Changes in farming methods enabled the fallows to be brought under permanent cultivation. Crop rotations were elaborated from the sixteenth century, developing out of simple grain-fallow or winter corn – spring corn – fallow systems into many and varied shifts of temporary grass or forage crops with cereals. Improved grasses and forage crops eliminated the need for fallow and added greatly to the effective productive acreage. Fifth, there were more conventional expansions of frontiers into lands occupied at low densities by tribal peoples and aliens. As time went on the lands of such people were seized or otherwise coerced more fully into the market system.

This last aspect of European economic history, internal or landward colonisation, may perhaps be thought of as a series of explosions along the eastern borders and a series of implosions into Celtic lands. Compared with the maritime expansion of Europe, particularly the struggle for British dominion over the oceans and the grasslands of the Americas, southern Africa, and Australasia, the internal (or adjacent landward) expansion has been neglected. In fact there had been a recurrent eastward expansion by land in Europe, involving at its most unexpected even a migration of Scots to Poland in the seventeenth century. A larger movement was that whereby Lorrainers and Germans took over the lands of Muslim herdsmen on the Great Hungarian Plain, which the Habsburgs recovered by the Treaty of Carlowitz in 1699 and returned to the earlier function as the mustering ground for cattle drifts to central European markets, and later converted to granaries of wheat and maize. Another big movement, part of the expansion of Imperial Russia, was the migration during the second half of the eighteenth century into the Ukraine, the Crimea and the entire northern shore of the Black Sea, which whole area subsequently became a breadbasket for western Europe. Eleven million acres were allotted to colonists in one early ten-year period, although not until the second half of the nineteenth century could it be said that this last internal frontier was fully occupied.

As to the pressure into the Celtic lands, the ancient territorial ambitions of the English and Lowland Scots regarding Wales, the Scottish Highlands and Ireland were renewed. Wales was formally joined to England by the Act of Union in 1536, guaranteeing the flow of pastoral products to England; the plantation of Ireland is a tale too tangled to be retold in a short space, but a particularly dramatic episode was the transfer of almost seven million acres to Protestant hands between 1652 and 1660; and the western isles of Scotland were violently invaded at the start of the seventeenth century, although only a final fit of exasperation after the 'Forty-five' caused the Highland clans to be put to the sword and the way to be cleared for sheep ranching. The Celtic lands were in truth not uniformly rich and much of the motive for subduing them was to deny Roman Catholic powers in Europe a backdoor for the invasion of England. Further, strenuous resistance bloodied the noses both of the land speculators whom James VI and I had licensed to commit genocide in the Hebrides, and of several swashbuckling entrepreneurs in Ireland. Certain of the very same individuals reappeared in the early history of colonisation in Virginia and New England. They sat on a see-saw which tilted between fully mobilising land resources within Europe and exploiting lands and seas outside.

Adam Smith considered that 'the discovery of America, and that of a passage to the East Indies by the Cape of Good Hope, are the two greatest and most important events recorded in the history of mankind'. By his day these events had had time to fructify and the exploitation of extra-European sources of food and raw materials was well established. There had, as it happened, been a long interval before the full benefits were established. During this, Portuguese and Spanish finds of silver, gold, and spices diverted attention away from an initial interest in 'real' resources and promoted the Price Revolution of the sixteenth century. In the fifteenth century the research institute established by Henry the Navigator at Sagres in Portugal had planned a thorough programme of island-hopping in the Atlantic, in search of land to grow grain and sugar, standing timber to cut, and colonies of seals for oil. The diversion from these goals was unfortunate. Spain, for all the silver of Central America, failed to transmute it into sustained growth.

The Spaniards used their meretricious riches to import manufactures from north-west Europe instead of building up their own industry. The north-western Europeans, apparently after capturing a very large share of Mediterranean trade by sheer commercial vigour, and after a few passages with fool's gold, turned back in search of 'real' resources outside Europe. This was a long time after Columbus and da Gama and it was an even longer time, into the late seventeenth or early eighteenth century, before markets outside Europe absorbed any quantity of European manufactures. Maritime expansion was initially a peripheral undertaking. As Adam Smith himself recognised, the discovery of the New World arose from 'no necessity'. This is not to say – quite the opposite – that there was not ultimately a massive boost given to European growth by the acquisition of almost 20 million square miles of land in the Americas, Australasia and South Africa (five times the area of Europe), plus of course the interposed marine fisheries. When the eastern agricultural frontier in Hungary, Poland and Russia is included, and the supply of raw materials to western Europe from the Baltic and Scandinavia, the eventual windfall of resources is staggering.

The categoriser of the phases of expansion is plagued by exceptions. What is taken as constituting Europe at a given date must determine what may properly be treated as interior colonies as opposed to external frontiers. Outward pressure against the Ottomans involved fairly evident frontier movements, but the role of Scandinavia and the Baltic lands is more ambiguous or at any rate changeable over time. In early modern times Scandinavia and the Baltic littoral were being used as resource colonies and markets by the Dutch and English. Eventually the Scandinavian countries proved able to imitate extra-European exploits, although up to the Second World War there were communities of expatriate Englishmen in ports along the southern shore of the Baltic, engaged in despatching primary products home from regions which retained some part of their old role as resource colonies. Outside Europe, of course, the resource grab by north-western European economies in particular went from strength to strength in the seventeenth, eighteenth and nineteenth centuries, although disturbed by conflicts among the colonial powers themselves and occasional colonial rebellions.

The chronology of overseas expansion may be complicated but the functional consequences for European economic growth are reasonably clear. It was as though by some magical process of continental drift the area of the seaboard countries of western Europe had increased. They commanded vast new or extra quantities of resources of three main kinds. First, there were the staples of the Commercial Revolution, which will not be dwelled on here, the imported lumber, cereals, and semi-tropical commodities like tobacco, tea, coffee and indigo. Second, there was a much wider range of crop plants which could be grown within Europe and raise its own productivity per acre. Third, there was a bigger intake of fish protein and whale and seal oil from the world's oceans.

The central effects may be indicated by a type of reverse staple theory, rather as sketched by Walter Prescott Webb in *The Great Frontier*. The 'metropolitan' economy of north-west Europe was stimulated by waves of utilitarian resources reaching it from its annexes, mainly overseas. This amounted to a gigantic extension of Europe's effective resource base, its 'ghost acreage' in the terminology of the fisheries scientist, Georg Borg-strom. 'Ghost acreage' is a measure of the extra tilled land which would be needed to produce at home, with given techniques, the equivalent quantity of food, of the same nutritive value, as that obtained from external sources. The measure is divided into 'fish acreage', the tilled land needed to raise animal protein equivalent to that supplied by fishing, and 'trade acreage', the tilled land needed to replace farm products imported for human and animal feed. 'Ghost acreage' must remain a notional concept because we lack historical data to calculate it, but the idea is instructive. Enormous additions of 'real' resources were made available and they came from a much wider climatic range than obtained in Europe. Risks of food and raw material supplies failing were thus spread more widely, over a range of extra-European territories that can be looked on as a giant portfolio of assets. Europe's total income rose and (in another classic welfare gain) it was spread more evenly over time. All these additions to Europe's resources were made at a low cost compared with the alternative of increasing output from the Continent's own acreage.

The cutting edge of the expansion was the grab for pelagic bounty. The English and French secured the richest sea fishery of all, the Grand Banks of Newfoundland. The cod caught there was sold in southern European countries which were short of protein and which being Roman Catholic had institutionalised the eating of fish. The north-western European countries did not themselves rely for food on their catches of fish but received the 'fall-out' of the fish trade in the form of capital and entre-preneurship. Their capital markets were stimulated by large numbers of people taking small individual shares in fishing vessels. The north-western Europeans got the lion's share of the work of ship-building, ship-fitting and provisioning. The growth of their port towns was advanced by the building of dwelling houses, warehouses, wharves, docks, and the atten-dant workplaces for thousands of bakers, brewers, coopers, ships' carpenters, smiths, net-makers, rope-makers, line-makers, hook-makers, and pulley-makers (the ship's block or pulley was to be one of the earliest standardised products of eighteenth-century industry). The same coun-tries benefited from the growth of trades which developed out of the fisheries, an example being the North American fur trade. They obtained a favourable balance of trade with southern Europe and took this out in Mediterranean wines and citrus fruits, products which as Thomas Mal-thus noted would otherwise simply not have been available at any price in cool, cloudy north-west Europe. Most valuable of all, perhaps, was the amassing of information about commercial geography which made the expansion of maritime activity self-sustaining. Cogitating enviously on the springs of Dutch wealth in 1680, William Petty wrote that 'those who predominate in shipping and fishing have more occasions than others to frequent all parts of the world and to observe what is wanting or redundant everywhere...and consequently to be the factors and carriers, for the whole world of trade'.

Whaling may be seen in a similar light to fishing. Species of 'right whales' (the term merely signifies the right whales to catch) were sought farther and farther from European shores. They were pursued to the edge of the Arctic, and by the early seventeenth century one thousand Dutchmen summered in Spitzbergen, at a permanent encampment called Smeerenburg (Blubbertown). Whalers next crossed the North Atlantic. Sperm whales enticed them into the South Atlantic, the Pacific, the Tasmanian bays, and Antarctic waters. It so happened that the whalers regularly found new grounds just when the old ones were on the point of being hunted out, and they were able as a result to keep up a barely faltering flow of oil to European markets. A similar Providential theme, of an almost mystical kind, has been commented on in the resource history of the United States. Perhaps it may be said that the Europeans made Providence work for them.

Whale oil was of prime importance as a lubricant and an illuminant. The oil was used to soften leather in days when the leather trades were in the front rank, before they were supplanted by rubber and petroleum-based synthetics. It was used for softening coarse woollen cloth, as a base for paint and tar with which to caulk and coat the planking of ships and houses, to make soft soap, and to grease ever-faster and more numerous machines. For this last purpose whale oil was vital throughout the early history of industrialisation, for the petroleum oil industry only dates from the sinking of Colonel Drake's well in Pennsylvania in 1859. Until the advent of coal gas at the start of the nineteenth century whale oil was an important means of lighting city streets, factories and large houses. The whalers also supplied ambergris for scent, malleable bones for stays and umbrella frames, and blubber and bone for fertiliser, but their main economic contribution was in the supplying of oil, the truly indispensable use of which was for industrial lubrication. The expansionary effects of the whaling industry on the economy generally may have outweighed those of fishing. Whaling vessels were heavier ships using stouter equipment than most fishing boats, their long voyages required greater capitalisation, and the use of the oil demanded a skilled knowledge of tribology, the science of lubrication. Whaling vessels were the oil tankers of the pre-petroleum world and besides this they made special contributions to its exploration.

As industry was served by new sources of whale oil from outside European waters, so agriculture was served by the introduction of new non-European food crops. Maize and potatoes were the outstanding newcomers. Both are climatic peripherals as far as Europe is concerned. In a period when the central bloc of western Europe agricultures was already stirring to raise its productivity they extended the zone of reliable food output to the south and north. Maize proved to be adapted to the hot summers and uneven rains of the Mediterranean basin and went a long way towards filling unmet food needs there. Potatoes were taken up on the former fallows and poor, untilled, soils of Europe north of the Alps, and along the wetter littoral in Ireland, western Scotland, the Low Countries and Norway, slowly at first, quickly from the late eighteenth century.

By domestic endeavour, the importation of new crop species, and the direct import of food, the aggregate food supply of Europe climbed and has gone on climbing throughout the post-Columbian epoch. This generalisation, certainly, brushes aside important short-term phenomena such as harvest failures, and persistent deficiencies of diet for some populations and social groups. Nevertheless the generalisation correctly captures the success of Europe in finding food for a growing, increasingly urban, population. By historical standards the achievement was remarkable and the demographic and economic consequences were boundless. Some of the significant episodes in the long-term achievement of adequate food supplies deserve to be picked out. In early modern times the diffusion of rye, supplemented with protein from salt fish and vitamin c from pickled cabbage, permitted denser settlement than before along the Baltic into Russia. This diet had made a sort of colonisation possible. Very soon these quasi-colonies along the Baltic were able to export enough cereals to supply the Netherlands, with an overplus which Dutch shippers re-exported to Italy and other Mediterranean countries. On an average of years in the late seventeenth century this supply fell off, but it remained as a buffer to be drawn on in any year when the harvest was short in western and southern Europe.

At that period, in the latter years of the seventeenth century, there was a new and growing stream of English grain exports to the Continent. England had been a small net importer of grain (for the London market) at the start of the seventeenth century and the shift to exporting was both unexpected and remarkable. To some degree this achievement in a north-western European country was a culmination of an old sequence of diffusions whereby forage plants had entered Mediterranean Europe through the Muslim world and spread northwards. Some of these plants had been adopted as feed crops by the specialist livestock farmers of the Low Countries and carried on into England to act as fodder courses in rotation with cereals. The productive cropping systems pieced together in England helped to turn that country into a grain exporter from the 1660s to 1750. The principle of these rotations was afterwards transmitted back to mainland Europe, doing away with the need to rest the land by fallowing, since the dung of animals fed on the forage crops restored fertility to the soil. This long process whereby plant species suitable for use as fodder crops drifted to north-west Europe from as far afield as south-west Asia owed something to Europe's location, to the permeable interface between Christendom and Islam. The biological and economic consequences of that culture contact were slower and less dramatic, but hardly less fruitful, than the post-Columbian dispersal of crops from outside Eurasia.

By the late seventeenth century Europe's food supplies were more varied and secure than ever before, notwithstanding the increase of population and occasional (but diminishing) runs of lean years. The European littoral especially benefited from new sources of supplementary import as distant as North America. The economy of the coastal regions was made more robust by the diversification of its food resources; the dampening of fluctuations in food prices and of famine mortality reduced a fundamental cause of economic instability. No single plant disease or particular inclemency of the weather could depress food supplies, or the supplies of farm-produced raw materials for industry, as much as heretofore. There may be some causal connection between this amelioration and the urgent stirrings of industrialisation in England.

By the end of the eighteenth century the population of Europe had again risen to the point where it pressed against food supplies. The nineteenth century saw this subsistence problem tackled in four ways: in England by the further development of farming methods; by upgrading soil fertility through the use of oil-cake obtained outside Europe to feed cattle for dung and through the import of guano from the seabird colonies off Peru; by the more energetic spread of English methods to mainland Europe; and by importing more produce directly from the newly-ploughed grasslands and newly-stocked ranges of other continents.

The more intensive production within European agriculture itself was not without cost, for reasons which present an apparent (though not a real) paradox. Whereas the overall food resources of Europe became more resilient, because more diverse, local tendencies towards specialisation and intensification actually increased the risks of loss to pests and disease in given regions, losses which were sustained in the case of the wine-growing parts of France when phylloxera struck, or even over a whole country in the case of Ireland when the potato blight appeared. Obviously there were advantages to raising only one crop, in the shape of specialised equipment needs and work routines and standardised arrangements for processing and distribution. On the other hand monoculture offered an ideal habitat to a few species which could multiply to become pests.

Agricultural pests, and in some degree the whole humanised landscape, may be looked on as true by-products of the dominant economic system. The relationship may be traced back into prehistory, when peoples moving into Europe from south-west Asia brought useful crops and grasses but almost unwittingly an entire 'living entourage' of unwanted species too. They introduced plants which being adapted to bare earth or open country habitats in Asia quickly spread as weeds wherever the land was cleared for farming in Europe. Specialised crop production greatly extended this type of relationship. It created super-habitats in which a handful of parasites, predators and pathogens could reach explosive levels. Thus when the rye crop was established across northern Europe a specific fungus, ergot, travelled with it. The heavy purple heads of ergot flourished among the rye in damp seasons. Threshed with the grain and ground into the flour, ergot was responsible at intervals for enormous psychotic outbreaks among humans. By the nineteenth century rye was being replaced by potatoes or wheat and some simple amendments had been made to husbandry routines, bringing ergotism within bounds, indeed abolishing all except rare, minor outbreaks in the West. The example of ergot demonstrates the link between extreme agricultural specialisation and the concomitant creation of favourable conditions for harmful organisms.

The most cataclysmic fungal infestations of the nineteenth century did not affect the final consumer in the direct way of ergot but instead destroyed the plant host. The consequences were of course just as tragic where populations relied exclusively on the one crop. The most striking manifestations, already mentioned, were the potato blight which caused the Great Famine in Ireland, the west of Scotland, the Low Countries and Norway, and the phylloxera which so devastated the French vineyards that they had to be replanted with rootstocks from California. In the absence of effective pest control by chemical biocides, themselves treacherous (by 1840 a copper sulphate solution used to protect seed wheat against smut was inadvertently poisoning partridges in Hampshire), these ecosystems had become hyper-developed.

Similar pest and disease problems were evident among livestock. Flocks and herds of only one species were efficient from the producer's point of view in the short- or even the medium-term, but were vulnerable to disease in the long-term. The most serious animal diseases were transmitted from Asia and had fortunately often lost their virulence by the time they reached the favoured shores of western Europe, especially those of Britain sheltering behind the Channel moat. But nowhere was entirely safe. The threat of plague was heightened by the build-up of livestock populations and more frequent and extensive trading in animals and feedstuffs. Cattle in western Europe were massacred by rinderpest several times during the eighteenth century and this phenomenon throws some light on the origins of the scientific research which eventually curbed losses due to animal disease. To illustrate, the loss from epizootics in France made them matters of concern to the *intendants*. A rinderpest outbreak in 1770–1, which quarantine failed to contain, inspired the Comptroller-General of Finances to engineer the founding of the Société Royale de Médecine. This society was charged with the investigation of epizootics and human epidemics, and also interested itself in sanitary conditions, occupational diseases, and (as it came about) a severe occurrence of ergotism in the Sologne district in 1777. These shocks to the economy thus aroused medical and biological science. The interesting question, of course, is why it was European society at precisely that period which responded so positively to agricultural upsets. Ecological disasters cannot by themselves explain the institutional reaction, but they were evidently the means of focussing scientific effort once a generalised concern for such matters had appeared. Progress of a strictly scientific nature was slow and stumbling, the big breakthrough awaiting the development of antibiotics in the 1940s, but the early emergence of a veterinary profession had ensured that such partial remedies as became available were being diffused.

On the cereal side, western Europe quite lost any comparative advantage in the 1870s. By 1890 the major sources of supply were the United States, Russia, Hungary and India. Faced with a waterfall of cereal imports far greater than any current deficiency in domestic output and cheap enough to bankrupt higher-cost home growers, several continental powers opted for tariff protection. Among them Germany most notably pressed ahead with a search for import substitutes, finding an alternative to cane sugar in home-grown sugar-beet and spurring her chemists to devise various *ersatz* products. In these ways Germany and some other nations were able to squeeze more food and raw materials out of the factor of production, land, which was scarcest for them since they had lagged in the race to colonise temperate grasslands outside Europe. The decision to seek and use substitutes was political, being an attempt to protect their own farmers' incomes and to reduce the national dependence on a 'ghost acreage' the routes from which were controlled by the British navy.

The biggest food importing economy remained Britain. As demand rose there and the technology of carrying freight was improved, so concentric bands of different land uses, specialising on particular products, were shaped and spread outwards across other lands. Perishable vegetables and dairy products were raised closest in to the chief British market centre, London, with grains being grown farther out, and meat, wool and hides beyond. 'The outer boundary', which comprised extensive stock-raising and lay beyond Europe, even beyond the northern hemisphere, 'pulsated in time to the beat of prices in London' (J. R. Peet). Precise rings of land usage were distorted by real world differences in production possibilities, differential accessibility, and political resistance to free trade, but the underlying pattern can be detected. Types of farming, the aspect of the countryside, and therefore the prospects for industrialisation and economic growth, all bore a relation to the linear distance from the biggest market, London. The notion may be jobbed back to early modern times when Amsterdam was the hub of the commercial world and the costs of supplying primary products to this focus already determined the nature of the ecosystems over a far wider area. The whole system, the entire arrangement of ecosystems, expanded outwards as the metropolitan market grew and transport costs fell. This process was in full swing during the Victorian era.

The nineteenth century saw an almost uninterrupted run of eighty years' deflation in western Europe. Unlike earlier great deflations this one was not the result of a forced contraction of demand caused by demographic setback but was the outcome of a fortunate combination of circumstances on the supply side. Methods of production and transportation were being improved constantly. The interiors of the new lands were being settled by populations of European stock whose connections led them to engage in producing food and raw materials for sale on the European market. Primary product prices went down and went on going down. This was obviously propitious for the economic growth of the industrialising countries, especially in the favoured case of Britain.

Nevertheless there were other ways to grow. Countries with less of a share in the extra-European economies (Germany is the obvious example) also experienced a powerful surge of economic growth in the second half of the nineteenth century. Evidently industrialisation could be generated at home, and domestic agriculture could be developed, given the prior example of British growth plus the political will to undertake a policy of import substitution. Germany, in particular, sought and found substitute raw materials for her industries and substitute crops to feed her people, and thereby compensated for the lack of a sizeable temperate zone empire.

In long perspective it seems that societies have usually found conquest and colonisation easier than massive technological change. A reason may be that the latter not merely expands the economy but alters its structure, and threatens derivative changes in society which would disturb the holders of power. Conquest and colonisation on the other hand are extensions of the existing system and hold out the prospect of additional land and jobs to those who are already powerful. At worst there may be a gradual dilution of their equity in the sense that there may come to be more rich and powerful individuals in the society – but not a traumatic rise of new élites. The singularity of European civilisation was to extend its territorial power across the seas and to a degree matched by no other, and at the same time to achieve a thorough industrialisation, something which had literally no historical precedent. Industrialisation involved the use of new production functions in which resources were combined more efficiently through technological advance, and it fed on cheap primary products from frontier areas. Securing these new supplies of food and raw materials, though fundamental in the rise of the Atlantic seaboard economies, was the easier task. Colonisation invited less social upheaval than bringing into being factories, machines, urban proletarians, parvenu entrepreneurs and scribbling intellectuals and it seems almost surprising that ruling groups in Europe submitted to the stresses of industrialisation without making much more determined efforts to speed up overseas settlement. Presumably the shadowy and ambiguous processes of growth were beyond their understanding or control.

Viewed from the grandstand of history, the 'Industrial Revolution' was a prime discontinuity. Yet it was contained within the somewhat more conventional discontinuity of the Discoveries whereby territory was effectively added to the European economic system. There never was an empire, an accession of 'ghost acreage', like the combined spheres of influence of the British, French and Dutch in the eighteenth century. The haul from this great, dispersed imperium raised per capita real incomes in the home countries to levels which compare favourably with the richer of the developing nations today. Europe had become a sink for global protein, raw materials, fertiliser, and energy. Resources were pulled in from farther and farther beyond its bounds. Rising marginal costs of obtaining resources, or obtaining them from a given area, were repeatedly collapsed by discoveries of new supplies or new areas of supply. The pressure of population was repeatedly deflated and the rise of the effective man : land ratio was slowed down. In such a fashion Europe became progressively more detached from its native ecological base until in the mid-twentieth century its prosperity hinged on the cheapness of imported food, raw materials and, above all else, energy in the form of petroleum oils. When stockpiles were run down and the Cold War stalemated in the wake of the Korean War, that prosperity seemed assured. Development economists came to elevate the over-supply of primary products to the status of a law. They neglected the gradual effects of rising resource consumption by the developing countries themselves and the latent political power which could be exerted through cartelisation. Subsequent events have shown the unwisdom of believing that resource inputs must be cheap.

An astonishingly productive and convoluted economic system had been founded on the assumption of cheap, extra-European resources. Europe was not the sole gainer, although that view is widely held. Without benefits of trade for the exporters of primary products the once-colonial world would have experienced less economic growth than it did. But the benefits were distributed asymmetrically. A grave imbalance in protein, raw materials, fertiliser and energy consumption marked the era of Europe's dominion over world economic and ecological history. Other polities have now begun to redress the balance, but the finite extent of ocean and grassland in the world implies that under any known technology they cannot replicate the means by which Europe rose. Future history looks to be informed by a bitter and more equal struggle for known reserves of natural resources; or more optimistically by technological advances which will economise on resource inputs; or in utopian vein by simpler ways of life, that is by a reduced consumption of material goods and hence of the resources needed to produce them; or most probably by varying, unstable combinations of these outcomes.

SELECT BIBLIOGRAPHY

Albion, R. G. *Forests and Sea Power: The Timber Problem of the Royal Navy 1652–1862*, Cambridge, Mass.: Harvard University Press, 1926

Algvere, K. V. *Forest Economy in the U.S.S.R.*, Stockholm: Studia Forestalia Suecica, No. 39, 1966

Bamford, Paul Walden. *Forests and French Sea-Power 1660–1789*, Univ. of Toronto Press, 1956

Bates, Marston. 'Man as an Agent in the Spread of Organisms', in W. L. Thomas (ed.), *Man's Rôle in Changing the Face of the Earth*, University of Chicago Press, II, 1956

Borgstrom, Georg. 'Ecological Aspects of Protein Feeding – The Case of Peru', in M. T. Farrar and J. P. Milton (eds.), *The Careless Technology: Ecology and International Development*, Garden City, New York: The Natural History Press, 1972

Bourlière, François. *The Land and Wildlife of Eurasia*, New York: Time-Life Inc., 1964

Braudel, Fernand. (Translated by Miriam Kochan). *Capitalism and Material Life 1400–1800*, London: Weidenfeld and Nicolson, 1967

Crosby, Alfred W. *The Columbian Exchange*, Westport, Connecticut: Greenwood, 1972

Cutting, C. L. *Fish Saving: A History of Fish Processing from Ancient to Modern Times*, London: L. Hill, 1955

Darby, H. C. 'The Face of Europe on the Eve of the Great Discoveries', in G. R. Potter (ed.), *The New Cambridge Modern History*, I, *The Renaissance (1493–1520)*, C.U.P., 1957

Darling, F. Fraser (ed.). *West Highland Survey: An Essay in Human Ecology*, O.U.P., 1955

Dovring, Folke. 'The Transformation of European Agriculture', in H. J. Habakkuk and M. Postan (eds.), *The Cambridge Economic History of Europe*, VI, *The Industrial Revolution and After*, Part II, C.U.P. 1965

Durand, J. D. 'The Modern Expansion of World Population', *Proceedings of the American Philosophical Society*, III (1967)

Evans, E. Estyn. 'The Ecology of Peasant Life in Western Europe', in W. L. Thomas (ed.), *Man's Rôle in Changing the Face of the Earth*, I, Chicago, 1956

Faber, J. A., Diederiks, H. A. and Hart, S. 'Urbanisering, Industrialisering en milieuaanstasting in Nederland in de period van 1500 tot 1800', *Afdeling Agrarische Geschiedenis Bijdragen*, 18 (1973)

Flawn, Peter T. *Mineral Resources: Geology, Engineering, Economics, Politics, Law*, New York: John Wiley & Sons Inc., 1966

Flinn, M. W. 'The Stabilisation of Mortality in Pre-Industrial Western Europe', *Journal of European Economic History*, 3 (1974)

Gray, Malcolm. *The Highland Economy, 1750–1850*, Edinburgh: Oliver & Boyd Ltd, 1957

Hannaway, Caroline C. 'The Société Royale de Médecine and Epidemics in the Ancien Régime', *Bulletin of the History of Medicine*, 46 (1972)

Harris, J. R. 'The Rise of Coal Technology', *Scientific American*, 231 (August, 1974)

Helleiner, K. F. 'The Population of Europe from the Black Death to the Eve of the Vital Revolution', in E. E. Rich and C. H. Wilson (eds.), *The Cambridge Economic History of Europe*, IV, *The Economy of Expanding Europe in the Sixteenth and Seventeenth Centuries*, C.U.P., 1967

Hirst, L. Fabian. *The Conquest of Plague: A Study of the Evolution of Epidemiology*, Oxford: The Clarendon Press, 1953

Howe, G. M. *Man, Environment and Disease in Britain*, Newton Abbot: David & Charles, 1972

Jenkins, J. T. *A History of the Whale Fisheries*, London: H. F. & G. Witherby, 1921

Jones, E. L. *Agriculture and the Industrial Revolution*, Oxford: Basil Blackwell, 1974 (Chapter 5, 'Agricultural Origins of Industry')
'Afterword' in William N. Parker and E. L. Jones (eds.), *European Peasants and Their Markets: Essays in Agrarian Economic History*, Princeton, New Jersey: Princeton University Press, 1975

Lane, Frank W. *The Elements Rage*, London: Sphere Books, 1968 (2 volumes)

Langer, William L. 'American Foods and Europe's Population Growth 1750–1850', *Journal of Social History*, 10 (1975)

Large, E. C. *The Advance of the Fungi*, New York: H. Holt & Co., 1940

MacLeod, W. C. 'Celt and Indian: Britain's Old World Frontier in Relation to the New', in Paul Bohannan and Fred Plog (eds.), *Beyond the Frontier*, Garden City, New York: The Natural History Press, 1967

Masefield, G. B. 'Crops and Livestock' in E. E. Rich & C. H. Wilson (eds.), *The Cambridge Economic History of Europe*, IV, *The Economy of Expanding Europe in the Sixteenth and Seventeenth Centuries*, C.U.P., 1967

McCracken, Eileen. *The Irish Woods Since Tudor Times: Distribution and Exploitation*, Newton Abbot: David & Charles, 1971

Mumford, Lewis. *The City in History*, New York: Harcourt, Brace & World, 1961

Netboy, A. *The Atlantic Salmon: A Vanishing Species?*, London: Faber, 1968

Ordish, George. *The Great Wine Blight*, London: J. M. Dent & Sons Ltd, 1972

Peet, Richard, 'Influences of the British Market on agriculture and related economic development in Europe before 1860', Institute of British Geographers, *Transactions*, 56 (1972)

Pipes, Richard. *Russia Under the Old Régime*, New York: Charles Scribner's Sons, 1974 (Chapter I, 'The Environment and its consequences')

Richardson, H. G. 'Some Remarks on British Forest History', *Transactions of the Royal Scottish Arboricultural Society*, 35 (1921) and 36 (1922)

Russell, W. M. S. *Man, Nature and History*, London: Aldus Books, 1967

Slicher van Bath, B. H. *The Agrarian History of Western Europe A.D. 500–1800*, London: Edward Arnold, 1963

Smith, C. T. *An Historical Geography of Western Europe before 1800*, London: Longmans, 1967

Te Brake, W. H. 'Air Pollution and Fuel Crises in Preindustrial London, 1250–1650', *Technology & Culture*, 16 (1975)

Tubbs, Colin R. *The New Forest: An Ecological History*, Newton Abbot: David & Charles, 1968

41

Utterström, Gustaf. 'Climatic Fluctuations and Population Problems in Early Modern History', *The Scandinavian Economic History Review*, III (1955)

von Viettinghoff-Riesch, Dr Baron. 'Outlines of the History of German Forestry', *Irish Forestry*, 15 (1958)

Wilkinson, Richard G. *Poverty and Progress: An Ecological Model of Economic Development*, London: Methuen, 1973

Woodham-Smith, Cecil. *The Great Hunger: Ireland 1845–1849*. New York & Evanston: Harper & Row, 1962

Woytinsky, W. S. & W. S. *World Population & Production: Trends and Outlook*, New York: The Twentieth Century Fund, 1953

Wrigley, E. A. 'The Supply of Raw Materials in the Industrial Revolution', *Economic History Review*, 2nd Series, XV (1962)

CHAPTER III

INDUSTRY

The forms of late medieval industry[1]

INDUSTRIAL activity in Europe in the late fifteenth century fell typically into five forms. Two of these were destined to decline over the following several centuries; one was to continue a vigorous life over the whole period covered in this essay, then virtually to disappear; and two, under pressures from changes in technology, were to blend

[1] Recent surveys have made this body of experience somewhat more accessible to English-language readers. On the subjects treated in this and the following section, see: Fernand Braudel, *Capitalism and Material Life 1400–1800* (New York, Harper & Row, 1973); *The Cambridge Economic History of Europe* (London, Cambridge University Press, 1952–67); Jan De Vries, *The Economy of Europe in an Age of Crisis 1600–1750* (London, Cambridge University Press, 1976); Hermann Kellenbenz, *The Rise of the European Economy* (London, Weidenfeld & Nicolson, 1976); Gino Luzzatto, *An Economic History of Italy from the Fall of the Roman Empire to the Beginning of the Sixteenth Century* (London, Routledge & Kegan Paul, 1961); H. A. Miskimin, Jr, *The Economy of Early Renaissance Europe 1300–1460* (Englewood Cliffs, New Jersey, Prentice-Hall, Inc., 1969); Domenico Sella, 'European Industries 1500–1700' in C. M. Cipolla (ed.), *The Fontana Economic History of Europe*, vol. 2 (London, Collins/Fontana Books, 1974) and Sylvia Thrupp, 'Medieval Industry 1000–1500' in volume one of the same series (1972).

Among the many articles, see: Max Barkhausen, 'Government Control and Free Enterprise in Western Germany and the Low Countries in the Eighteenth Century' in Peter Earle (ed.), *Essays in European Economic History 1500–1800* (London, Oxford University Press, 1974); Eleanora Carus-Wilson, 'The Woollen Industry' in M. M. Postan and E. E. Rich (eds.), *The Cambridge Economic History of Europe*, vol. II (London, Cambridge University Press, 1952); Hermann Kellenbenz, 'Rural Industries in the West from the End of the Middle Ages to the Eighteenth Century' in Peter Earle (ed.), *Essays in European Economic History 1500–1800*; Herbert Kisch, 'The Impact of the French Revolution on the Lower Rhine Textile Districts – Some Comments on Economic Development and Social Change', *Economic History Review*, 2nd ser., 15 (1962), 304–27, and 'Textile Industries in The Rhineland and Silesia, A Comparative Study', *Journal of Economic History*, 19 (1959), 541–69; Marian Malowist, 'The Economic and Social Development of the Baltic Countries from the Fifteenth to the Seventeenth Century', *Economic History Review*, 2nd ser., 12 (1959), 177–89; Joan Thirsk, 'Industries in the Countryside' in F. J. Fisher (ed.), *Essays in the Economic and Social History of Tudor and Stuart England* (London, Cambridge University Press, 1961); Herman Van Der Wee, 'The Structural Changes and Specialization in the Industry of the Southern Netherlands, 1100–1600', *Economic History Review*, 2nd ser., 28 (1975), 203–21; H. Van Werveke, 'Industrial Growth in the Middle Ages: The Cloth Industry of Flanders', *Economic History Review*, 2nd ser., 6 (1953–4), 237–54.

For older literature, see: Karl Bücher, 'Gewerbe' in the *Hand-wörterbuch der Staatswissenschaften*, vol. 4 (Jena, G. Fischer, 1892) and *Industrial Evolution* (1901; reprinted 1967; New York, Burt Franklin); J. U. Nef, 'Industrial Enterprise at the Time of the Reformation, *c.* 1515–*c.* 1540' and 'Mining and Metallurgy in Medieval Society' in *The Conquest of the Material World* (Chicago, University of Chicago Press, 1964); George Unwin, *Industrial Organization in the Sixteenth and Seventeenth Centuries* (1904; reprinted 1965; New York, Augustus M. Kelley); Max Weber, *General Economic History* translated by Frank Knight (New York, Greenberg, 1927).

together to create the industrial technique and organisation, larger-scale and continuously dynamic, that we recognise as characteristically modern.

The *village industry*, descended from the specialised crafts on manorial estates was perhaps the most widespread of these forms. The serf status of the artisan, continued or restored in eastern Europe, had been permanently transmuted in the West to that of free worker owning his tools and materials. But markets were local, pay was often made in kind, and the artisan, particularly if he held a bit of land from a lord or one of his subtenants, was effectively immobilized. The shoemaker, the smith, the carpenter, the thatcher, the mason, the miller, the butcher, the baker, the weaver – all were distributed in local markets over the countryside, drawing upon the locality for most materials and serving the households of village and rural families. Their work was supplemented by the industry of itinerant craftsmen who transported their capital – i.e. their skills and a few tools – from place to place, eating their way through the countryside, sometimes in the training years of an urban apprenticeship, sometimes in a permanently gypsy-like existence. Below the level of village industry, the primitive *industry of peasant households* for their own or local consumption continued in many more remote areas. Except for the basic tasks of food preparation, it is difficult to find in fifteenth-century Europe, or thereafter, examples of the degree of self-sufficiency in a rural household that characterised the extreme conditions of the American frontier. The village form of social organisations was designed, one might almost suppose, to avoid it, and to afford to an agriculture of low productivity the means to release a few specialised workers for industrial tasks.[1]

An immense gap in skill and organisational complexity existed between village and peasant industry and that of the *workshops of urban artisans*. In north Italian cities and the Flemish towns they are as well known to us

[1] The standard references on the history of Renaissance technology are the rather widely known and compendious volumes: Maurice Daumas (ed.), *A History of Technology and Invention*, vol. 2 (New York, New Crown Publishers, 1969); T. K. Derry and T. I. Williams, *A Short History of Technology* (London, Oxford University Press, 1961); Melvin Kranzberg and C. W. Pursell, Jr (eds.), *Technology in Western Civilization*, vol. 1 (New York, Oxford University Press, 1967); Charles Singer *et al.* (eds.), *A History of Technology*, vol. 3 (London, Oxford University Press, 1957).

My own knowledge owes most to A. P. Usher's classic treatment, *A History of Mechanical Invention* (revised edn, New York, McGraw-Hill Book Company, Inc., 1954) and to the books and articles of J. U. Nef, especially *The Rise of the British Coal Industry* (London, G. Routledge & Sons, Ltd., 1932) and his essays reprinted as *The Conquest of the Material World* (Chicago, University of Chicago Press, 1964); also to C. M. Cipolla's interesting little books, *Clocks and Culture 1300–1700* (New York, Walker and Company, 1967) and *Guns and Sails in the Early Phase of European Expansion 1400–1700* (London, Collins, 1965) and Samuel Lilley, *Men, Machines and History* (London, Lawrence & Wishart, 1965) as well as his chapter 'Technological Progress and the Industrial Revolution 1700–1914' in C. M. Cipolla (ed.), *The Fontana Economic History of Europe*, vol. 3 (London, Collins/Fontana, 1973) and Hermann Kellenbenz's chapter 'Technology in the Age of the Scientific Revolution 1500–1700' in volume two of the same series.

through the history of the decorative arts, producing at their highest the masterpieces of painting and sculpture of the Italian and north European Renaissance, as through the history of useful industry. The form of organisation was much the same in the fine and the practical arts and had not much changed since the flourishing of the craft guilds in the twelfth to fourteenth centuries. A master workman trained journeymen and apprentices, the latter bound to him, almost as family members, for a period of years. The master in turn was controlled to a degree through the guild, which set prices, terms of apprenticeship and standards of quality. The master workman had his own customers, or dealt with a merchant who also brought in supplies. The system, like the village agriculture of the period, remained a mixture of group control, individual initiative, and private property. The resurgence of princely authority since the late Middle Ages had destroyed some of the political power of the guilds but in many cities in 1500 they still formed an important component in town government.

A fourth industrial form present at the outset of the expansive period of European capitalism was *Montanindustrie*, mining, smelting, charcoal burning and quarrying, located with reference to the sources of supplies of the natural raw material. Since these were deep in the mountains and forests, the industries exploiting them tended to be part of landed estates, with labourers closer still to a serf-like status and controls altogether less capitalistic than in the village or urban workshops. The iron industry, often considered in this category, was in fact only partly so. Small iron deposits in shallow diggings were exploited at many scattered locations. Iron production was located with reference to ore and charcoal supplies and, with the fifteenth- and sixteenth-century development of the blast furnace and rolling mill, to waterpower sources as well. But the further working of bar iron occurred at forges near market locations.

Finally, *merchant-organised networks combining rural and urban labour* were widely employed. In the medieval wool trade a famous division of labour had existed between England which grew the wool, Flanders which spun and wove it, and Italy which dyed and finished it. The growth of the Italian woollen industry in the fourteenth century had displaced this trade by putting out materials within the Italian countryside. But in East Anglia and the west country in England, and in patches on the Continent – in Flanders, Switzerland, parts of northern France – forms of a putting out system had begun to flourish wherever rural labour could be put to use or where waterpower in the fulling operation had drawn that part of the finishing trades to the countryside.

In 1500 the forms of industrial organisation in western Europe then were the following: (a) village and local specialised industry; (b) peasant industry for the household; (c) urban artisan industry; (d) materials-oriented industries in the countryside; (e) merchant-organised systems, combining rural and urban labour. All these forms had been present in the thirteenth century, and all persisted in one corner of Europe or another up through the nineteenth century. The changes of the early and middle modern period, i.e. from 1500 to 1850, which are the subject of this essay, occurred steadily throughout these 350 years, in response to a number of economic and technical factors, in particular as a result of the interaction between market growth and technical change. Before the mid-eighteenth century much the major causative factor, insofar as it is possible to weigh such things, was, as Adam Smith discerned, the steady growth of markets – the increase in the volumes of industrial goods which could be sold.

The growth of the market

To analyse the reasons for the market growth would lead the discussion far into the total economic, social and political history of the early modern period. Evidently a mass of self-reinforcing expansionary processes lay implicit in the European environment and social system of the fifteenth century. They have been only very incompletely laid bare. Population growth, resuming its upward course after the catastrophes of the fourteenth century must have expanded the margin of cultivation, and in so doing have increased the absolute surplus available to support a non-agricultural workforce. If then economies of scale were present in industry taken as a whole, a rise in industrial productivity would ensue and with it a rise in the market for both manufactures and agricultural products. Or again the growth of the state – the notable feature of Western political history in the sixteenth and seventeenth centuries – centralised and magnified demand for certain specific industrial products – for military equipment, for ships, for coinage, for the constructions and luxury consumption of princely courts. The stream of landed revenues must have been in part diverted to the hands of those who demanded goods with a higher skill and materials component and a lower component of sheer labour services. The growth of taxes, with royal imposts piled on top of feudal dues, must have increased the slice taken from the peasantry whose localised demand patterns were less favourable to concentrated industrial activities. In this same category of explanation must be placed the famous sixteenth-century inflation – perhaps four-fold over the century and affecting agricultural goods more strongly than manufactures. Whatever the distortions produced in the distribution of income, it would not be surprising if a price rise in the presence of some reserves of rural under-employment should have stimulated total demand. It would be interesting, too, to speculate on whether larger supplies of the precious metals and the growth in credit instruments and forms of debt did not itself extend the market simply by facilitating trade, encouraging the conversion of barter transactions to monetary ones and permitting the accomplishment of trading transactions which under a scarcity of money would not have been consummated at all.

The growth of trade itself may be looked on as an exogenous prime mover insofar as improvements in navigation, ship construction and the increase of geographical knowledge were involved. Here within the growth of trade itself occurred a reciprocal process, moving from its expansion to the knowledge, growth, and technical changes which made further trade possible. Beyond that, the distributional shifts and social and organisational changes accompanying the trade expansion both affected the growth of the market for industrial goods and the changes in the organisational forms within industry itself; this will be shown in more detail below. Directly, one can attribute major economic effects before the eighteenth century not to the overseas expansion, but to the growth of trade within Europe, the Dutch–Baltic trade, and the trade between the North Sea and the Mediterranean. Yet the overseas trade – round Africa and to the Americas – must have acted as an important exogenous stimulus, whose effects were multiplied within Europe itself. Closely related were the social and intellectual changes which, intertwined with the contemporary religious and political change, made western Europe in the sixteenth century a seedbed of individualistic mercantile and capitalistic industrial enterprise.

The market growth then was accompanied by changes in the shape of demand, by the development of forms of business and market organisation, and by a spirit of enterprise which, taken within its institutional forms, we call capitalistic. It should be emphasised that the effects of market expansion were felt in the sixteenth to eighteenth centuries not only in the mercantile sector, but in industry as well. Village and peasant industry for immediate consumption probably did not flourish, although it maintained its share of local markets until the displacements produced by the technical changes of the eighteenth and nineteenth centuries. But urban workshops, mines, and smelting works prospered, the latter benefiting from some notable technical improvements. To them were added, particularly in the France of Colbert, the royal manufactories, the mints, arsenals, potteries, and textile factories under royal sponsorship and finance. Growth of a state sector was accompanied by the sponsorship of technical discovery and of science, described in the following section.

Among the industrial forms, it was the merchant-organised and merchant-dominated rural industry which enjoyed the greatest expansion. Where trade and mercantile influence was strongest – in the Midlands and the north of England and along the great river of industry that ran from the Low Countries up the Rhine, across south Germany and over the north Italian plain – the activity was most striking. The actual penetration of the countryside, the use of surplus rural labour, the complex movements of materials and foods had gone far beyond the mere absorption of seasonally idle agricultural workers, or of women of farm households. A rural industrial labour force was present in these locations, engaged in full-time industrial activity for the market. Tasks were divided, small pieces of capital intruded themselves at each point. The demand patterns, wealth patterns, and especially the demographic behaviour of this labour force were radically different from those of a peasantry or of industrial workers in cities. At the same time, an alternative system of industrial organisation had not died out. Urban workshops, mills and mines, royal manufactories had increased in number and benefited from the technical changes of the sixteenth century more perhaps than the cottage industry could.

The path of technical change

Modern industrial society takes its origin in the eighteenth century at the intersection of two historical processes which, though never completely separate from one another, had developed during the Middle Ages and Renaissance in relative independence. One of these was the organisational development identifiable as early capitalistic enterprise. The other was the complex and uncertain process of technical changes.

That these two features of industrial history had existed in isolation in earlier periods is undeniable. Trade and production for private profit occurred in ancient Greece, in South Asia, and in medieval Europe, together with the introduction and diffusion of money as a means of payment. Technical changes were not notable in mercantile capitalism of this sort; indeed it is not clear that the mercantile mentality with its quick calculations and short time horizons is best suited to understanding and fostering the uncertain, obscure and capital- and skill-intensive activities by which production processes are improved. On the other hand, technical changes had appeared in societies – for example in China – where the drive for maximum profit or the pressure of market failure was relatively remote. The very slowness of technical change over mankind's history, its spottiness, the lack of ready diffusion of its results, may be attributable to the relative isolation of peasant producers, royal households and craft workshops from the force of competition on capitalistically organised markets. So long as merchants dealt in the natural surplus of a region's agriculture, or in goods produced in the local monopolies of the countryside or the guild-dominated city, capitalist competition did not systematically penetrate the structure of production. Technology remained largely a matter of the transmission of the considerable body of hand skills, the arts of industry and agriculture, acquired painfully over thousands of years of industrial history and held tenuously in the brains and trained muscles of the living generation of craftsmen or in the pages of a very few hand-copied texts and treatises. In technology's long and uncertain development before 1800, new ideas appear rarely and when they do, it is as if in the thought processes of an absent-minded man. They do not diffuse readily over space, nor are they followed up in all their refinements and implications even at their points of origin. There is a lack of concentration in the history, a lack of cumulative effect in the development.

Nevertheless the industry of the sixteenth century benefited from an accretion of inventions that had occurred in Europe during the preceding 500 years. Among power sources, to be sure, no striking innovation occurred. Only in the development of firearms was the expansive power of gases harnessed to any use. Wind and water remained, and were to remain till the late eighteenth century, the only inanimate prime movers with appreciable industrial use. Except for water in mill ponds and dams, they could not be stored; hence industrial operations beyond the strength of men or beasts were as dependent on the variability of natural forces as was agriculture. In the face of this restriction, the main development in the sixteenth and seventeenth centuries was the diffusion, development and generalisation in a variety of uses, of the water wheel. In mining, in iron working, in fulling and other operations requiring a stamping and hammering motion, the water-wheel hitched to many ingenious gearing devices came into much wider use.

Connected to this development were several improvements in the other components of an integrated technology: the provision of raw materials and the transmission of power. Materials supplies were increased in the sixteenth century by improvements in mining, in paper-making, and through the development of the blast furnace, which spread probably from the neighbourhood of Liège up the Rhine to the south-east, and also north across the channel. The largest branch of industry – textiles – remained dependent, however, on traditional raw materials: wool from England and Spain, flax from the North Sea coast, and a little cotton from Egypt and the Middle East. It was the extension of trade within Europe and the geographical exploration overseas rather than technical change that widened European industry's resource base. Precious metals from the New World, and increased supplies of Baltic timber and Swedish bar iron were important accessions.

On the whole industry improved most through the further development of mechanisms for the transmission of power. Here the structure of the technology was, in a sense, best able to yield to the pressures and incentives of a growing demand. The lathe, that marvellous late medieval tool, was developed, improved and adapted to many uses. The products of the smithy, forge and machine shop were not the complex forms of machinery for further production known to the late eighteenth century, but direct consumer goods: firearms, clocks and watches, scientific instruments, furniture, hardware of all sorts, crude agricultural implements. No invention in the operations of the textile industry in its many branches approached that late medieval invention, the spinning-wheel, in productivity-raising effect. Where inventions occurred, for example, the stocking frame and the ribbon loom, they had a striking, but rather localised impact. Diffusion was slow, and the basic operations of cloth-making remained unaffected. Most characteristic of the sixteenth and seventeenth centuries was the strenuous activity of the industries involving the largely unmechanised assembly of parts and materials – construction and ship-building. Here organisation was important; although designs, styles and materials altered, the crafts and their tools remained much as the Middle Ages had left them.

In the three centuries prior to 1750, then, some changes occurred in the three branches of technology: power generation, power transmission and materials production. Particularly between about 1450 and 1600, a mini-revolution may be identified in the application of waterpower in mining and iron-making, the developments in smelting, and in the invention of ingenious mechanisms, especially in branches of production specifically stimulated by a spreading luxury demand – firearms, printing, clocks. Many of the improvements originated in south Germany, and the diffusion of inventions was fairly rapid after the invention of printing and where the items themselves moved in trade. In the imaginative notebooks of Leonardo da Vinci sketches of these Renaissance inventions went far beyond actual practice, but retained that scattered quality characteristic of all pre-modern technical change. They depended in no respect upon the introduction of any drastically new scientific or engineering principle, such as was to characterise invention in the late eighteenth and early nineteenth centuries and they had little interaction with one another. No chains of rapid inventive progress were forged to pull productivity along in one industry after another, with the steady upward movement that became the mark of the Industrial Revolution and the industrial history that followed it. The productivity growth may have contributed to the relatively less rapidly rising prices of industrial goods in the six-teenth-century inflation but the growth of demand appeared still largely dependent on the factors mentioned above – population movements, political change, geographical discovery, the increase in trade. Technology was learning, in a sense, to respond to market incentives, but it could not yet lead the way to continuous market growth.

The generating institutions of scientific and technical knowledge[1]

The historian, at least when he works on a period where data are scarce is always part-novelist, employing a narrative rhetoric in which the tone and emphases of the discussion and the arrangement of its parts contribute to its interest and its verisimilitude. At this point in this essay, it would be appropriate and straightforward to move directly into the English Industrial Revolution. When we do that, in the following section, it will become apparent how readily that central development follows upon the general market growth, the articulated economic institutions and the rather diffused technological change of the sixteenth and seventeenth centuries. For a treatment, which encompasses the nineteenth century, even in part, on the Continent, however, it is necessary to consider another early modern development, whose connection with the inventions of the fifty years following 1750 is thought by most scholars to have been tenuous, but whose underlying importance for the path of modern industrial development as a whole can hardly be denied. This development is, of course, the growth of fundamental science, with a particular body of social institutions to carry it on, and a particular mentality, a way of looking at the world that we now recognise as 'modern'.

Scientific thought is akin to the rising capitalism of the Renaissance in several respects. Both are materialistic philosophies *of this world*, and both – at least in their European form, were conceived as activities of individuals rather than of social or corporate entities. Both began to grow in European society before the Protestant Reformation and were

[1] Some useful references from the large literature in this field include the following: J. D. Bernal, *Science in History*, vol. 2 (London, Penguin Books, 1969); A. F. Burstall, *A History of Mechanical Engineering* (Cambridge, Massachusetts, M.I.T. Press, 1965); E. A. Burtt, *The Metaphysical Foundations of Modern Physical Science* (New York, Doubleday, 1955); Herbert Butterfield, *The Origins of Modern Science 1300–1800* (London, G. Bell and Sons Ltd., 1950); G. N. Clark, *Science and Social Welfare in the Age of Newton* (second edn, London, Oxford University Press, 1949) and *The Seventeenth Century* (New York, Oxford University Press, 1961); A. C. Crombie, *Mechanical and Early Modern Science*, 2 vols. (New York, Doubleday, 1959); A. R. Hall, *The Scientific Revolution, 1500–1800* (Boston, Beacon Press, 1956) and 'Scientific Method and the Progress of Techniques' in E. E. Rich and C. H. Wilson (eds.), *The Cambridge Economic History of Europe*, vol. IV (London, Cambridge University Press, 1967); Peter Mathias, 'Who Unbound Prometheus? Science and Technical Change, 1600–1800' in Peter Mathias (ed.), *Science and Society 1600–1900* (London, Cambridge University Press, 1972); R. K. Merton, *Science, Technology and Society in Seventeenth Century England* (New York, Harper Torchbooks, 1970); René Taton, *Reason and Chance in Scientific Discovery* (New York, Philosophical Library Inc., 1957); A. N. Whitehead, *Science and the Modern World* (New York, Pelican Mentor Books, 1948); Edgar Zilsel, 'The Sociological Roots of Science', *American Journal of Sociology*, 47 (1942), 544–62.

On the ancient argument over Protestantism and Capitalism, an article by Herbert Lüthy, 'Once Again: Calvinism and Capitalism', *Encounter*, 22 (1964), 26–38, contains a new point of view which I have adopted here. A very recent thoughtful statement of a different, but by no means contradictory view, is made by Albert O. Hirschman, *The Passions and the Interests* (Princeton, New Jersey, Princeton University Press, 1977).

indeed part of the social and intellectual ferment from which the Renaissance, the Reformation and the modern national state arose. Both involved a trust in tangible sense data and both were rebellious against authority, especially when it interfered with the individual pursuit of gain, or of scientific truth. The medieval Catholic world had furnished not only a relation of man to God and His Church, but also a sense of the social whole. It was a world in which ideally every part and person depended upon every other, the whole bound together by a common belief in another world, and by a common magic – the magic of the church and its sacraments – as much as in any primitive society studied by anthropologists in recent times. Against this social sense, with its supernatural sanctions, capitalism put the pursuit of individual gain, without regard to just prices, usury restrictions, or any ultra-mundane devotion. Science, though long retaining a magical and religious aura, depended in Galileo or Bacon on an individual mind's search for truth by observation and experiment. The Protestant Reformation then expressing a similar individualism in the search for the soul's salvation, achieved a rapid, religious symbiosis with both capitalism and science which Catholicism never could attain.

Yet neither capitalism nor science could avoid or dispense with the institutionalisation of their thought and behaviour patterns, the regularisation of the norms by which both money-making and truth-finding might be legitimately achieved and success tested and identified, and the development of devices for communicating their culture to others and to successive generations. These tasks were vested only partially in the state; private business activities, private agreements and codes of behaviour, private meetings and correspondence formed the basic stratum of a developing modern culture in the economic and intellectual life of northern Europe in the seventeenth and eighteenth centuries. The small peer groups – companies of merchants, societies of amateur scientists, corresponding members of university faculties – began to form a significant social class, an aristocracy of money, enterprise or intellect within which the rewards and sanctions exceeded anything that a king or his courts could have imposed.

The free European market both in goods and ideas developed, however, in the presence of – one might almost say under the very nose of – a state apparatus which in the sixteenth and seventeenth centuries did not remotely resemble that of the nineteenth century when capitalism and science had become dominant. The relation to this state – the royal and centralist state of sixteenth-century England and seventeenth-century France – was ambivalent and, like most ambivalent relationships, stormy. Merchants and manufacturers depended on the growing power of the central government for many things: first, for special privileges, grants of monopoly, contracts and trading rights; second, for the establishment of a currency system and the chartering and protection of financial institutions; third, for the legitimising of commercial contracts, the protection of property, and to a considerable degree the control of the labour force. On the other hand, their interests were not synonymous with those of the state, and the presence both of the landed interest and the monarch himself ensured a conflict. Clearly for commercial expansion, the optimal arrangement was that experienced in the Dutch Republic after its successful revolt against the Spanish emperor and in England after the 'Glorious Revolution' of 1688: i.e. the substantial hegemony of the mercantile interest in the conduct of government. In France, the policies of Richelieu, Mazarin, and Colbert directed toward fostering trade and industry were a rather weak substitute for the stimulus given to trade by the provision of a greater degree of bourgeois freedom in the Protestant lands.[1]

However, for the development of science, as distinguished from practical improvements in technology, it is not clear that the dominance of society by the commercial classes was the most favourable arrangement. The role of scientist, even in the amateur or non-institutionalised science of the Renaissance, is closer to that of the theologian or scholar-priest than to that of the inventor of practical technology. He is the elaborator of the true view of the world, employing a method involving both reasoning and appeals to sense data, to give men an understanding of where they are in relation to the universe, and what is the ultimate constitution of matter and material forces. The sponsorship of such an institution devolved naturally upon those who in previous ages had sponsored the church and ecclesiastical foundations and activities. Included among these foundations were the universities, which in the sixteenth and seventeenth centuries were beginning to change from the monkish groups of the Middle Ages engaged in theological disputation into the general purpose institutions of knowledge we know today.

Science then, of the more or less 'pure' variety – the natural philosophy which investigated astronomy, mechanics, and even chemistry – found the growing interest in its methods and its findings institutionalised and sponsored in several directions: first, in small private groups and societies of interested men, rich enough to pursue such a hobby; second, under specific sponsorship and financial support by noblemen and monarchs and even by wealthy bankers or merchants, as part of a general sponsorship of the arts; third, in the universities, as separately endowed foundations under royal or ecclesiastical patronage. In the Protestant states, private groups with some royal sponsorship were largely responsible for the growing body of experimentation and research; in southern Europe,

---

[1] Nothing has surpassed the treatment of French and other mercantilisms by C. H. Wilson in 'Trade, Society and the State' in E. E. Rich and C. H. Wilson (eds.), *The Cambridge Economic History of Europe*, vol. IV (London, Cambridge University Press, 1967).

science had to live under the watchful eye of the church and the Inquisition; in France, a characteristic mixture of Catholic and Protestant forms, in this as in many other things, offered perhaps the most favourable climate for the development. The Inquisition was absent; sponsorship by the crown, eager to exhibit itself as the source of all knowledge and all light, was generous, yet a spirit of free rationalism was not smothered. By the eighteenth century, these institutions had matured into a strong network of intercommunicating groups. Even in Prussia, Russia and Austria, the monarchs of the Enlightenment, affected by a culture that had its home and origin in France, founded schools and academies. At length that Black Prince of the Enlightenment, the Emperor Napoleon I, in France itself, established a legal, educational, and professional structure for the country which crystallised and routinised the seventeenth- and eighteenth-century practice.

From Galileo to Darwin, then, European science participated in, and even led, the general development of a triumphant and glorious secular culture, its rationalism animated by a glowing faith in reason, its materialism made endurable by a strongly felt esthetic, its potentially corroding individualism checked and channelled by an emergent nationalism, by strong state power, and the sense of participation internationally in a developing bourgeois culture, replacing the universal aristocratic and ecclesiastical culture of Catholic Christianity. In this cultural climate the Protestant sects – Lutheran, Calvinist, Puritan, Baptist, and even the national churches that had broken with Rome – flourished. But the back of ecclesiastical domination of thought, science, and the fine arts had been broken by Luther's revolt and Henry VIII's bullying, and by the wars of religion in the Netherlands, France, and the German states. Theology was no longer the queen of the sciences. Catholicism was no longer Europe's state religion. Despite the emphatic personal ethics of its sixteenth- and seventeenth-century founders, and the persistence of such an ethic far into the nineteenth century, Protestantism was in fact a much weaker form of social control than Catholicism had been. By the nineteenth century, the scientist, the political economist, the politician and the businessman had replaced the courtier and the priest.

From the viewpoint of industrial history, it is not clear that European science until the middle of the nineteenth century was of much practical value. Industrial technology, and agricultural technology too, developed by 'tinkering', i.e. by rather random experimentation aimed at some useful object. The details of the process are considered in the next section, where it becomes evident that the accumulation of various series of such efforts, produced at length the climax of interaction that we call the Industrial Revolution. The scientific investigation of nature proceeded along somewhat different lines. Yet parallelisms or interconnections between technological and scientific progress may be observed. For one thing, it seems quite apparent that much the same attitudes of mind motivated and guided both processes. A rational faith in the orderliness and predictability of physical processes and the stability of physical materials was combined with a refusal to accept any evidences of this faith except those offered by direct observation and material demonstration – a rejection of authority and of history, of all that could not be personally and individually seen, communicated, and made available to be confirmed by others. The difference between scientists and practical men before the nineteenth century lay in the scientists' effort to generalise their results with the instrument of mathematics, so as to produce 'laws' of nature. Where technological change stopped with the development of a useful device, process or material, going on only to employ it in further uses or in other inventions, the effort of scientists was to produce a general statement which would state the enduring relationship, preferably with a formula showing the magnitudes of the quantities and effects involved.

Given the similarities in the basic animating attitudes, it is no accident that both 'pure' science and applied technology experienced a lift in the intellectual climate of the centuries in which protestantism and capitalism grew, and a culture of rational humanism spread out from Italy over western and northern Europe. Nor is it an accident that the branch of science and technology which was first to yield up its secrets to the curiosity and contrivances of men in these centuries was that in which natural forces and materials are most ostentatiously displayed to the naked eye: the science and art of mechanics. By the eighteenth century, both the science and the art were well advanced, and one can then see forming between the two, the profession so important for nineteenth-century development, the mechanical engineer, acquainted with scientific principles, possessed of an adequate knowledge of mathematics, concerned with the exact and quantitative statement of a phenomenon or relationship, and interested in relating this knowledge and technique to the improvement of the useful arts, of machinery construction, bridge-building, road-building, mining, navigation. The development of such a profession requires that both the science and the technology in a field be at a certain point of development, each having arrived there separately to a degree and by empirical methods, a point which makes it possible to relate theory and practice in a stream of systematic improvements. But to say that this relationship could occur, first in mechanics, then in hydraulics (a branch of mechanics), then – beginning in the mid-nineteenth century in chemistry, finally in electricity, and the life sciences – is not to argue of either scientific progress or of technological change that one was the cause of the other. Bits of interconnection can of course be found. The devices and materials developed in industry were available for scientific experimentation, and the demands of scientists had a stimulating effect on the development of measuring, timekeeping, and other instrumental equipment. But relative to industrial markets generally, the demands of scientists were but one of many luxury demands of individuals and the state – fine tapestries, firearms, china – which a developing body of industrial crafts could serve. By and large, in the seventeenth and eighteenth centuries science and technology grew up together like twins in a family out of a common culture which had deep-hidden social and socio-psychological, and ideological, origins.

The Industrial Revolution: technological aspects

The brilliant mercantile expansion of northern Europe in the seventeenth and eighteenth centuries was accompanied by a measure of technical change. Europe was here involved in a complex social process in which three aspects were of predominant importance: mentality, scale and feedbacks. Of the mentality we have already spoken: an inquisitiveness about nature and a greedy desire to improve on her workings for practical ends. The scale depended partly on the diffusion of these attitudes and the links of communication between inventors and producers at points as distant as Italy and England, Sweden and Spain. With the economic and industrial awakening of northern Europe after 1550, a sharp increase had occurred in the area and in the population over which trade and the exchange of ideas and devices of technology were diffused. The growth in intra-European trade, plus the small but marginally very significant links with the nascent overseas empires in the Indies, the African coast and the Americas, meant a growth in market size which had many economic and productivity-raising effects. These depended largely on the spreading of fixed costs in the tangible and intangible social capital of which the new nation states could avail themselves. Rivers, harbours, shipyards, dock facilities became more crowded and more fully used. Knowledge of ship construction, the shipping lanes, and navigation became more widely spread and shared. As shipping routes became more complex, with numerous burgeoning ports of call, waste space and empty return hauls diminished.[1] The states grew strong enough to war on each other, which was a waste, but also to suppress internal tolls, bandits and marauders on land and sea, and to establish that chief public good of the modern state, internal peace and order, so as to permit the easy development of commercial practices, and laws of property and contract, enforced by the king's courts.[2] The growth of navies made possible the convoying of unarmed merchant ships, and the use for cargo of the space previously taken up by guns and fighting men. As such extensions of

[1] D. C. North, 'Sources of Productivity Change in Ocean Shipping', *Journal of Political Economy*, 76 (1968), 45–69.
[2] D. C. North and R. P. Thomas, *The Rise of the Western World* (London, Cambridge University Press, 1973); W. S. Holdsworth, *A History of English Law*, vols. 8, 10, 11 (seventh edn revised, London, Methuen & Co. Ltd., 1973, 1966, 1973).

scale lowered production and transport costs, incomes rose and the effective scale of the market was further increased. This purely economic feedback, dependent upon the phenomenon of decreasing social costs, was not, however, the most important effect of the expansion in the European economy and its interconnected commercial and industrial culture. To understand the crucial effect on the process of technological change, it is necessary to consider that process in a little more detail.[1]

Technological change, at least before the age of the research laboratory and a developed engineering and scientific base, depended upon the unorganised ideas and obsessions of individual inventors. These men came from various occupations, and often were themselves tool-users, conversant with some branch of production and observant of means of improving it. They became characteristically seized with a specific problem – the mechanising of stocking knitting, the casting of large pots, the working out of a control mechanism for a clock, the smelting of iron ore with coal – which they pursued with single-minded intent. Whether they solved it or not was partly a matter of luck, but it was also dependent on the ideas, materials, instruments and auxiliary devices with which their minds and their workshops were furnished. Given that an inventor was seized by a problem, his efforts to solve it were carried out on a stage which was set by all that he knew, and all the equipment and materials available at the time. At some point, in a successful invention, a moment arrived when, after weeks or years of conscious and unconscious concern with the solution, the combination of elements in the environment was hit upon, by accident, even in a dream, or sometimes with conscious design, which provided a feasible, economical solution. Following this, a period, called by Usher the period of 'critical revision', occurred in which the invention was refined, ancillary improvements were introduced, a model was made, a patent acquired and production begun. Even here, and in the early stages of the production process, many small inventions,

[1] See references cited in note 1, p. 44 above. A good bibliography on all the subjects in this and the following section is given in David Landes' contribution to *The Cambridge Economic History of Europe*, 'Technological Change and Development in Western Europe, 1750–1914', in vol. VI, part 2, H. J. Habakkuk and M. M. Postan (eds.) (London, Cambridge University Press, 1965), extended and published separately, without bibliography, as *The Unbound Prometheus* (London, Cambridge University Press, 1969). The role of science and technology has been re-examined by A. E. Musson and Eric Robinson, *Science and Technology in the Industrial Revolution* (Manchester, Manchester University Press, 1969) and D. S. L. Cardwell, *Turning Points in Western Technology* (New York, Science History Publications, 1972) and *The Organisation of Science in England* (revised edn, London, Heinemann, 1972). The coal technology and its effects on industrial skills and locations have been the subject of researches by J. R. Harris and his students. See J. R. Harris, 'Skills, Coal and British Industry in the Eighteenth Century', *History*, 61 (1976), 167–82; Jennifer Tann, 'Fuel Saving in the Process Industries during the Industrial Revolution', *Business History*, 15 (1973), 149–59. Two other recent treatments with new materials are R. L. Hills, *Power in the Industrial Revolution* (Manchester, Manchester University Press, 1970) and C. K. Hyde, *Technological Change and the British Iron Industry, 1700–1870* (Princeton, New Jersey, Princeton University Press, 1977).

small novelties were introduced. The whole was an act of creation perfectly analogous to the creation of a pure work of art or of the intellect.

Now the function of the environment in this process was to provide the inventor both with the problem and the means and stimulus for its solution. But the availability of such ideas and materials depended much upon how wide was the inventor's world and vision. The growth in the scale of the economy, and of western European industrial society, was a widening of this world. To provide in England, Swedish iron, or ideas published in German books, was to offer to English inventors materials and information which greatly facilitated their efforts. The function of scale expansion then, apart from spreading the fixed costs of equipment, transport, public goods and knowledge, was to increase the communication of such ideas and the availability of such materials and equipment. Across western Europe, in all the industrial areas, a race of inventors appeared in the wake of the industrial and commercial expansion. But it required a particular intensity of economic life, a rather strong concentration of industrial opportunity, a rather close-knit nexus of communication to produce a flowering of inventive activity. The combination of attitudes, ideas, knowledge, ambitions, commercial opportunity and the protective institutions of property and patent rights – all this was required to coax out invention and then, once it was begun, to give it its head.

Hence it was that 'the' Industrial Revolution occurred not in the old industrial areas of the Continent, in royal factories, or towns dominated by princes or the remains of guilds – but in England where trade expansion, capitalist institutions, a pragmatic view of the world, and a social structure that gave common tradesmen and mechanics appreciable freedom, were all simultaneously present and on an adequate scale. The Netherlands, a closely analogous case in many respects, could not furnish so large an internal market or so broad a base in industry and industrial resources. England, on the other hand, which had shared but not dominated the European expansion in scientific knowledge, maintaining her connection with the intellectual sources of invention, offered a commercial climate in which the activity could flourish.

Given this locus for inventions, it is of interest to examine their specific interconnections. Figure 1 divides inventions into three groups: the production of materials, the generation of power from inanimate sources, and the transmission of power – its 'harnessing' to move the right part, at the right speed, in the right direction. These branches of technology in the eighteenth century existed in what may seem by some retrospective standard to have been uneven states of development. The third, being mainly the province of mechanical technology, was the most advanced. Using parts made of wood or of iron, employing the power of animals (including men), of gravity, generally with the medium of falling or mov-

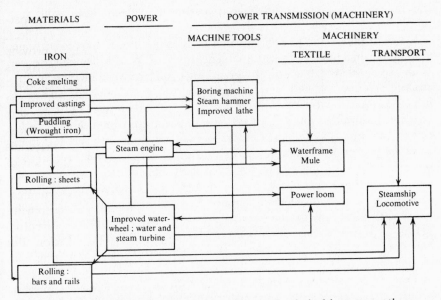

Fig. I. The Industrial Revolution: sequence and technical interconnections, 1750–1850.

ing water, or of the wind, a body of equipment had developed since antiquity, which under the inducements of the sixteenth and seventeenth centuries had acquired considerable sophistication. Until the middle of the nineteenth century, it was these mechanisms which showed the greatest development. Most of the industrial revolution was the extension of machinery – now built of iron – into new types of operations and new branches of manufacture and agriculture. Underlying the whole development of the mechanical side was the elaboration of machine tools and the development of a profession of mechanical engineering whose calculations could improve design and efficiency. The mechanical inventions of the period 1760–1850 make a very long list indeed, and developed partly out of one another, employing parts, devices, or ideas to produce a widening array of products.

Alongside these inventions, the other two branches of technology have only two major changes to offer: in materials production, the improvement and cheapening of iron through smelting, refining, and further working; and in power generation, the development of the steam engine, itself largely a mechanical invention except for the novel power source employed. The important improvements in the water-wheel came largely as the result of careful application of principles of mechanical and hydraulic engineering to an old device. It may be thought a convenient formulation to call these 'enabling inventions', which occurred at just the time and to just the degree to permit the mechanical industrial revolution to flourish.

It would take a long book to begin to specify all the interconnections among the mechanical inventions. The story of Watt's dependence on Wilkinson's boring machine to give him cylinders machined to a fine enough tolerance is but one example. Through the mass of technical interrelations an evolving body of machine technology was initiated. Its creation required a number of economic, social and intellectual conditions, notably: (1) a moderately large and well-organised market sufficient to make invention profitable; (2) within that market, some bottlenecks focussing attention on specific points in the technical processes of manufacture, offering rewards for the solution to specific technical problems; (3) a body of skilled mechanics, tool-users and ingenious practical men who kept in touch with one another and with manufacturers; (4) means of finance at least at the very modest levels required in this sort of research and development; (5) an absence of interference or excessive direction or planning from a central authority, whether the state or the money market. In these circumstances, invention could become a kind of folk activity, done repeatedly, on very small scale, by very many different operators. An attack of this kind on the secrets of nature is sometimes called a 'shotgun approach' – the firing of many small missiles at the target. Obviously such a process entails great individual loss, many bankruptcies and much suffering. In the absence of full knowledge of the underlying science, no other way of guiding invention was possible.

Given this social technique of invention, it was certainly no accident that mechanical invention flourished while subtler forms and problems of technology – in chemistry or physics, animal breeding or the plant sciences for example – lay untouched. Most of its basic knowledge goes back to Aristotle and Archimedes and the development of mechanisms for specific tasks was not a matter of research but of contrivance. Ingenuity and imagination were required, but the instrument of observation was the naked eye and, unlike the case in agricultural sciences, the success or failure of an experiment could be immediately known. No historian of technology has yet arrayed discoveries in various branches in order of their inherent difficulty, or in relation to the capital equipment in instruments, scientific knowledge, and experience required to bring them to light. Yet such an investigation must underlie the understanding of why modern technology developed in the forms and sequences that in fact it did.

The fact that mechanical inventions came first, employing iron and moved by waterpower or by the steam engine using wood or coal is, however, a fact of vast significance for modern industrial history. Its significance for the development of the organisational form of modern industry – the factory – built around a central power source is considered in the next section. Equally important was the way it reinforced, almost as if by design, the commercial supremacy of England for the hundred years after 1770. The technology of coal and iron was, by modern standards, a crude and simple technology which favoured, locationally speaking, areas well-endowed with those minerals. Such accidents happen in economic history where the effects of resources, techniques, and commercial culture are so closely intertwined. How different might the picture of industrial location in the nineteenth century have been had not coal, but oil, been the first prime industrial fuel, and water-power or water vapour figured less prominently! The large coal and ore resources conveniently located near water transport in Great Britain set the seal, as it were, on the predominance that Britain's commercial expansion had already initiated. Other coal and iron areas at that period of history had generally one raw material or the other, but not both, or were themselves remote from intense commercial activity, and British capital was not yet moving out to such locations with the vigour and abundance that appeared in its worldwide expansion after 1850. Other strongly commercial areas, the Netherlands or later New England, did not overlie, in close contact, the extensive subsoil deposits that could create a local mining industry. In Britain, both parts of the puzzle fell into place and a complex industrial development suffered no check from any direction. But while this was true, it was also the case that Britain really held no secrets in the minds and equipment of her inventors which others could not readily copy. If the Industrial Revolution was built on a combination of aggressiveness and physical advantage, there might come a time when others who had or could acquire similar endowment could adopt the attitudes that produced so exciting a result. The British development was like the growth of a tropical forest in a favourable climate and on the soil of a shallow technology which proved exceedingly fertile for a short space of historical time. As technology advanced in step with a developing body of science and scientific techniques of gaining more knowledge, its roots went deeper, its variety became richer, and its applications in the world's areas came to depend less on climate, harbours and mineral wealth at home, and more upon the adaptability to local conditions that a profound knowledge of the ways of nature would permit.

As the Pandora's box of modern technical knowledge was opened, the creatures which lay on top swarmed out first. And the situation was made the more complicated by the fact of not one, but two Pandora's boxes – one labelled Technology and one labelled Science. It is not fair to British science to suppose that because inventions poured out of the Technology box in such profusion, the Science box lay unopened. But in fact for British technology the commercial opportunities in the late eighteenth and early nineteenth centuries were so rich that the mass of inventions of immediate practicality darkened the sun. Like rich lumps of ore lying on the surface of a deep deposit, the mechanical inventions, involving simply the physical relations of one piece of visible matter to another, lay open, shiny and attractive, available at the cost of a little ingenuity and cleverness. What lay below the external appearance of matter, what forces bound it together, even giving it life, could not be known and worked for the practical power it gave over nature until the Science box had been opened for several generations. A science of mechanics could be developed in the eighteenth century, and a mechanical conception of nature, originating in the study of celestial mechanics, could take hold of men's imaginations at the same time that mechanical technology could proliferate in practical uses. As the profession of mechanical engineer developed, the science could even be of use in the art of invention, particularly in perfecting its details and increasing its efficiency. And purely empirical research could go a long way towards harnessing even forces as remote and dangerous as electricity or the chemical processes of metallurgy or the explosive power of gunpowder or combustible vapours. But as the mechanical technology presupposed a certain level of familiarity with mechanics, these later technological developments came about in the presence of an advancing science already looking into their essential nature and causes. The growth of that sort of knowledge in turn required experience with, and improvements on, the methods, instruments, and language of science itself.

The Industrial Revolution: organisational aspects

The path of mechanisation and its attendant industrial change through the industries and regions of western Europe is sketched briefly in the final section of this essay. Before discussing the spread of the technology, however, it is important to specify more exactly the old and the novel elements in the socio-economic organisation which surrounded, permitted, and even stimulated it, and ultimately were so strongly shaped by it. Changes in the status and condition of the working class were the most sensational social effects of the new industrial forms and techniques. A subtle analogy exists, however, between the balance of liberty and authority in labour organisation and similar balances in capital markets and in the social and intellectual history more generally.

In all respects English society appears to have been freer, more fluid, closer to an ideal market economy, even in the eighteenth century, than were the kingdoms of continental Europe. Much erosion of medieval and even of mercantilist restrictions and conceptions had occurred with the development of trade and the trading class. The almost purely capitalistic form on which English trade was conducted and financed promoted the diffusion of a money economy and market relationships and motiva-tions from international commodity markets into the markets for capital, technology and labour. The wide extension of the putting-out system – the creation of mercantile enterprise – gave entrée for capital into industrial processes, but it was not wholly responsible for the revolutionary result. Putting-out existed on the Continent, too, without leading readily into a dynamic process of technical change. But the fact that some mobility of capital, ideas and labour was good does not imply that more would have been better. English society of the late eighteenth century must have contained a balance of mobility and rigidity, of fluidity and 'lumpiness', of freedom and authority very nearly optimal for economic growth in that stage of technology and markets. To make this point more explicitly, we must consider the function played by monopoly and immobilities in productive factors in three areas: the generation of technology, the accumulation of capital, and the organisation of the labour force.

Technological change.[1] In a competitive economy organised by small-scale producers, the generation of new techniques is both stimulated and directed by economic circumstance. If a new product or new process can be devised and temporarily or permanently monopolised by a producer, monopoly profit can be derived from it. The incentive to innovate should be high, particularly if the market is wide, but not so wide as to make its monopolisation wholly beyond the reach of any single producer who can obtain a modest cost or sales advantage by an invention. Or in a competitive industry producers may be threatened with the narrowing of profit margins, or even with bankruptcy by sudden external developments. Competing products suddenly coming in from abroad or from regions opened up by transport improvements, a tightening of the labour market, or rises in raw materials costs, may produce this threat. Producers then may feel pressure to seek for innovations, to shift out of production, to find other sources of labour or supplies and to apply any other available profit-maintaining or cost-reducing devices.

Innovation induced in these ways is part of competitive producers' efforts to escape from the pressure of competition on profits by whatever means are at hand. The effectiveness of the incentive was recognised in England and on the Continent in the eighteenth century by the development of patent laws, themselves a device drawn from the arsenal of state mercantilist policy. Patents, by giving a monopoly, or property right, in an invention, need not have a total social effect of stimulating the competitive search for innovation or efficiency. The effects of royal grants of monopoly in the seventeenth century differed little from the effects of the guild restrictions of medieval industry. But given for a limited period

---

[1] Some of the extensive literature on induced innovation and related topics is examined, and many important insights given, in Nathan Rosenberg's collected essays, *Perspectives on Technology* (London, Cambridge University Press, 1976) especially chapters 4–6.

in an atmosphere of competition, patents may offer the promise or the illusion of encouraging invention without perpetuating monopoly. On the whole patents appear to have added a bit to the incentive to innovate without much encumbering the spread of knowledge. Furthermore, as an unintended side-effect, patenting created a new product: technology, which could be licensed or sold. It helped to professionalise the trades of inventor and engineer and to separate invention from production, creating a specialised activity with its own organisation and rewards. This aspect of the development did not become prominent until late in the nineteenth century.

Now the special historical conditions under which patents and property rights in knowledge could have an incentive effect on the creation of new technology appear to have obtained in the hundred years from 1750 to 1850 in Great Britain. Most important in the result was the relatively small scale of production. An industrial production derived not from the monopolies of craft shops but in large measure from the mercantile organisation of the putting-out system was animated less by the 'instinct of workmanship' than by the drive for profits. Even in a monopoly, if a profit-maximising spirit is preserved, the possibility of adding to profits acts as an inducement to invention. But the atmosphere was one of a world not of monopoly but of small competitive ventures, each seeking to capture a bit of profit, as in a trading venture, and needing some special place in the production structure to do so. Capital was fairly mobile within the trades and competition was keen. How much more then must the drive for profits have been active where profits were continually threatened, where competition or external developments brought the face of bankruptcy and ruin up close, pressed stark against every producer's window! Not monopoly, not pure competition, but the uneasy monopoly in a competitive world offered the economic – as distinct from a sheer intellectual – stimulus to invention.[1]

A rush to invention as a means to gain or maintain profits in a competitive economy suggests that invention is in some sense easier to come by than the rearrangement of capital and productive factors through markets along different lines. Indeed this is what is meant when it is said that invention is spurred on by the fear of loss along a given line of production. Such loss can be felt only if productive factors are immobile, if sunk capital or acquired skills cannot be converted or liquidated and shifted to other use, if the supply of a factor to an individual producer is not perfectly elastic. In order for bottlenecks in production to arise, creating quasi-rents for some and threatening ruin for others, a degree of factor immobility is necessary, and it must appear to producers more

[1] F. D. Prager, 'A History of Intellectual Property from 1545 to 1787', *Journal of the Patent Office Society*, 26 (1944), 711–60. See also the remarks in D. C. North and R. P. Thomas, *The Rise of the Western World* (London, Cambridge University Press, 1973), pp. 152–6.

nearly possible to break such bottlenecks cheaply, not by shifting factor proportions, or moving out of the industry, but by focussing inventive talent on some portion of the production process. Inventors must be, in a sense, more mobile than capital or labour, if economic circumstances as such are to produce a spur to invention. But in fact it is just this generalisation of mechanical and inventive talent, this flexibility and mobility that appear to have existed in eighteenth-century England and nineteenth-century USA – perhaps even more strongly in the latter where a 'jack of all trades' tradition had been stimulated by the conditions of the frontier.

The scale on which inventive activity occurs and the openness of lines of communication among inventors and between them and producers is also an important feature. Large-scale organisation, with good communications, makes for specialised activity which narrows an inventor's focus, but a large economy also provides a mass of industry over which inventive talent can work. Were the market to reign supreme, without other means of communication or other incentive to inventors, specialisation might become too narrow and invention too closely directed to specific ends. The inventor must see beyond the end of his nose, or of a profit and loss account. Were the market not to exist at all, an inventive culture might intercommunicate, but the spurs and the signals to move and direct useful activity would be absent. Here, as at so many other points, an appropriate mix of market and non-market organisation and motivation appears to have been required for economic and industrial growth.

The incentive effect, as just described, is supplemented in modern technical change by another effect of economic circumstances, called by Rosenberg, 'focussing', – the steering of an inventor, or a group of inventors in an industry, toward a specific problem. In what has been said above there is no clear reason why the economy should cause invention to focus on one problem rather than another. Invention may be induced in response to external circumstance but in general not located or focussed by changed economic conditions. If labour grows expensive, there is no particular reason for producers looking for labour-saving techniques, rather than some other sources of savings. The structure of production and technology should adjust where it is weakest, i.e. where factors are most mobile or where technical changes are closest to the horizon. However, the small-scale competitive firms of eighteenth-century England utilised rigid and rather narrow techniques. If costs in a process rose, the option was not open to reduce costs in other firms or branches of production; the process itself had to be adjusted or the trade abandoned by the producer. In coke smelting, for instance, a rise in the price of charcoal might in theory have caused capital to move elsewhere. But in the smelting firms, it may plausibly also have focussed inventive activity on efforts to find a substitute fuel. A rise in the price of yarn, derived from increased demands of weavers using the flying shuttle in the eighteenth century, or by suspension of English yarn imports on the Continent in the Napoleonic wars, might have been compensated by some shifts of workers into spinning. But it would also understandably focus inventive activity on improving the productivity of the spinners already at work. And if, as it happened, that was just a place where invention was practicable, where the structure of the existing technology was relatively easier to change, then spinning inventions would be the result.

The mechanical technology of the eighteenth century appears to have been particularly susceptible to such economic inducements and focussing. The situation in industry indeed was not as dissimilar to that in agriculture as has sometimes been supposed. In both sectors the skills of workers trained in the specific trade since youth had formed the basis of the technology. In both sectors, the excitement of market growth, stirring the imagination of materialistic and money-minded men, encouraged efforts to improve existing techniques. In both cases under such pressures the body of existing technology proved itself capable of extensive improvement without undergoing striking change in fundamental principles. In industry the improvement was accompanied by the perfecting of a science of mechanics (which could later be applied to agriculture as well); both art and science were capable of being improved by the unaided power of the mind and the eye, by observation, thought and contrivance, and the technology could move on within half a century to more complex realms.

Organisation of capital and labour.[1] Strictly speaking, a 'market for technology' did not exist before very recent decades in industrial history. In the eighteenth century there was a market for products, and not a very perfect market at that. But where it was active, thanks to mercantile activities, it made its influence and excitement felt backwards into the structure of production and even of technology. In doing so, the mixture of market and non-market elements, of old and new motives, of pockets of security and profit in the blowing wind of competition created an

[1] The *loci classici* for a discussion of these subjects are the famous chapters in Adam Smith, *The Wealth of Nations*, book 1, chapters 1–3, and Karl Marx, *Capital*, vol. 1, chapters 13–15. An interesting, and provoking, recent addition to the discussion is by S. A. Marglin, 'What Do Bosses Do? The Origins and Functions of Hierarchy in Capitalist Production', *Review of Radical Political Economics*, 6 (1974), 60–112. On the supply of capital to industry in the Industrial Revolution, see the essays collected by François Crouzet, with a valuable editor's introduction: *Capital in the Industrial Revolution* (London, Methuen & Co. Ltd., 1972). Management methods are discussed in Sidney Pollard, *The Genesis of Modern Management* (Cambridge, Massachusetts, Harvard University Press, 1965) and sociological aspects of labour force organisation in Neil Smelser, *Social Change in the Industrial Revolution* (Chicago, University of Chicago Press, 1959) and the work of E. P. Thompson, *The Making of the English Working Class* (New York, Random House, 1963).

excellent environment for rapid, simple technological change. As the techniques were derived from production experience, so did they remain closely entwined with industrial activity, providing a growing inventory of tools and ideas for further development.

The situation was not greatly different with respect to the accumulation of capital. Capital was thought of as either very short- or very long-lived. The national wealth, when it was thought of at all, was viewed either in the mercantilist notion of a stock of precious metal, or in Adam Smith's enlightened view, as land improvements and public buildings, and the energies and skills of the population. Private capital was a merchant's stock in trade or a manufacturer's inventory of materials and goods in process or a fund of money to be turned over in trade or through wage payments in the somewhat more lengthy processes of manufacture. As in the case of technology, there was not so much a market for capital as a responsiveness on the part of capital to market facts and opportunities. The liquidity which a primitive capital market afforded, and the communication of knowledge of investment opportunities encouraged saving and directed capital into profitable uses. But most of the industrial capital in England appears to have derived from industrial operations; indeed in early firms the distinction between capital and income, or capital expenditures and current expenses, was not made at all clearly. Such a situation was conducive to industrial saving, and to reinvestment at points where a hard-headed entrepreneur could see prospects of a sizeable gain. Money and credit, and even mercantile banks, were essential to keep the system running, but one may wonder whether a sensitive market for industrial capital would have improved the rate of accumulation or the direction of its investment. As it was, with each firm depending largely on its own resources the incentive to save was high, and the investment was made by those with best knowledge of the opportunity. It is doubtful whether the collection of brokers and stock-jobbers accompanying the capital markets of the 1870s and 1880s would have either induced more saving or known how to advise investors more wisely than the entrepreneur-savers of the Industrial Revolution were able to do for themselves.

If the organisation of capital and enterprise in the Industrial Revolution involved no separation of ownership and control, the reverse may be said for the organisation of labour. I do not refer here to the notorious separation of the worker from his 'means of production', the tiny physical capital of which he had availed himself under the putting-out or craft shop systems of organisation. Within both those organisational forms, a hierarchical organisation prevailed, based on the hierarchical organisation of the family. In a shop the master controlled the labour of his family and, for the length of their terms, that of journeymen and apprentices. Within such tiny political units, each man had his duties and station, and no doubt customary rights and obligations assumed the form of informal law, just as had occurred on manorial estates on a larger scale. Similarly also in rural domestic industry, a man commanded the labour of his wife and children, subject to all the sanctions which through proximity and affection they could inflict upon him. Nor is it clear that the position of women was distinctly inferior to that of men in the peasant or peasant-industrial household. What distinguished the fully developed putting-out system from these was the intimate and customary tie of the head of the family or para-familial labour unit to the furnisher of the materials and the market. To the degree that the merchant employer held a regional monopoly over 'his' cottage workers, the latter were subject to close bargaining whether they 'owned' their tools or not. Materials could be allotted and piece rates fixed to keep labour's share at a minimum, and the difficulty of organising a group of workers established that preponderance of bargaining power on the side of the merchant employer which was to become so marked in the developed factory and wage labour system.

In these conditions, the establishment of a few factories, i.e. collections of workers or worker family-groups under one roof and subject to one direction, may have made capitalist control of a labour force easier in the short-run. But ultimately, as Marx first pointed out, factory organisation, though facilitating longer hours, stricter discipline and more careful supervision of time and materials, in the end removed the capitalist's great advantage over his workers: the difficulty they had in communicating with one another when they worked at dispersed locations. Instead of coming together at church or tavern on social occasions only, under the eye of priest or constable, the workers in a factory were thrown together in daily, intimate, professional contact. It is little wonder that workingmen's associations, which had led a marginal existence among apprentices or rural workers pushed beyond the limits of endurance, began to grow into regular and continuing bodies as factory organisation extended its scope. The titular loss of independence through loss of ownership of a few tools was finally more than balanced by the gain in easy access to the means of group solidarity, though this did not necessarily help the workmen immediately affected.

In those trades where the advantage of a factory organisation was confirmed by the grouping of complex geared and belt-driven machinery around a single power source, it was almost inevitable that the organisation would be carried out by a capitalist grouping workers at just the right points in the machine process, supplementing the failings of the machine by manual skills and human muscle power. The family system indeed was preserved anachronistically within some early spinning factories, and systems of piece rate and time rate competed with each other for dominance. 'The market' appeared in the buying and selling of labour power as of any other commodity, but it is equally important to note the points into which the market did not penetrate. Labour was sold, but not by the minute on a perfect market, subject to close calculation and instantaneous renegotiation. The workers could not hire capital in the same sense that capital could hire workers; rather the hierarchical form of family organisation was preserved and transferred here, and without many of the protections that customary law in a small political unit gave to family and workshop. Workers sold themselves for a space of time, in a form of daily slavery, agreeing to do each day what job the employer required in exchange for a wage. Such an organisation is not truly a market organisation in the same sense as foreign exchange markets, for example, where supplies are offered and withdrawn at a slight titillation of the price, and negotiators change sides from supplier to demander as quickly as a thought passes through the mind. The capitalist firm was a political organisation in its internal structure, bound by markets at either end.

The question is: how well was this form, derived so naturally from the historical circumstances in which the new technology was created, adapted to those techniques? It is not possible to argue that the techniques themselves were created and adapted to the form without ignoring the immanent constraints of the technology. Are we not rather in the presence again of one of those historical coincidences without which the surprising growth of modern industry could never have occurred? Remarkable developments require remarkable explanations and England's sudden industrial development in textiles and iron was a wholly unexpected and, in the long run, unsustainable and extraordinary event. Why then should it appear inevitable or yield to some deterministic and holistic explanation?

Whatever the explanation, it is possible to argue in retrospect that the adaptation was a good one for establishing machine industry and for ensuring its spread. The factory built around a central power source – a water-wheel or large steam engine – possessed significant technical economies of scale, particularly since the steam engine was never as successful as was later the electric motor in adapting to a wide range of capacities. The scale economies made it profitable to keep machinery in continuous operation – particularly water-wheels during seasons when water power was strong. (In many cases the steam engine was first used to supplement water power in dry seasons.) It meant also attaching as much machinery as possible to the wheel or engine once its fixed installation was accomplished, and so of producing a large volume of output. These economies of scale were closely allied with economy of continuous operation, particularly evident to private owners of capital who thought in terms of turning over their stock. Whether working with his own or borrowed money, it paid a manufacturer not to let his equipment stand idle. But continuous operation had another aspect. While the machinery was attached to the power source, it all moved together. Belts or specific machinery might be temporarily detached, but on the whole workers had to operate with the machine and to time their motions to its requirements. This was the principal advantage that a wage system, with an authoritarian organisation, held over a system in which labourers might sell not their labour but their product as it passed from one form to another, or might renegotiate their labour contract minute by minute, or hour by hour. The resemblance of factory organisation to that of an army, in which each member had to respond quickly and on command, without knowing all the reasons why, did not escape notice. And, as in an army, the operation of the market principle within the organisation was rendered impossible, at least unnecessary, by the fact that a few men – the managers – planned the whole operation and had no need of any inputs from below.

It remains to ask why, if slavery on the job was the technically most efficient status for the labourer, the freedom of the labourer off the job appears to have been wedded so closely to nineteenth-century industrialism. In Russia and in the American South, serf- or slave-operated factories were not unknown. Their limited success makes them the exceptions that prove the rule. The answer – that it is cheaper for an individual capitalist to avoid responsibility for workers off the job – is not wholly satisfactory since it confounds the individual with the social perspective. Unemployed or ill workers had to be supported by someone, and ultimately the capitalists would have to pay a sizeable share of the cost. The advantage of freedom over slavery for the workers in nineteenth-century growth appears to have lain in the value of mobility in an economy where new industries, firms, locations and tasks were appearing every week. Where entrepreneurs were locked in to their already adopted technique and where capital was not nearly as liquid as it was later to become, ownership of workers by masters, or even binding patriarchal relations deprived an economy of an important element of flexibility. And, too, wherever freedom won out over slavery the drive to individual self-advancement could remain for workers as for entrepreneurs a strong engine of economic growth.

In England, the peculiar mixture of markets and authority could prevail because state controls had been relaxed to a greater degree than on the Continent. Here again the vestiges of an earlier, more authoritarian organisation remained, enough to preserve the regularity of life and of expectations. It is not that the state was weak; there was no question of who retained the monopoly of force. The central authority of the Tudor state, indeed of the Norman kingship, was retained. The writ of the king and the king's courts ran into every county, and the lords lieutenant and the state church kept watch on the vagaries of local and town government. Below that and well integrated into it, a social structure of classes sustained by a class deference derived from feudalism persisted in England as elsewhere in western Europe. The beginnings of a democratisation, or even a thorough embourgeoisement of this society were still a hundred years in the future, and a full modernisation and proletarianisation still farther off. The difference between England and the Continent lay not so much in the balance of central and local authority as in who controlled that authority. Here thanks to the intrusion of a strong mercantile interest in the struggle between king and landed aristocracy, the power of the Renaissance and seventeenth-century monarch, so strong in France and on a miniature scale in the German states, had been balanced by the wealth of London and the Puritan independence of large areas of the countryside. The Revolution of 1688 was to set the seal on a political compromise which lasted till the Reform Act of 1832 – rather less a compromise than a combination of the heavy weight of a Protestant landed interest and a Protestant merchant and banking aristocracy to establish a limited monarchy. With things so arranged on top, and with enough flexibility to adjust squabbles within the ascendant Whig and Tory aristocracy, a government of incredible strength and toughness evolved, able to survive and surmount financial instability and crises, massive fraud and corruption, wars on the Continent and overseas, the loss of one empire and the development of another, and finally to organise the conservative forces of the Continent to the defeat of Napoleon. Little wonder that such a structure could also almost unconsciously control and channel the forces of a rising industrial development. No doubt its congeries of policies and laws, a fantastic scrap basket of bits left over from feudal and medieval restrictions, mercantilist encouragements, and responses to the pressures of particular situations and interests, produced a less than ideal or optimal effect on the development. One thing was clear: it was fully capable of providing stable support for the evolving body of commercial law, for the 'rights' of the individual property-holder, and for domination over the labouring poor. It was not a 'tool' of the propertied classes in any conscious, planned, or conspiratorial sense; had it been so, its evolution into full parliamentary democracy and twentieth-century socialist industrial organisation would have been far less steady and more bloody. But in the eighteenth century and the early nineteenth, it produced just the balance of authority and free markets that an early and unsteady capitalistic industrial organisation required to take its first steps toward maturity, strength and dominance. On the Continent, developments were otherwise, as the following section will indicate.

The spread of modern industry[1]

The spread of mechanical techniques through industries and through geographical regions is a pair of processes with many common characteristics. The mechanisation of a new industry required adaptation of the power and inventions to harness power to specific operations. The spread of a given machine technique, e.g. mechanical spinning, from one region required interested entrepreneurs, favourable factor cost conditions, suitable government policy, and supplies of capital and workers adaptable to the machine process. It too required minor inventions to adapt the equipment to specific raw materials, markets, climate, and labour force. The timing, speed, and form of the diffusion in both cases depended on special technical, economic or sociological conditions of the industry or region in question. In the competitive economy of northern Europe, the spread of mechanisation among industries was in one sense the more fundamental sort of diffusion since the minimum physical cost locations of new industries were determined by cost characteristics of the new technique. Given these characteristics, the ultimate dispersion of an industry was largely a matter of economic geography. Social and economic differences – the availability of capital, the training and immobility of the local labour force, the policy of the region's government – determined the lags, however, before the 'natural' economic factors and the force of competition took effect. This was especially true where the natural locational advantage of one region over another was rather small. In textiles, for example, differences in the location of enterprise, capital, cheap labour, and close relations with overseas outlets could set the advantage.

[1] W. O. Henderson, *Britain and Industrial Europe 1770–1870* (2nd edn, Leicester, Leicester University Press, 1965) traces some of the direct lines of connection from Britain to the Continent. Rondo Cameron's original and well-researched book, *France and the Economic Development of Europe 1800–1914* (Princeton, New Jersey, Princeton University Press, 1961) and the monumental work of Maurice Lévy-Leboyer, *Les Banques Européennes et l'Industrialisation Internationale* (Paris, Presses Universitaires de France, 1964) treat the Continental industrialisation, as does the earlier work of A. L. Dunham, *The Industrial Revolution in France 1815–1848* (New York, Exposition Press, 1955) and the essays by Jan Craeybeckx and Claude Fohlen in Rondo Cameron (ed.), *Essays in French Economic History* (Homewood, Illinois, Richard D. Irwin, Inc., 1970). To the classic textbook of J. H. Clapham, *The Economic Development of France and Germany 1815–1914* (4th edn, London, Cambridge University Press, 1963) and David Landes' treatment of the western European area as a whole (see *The Cambridge Economic History of Europe*, vol. VI, part 2, H. J. Habbakuk and M. M. Postan (eds.) (London, Cambridge University Press, 1965) and *The Unbound Prometheus* (London, Cambridge University Press, 1969) have now been added very good chapters in A. S. Milward and S. B. Saul, *The Economic Development of Continental Europe 1780–1870* (London, George Allen & Unwin Ltd., 1973) and in C. M. Cipolla (ed.), *The Fontana Economic History of Europe*, vol. IV, especially chapter 1, 'France 1700–1914' by Claude Fohlen, and 2, 'Germany 1700–1914' by Knut Borchardt. The conference volume of the International Economic Association, edited by W. W. Rostow, *The Economics of Take-off into Sustained Growth* (New York, St Martin's Press, 1965) also contains a number of valuable articles on early development in various countries as well as an evaluation of the 'take-off' hypothesis of W. W. Rostow.

Diffusion among industries. In an earlier section, indication was given of the path of the Industrial Revolution among industrial processes. One may observe certain clusterings in the history of its progress. One was the spread of the power process from cotton-spinning through other branches of the textile industry – to wool and linen, and after a delay to mechanised weaving. Hand processes in the garment industry – e.g. shoemaking and sewing – presented specific technical problems which yielded, one after another between 1800 and 1850, to British and American ingenuity and enterprise. All this development was brought on partly by the force of economic pressures within the structure of textile and clothing production which focussed inventive activity, and partly by the rise in the level of technical opportunity for solving problems through improvements in materials, machine tools and control mechanisms. The history of the development of the sewing machine may be cited as a notable example of the eco-technic process at work.

Beyond the 'light' industries – textiles, boots and shoes, machine tools, and farm machinery – the latter developing more rapidly under favourable market and terrain conditions in North America after 1850 – there lay the engineering problems of heavier equipment in transport and power generation. Continuous improvements in the steam engine increased its efficiency and extended the range of capacities and pressures generated and contained. Such improvements occurred at all the locations where engines were used and produced, in England, Wales, Belgium, Germany – even on the banks of the Ohio in America. The adaptation of steam to water navigation is a classic story in the history of invention, and from Trevithick to Stephenson, the development of locomotives, braking mechanisms, and all the vast array of railroad inventions created the mid-century transformation of land transportation. In stationary engines, the first half of the nineteenth century saw the development of the water and steam turbine in France and England through the inventions of Fourneyron and the thorough investigation of the science of thermodynamics by Carnot.[1]

We have seen that mechanical inventions, as they spread to various industries and locations in northern Europe and North America, presupposed a large interconnected industrial region. This was required to ensure both adequate market size and the mass of intercommunicating inventive activity necessary to keep economic expansion and technical change in motion. In the eighteenth century, it appears that central England itself was a large enough area. A striking fact about the Industrial Revolution is the speed with which improvement extended from iron and machinery production to the manufacture of machine tools. Machine tools lie deep in the production processes of modern industry. To make

[1] D. S. L. Cardwell, *From Watt to Clausius* (Ithaca, New York, Cornell University Press, 1971).

it worthwhile to devote efforts to improve the machines which make machines, a large market for machinery is essential. The increase in the productivity of machinery and in its durability when iron was used worked in exactly the reverse direction. A market for machinery of unusual scale must have been present to give the impetus. This is true in early nineteenth-century north-eastern United States, where the level of income, its distribution, the protection afforded by distance from English competition and (some allege) the scarcity of labour relative to capital, and of both relative to the ambitions of the population, helped also to allow an industry of specialised machine tool manufacture to grow quickly out of the machine shops of the textile mills. Once developed, the machine tool industry, employing water or steam power, improved and cheapened iron, and better and more closely machined parts in its own equipment could lift machine production out of the workshop of the mechanic and make it too a factory industry. The cheapening of machinery, rather than a fall in the rate of interest, has been largely responsible for the greater physical capital intensity of modern processes.

In England and Belgium, the close link of machinery production to the local iron industry cannot fail to be observed. With the possibilities of steam-powered machinery, an engineering industry was growing up around iron works, and the massive fuel requirements of coke smelting and puddling brought iron works to locations at coal beds. In Britain by 1850 most major coal beds were thus the site of iron smelting and fabricating industries. There can be little doubt that even before the steel inventions of the 1850s, the coal-based industrial complex was an economic unit. Because of the saving in fuel transport costs and the further advantages of agglomeration and communication in a concentrated area, its products could undersell those of producers at scattered locations. By 1850 the Industrial Revolution, as a revolution in both technology and plant and enterprise organisation, had spread from cotton-spinning to other 'light' easily mechanised industries, then to the heavier industries of transport equipment and machine production itself, the latter based also on the improvements in the iron industry that were part of the eighteenth century development. Lodged between light and heavy industries, the machine tool companies expanded and extended the varieties and uses of their products. As these industries, particularly those using coal and iron, clustered around coal or ore mining areas, the typical industrial complex of the later nineteenth century was formed. The railroad added to the advantage of these dark and smoky districts even as it increased the demand for their products, and the Bessemer and open-hearth processes coming in after the 1850s ensured their stability for the half-century following 1870, not only in Britain and Belgium, but around the coal beds of the valleys tributary to the lower Rhine, and the upper Ohio.

One must remember that the Industrial Revolution was based on a certain group of inventions and an accompanying organisational form, which could not spread beyond the industries where coal, iron and machinery could be introduced. In Britain in 1850 many industries and operations were not power driven, or mechanised. The largest component of the non-agricultural labour force in 1850 was, after all, domestic service, and the mechanisation of the household lay beyond anyone's imagination. Construction, including ship-building and road-building, was relatively untouched, similarly most food-processing operations and, of course, agriculture. The very growth of the larger-scale industries, and the swarming of populations to new locations gave occupation to vast numbers of small-scale producers, and furnishers of service. Office work, too – except for the development of the typewriter and the telephone and telegraph after 1850 – experienced no productivity increases, and the way was laid in all these respects not only for the perpetuation of the class of small shopkeepers and professionals, but also for the growth of the 'white collar' staff of the larger establishments. The whole society then was not industrialised, much less proletarianised. Industry, industrial capital, industrialists, and industrial wage workers assumed a place on the front bench of society and politics, constituting a special 'interest' alongside the interests of the mercantile community, the bankers, the professional and white collar class and the landed interest of ancient origin. It assumed a place beside the others, but did not crowd them off the scene.

Diffusion among regions of north-western Europe. The advances in the cotton, iron and machinery industries between 1780 and 1840 were the whole bases on which the English Midlands, with extensions in South Wales and Scotland, in 1850 rested a remarkable industrial leadership over the long-established industrial regions of the Continent. In textiles, technical obstacles which lay in the way of mechanising operations in flax, silk, or even wool did not obstruct the application of machinery to cotton. England's lead in the cotton industry then must be attributed to her superior trading position and access to markets and to raw cotton supplies. Possibly also, the long experience in wool made an easier transition to cotton than could be achieved by silk or linen producers. The development of a cotton industry on the Continent had to depend initially on the importation of English machinery and a few English workmen and plant designers – an expensive and unsatisfactory way to overtake a foreign competitor. Still machinery was eventually applied to the branches of textiles in which continental producers specialised and the slower pace of development in machinery and the iron industry on the Continent cannot be attributed to technical reasons. Clearly before 1840 the continental industrial regions – the cities with their workshops and the rather widely separated and disconnected areas of rural industry – lacked the intensity in industrial activity closely linked to machine shops, which gave British industry the critical mass necessary to a continuous and self-reinforcing economic and industrial development. The imported English spinning machinery at Ratingen in the Rhineland, in Normandy along the Seine tributaries, and later in Ghent, were sparks of modernisation which did not light a fuse to set off the fireworks.

The Belgian case is the exception on the Continent which proves the point at issue here.[1] In Flanders the dense textile industrial district lay close to a large foreign market and to the iron- and coal-based industry of Liège and the Belgian coalfield. Even under Napoleon, industrial development began, when the area was joined with the Dutch provinces in 1815, overseas markets were opened and access given to Dutch capital. The Dutch areas themselves failed to industrialise – possibly because of a history and social structure based solely on commerce, possibly also because of lack of cheap coal. Instead, the Dutch king invested in the Belgian areas which lay under his government between 1815 and 1830, and a little borrowing of workmen and machinery from England developed mechanised spinning and a domestic machinery industry. By 1850 – twenty years after the separation from Dutch rule, the Belgian Netherlands had become the world's second coal-based industrial district in which the light and heavy industries of the Industrial Revolution were joined.

The persistence of traditional and typically 'early modern' barriers to industrialisation on the Continent is shown best in France. The Revolution had swept away the remains of feudal forms – feudal land tenures and the power of the guilds in cities. It had not destroyed, indeed it had confirmed, governmental centralisation and mercantilist policies of the state. The revolutionary governments and Napoleon had strengthened the state much as Louis XIV had done, though more intelligently, and much was provided for the new (and not so new) commercial and industrial bourgeoisie. Commercial and property law was regularised through the *Code Napoléon*, scientific and technical education was extended and strengthened. An educated scientific and engineering élite was enlarged. The Bank of France helped stabilise the currency and brought French public finance up to the degree of modernity that England had achieved a hundred years earlier. Modernisation and regularisation of the tax system added greatly to the regularity with which business expectations could be pursued. By reducing its personal and arbitrary character, the post-Revolutionary government helped to create a climate of reduced uncertainty for mercantile and business interests.

The regimes from Napoleon I to Napoleon III offered also many direct

[1] To the references cited in note 1, p. 72 above including an excellent chapter in Rondo Cameron's *France and the Economic Development of Europe 1800–1914* (Princeton, New Jersey, Princeton University Press, 1961) may be added a recent treatment of the Belgian 'case' by Joel Mokyr, *Industrialization in the Low Countries 1795–1850* (New Haven, Connecticut, Yale University Press, 1976).

opportunities to business enterprise. Interruption of trade with England from 1790 to 1815 reserved the Continental market to Continental – and largely to French or Belgian – producers. The inflation and the wars themselves offered the usual opportunity for short-term and individual gains. Enough venality was present, enough luxury demand, enough waste to nourish the greediest entrepreneur. Yet for all that, one cannot speak of any French government until the parliamentary democracy of the Third Republic, as an oligarchy like that in seventeenth-century Netherlands or eighteenth-century England. The peasantry, the church, the remaining aristocracy, the army, the bureaucracy – all were too strong to furnish a clear climate for modern capitalism. If the balance in England by 1780 was about right to allow an eco-technic, industrial revolution to proceed, the balance lay in France a bit too strongly on the side of what Marxists call pre-industrial economic formations. Much is made in history books of England's political gradualism, in contrast to France's recurrent revolutions. But in economic modernisation, it was in France that gradualism prevailed. Napoleonic government and its successors under the Restoration and the July Monarchy maintained a stance which combined liberalisation, protection, and paternalism until more classic liberal policies were introduced. By that time, industrialisation had developed into something different from what it had been seventy years earlier, and what France had preserved of the older forms and values – the system of technical education, the aristocratic spirit of scientific research, the balance between population growth and her own food supplies – began to pay off.[1] The nation then could lay the base for continued economic progress as a national unit, even up to the present day, through all the devastations of war and political and moral catastrophe.

The situation in the scattered German textile and metal-working regions of the eighteenth century was not greatly different from that in France.[2] But they lacked two developments that English and French regions had experienced: incorporation in a national state, and within it, a political revolution. Even by 1700, the physical depredations of the Thirty Years War had been repaired, but within the notoriously numerous political districts, a mixed medieval and Renaissance political economy survived and flourished. The states were not inactive in efforts to advance

[1] French technical education is interestingly treated in F. B. Artz, *The Development of Technical Education in France 1500–1850* (Cambridge, Massachusetts, The M.I.T. Press, 1966). A recent dissertation by Bernard Gustin, 'The German Chemical Profession: 1824–1867' (Department of Sociology, University of Chicago, 1975) throws needed light on German chemical training and research before Liebig, and the role of the apothecaries in the development.

[2] See the articles by Herbert Kisch in note 1, p. 43 above and also Gerhard Adelmann, 'Structural Change in the Rhenish Linen and Cotton Trades at the Outset of Industrialization' in François Crouzet, W. H. Chaloner and W. M. Stern (eds.), *Essays in European Economic History 1780–1914* (London, Edward Arnold Ltd., 1966). On metallurgy, see N. J. G. Pounds and W. N. Parker, *Coal and Steel in Western Europe* (Bloomington, Indiana, Indiana University Press, 1957).

industry; they encouraged it by all the best principles of mercantilist economic policy. Nor was there any lack of skill or enterprise in many areas; we have seen earlier how extensive was the diffusion of the Renaissance technology in the south, central and western German states. Rhine merchants and bankers were active throughout the whole period before 1850, and in south-west Germany, the activity and ambitions of apothecaries, along with the princely sponsorship of 'pure' science in the universities, laid the foundations for Germany's later successes in chemicals. The tariff history, of which so much has been written, indicates that barriers to internal trade were overcome, but the Zollverein, too, was a mercantilist measure pursued from political motives, not only on the part of Prussia but also of the petty princes who hoped, in typically seventeenth-century fashion, to increase net revenues from a source outside the control of assemblies and nobility. Even after the industrialisation got under way in the Prussian territories and in the Empire, no one would ever have mistaken the Imperial German government for a businessman's state.

By 1850 what was lacking in both Germany and France in 1800 had been partially supplied. The social and political basis for modern capitalistic industry had inched its way toward a condition which could tolerate capitalist expansion without the continual drag of medieval or mercantilist restrictions or the unexpected and disrupting assertions of authority of divine right monarchs and their bureaucracies. Then between 1850 and 1870 two decades of classical liberal policies in both France and Prussia expanded trade, strengthened financial institutions, encouraged capital accumulation. What had been lacking in the earlier textile industrialisation was the opportunity to make the link with the iron industries, and this the railroad had only partly supplied. But the social and physical elements in modern industry were present – the intangible social capital of laws, skilled mechanics and engineers, educational institutions, a still disciplined labour force, and the physical capital of transport improvements. As contact between regions improved, the disadvantages of the small- and scattered-scale of the earlier textile and light machinery industries began to be overcome.

Into this atmosphere in the 1860s came as a supplement and substitute for wide geographical scale, the opportunity for heavy industry localisation. Through the accidents of politics north-western Europe's coal was distributed in bits across all of the major north-western countries. It had long been known and mined in spots – in the Saar, in the Liège region, and at a few shallow diggings in France. With the opportunity opened by market growth and the steel inventions of the 1860s, the clustering around these deposits began to take shape, and the immense industrial strength of the Franco-German–Belgian area began to make itself felt.

The development of coal, steel, chemicals and electricity on the

Continent belongs to the history of the latter part of the nineteenth century. It would take another chapter, or another book, to fill it in. It exhibits similarities in form and timing to the American development south of the Great Lakes, between Chicago and Pittsburgh in these same decades. But European industrial history prior to 1850 shows that it grew up on an industrial base very different from that of both England and the USA. Unlike the eighteenth- and early nineteenth-century developments in England, continental industrialisation after 1850 was not based simply on the scale economies of wide textile markets, and the accompaniment of a mechanical engineering technology. That was a combination which the continental locations, for reasons of economic and social organisation in the late eighteenth century, had not been able to achieve. But at length after half a century of sporadic, artificial and pale imitations of British technology, continental industry hit upon a rich vein which its own tools and traditions were able to mine. In the technology of coal-based chemistry, in metallurgy scientifically developed, and in inventions leading into the lighter but even more science-based industry of the twentieth century, the Continent's long industrial traditions and its institutions of pure scientific research and of applied training could at last come into their own. With the concentration of activity around coal-fields, the industrial strength was developed which, by permitting further developments away from coalfields, could lead continental industry into its upsurge after the calamities of the 1940s.

This essay develops ideas offered in lectures to graduate economics students at Yale University over a number of years, and exposed also at seminars at European and American universities since 1972. I wish to express thanks to many participants in those seminars for useful comments, and in particular to Richard Levin, Jan De Vries, Harry Miskimin and Quentin Skinner for reading and commenting on the manuscript. I am especially indebted to Peter Mathias, Eric Jones and Peter Burke for initial encouragement, even though they may, like St Peter, wish now to deny it thrice before the cock crows. The work could in any case not have been brought into this form without a generous grant from the Concilium on International and Area Studies and the Department of Economics at Yale, and the diligent and informed research assistance of Laurie Nussdorfer.

My debts to the authors in the field are only imperfectly acknowledged in the footnotes, but will be evident to anyone acquainted with some of the literature, including, I trust, the authors themselves. The footnotes indeed are intended not as source references or elaborations of the text, but as suggestions for further reading, primarily in English-language sources. A full bibliography of the main writings published in English, French, German and Italian since the publication of the major bibliographies of David Landes, *Cambridge Economic History of Europe*, vol. VI, part 2 (1965) and Maurice Lévy-Leboyer, *Les Banques Européennes et l'Industrialisation Internationale* (1964) is in preparation. I regret that I have been excluded from writings in Dutch and Swedish by 'ignorance, pure ignorance'.

CHAPTER IV

POPULATION

BEFORE AND AFTER

LET us first take a look at the birth and death columns which appear regularly in our newspapers: most of the announcements are to do with elderly people; there are some deaths of young adults or children, of course, usually the victims of accidents, but the typical announcement is that of the funeral of a widow of about 80, attended by two of her children and about four or five grandchildren. We have hardly any similar evidence for the sixteenth century, with the exception of a few family records, but by using the method of family reconstitution we could find analogous cases. To leave behind one or two children and four or five grandchildren, if one was lucky enough to live to 80, was not unusual.

At first sight, there seems to be little difference in the composition of families and in the kinship relations: in the sixteenth century, as in the twentieth, the dominant type is the nuclear family, made up of father, mother and children. The gap between generations has not changed much either: about twenty-five to thirty years, as a result of a relatively high age of marriage; western Europe has never known adolescent marriage: in India, in 1891, the average age of girls on marriage was only $12\frac{1}{2}$, while in western Europe it was as high as 23.

The maximum life span has not changed much either: in the twentieth century as in the sixteenth, this does not exceed 115 years; and the reported cases of extreme old age owe more to the lack of official records or to general ignorance, than to the quality of life or the progress of medical science.

Another biological constant: the ratio of male to female births remains at around 105 : 100, and if it seems to have been slightly higher in the past (109 in the seventeenth century?) this is perhaps due to an error in measurement.

Finally, in the England of 1977, as in that of 1577, the generations scarcely replace one another: the net reproduction rate is near to 1, and the growth rate near to 0. It is the same in almost all of north-west Europe.

Taking into account the fact that migration has decreased in recent years, the exchange of population between nations is hardly more important today than 300 years ago. Populations are no doubt more mobile, but within their own frontiers.

Nevertheless, the demographic situation in Europe in this last quarter of the twentieth century is fundamentally different from the situation at the end of the sixteenth century, before the 'industrial revolution'.

POPULATION

(1) *Statistics*

It must first be said that we know more than we did. Each month, information bulletins published by the national institutes of the main countries in Europe give so many details about population distribution, the number of births, the fertility of women, the causes of death, etc., that it becomes difficult to assimilate this mass of facts. Twelve demographic journals are published in Europe alone. Finally, each year the *Demographic Directory of the United Nations* presents the essential statistics about all the countries in the world. The only countries in Europe we are not very well informed about are the USSR and Albania, where some of the facts (causes of death, age structure of the population, etc.) are still kept secret.

For the sixteenth century, on the contrary, we have only fragmentary data: a register of the citizens of such-and-such a town, a tax roll for such-and-such a village. Where a national census was made, there is practically no trace of it left. The records of baptisms, marriages and burials, which would have made it possible to calculate changes in the population, were not exploited at the time. Writers who were interested in the population of Europe were therefore reduced to guesswork. Despite the progress made in the seventeenth century, most Western thinkers remained convinced for more than a hundred years that the population of the world was getting smaller every day and that 'in a thousand years it will be no more than a desert' (Montesquieu, 'Lettres Persanes').

(2) *Numbers*

On 1 January 1977 Europe had 670 million inhabitants, which represents approximately 17 per cent of the world population. At the beginning of the sixteenth century, as far as we can tell, the population of Europe must have been of the order of 60 or 70 millions, or 18 per cent of the world population (66 million inhabitants in 1500 to the west of the present borders of the USSR, according to Dr Biraben).

This population was not distributed in the same way: whereas today the record is held by the Soviet Union with 260 million inhabitants (190 millions in European Russia) followed by West Germany (62 millions), the United Kingdom (57 millions), Italy (57 millions) and France (54 millions), it seems that in the sixteenth century the four most densely populated countries were France, Italy, Germany and the Turkish Empire, each with between 10 and 20 million inhabitants.

For the sixteenth century it is difficult to be so precise, but the table that can be drawn up for the year 1750 (figure 2) gives an acceptable picture of pre-industrial Europe: 140 million inhabitants, 30 or 35 millions of whom were within the present frontiers of the USSR.

Inside each country, the distribution differed noticeably from that

POPULATION

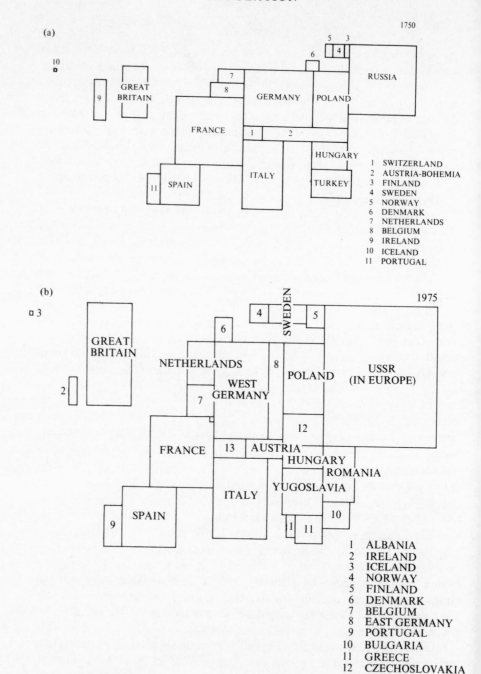

Fig. 2. The population of Europe (a) in 1750 and (b) in 1975. Each country is represented by a rectangle with an area proportional to its population.

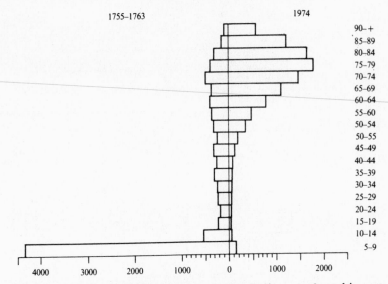

1755–1763   1974

	90–+
	85–89
	80–84
	75–79
	70–74
	65–69
	60–64
	55–60
	50–54
	50–55
	45–49
	40–44
	35–39
	30–34
	25–29
	20–24
	15–19
	10–14
	5–9

4000   3000   2000   1000   0   1000   2000

Fig. 3. Mortality relative to age groups in Sweden in 1755–63 and in 1974. Calculated from 10,000 deaths.

of today: only 10–20 per cent lived in what was called a 'town' at the time, that is to say a privileged community, sometimes self-governed and usually surrounded by ramparts. Around 1600, only thirteen towns in Europe had a population of more than 100,000: Constantinople, Naples, Paris, London, Adrianople, Venice, Seville, Milan, Lisbon, Rome, Grenoble, Palermo and Prague. Today 660 European or Soviet towns exceed this figure: there are thirty-nine agglomerations of over a million, and three of these have more than 5 million inhabitants (Paris, London and Moscow).

It is estimated that altogether 60 per cent of Europeans live in towns, and about 40 per cent in large agglomerations (with more than 100,000 inhabitants).

(3) The reduction of the death rate

Figure 3 shows the age distribution at death in Sweden in 1760, and in 1974. Unfortunately we do not have any similar table for Europe in 1600, nor even for 1700, but Sweden in 1760 is probably representative of a 'pre-industrial' population.

It can be seen that in 1760 it was above all the young who were dying: out of 100 newborn babies only 78 reached their first birthday, 66 their fifth, and 57 their twentieth. Today, on the other hand, it is above all the elderly who die: out of 100 newborn babies, 78 reach their sixty-eighth birthday, 66 their seventy-fourth, and 57 their seventy-seventh.

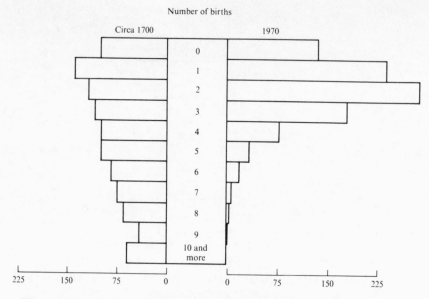

Fig. 4. Birth rate in 1,000 French families towards 1700 and in 1970. The seventeenth-century birth rate was calculated from nineteen village monographs dealing with Normandy and the Ile-de-France; the twentieth-century birth rate was calculated for the whole of France from the 1968 census.

It is, then, among the younger age groups that the reduction in the death rate has been most noticeable: to be schematic we can say that it has dropped by $\frac{7}{8}$ for children, by $\frac{3}{4}$ for young adults and by $\frac{1}{2}$ for old people. The infant mortality rate was certainly higher than 200 in 1,000 in pre-industrial Europe; it has now fallen to 24; whereas for people of 80 years of age it has been reduced to about 100 to 150 per 1,000.

We can estimate that, for the whole of Europe, the average expectation of life has risen from 25 years to 70 years in three centuries.

(4) *The reduction in the legitimate birth rate*

Figure 4 shows the distribution of families according to the number of recorded births, first of all in France in the eighteenth century, and then in 1975. Despite quite substantial regional variation in fertility, these two figures can stand for the whole of Europe. It can be seen that, in spite of a high death rate which broke up many couples prematurely, the proportion of large families (more than three children) was about 55 per cent before the Industrial Revolution; it has now fallen to 14.3 per cent.

From this it may be concluded that birth control was little practised in the past, except perhaps at the opposite ends of the social scale: in the world of the aristocracy and in that of prostitution. Today it is more or less widespread.

It is obvious that the high rate of infant mortality acted as a corrective to high fertility: the number of children who reached their twentieth birthday was not much higher than today.

This is how the artificial resemblance between certain sixteenth-century family structures and contemporary ones, as we have described them in the introduction, can be explained.

All the same, if we go a little deeper we notice that these analogies can only have been exceptional – to die at 80 or more made you quite a phenomenon in the sixteenth century – according to Wargentin's table of mortality only one newborn girl in seven survived to this age; according to the most recent Swedish table, virtually one girl in two.

Pre-industrial societies were weighed down with children much more than our own, although the replacement of generations was hardly more secure – in the statistics for the Vezelay *élection* drawn up by Maréchal Vauban in 1698, girls under 12 years old made up 37 per cent of all women, while in France today they represent no more than 18.5 per cent – exactly half.

This entails two important differences in population structure. With a much higher birth and death rate than today, traditional Europe had an age pyramid in the shape of a Chinese hat – very wide at the base, with concave sides. Whereas all contemporary pyramids look rather like helmets which bulge half-way up. With more children to feed, families were larger on the average than they are today. This was true even in less fertile regions like Corsica.

So even in regions like England or northern France, where the great majority of households were composed of nuclear families, the average size of these households was equal to, or higher than, four members, whereas today it is only three.

(5) *The flattening of the curves*

In pre-industrial Europe, death was at the heart of life, just as the cemetery was at the heart of the village. But what made death even more alarming was that it struck suddenly and violently. As P. Goubert puts it, 'For several months on end, sometimes for a year and occasionally longer, the number of funerals would double, treble (and sometimes even worse) in a parish, a bailliage, or in one or more provinces. A tenth or a fifth of the population (sometimes more) would go to their graves. People could not make proper sense of this, and attributed it to divine anger, the punishment of accumulated sins, or the vengeance of demons . . .'

For example, in the little parish of Maumusson, where the average number of burials had not exceeded 10.3 in the decade 1574–83, there

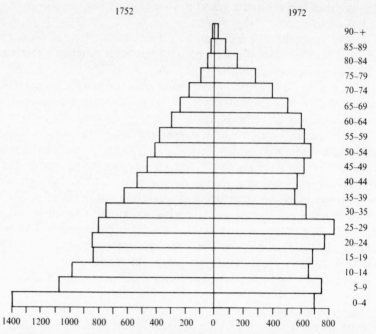

1752   1972

Fig. 5. Age pyramid in Sweden (for 10,000 people) in 1757 and in 1972. On the left, an example of a 'young' population, with a high birth rate and a high death rate. On the right, an example of an 'old' population – but the effects of the 'baby boom' which followed the Second World War are clearly visible.

were 146 deaths registered in 1584 alone; similarly, in London, the plague of 1665 carried off 97,306, whereas the highest total for a single year in the previous period had been 16,665. As soon as the statistics allow us to look at things on the national scale, we find similar results.

The flattening out of the curves of births and marriages is less noticeable, since they continue to reflect varying economic trends; besides, the behaviour of different populations changes more quickly than in the past. All the same, the coefficient of variation of marriage has itself diminished: it is only 7.8 per cent in contemporary France (1963–74), whereas it reached 9.3 per cent in France under the old regime (1763–74).

Finally, the seasonal variations themselves are less important now, at least as far as births and marriages are concerned. In Paris, for example, during the period 1670–83 the annual figure, measured in indices, reached 30.5 for births, 166 for marriages. The figures for the contemporary period (1958–67) have fallen to 16 and 86.2 respectively.

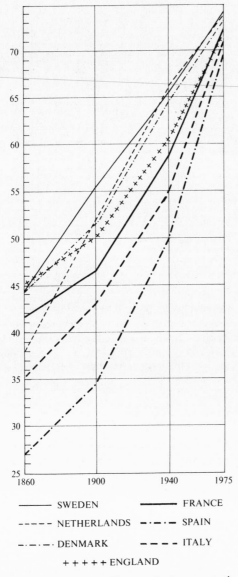

Fig. 6. Convergence of death rates. Changes in the expectation of life since 1860 in a number of European countries.

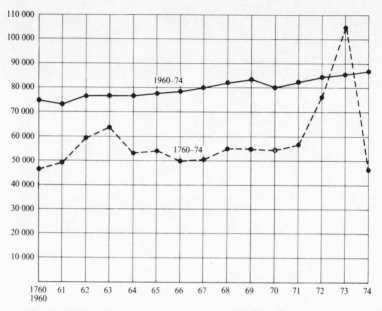

Fig. 7. The decrease in annual fluctuations. Although the population of Sweden has increased almost five-fold between 1750 and 1975, the present number of deaths a year is not much higher than it was in the eighteenth century. The most striking phenomenon is the decrease in annual fluctuations. Today the worst annual figures for deaths are only 17 per cent higher than the best ones, while the 1773 figure was 136 per cent higher than that for 1774.

(6) *The convergence of demographic regimes*

We have no way of measuring the birth and death rates in Europe before the nineteenth century, but monographs on villages show important regional variations in the seventeenth and eighteenth centuries. Infant mortality, for example, seems to vary between 120 and 360 per 1,000; and legitimate births to mothers in the age range 35–9 years seems to vary from 0.215 to 0.412.

Similarly, around 1750, life expectancy reached 35.8 years in Sweden, whereas it was only 24.8 years in France. Today, the Swedes live to an average of 74.2 years, the French to 72.1: a difference of only 2.8 per cent. In Albania, the least developed European country, life expectancy has already reached 65 years. The same thing goes for infant mortality, at least if this is measured in absolute terms.

The birth rate in all European countries is now less than 20 per 1,000 (except for Ireland and Albania); the death rate is less than 12 per 1,000 (except for East Germany, Austria and Belgium); and the infant mortality rate is less than 50 (except for Albania, Portugal and Yugoslavia).

Nevertheless, this similarity in demographic patterns is relatively recent – it was preceded by a period of divergence to which I shall return. To take up Alfred Sauvy's metaphor, the race towards progress began by a long bottleneck, in which the leaders were only a little ahead of the others. As soon as the track opened up the leaders got away at top speed while those behind stayed on the spot. At the end of the race those in front have had to slow down and those behind have now almost caught up.

The convergence between demographic systems is clear not only for countries, but also for regions, and for social groups: every day differential demography loses some of its importance.

One of the most interesting aspects of this state of affairs is the closing of the gap between the two systems that once divided Europe: that of late marriage in the West, and of adolescent marriage in the East.

Previously, the demographic equilibrium of western Europe was assured by three laws, unwritten but deeply rooted in the social consciousness:

(a) one married couple to each home
(b) no marriage without a home
(c) no babies outside marriage.

No couple could marry until a smallholding became available: young men and girls had to find work as servants until they inherited or saved a sum enabling them to buy a shop or a piece of land. The age for first marriage was therefore late (27 years on average for men and 25 for women in France), and the proportion of girls who remained unmarried was fairly high (about 13 per cent in France in the second half of the eighteenth century; 10.4 per cent in Sweden in 1750).

On the other hand, in eastern Europe, and in a large part of central and southern Europe too, young couples (or at least one of them) were willingly received into their parents' household. These countries could therefore practise adolescent marriage. This is why around 1900 in the age group 20–4, 76 per cent of young Bulgarian girls, 65 per cent of Romanian girls, and 84 per cent of Serbian girls were already married. Only 0.8 per cent of the Bulgarians, 0.7 per cent of the Serbs and 4.7 per cent of Russians remained old maids.

The population was nevertheless regulated after a fashion – partly by a high mortality rate, partly by social custom (emigration of the youngest sons) and sometimes by deliberate birth control.

Today there is a tendency towards earlier marriage in western Europe, and towards later marriage in the East. The average age of girls marrying for the first time in the cohort born between 1936 and 1940 was 22.7 years in France; 22.3 years in England and Wales; and 23.4 years in Sweden; it reached 20.7 years in Bulgaria and 22.2 years in Yugoslavia. In Ireland, where the average age was 28 years in 1946, it had come down to 24.8 years in 1973.

As for the proportion of unmarried women (measured in the age group 45–9), this has now dropped to 8.2 per cent in France, 7.8 per cent in England, and 7.8 per cent again in Sweden; whereas it has risen slightly in eastern Europe to 2.2 per cent in Bulgaria and 6.3 per cent in Yuogslavia.

The only exception is Ireland, which, after a major crisis in the nineteenth century, has adopted a hyper-Malthusian demographic system (i.e. one based on continence and late marriage). This is simply the traditional self-regulating mechanism, adapted to the circumstances. Girls marry there at an average age of 24.8 years; 17 per cent of them remain celibate; the proportion of illegitimate births does not exceed 3.2 per cent and the birth rate among married women still reaches 146 per 1,000 in the age group 35–9.

With the exception of Ireland and Albania, all the countries in Europe, including the USSR, are engaged in a process of demographic standardisation.

HOW AND WHY

The system just described has sometimes been called the 'demographic old regime'. It is a useful expression since it reminds us that the idea of 'old regime' is defined in relation to that of revolution. But it is a deceptive expression – like that of 'demographic revolution' – in that it suggests a complete opposition between two systems separated in time by a definite break.

In fact, the transition has been very slow; so slow that it is no doubt not completely finished today. Apart from biological constants, let us remember that much of our demographic behaviour is directly inherited from the past: for example, our attachment to the nuclear family (which seems to be harder to get rid of than many sociologists in a hurry would allow), and, more generally, everything which is concerned with marriage, social phenomenon *par excellence*, and one which is the most effective regulator of the birth rate even today.

This is why the expression 'demographic transition' seems to be better adapted to our needs than 'demographic revolution'. Unfortunately, a few specialists have tended to restrict its use, taking the term 'demographic transition' to mean merely the changeover from a high birth rate to a system based on widespread birth control. In the rest of this chapter, I shall be using this term in its wider sense, so that it includes all the demographic changes that have happened between the seventeenth century and our own time, whether it is a question of the birth rate, the death rate, marriage patterns, or the structure or mobility of the population – in short, everything I have discussed under the six headings of the first section.

The idea of a demographic 'old regime' can also be criticised in so far as it implies a coherent model. As we have seen, the most obvious characteristic of traditional Europe was its diversity. Without pushing the paradox so far as to write 'the rule is, that there are no rules', it is still possible to speak in terms of the region of chance, contrasts, and accidents. It is true that much the same thing applied to the political old regime, but this idea of a political old regime is specifically French and corresponds to a well-defined model (absolute monarchy as established by Louis XIV) whereas the demographic old regime encompasses several models, based on different conceptions of the family, the boundaries of which cheerfully overran national frontiers, dividing Europe into three or four more or less distinct cultural zones.

All the same, the idea of the old regime seems preferable to that of 'pre-industrial populations', since the latter expression implies that it was the process of industrialisation that provoked the demographic changes – a proposition that is neither proved nor possible to prove, as we shall see later.

The stages of the transition are all the more difficult to follow because historians have not yet managed to draw up a complete picture of the demographic situation in Europe for the eighteenth century, let alone for the seventeenth century, and even less for the sixteenth. We are therefore led to believe that the earliest situation we know about went back indefinitely, which is no doubt an illusion. In all places and at all times there has been development, and nowhere has this development been really linear.

We shall begin, therefore, by striking a brief balance of what we know and do not know about demographic 'old regimes'; we shall pause to consider the enigmas of the 'take off'; then, as we reach the more solid ground of the 'age of statistics' we shall try to establish the timing of the transition.

(1) *The demographic old regimes: light and shade*

As we have already seen, men in the sixteenth century knew very little about population problems; to tell the truth, they did not even know what questions to ask; the first work on demography, the *Natural and Political Observations upon the Bills of Mortality . . . of the City of London*, of Captain John Graunt did not appear till 1661.

There is little to be gleaned from the writings of the period, apart from evidence of attitudes which might throw some light on demographic patterns. These patterns are, moreover, little known. Several modern specialists have examined the old parish registers. They have derived from them annual and monthly statistics of weddings, baptisms and burials; some clues to the average age of death or the frequency of illegitimate births; but very few have had the courage to undertake family reconstitution, a technique developed in France by Louis Henry, and

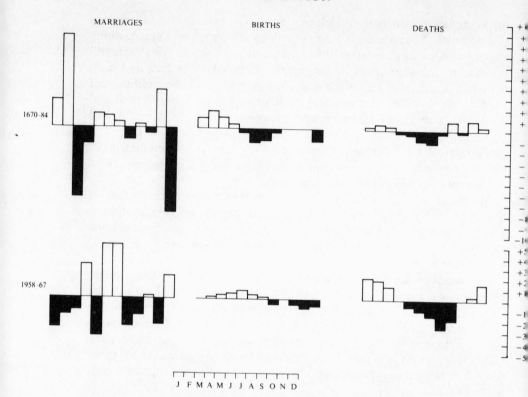

Fig. 8. Births, marriages and deaths in Paris in 1670–84 (above) and 1958–67 (below). The monthly marriage rates have completely changed. The old system was to marry above all in February and November, before the 'closed seasons' of Lent and Advent. Now the peak periods for marriages coincide with holidays (Easter, summer, Christmas). The monthly birth rate has also shifted relative to that of the old regime. The peak has moved from February to May, meaning that the peak for conceptions has moved from spring to summer. A reduction of intra-uterine mortality has also occurred. As for the death rate, the monthly variations have become sharper because it is virtually only the old who die now (most of all in winter), while under the old regime there was also a high death rate for infants, above all at the end of summer.

which alone enables us to discover the parameters of a demographic system: the marriage rate and the legitimate birth rate. Elsewhere, a few lists of names, a few tax records or ecclesiastical censuses, or lists of admission to citizenship have given us some evidence on the structure of local populations, their division by age, sex and occupation, and the composition of families.

These studies have only really been undertaken in England, France, Spain, Italy and Poland. For the rest of eastern Europe we are reduced to

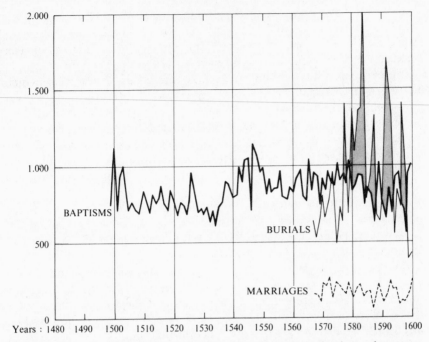

Fig. 9. Baptisms, burials and marriages in the Nantes region in the sixteenth century.
This graph is based on the statistics published by A. Croix. Note the rise in baptisms
in mid-century and the tremendous rise in mortality at the end of the period.

crude calculations (11 or 15 millions at the beginning of the sixteenth
century?) and to indirect evidence about demographic expansion.

Even for western Europe, the experts' estimates vary considerably:
J. C. Russell attributes 5.5 million inhabitants to Italy at the beginning of
the sixteenth century, but C. M. Cipolla claims that there were more than
10 millions. We would be wise to keep to an approximate estimate – 60
to 80 million inhabitants in Europe in 1500.

This population bracket is in any case very low, well below that of the
fourteenth century: the Black Death, war and political troubles had taken
their toll and disturbed the bases of economic life.

There is nothing surprising, then, in the fact that the sixteenth century
was marked by demographic expansion, which was to a large extent only
a recovery. We find traces of this everywhere: in the compoix of Languedoc, studied by E. Le Roy Ladurie; in the surveys of the Tver district;
in the baptism and marriage statistics published by A. Croix (figure 9);
in those of the Wapentake of Morley, edited by Michael Drake, etc.

It is estimated that the population of Castile rose from 3 to 6 millions
in sixty-four years (1530–94); the population of Sicily from 600,000 to
1,100,000 in the course of a century; the population of Germany from

12 to 20 millions; and that of the province of Holland from 275,000 to 627,000 between 1514 and 1622. For the whole of the United Provinces, estimates vary between 1,200,000 and 1,300,000 for 1550: between 1,400,000 and 1,600,000 at the end of the century.

The expansion was uneven owing to severe crises of mortality, which hit towns in particular and which seem due, for the most part, to a new outbreak. In the last third of the century, the death rate ended up higher than the birth rate, because civil and foreign wars helped to make the situation worse and to ruin any chance of recovery. The population remained the same or decreased, according to local conditions, but all the same it never fell to the catastrophic levels of the fifteenth century.

We have only an extremely incomplete picture of the demographic system, and what we have is thanks to the works of G. Cabourdin, L. Henry, T. H. Hollingsworth, E. A. Wrigley and some of the pupils of M. Lachiver.

One has the impression that the age of marriage was a little lower than it was to be in the seventeenth century (22 years for girls in the Lorraine countryside); that pre-marital conceptions and illegitimate births were a little more frequent; and that the birth rate amongst married women was a little lower – but all this awaits confirmation.

For the seventeenth century, we have a little more information: kings and their ministers began to concern themselves with the number of their subjects, for fiscal reasons as much as military ones. They ordered censuses which were more and more extensive, and more and more detailed. At the same time they took an interest in registers of baptisms, marriages and burials, and made it compulsory to preserve them. For its part, the Catholic Church ordered its priests to register deaths as well as baptisms and marriages, and also to keep a *Liber status animarum* or *Book of Souls* (1614).

As far as recording population movements is concerned, the seventeenth century took over from the sixteenth. What was new, was that people began to exploit the sources, and to publish them: the facts about the city of London, which had only been published spasmodically in the sixteenth century (notably in 1578–82) appeared regularly from 1603 on, thanks to the parish clerks. The analysis of these bills of mortality was soon going to form the basis of the pioneer work of John Graunt.

This example was followed in France, where Colbert ordered the publication of monthly figures for population movements in the city of Paris between 1670 and 1683); and then by some German towns (Leipzig, Stuttgart).

The results of the censuses were kept secret for a long time: the first publication dealt with Sicily in 1642. As for France, we had to wait for the 'Census of the kingdom' published by the bookseller Saugrain (1709) –

Table 1. *Life expectancy of the British and Danish aristocracy in the sixteenth and seventeenth centuries*

Generations born in	Britain		Denmark	
	Males	Females	Males	Females
1550–74	36.5	38.2	34.7	37.7
1575–99	35.3	38.1		
1600–24	32.9	35.3	31.7	32.7
1625–49	31.2	33.2		
1650–74	29.6	32.7	30.3	36.1
1675–99	32.9	34.2		
1700–24	34.4	36.3	34.8	36.5
1725–49	38.6	36.7		

statistics which were in any case out of date by the time they reached the public.

Given these conditions, one can only admire the relative accuracy of the estimates of Europe's population made for the first time in Father Riccioli's geography, published at Bologna in 1661 – 11 million inhabitants for Italy, 9 millions for Spain and Portugal, 19–20 millions for France; the same for Germany, Bohemia and Hungary together; 6 millions in Poland, Lithuania and Pomerania. The underestimate of the population of the British Isles (4 millions) and of Muscovy (3 millions) were more or less cancelled out by the overestimate of the population of Scandinavia (8 millions) and of the Balkans (16 millions), so that one ends up with a plausible total of 100 million Europeans. Gregory King also settled for this figure at the end of the century. Around 1750, the total figure was thought to be between 130 and 140 millions, of which 25 millions were attributed to France, 25 millions also to Russia, 20 millions to Germany, about 16 millions to Italy and 12 millions to the Habsburg Empire.

In comparison with the estimates we have put forward for the beginning of the sixteenth century, the growth is considerable, especially in eastern Europe. On the other hand, despite increased urbanisation, the list of towns with over 100,000 inhabitants hardly lengthened after 1600: Seville, Granada, Adrianople and Prague no longer feature, but nine cities must be added to the list: Amsterdam, Vienna, Moscow, St Petersburg, Dublin, Madrid, Milan, Lyon and Berlin.

It does not, however, seem to be the reduction in the death rate which explains this European expansion: as far as we can tell, life expectancy in the seventeenth century was lower than in the sixteenth. At least this conclusion is suggested by the studies of T. H. Hollingsworth on the aristocracy in Britain and of H. O. Hansen on that of Denmark.

The estimate in Table 1 is concerned with a very narrow social group,

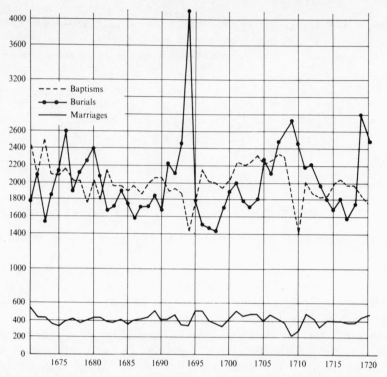

Fig. 10. Population trends in the Paris basin, 1670–1720. This graph is based on statistics drawn from the registers of ninety rural parishes of the Paris basin, taken at random by the INED (National Institute for Demographic Studies) in the course of research into the population of France between 1670 and 1829. Note that the fluctuation in the death rate is much greater than that for marriages and baptisms.

A major rise in the death rate, which was usually linked to an increase in grain prices and to plagues, had an immediate effect on the rate of marriages and baptisms. As soon as the crisis was over, there was a rush to get married and the population soon rose to its former level. It is possible to see movements of ebb and flow over a period (30 years) which more or less corresponds to a generation.

but it certainly seems to reflect the poor conditions, linked perhaps to the 'little ice age', which were prevalent in Europe from the end of the six-teenth century. In any case, the death rate was rising: the parochial and even the regional mortality curves bristle with peaks which sometimes, but not always, correspond to a period of high grain prices (figure 10): it was the period of subsistence crises, studied in France by J. Meuvret and P. Goubert. It was also the period of great epidemics – in Colyton in 1645 a quarter of the population were carried off, and the community did not recover from the blow.

Indeed, these mortality crises were severe enough, and sufficiently widespread, to slow down population growth altogether in part of Europe. There were even areas whose population was reduced – this was usually associated with large-scale international conflict: for example, the Thirty Years War reduced the population in Germany and the Northern Wars had the same effect around the Baltic.

Meanwhile, without much fuss, western Europe had just gained its first victory over microbes: the plague, which had struck more and more fiercely in the first two-thirds of the seventeenth century and had claimed 100,000 victims in London as late as 1665, virtually died out after this, apart from an isolated outbreak in Provence in 1720. This important victory does not seem to have happened by chance, nor as a result of a mutation of the virus, for the plague continued to rage in eastern Europe. The disease was defeated by the isolation of its victims and the implementation of rigorous measures of hygiene imposed by the public authorities.

Unfortunately, the population of Europe was slow to gather the fruits of this great victory: at the time, other diseases, which no one thought of fighting in the same way, took over: smallpox, typhus, dysentery. Wars helped to spread them by provoking the movement of troops and refugees. In France, the years 1693 and 1719 were particularly catastrophic; in England the year 1727 was marked by a record mortality.

These losses were, however, made up each time thanks to the self-regulating system which had gradually been established. Populations in the West, subject to the laws of Christian morality, could draw on considerable reserves. The young unmarried formed a matrimonial reserve force whose function was to enable society to keep the number of households, that is to say, the number of basic economic units, at a more or less constant level.

The rules regarding celibacy and marriage were never enforced so strictly, nor so much respected by the population, as in the seventeenth century. In France, the Catholic Counter-Reformation insisted on the publication of the banns of marriage, reduced betrothal to a simple formality often celebrated on the eve of the wedding ceremony, hunted down irregular liaisons, and even preached continence within marriage. In England, Puritanism had the same effect. If it did not get rid of trial marriage – as the proportion of pre-marital conceptions, much higher than in France, would suggest – it helped to reduce the number of illegitimate births quite substantially (figure 11).

It is likely that this sexual repression, which in any case was never totally effective, as J. L. Flandrin has shown, had repercussions on the legitimate birth rate, which seems to have been lower in the seventeenth century than in the first half of the eighteenth century. In any case, the average age on first marriage continued to rise: in Colyton, where it was already 27.2 years for men and 27 years for women between 1560 and

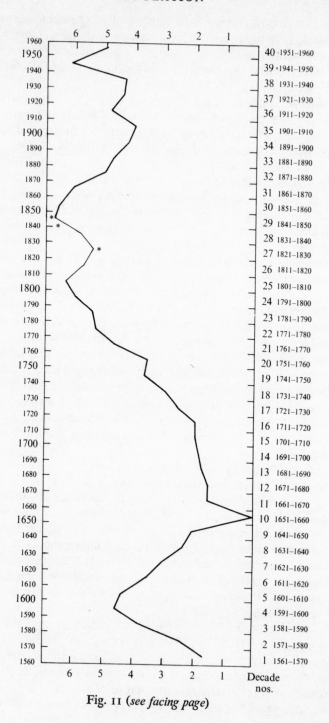

Fig. 11 (*see facing page*)

1646, it rose to 27.7 years and 29.6 years respectively in the period 1647–1719.

Amongst the bourgeoisie of Geneva, it developed as follows:

Date of birth	Males	Females
1550–99	27.2	21.4
1600–49	29.1	25.6
1650–99	32.6	25.7

Of course, these remarks are only valid for western Europe. We still know nothing about the demographic patterns of eastern Europe, based no doubt on early marriage and the extended family: the only clue is a list of inhabitants in the Serbian quarter of Belgrade for 1733–4: it included 1,356 people, of whom 384 were described as guests or foreigners. The average size of families was 7.14; or 5.45 if guests and foreigners are disregarded. These figures are considerably higher than those for England (4.75 between 1574 and 1821 according to P. Laslett) and also higher than the figures H. K. Roessingh found for the families of farmers in the Veluwe in 1566 (6.8).

(2) *The enigmas of the 'take-off'*

The growth in the European population began again in the eighteenth century but it is very difficult to date its progress exactly, partly because its original position is not known exactly, but especially because the growth was not smooth: it was punctuated by severe mortality crises which continued those of the seventeenth century and interrupted the rhythm. Iceland suffered in this way in 1707, England in 1726–9, France in 1783–4, and Scandinavia in 1772–3.

Towards 1800, Europe had about 190 million inhabitants; 45 millions in the Russian Empire, 29 millions in France, 25 millions in Germany, 23 millions in the Habsburg Empire, 19 millions in Italy, 16 millions in the British Isles and 12 millions in Spain. Assuming that the population did

Fig. 11. Illegitimacy ratios (percentage of registered baptisms, percentage of registered births) in England 1561–1960, by decade. From P. Laslett and K. Oosterveen, 'Long-term Trends in Bastardy in England' in *Population Studies*, 27, 2, 1973.

This graph is based on the research of the Cambridge Group (up to the decade 1801–10) and on official statistics (from 1841–50 onwards). There is little to say about the sixteenth-century increase; it is perhaps the result of more thorough registration. On the other hand, the decline in the first half of the seventeenth century is extremely significant; it corresponds to the rise of puritanism. Note that the level remains low until about 1720. Afterwards it rises sharply, partly owing to the rise in age at marriage and partly to the increased mobility of the population.

not exceed 100–110 millions at the beginning of the century, the increase was at least 75 per cent.

All the same, the rate of growth did not remain constant throughout the century; it was faster and smoother in the second half of the century than in the first. It also varied widely in different countries.

Let us confine ourselves to the period 1750–1800, for which we have reliable statistics; especially for Scandinavia, where the figures were collected at the time by the pastors themselves; for France, where they have just been established by the large-scale survey of the National Institute for Demographic Studies; and for the Netherlands, where they were published by Slicher van Bath and his team.

For these countries, the table appears as follows (%): Finland, +96; Norway, +37; Sweden, +32; France, +19; Denmark, +15; Netherlands, +10; Iceland, −4.

The picture is much less clear as far as other countries are concerned Ireland probably went from 3 million inhabitants to 5.2 millions (+73 per cent); England and Wales from 6.1 millions to 9.2 millions (+51 per cent); Italy from 15.5 to 19.5 millions (+26 per cent).

To sum up: it seems possible to distinguish two demographic patterns within Europe: (a) those of the new countries, in which the annual growth rate reached or exceeded 10 per 1,000. This category would include Finland, and no doubt also Russia, Poland, Hungary and the Balkan States. Ireland, too, must be added to this group, for rather special reasons (the re-distribtion of small-holdings by the landlords, which triggered off the self-regulating mechanism); (b) those of the old countries, where the annual growth rate stayed below 5 per cent, as in Italy, France, Spain, Denmark and the Netherlands.

Sweden and Norway, which were new countries in part, were in an intermediate position; and the same goes for Great Britain, where industry and commerce began to create more jobs.

It is important to note in the first place that growth was virtually universal in Europe, and that it is completely useless to try to explain it in national or regional terms, all the more because other parts of the world seem to have experienced it as well.

In the second place, growth began well before 1750: in Sweden it reached nearly 20 per cent between 1700 and 1750, despite the Great Northern War; the population of Finland increased by 49 per cent, Norway by 27 per cent, Italy and France by 16 per cent, etc.

Finally, the regional distribution of growth does not at all correspond with that of industrialisation. All over the Continent, demographic increases preceded the economic developments inaccurately known as the 'Agricultural Revolution' and the 'Industrial Revolution'. It was indeed demographic pressure that forced the peasants of Europe to cultivate the land more intensively and to bring more land under cultivation. If food supplies had increased before the population did, supply would have exceeded demand and prices would have been on the decrease, whereas we can see a continuous increase in prices throughout Europe from 1750 onwards. Now at last the landowners made large profits, which encouraged them to invest, to take better care of their land, to stockpile grain, and to put it on the market. At the other end of the social scale life became more difficult: the poorer peasants tried to limit their purchases by having recourse to substitutes for grain (maize, potatoes, vegetables); they improved their gardening techniques. Agriculture made progress on all sides as a result of demographic pressure. It was not technological innovation which burst the constricting framework of peasant production, but a widening range of needs which gave rise to technological innovation.

However, this development took different forms in France, England, Ireland and in eastern Europe.

As far as France is concerned, the signs of crisis increased from 1770 onwards: the age of marriage rose again, which perhaps partly explains the higher incidence of illegitimate births and pre-marital conceptions. On the other hand, the birth rate within marriage decreased a little. It has been noted that number of vagrants increased, along with the floating population of large towns; it is quite probable that this situation contributed to the unleashing of the Revolution. The same signs were evident in Sweden until 1785.

In England, on the other hand, the development of capitalism meant that there was work for young people; and this in turn facilitated early marriage. Workers with a job could marry right away; those who were not qualified no longer had to wait till the end of their apprenticeship, and those who came from the country were no longer frustrated by the difficulties of establishing themselves. Finally, improvements in the transport system increased geographic mobility and encouraged the mixing of social groups. D. Chambers has shown that in the Vale of Trent industrial villages had, from the beginning of the eighteenth century, a higher surplus of births over deaths than purely agricultural villages, and that this difference was even more marked after 1740, thanks to a higher rate of marriage and fertility.

In Ireland, the population, which scarcely exceeded 3 million inhabitants in 1725, reached 4 millions in 1780 and 5.2 millions in 1800. Since we have no studies based on parish registers, we are not in a position to analyse the causes of this increase. It is difficult to believe that it can be explained entirely in terms of the lower death rate, although changes in diet, which had previously consisted mostly of dairy produce and potatoes, might have had a good effect. The rate of legitimate births seems always to have been high, and illegitimate births unusual. We are therefore led to believe that acceleration in demographic growth must have been the result of a reduction in the age of marriage, although this is disputed by

M. Drake. In order to increase their income, go over to intensive agriculture and bring more land under cultivation, the landowners pressed for the division of holdings, a tiny plot now being sufficient – thanks to the potato – to feed a family. In this way, with all demographic controls removed, Ireland moved towards catastrophe, offering a late, but tragic, illustration of the theory Malthus formulated for the first time in 1798.

In eastern Europe, the same causes did not produce the same effects because there were reserves of land available. The ruling classes acted in the same way as English landlords in encouraging young people to set up for themselves, but huge areas of land were ready for settlement. The frontier was open to pioneers. On this edge of Europe, population growth was at the same time the cause and the consequence of territorial expansion.

Having said this, the mysteries of this increase remain unsolved. For a long time historians tried to explain it in terms of technical progress, such as advances in medicine which were thought to have overcome disease, and advances in agronomy which provided Europeans with a larger food supply, which in turn reduced the death rate. The controversy was particularly animated in England. Most authors, especially G. T. Griffiths and J. Brownlee, do indeed attribute the increase in population to the lowering of the death rate, but from the 1950s on it began to be doubted whether there had been much real progress in medicine and hygiene, and this led scholars to question the drop in the death rate. J. T. Krause went so far as to declare that this drop was quite illusory, and due partly to the methods of registering deaths.

Today, local studies, in particular those of Chambers and Eversley, have proved that the drop was a real one, although we have no means of explaining it. Moreover, this agrees with what T. H. Hollingsworth had demonstrated for the peers of the realm. Whereas in this privileged group the average life expectancy had fallen to 29.6 years for men and 32.7 years for women during the period 1650–74, it had risen to 38.6 and 37.7 years respectively in the second quarter of the eighteenth century (see above, p. 95). In the third quarter, it went to 44.5 and 45.7 years; and in the last quarter, to 46.8 and 49 years.

We can see a movement in the same direction in Sweden, where life expectancy for women went from 36.6 years (1751–90) to 38.4 years (1791–1815), and also in France, where it rose from 25.7 (1740–9) to 32.1 (1790–9).

Since the increase in population seems to have been not just an English or even a specifically European but a world-wide phenomenon, we must reject local explanations. Unless there was a miraculous similarity in human behaviour from one end of the globe to the other the only explanation must lie in a change in the death rate, after the crisis of the seventeenth century. It is very disappointing for the historian to reach this conclusion which he cannot justify, but why did the Black Death come to Europe in the fourteenth century and not in the thirteenth? For the moment we have no answer to this kind of question.

(3) *The timing of the transition*

When we look at the curves of births and deaths for all the countries of Europe, we can generally pick out a first downward trend around 1880, a sudden recovery from 1945 onwards, and a new drop in 1965. This leads us to distinguish four periods in the 'demographic transition': from about 1760 to 1880 – the 'belle époque' of European expansion; from 1880 to 1940 – a general decline in the levels of both birth and death rates; from 1945 to 1965 – expansion again; from 1965 to today – towards zero growth.

(a) *The 'belle époque' of European expansion.* From 1760–1880 the population of Europe rose from about 150 to about 330 million inhabitants, an increase of 120 per cent. At the end of this period it represented 22 per cent of the world population and the average density per square kilometre reached 33 (figure 12).

As far as eastern Europe is concerned, we do not know enough about the rates of growth and the first statistics about the movement of the population did not appear until about 1860 (Romania, Serbia). As far as we can tell, the population was multiplied by 2.5 during the period.

We find more or less the same increase in Scandinavia (Denmark, Norway, Sweden) although the demographic system in these countries seems to have been quite different.

The growth records seem to have been broken by England, Germany and Finland, whose populations nearly quadrupled during these 120 years. After these countries comes the Austro-Hungarian Empire, where we can talk in terms of a three-fold increase.

On the other hand, the Latin countries (Italy, Spain, Portugal) only doubled their numbers; the Netherlands, Belgium and Switzerland seem to have been held back in their development; and as for Ireland and France, they appear to be special cases since the former only increased by 58 per cent and the latter by 45 per cent.

The increase in the German-speaking countries is particularly remarkable in view of the fact that these countries provided about 80 per cent of the wave of emigrants which took about 3 million Europeans across the Atlantic between 1841 and 1880.

The increase in the population of Europe from 1760 to 1880 is closely linked to the decline in the death rate, especially the juvenile death rate. It was in 1796 that Jenner developed the technique of vaccination, which allowed man to win a second great victory over death. Although infant

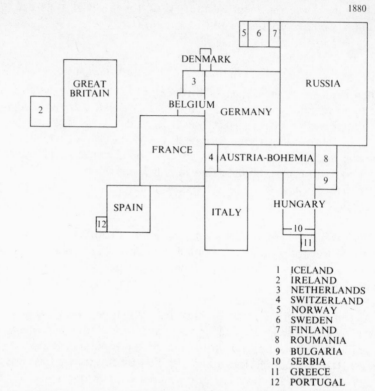

Fig. 12. Population of Europe in 1880 (compare figure 2). The population of Europe had almost doubled since 1760. It would double again between 1880 and 1970. The first period favoured Protestant Europe (Great Britain, Germany, Scandinavia) while eastern and southern Europe had its turn in the second period. In 1760, Great Britain represented only 5 per cent of the population of Europe; by 1880, its share had increased to 9 per cent.

mortality remained high everywhere, life expectancy increased as shown in the table on p. 105.

All the same, until about 1880 advances in medicine were not decisive: the plague was only eliminated from eastern Europe after 1841 and from the Balkans after 1849. Cholera took over: it appeared for the first time in Orenburg in August 1831 and ravaged the whole of Europe, claiming more than 100,000 victims in France. Later there were new epidemics in 1847–9, 1851–4, etc.

In the last analysis, the death rate hardly seems to have gone down between 1760 and 1880, apart from infant mortality, and no doubt also that among the higher classes of society. In the third quarter of the nineteenth century, then, the geography of European mortality seems to have shown

	Period	Males	Females
England and Wales	1838–54	44.5	46.4
	1871–80	47.5	52.5
France	1760–9	26.4	28.1
	1820–9	38.3	39.3
	1877–81	40.8	43.4
Sweden	1755–7	34.8	36.9
	1816–40	39.5	43.6
	1871–80	45.3	48.6

the same characteristics as 100 years previously, but in an even more pronounced way: the death rate is low in Scandinavia and in north-west Europe, but rises progressively as one moves towards the Mediterranean and especially towards the Black Sea. This partly explains the distribution of the population growth, roughly sketched earlier.

All the same, another factor played a decisive role – fertility. E. van de Walle undertook to measure this for most countries in Europe between 1840 and 1960, using an index based on the general level of fertility as compared with that of the Hutterite women. For 1880, the highest indices were those of Hungary (0.430), Germany (0.404), and the Netherlands (0.402), but these records would certainly have been beaten if the same information had been available to him for Russia (0.546 in 1900), Greece (0.491 in 1900), and the Balkans.

This fertility index is itself composed of three elements: the proportion of married women (of fertile age), the birth rate within marriage and, in addition, the illegitimate birth rate.

The first element favours eastern Europe, which practised early marriage, as we have seen: in 1880 the proportion of married women (of fertile age) reached 0.680 in Hungary; 0.687 in Russia in 1900, and 0.632 in Greece at the same date, whereas in western Europe it was universally lower than 0.550 and even fell to 0.409 in Sweden. In this way, a high marriage rate, making up for a disastrous death rate, enabled eastern Europe to grow demographically at the same rate as Scandinavia, and to overtake Latin Europe, but without reaching the record levels of Germany and England.

From this point of view it must be noted that the Industrial Revolution, by multiplying the number of jobs available, helped to bring about a higher marriage rate throughout western Europe, except in Sweden, Italy and in particular Ireland (scarcely industrialised in 1880). In this way, the proportion of married women rose from 0.375 to 0.436 in Belgium, from 0.389 to 0.469 in the Netherlands, from 0.516 to 0.538 in France and from 0.421 to 0.456 in Denmark, all in the space of thirty or forty years (1840–50 to 1880).

On the other hand, the legitimate birth rate, also measured in comparison with that of the Hutterites, hardly seems to have changed before 1880, except in France. Elsewhere, all the indices fall between 0.628 and 0.845 including those of eastern Europe; and for the states where the series begins around 1840, we can hardly seen any change, as shown in E. van de Walle's indices of legitimate fertility:

	1850	1880
Belgium	0.784	0.751
Denmark	0.677	0.686
Netherlands	0.831	0.831
Sweden	0.673	0.704

The only exception is France, where van de Walle's index is only 0.515 in 1840; 0.478 in 1860; and 0.460 in 1880. France is therefore the only country in Europe where voluntary birth control was practised systematically and on a wide scale. This touch of originality, which was to have important consequences on the balance of power in Europe (the proportion of the French population in the total European population fell from 17 per cent in 1760 to 12 per cent in 1800) is no doubt linked to the French Revolution, to the destruction of old traditions and to the gradual victory of an individualistic moral code, but historians are far from exhausting this subject.

In Ireland, too, events took an unusual course. We have seen that the upheaval in economic and social conditions had multiplied the number of holdings there from the end of the eighteenth century, and thus favoured early marriage. This, added to a high legitimate birth rate and a moderate death rate, provoked a real demographic explosion in 50 years: the population went from 3,740,000 inhabitants in 1777 to 7,764,000 in 1830, a growth rate of 108 per cent in fifty-three years (whereas England and Wales increased by only 85 per cent between 1780 and 1830). The potato blight, which appeared in 1845, caused a demographic catastrophe: more than 500,000 died and 892,000 emigrated between 1851 and 1855 alone, and it had an important, lasting effect on the marriage rate: the average age of girls at first marriage rose progressively to 30 years, and the proportion of unmarried women to 25 per cent. In 1851 the island had 1,623,000 fewer inhabitants than in 1841, and its population had fallen again to 5,175,000 by 1881.

(b) *The general drop in the death and birth rates (1880–1945).* From 1880 onwards, the death rate fell throughout the whole of western, central and southern Europe. We cannot make such categorical statements about eastern Europe since the records of deaths registered at the beginning of the period are clearly incomplete. However, it is probable that the death

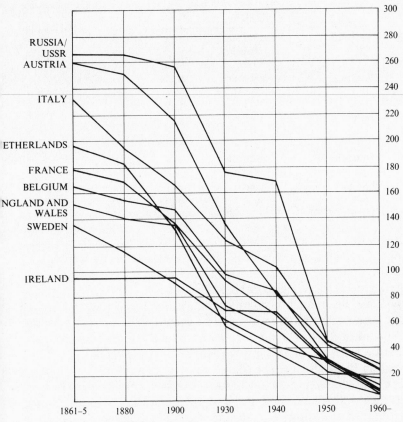

Fig. 13. The fall in infant mortality in Europe over the last 100 years. Compare figure 5. Infant mortality scarcely declined before 1880, in some places even a little later. The higher the original death rate, the more obvious the progress. Austria was still losing over 25 per cent of new-born babies in 1881–5, but had declined to 81 per thousand in 1936–40; while Ireland, which held the European record for low infant mortality in 1861–5 (95 per thousand) had only improved to 70 per thousand in 1936–40. Today the major countries have reached similar figures.

rate fell here too, since the population growth accelerated: the annual rate of increase of the population of Russia, which had been 1 per cent in the middle of the nineteenth century, rose to 1.5 per cent at the beginning of the twentieth. This reduction in mortality did not take effect only amongst the newly born (figure 13) but was spread throughout the population. The figures for life expectancy in different countries were already beginning to converge, as was pointed out at the beginning of this chapter. (See table on p. 108.)

The decrease in the death rate is no doubt due this time to advances in hygiene and medicine: the work of Pasteur and of numerous other

	Period	Males	Females
Sweden	1871–80	45.3	48.6
	1901–10	54.5	56.9
	1936–40	64.3	66.9
France	1877–81	40.8	43.4
	1908–13	48.4	52.4
	1933–8	55.9	61.6
Italy	1876–87	35.1	35.5
	1910–12	46.6	47.3
	1930–2	53.8	56.0
Hungary	1900–01	40.3	39.4
	1930–1	59.8	63.7
European Russia	1896–7	31.4	33.3
	1926–7	41.9	46.8

scientists on microbes led to the development of asepsis and antisepsis. The typhoid, cholera, diphtheria, tetanus and plague bacilli were identified and triumphantly defeated. Death from infection – particularly from post-operative infection – was dramatically reduced.

All the same, this reduction did not produce all the effects we might have expected, because the birth rate began to decline too, and the marriage rate did not altogether make up for this. In 1930 the birth rate had fallen below the French level of 1880 everywhere except in Ireland, in the Latin countries and in eastern Europe (figure 14).

At first the reduction in the death rate was faster than that in the birth rate, but then this was reversed at the beginning of the twentieth century, so that the rate of natural growth (per 1,000 inhabitants) developed as follows:

	Period		
Country	1876–80	1901–5	1931–5
Denmark	12.7	14.2	6.9
Norway	15.1	14.1	4.8
Sweden	12.0	14.6	2.5
Finland	14.2	12.7	5.8
Ireland	6.9	5.6	5.4
England	14.6	12.1	3.0
Scotland	14.2	12.2	5.0
France	2.9	1.8	0.8
Belgium	1.5	10.8	3.9
Romania	4.7	13.8	12.3
Germany	13.1	14.9	5.4
Switzerland	8.4	10.4	4.6
Austria	8.2	11.3	0.8
Hungary	7.0	10.8	6.6
Czechoslovakia	9.2	10.1	5.8

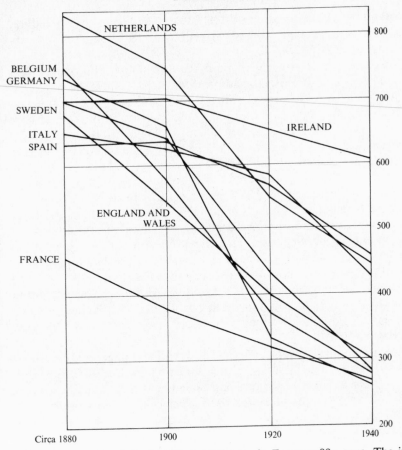

Fig. 14. Reduction of the legitimate birth rate in Europe 1880–1940. The indices have been calculated by E. Van de Walle, using the fertility of Hutterite women (who do not practice birth control) as a base. The greatest reduction was in Germany, which had almost caught up with France by 1925; the birth rate continued to fall during the crisis. By 1940 no country of northern or western Europe was replacing its population except Ireland and the Netherlands. Southern Europe (Italy, Spain, Portugal) and Russia (after the prohibition of abortion) came closer to replacing themselves.

This partly explains the slowing down of growth in the population of Europe from 1914 onwards. It is nevertheless quite remarkable that this growth should have first of all increased at the end of the nineteenth century and at the beginning of the twentieth, despite the almost universal decrease in fertility – a good example of the inertia of demographic phenomena.

In 1914 Europe had around 480 million inhabitants, including 140 millions in European Russia, which represented approximately 25 per cent of the world population. Since 1880 it had gained 150 million inhabitants; the average annual growth rate had therefore slightly exceeded 1 per cent.

During this period, however, more than 30 million Europeans had emigrated overseas. The British had provided 80 per cent of the emigrants until 1850, and still 50 per cent in the following period. German and Scandinavian emigrants were next to follow, and then from 1885–90 they came from all over Europe: from Portugal, Spain, Italy, the Austro-Hungarian Empire, the Balkans, Poland and the Ukraine. In the year 1910 alone, more than 2 million people crossed the Atlantic.

The period 1880–1914 marked the decisive turning point in European demography. Whereas until this time the rural population was more or less stable throughout Europe – the towns merely absorbing the rural surplus – the European countrysides now began to empty, adding no doubt to the economic crisis, and the proportion of the population living in towns rose to nearly 40 per cent, at least in western Europe. Whereas in 1850, only forty-five European towns had more than 100,000 inhabitants, by 1900 there were 143. London was then the largest city in the world, with 4,500,000 inhabitants, followed by Paris (2,700,000 inhabitants), Berlin (1,890,000), Vienna (1,675,000) and Moscow (989,000).

These developments went hand in hand with a change in the occupational structures: around 1900, in the whole of north-west Europe and even in central Europe, agriculture had ceased to be the dominant activity. In England it now accounted for only 9 per cent of the workforce, in Belgium for 20 per cent, in Germany for 35 per cent, and in France for 42 per cent.

Moreover, the age structures had changed considerably – the proportion of 'under twenties' had altered as follows between 1880 and 1930.

	1880 (%)	1910 (%)	1930 (%)	
Germany	44.8	43.7	29.8	(1936)
Belgium	42.7	39.8	31.0	
Austria	43.4	44.5	29.5	(1934)
Denmark	42.8	42.7	34.1	(1935)
France	35.4	33.9	30.4	
United Kingdom	46.3	40.1	32.8	
Sweden	42.5	41.0	30.8	(1935)

It is to be noted that the influence of the First World War was not the only factor, though it contributed to the narrowing of the base of the age pyramid in the countries involved.

This war was the immediate cause of about 13 million deaths, but the real losses were much higher if one takes into account the high death rate among the civilian population, the lost births which were never entirely replaced, and the troubles which resulted from the war: in Russia, for example, civil war caused about 4 million deaths, and the famine that followed, another 5 millions. In addition, the epidemic of Spanish flu in 1918–19 killed more than a million in western Europe alone.

In these conditions, the growth of the European population was severely restricted: in 1930, with 515 million inhabitants, Europe had only 35 millions more than in 1914. In 1940 it had reached 540 millions, including the European part of the Soviet Union. Out of the 25 millions gained between 1930 and 1940 at least 11 million had been produced by totalitarian regimes pursuing a high birth rate policy (Germany, Italy, the USSR).

During the inter-war period emigration from Europe was considerably reduced, despite the economic crisis and unemployment, because the United States began to close their doors: in 1928, for example, they only accepted 153,000 people, which was not even 10 per cent of the record levels before 1914.

The Second World War seemed to confirm demographic decline in Europe: losses – including Soviet losses – were three times as high as in the First World War: there were probably 40 million killed, half of them civilians. There were also large-scale and painful movements of population, and several tens of millions of lost births, but it is difficult to draw up a balance, since the record offices were disorganised and part of the information, especially the Soviet losses, was kept secret. Moreover, the recovery of the birth rate, which became evident sometimes in the middle of the war, masked the failure to increase and makes it impossible to calculate.

(c) *The recovery and further decline (1945–76)*. I shall not spend long on this period which is supposed to be better known, although its history is not yet complete. The basic fact is the general rise in the birth rate from 1945 onwards, but sometimes a little later, as in Germany and the USSR. It was thought at first to be just a period of recuperation like the one following the First World War, but the trend towards a higher birth rate continued, and even accelerated during the 1950s. The strangest thing is that the non-combatant countries experienced a similar development, though rather less pronounced.

The rise in the birth rate was particularly noticeable in western Europe in the following countries: Austria, Belgium, France, Norway, the United Kingdom and Switzerland; and in eastern Europe in Poland, Romania, and Yugoslavia. It was, on the other hand, relatively low in the two Germanies, in Czechoslovakia, Italy and Sweden.

Since the marriage rate increased slightly, and the death rate continued to fall everywhere (at least until 1965) the population began to grow again. Including European Russia, the total population reached 576 millions in 1950 and 636 millions in 1970. The annual growth rate, therefore, almost equalled the record levels of the beginning of the century.

Another curious fact is that this rising trend did not provoke the wave of emigration which seemed to be beginning in 1945, with the movement of refugees. Altogether, 3 million Europeans were expatriated during the twenty years after the war, but in return western Europe attracted about 15 million immigrant workers, some coming from the poor countries of southern Europe, but a good half from the Maghreb, Turkey, black Africa, the Antilles and even from India.

It is clear that for a long time the rapid industrialisation of western Europe created a level of employment higher than the demand: indeed, the two World Wars and the economic crisis, by accelerating the drop in the birth rate, had made the age pyramid concave; it was only from 1945 onwards that the population began to recover, and it took twenty years for the new generation to reinforce the working population. In France, for example, the number of workers, which had been 20.5 millions in 1906, only reached 20 millions in 1962 (despite the recovery of Alsace-Lorraine in 1918).

Eastern Europe has experienced a rather different development: from 1950 onwards the birth rate returned to the downward trend begun before the war: in fifteen years it fell by 32 per cent in Poland; 30 per cent in Bulgaria and Hungary; 28 per cent in Yugoslavia, and 22 per cent in Czechoslovakia. The USSR itself was not slow to follow, and East Germany broke all records for low growth, reaching the point where the death rate was higher than the birth rate. This development seems to have been the result of several factors: rapid urbanisation, the housing crisis, the increase in female employment, and the liberalisation of abortion laws. In Czechoslovakia, for example, where abortion was widely authorised in 1956, the birth rate fell by 16 per cent in the following five years, whereas it had only fallen by 6 per cent in the preceding five years. In Romania, where abortion was suddenly banned in 1966 the birth rate doubled in one year, and it remains today 36 per cent higher than its previous level.

With this exception, the birth rate in western Europe was universally higher, in 1964, than in east European countries. But that year, suddenly and without any apparent reason, the trend was reversed, especially in Great Britain, the German Federal Republic, the Netherlands and Scandinavia. In these cases it was not the liberalisation of abortion laws that set the process in motion, but it did speed it up. From 1964 to 1973 the birth rate dropped by 38 per cent in the German Federal Republic, by 34 per cent in the Netherlands, 30 per cent in England, and 25 per cent in Sweden. France resisted rather longer (22 per cent), like Spain and Italy, but the trend is continuing and today, to the west of the Elbe, the older generation is no longer being replaced.

On the other hand, in east Europe, thanks to a policy of family allowances and a more severe attitude towards abortion, there has been a slight increase since 1972.

Even in our twentieth century, therefore, there does not seem to be an obvious correlation between economic changes and the development of demographic systems. Why did the first industrial revolution encourage – except in France – demographic growth? Why the fall in the birth rate between 1880 and 1940? Why the divergence between east and west Europe from 1950 on? Why the demographic turning point in 1964? The careful study of economic statistics does not enable us to answer these questions.

What is clear, is that the whole of Europe is now involved in a demographic adventure from which it will not easily emerge: the social and educational policies and the structure of employment in its member countries will be affected by it for a long time, at least until the middle of the twenty-first century. Moreover, Europe's share in world population, already reduced in one century from 22 to 17 per cent, seems likely to shrink still further: including European Russia, it today accounts for only 9 per cent of world births: a situation without precedent for thousands, and perhaps tens of thousands, of years.

SELECT BIBLIOGRAPHY

André, R. and Pereira-Roque, J. *La Démographie de la Belgique au 19e siècle* (Brussels, 1963)

Ariès, P. *Histoire des populations françaises*, second ed. (Paris, 1971)
   Centuries of Childhood (London, 1962)
   Western Attitudes towards Death (Baltimore, 1973)

Armengaud, A. *La Famille et l'enfant en France et en Angleterre du 16e au 18e siècle: aspects démographiques* (Paris, n.d.)

Beloch, J. *Bevölkerungsgeschichte Italiens*, 3 vols (Berlin, 1937–61)

Beltrami, D. *Storia della popolazione di Venezia dalla fine del secolo 16 alla caduta della Repubblica* (Padua, 1951)

Biraben, J-N. *Les Hommes et la peste*, 2 vols (Paris, 1976)

Carr Saunders, A. M. *World Population* (Oxford, 1936)

Cipolla, C. M. *The Economic History of World Population* (Harmondsworth, 1962)

Creighton, G. C. *A History of Epidemics in Britain* (Cambridge, 1891)

Drake, M. *Population and Society in Norway 1735–1865* (Cambridge, 1969)

Dupâquier, J. *Introduction à la démographie historique* (Paris, 1975)

Faber, J. A. *et al. Population Changes and Economic Developments in the Netherlands*

Flandrin, J. L. *L'Eglise et le contrôle des naissances* (Paris, 1970)
   Familles (Paris, 1976)

Glass, D. V. *Numbering the People* (Farnborough, 1973)

Glass, D. V. and Eversley, D. E. C. (eds.), *Population in History* (London, 1965)

Gonnard, R. *Essai sur l'histoire de l'émigration* (Paris, 1928)

Henry, L. *Anciennes familles genevoises* (Paris, 1956)

Henry, L. and Fleury, M. *Manuel de démographie historique* (Geneva–Paris, 1970)

Hollingsworth, T. H. *Historical Demography* (London, 1969)

Imhof, A. E. *Aspekte der Bevölkerungsentwicklung in den nordischen Ländern, 1720–1750* (Bern, n.d.)

Knodel, J. E. *The Decline of Fertility in Germany 1871–1939* (Princeton, 1974)

Köllmann, W. *Bevölkerung und Raum* (Würzburg, 1965)
Bevölkerung in der industriellen Revolution (Göttingen, 1974)

Laslett, P., Eversley, D. E. C. and Armstrong, W. A. *An Introduction to English Historical Demography* (London, 1966)

Laslett, P. (ed.). *Household and Family in Past Time* (Cambridge, 1972)

Lebrun, F. *La Vie conjugale sous l'ancien régime* (Paris, 1975)

Livi-Bacci, M. *A History of Italian Fertility During the last two Centuries* (Princeton, 1976)

McKeown, T. *The Modern Rise of Population* (London, 1976)

Mols, R. *Introduction à la démographie historique*, 3 vols (Louvain, 1954–6)

Nadal, G. and Giralt, E. *La population catalane de 1553 à 1717* (Paris, 1960)

Population. Special number on 'Démographie historique', Nov. 1976

Romero de Solis, P. *La poblacion española en los siglos 18 y 19* (Madrid, 1973)

Russell, J. C. *Late Ancient and Medieval Population* (Philadelphia, 1958)

Shorter, E. *The Making of the Modern Family* (New York, 1975)

Sur la Population française au 18e et au 19e siècles (Paris, 1973)

Wrigley, E. A. *Population and History* (London, 1969)

CHAPTER V

PEASANTS

I

THE twentieth century, if one is to believe Eric Wolf, is a century of peasant wars; but the sixteenth or eighteenth centuries were great peasant ages *tout court*. On the Continent, the overwhelming majority of the population – 80 to 90 per cent – lived in the country and for the most part worked on the land. The time is past when peasant society could be compared – as in Marx's epigram – to a 'sack of potatoes', incapable of the solidarity, the consciousness or the existence 'in itself' or 'for itself' of a social class. Let us not get involved in a futile debate about the essence of a social class, but simply note that research on seventeenth-century revolts, on the *Chouans*, and on the peasant wars of our own time has shown quite clearly that peasants are capable, when they feel themselves threatened, of reacting as one against their enemies of the moment, whether nobility, church, townsmen, or the bureaucracy of an absolute monarch or a totalitarian state. The peasantry does indeed exist as a distinctive group of men tied to the land, growing crops and raising stock, whether to sell their produce on the market, or, more commonly, to consume it themselves or to barter it. This was the situation throughout Europe in the whole period covered by this chapter, from 1500 to 1950.

In spite of this basic unity, it is necessary to make some finer social distinctions. Until the coming of the tractor (1950), which was to change this social landscape without totally obliterating it, the crucial distinction was that between those who (whether they worked for themselves, or, more often, for others), disposed of nothing but their own labour, and those who had their own plough teams: horses in northern France, Belgium, England and most of northern Europe, oxen and/or mules in the Mediterranean countries.

The basic opposition was between (a) the day-labourer, *manouvrier* or *brassier* (that is, those who have nothing but their arms), and (b) the yeoman, farmer, *laboureur* or *ménager*, those who own and use plough teams. This kind of farmer is already identifiable in the Middle Ages and the Renaissance. He cultivated enough land to feed his family, and possibly his farm-hands. This means that he must have disposed of a minimum of twenty-five acres of good land, or half as much again if the land was less fertile, as was usually the case. He might even have a much larger estate (125, 250 acres or even more), forming part of a feudal or capitalist economy; examples can be found in England, but also on the Continent, both in developed regions (the Paris basin) and under-developed ones (Spain). The average yeoman (twenty-five to fifty acres) was not necessarily the owner or the long-term tenant of the land he cultivated. Very often he just took the land on a short lease, perhaps as a share-cropper, from a noble, bourgeois or ecclesiastical landowner. These different forms of land tenure affected the yeoman's costs, but from the technical point of view, the result was the same. The yeoman remained the true head of the farm. He worked to make a decent living for his family, which might or might not imply a narrow profit margin. He was also liable for a number of payments (taxes to the king, tithes to the church, rent to the lord of the manor, etc.), and he had his investments to think of (in enclosures, plough teams, seed). All in all, the fundamental aim of the system was not profit or the accumulation of capital. The aim, con-sciously or unconsciously pursued, was rather to ensure the continuity of the family and its lands from one generation to the next.

Even if they were not capitalists, these yeoman families, who flourished between the sixteenth and the nineteenth centuries, were often oriented towards the market. The towns had to be fed – towns of just a few thousand inhabitants, tens of thousands at the most (not counting urban monsters like Paris or London, with their half-million inhabitants each in the seventeenth century). These towns contained only 10 to 15 per cent of the local population, but they needed large areas of land to provide their food because of the low productivity of agriculture. Hence they exploited the yeomen of the neighbourhood in two ways. On the one hand, the wealthy townsmen bought up the land worked by the yeomen, thus turning them into tenant-farmers (around Rouen) or share-croppers (around Florence: the *mezzadria* system). On the other hand, by keeping the market price of food down and/or by demanding rent in kind, the town appropriated for its own consumption the surplus produced by the farmer. Each French or Italian town of the sixteenth and seventeenth centuries exercised a kind of urban imperialism and surrounded itself by a ring of countryside depen-dent on it. Great cities like London or Paris did this even more obviously and on a vast scale, and literally reshaped whole regions. The leading citizens of Paris bought up parcels of land and grouped them into large units of production of 250 acres or more and leased them to rich farmers. These farms fed the town and paid a good rent. It should be noted, how-ever, that this development was not inevitable, as the fervent supporters of the English or physiocratic model think. In the Netherlands in the seventeenth century, it was a system of small-scale but supremely efficient farming (with Flemish methods of intensive agriculture reminiscent of the Chinese system), which fed (and how!) the growing urban sector of the richest country in Europe.

If the yeomen were the central figures in the village, the farm-hands were the majority of its population. The *manouvrier*, *brassier* or day-labourer had only his own labour with which to earn his living, plus that of his wife when she was fit and those of his children when they were old enough to work. He did not own horses or oxen and so he could not use a plough, not even the simple light plough of southern Europe. However, he did own or rent a little land, a house, a garden, and a cow or a goat. These few possessions provided him with shelter and supplementary food, but not enough for his family to live on. It was not a question of his producing a surplus for the market (except, perhaps, a few vegetables, eggs and some spinning done by his wife). In order to get enough to live on, he had to hire out his 'labour power' and that of his family to a local farmer, who would take them on on a seasonal basis and when there was a lot of work to be done. The day-labourer's family was therefore subject to unemployment and to fluctuations in real wages, and so dependent on the fundamental unit of production, the household of the farmer, as Guy Bois has made abundantly clear in his recent study. European villages generally had a minority of independent yeomen and a majority of dependent day-labourers.

In addition to the basic couple of farmer/farm-hand, the village also contained artisans who worked for the peasants, the landlord, and the tiny local élite (the parish priest, for instance). They worked in wood (coopers), iron (smiths), and textiles (tailors). The countryside in the developed regions (the Paris basin, for example), contained a substantial minority of artisans. The underdeveloped regions (Brittany) had only a small minority.

In the case of the Breton interior, one of the most backward regions in France during the old regime, it was the peasants themselves who became handymen during the winter to make up for the lack of local craftsmen.

The wives of the farm-hands and even of the farmers increased their income by becoming temporary wet-nurses to babies from middle-class and even lower middle-class families in the neighbouring town. Spinning and weaving, practised by women and men respectively, could become a real rural industry, often working for distant markets (linen from Maine, woollen cloth from Languedoc). In this case the peasant family became part-time craftsmen, which made the social structure of the village more complex if not more complicated.

Finally, we must include in the peasant community, or in the spaces between villages, the world of migrants, tramps and beggars of all kinds, living on the margin of society and often despised. In certain extreme cases (Aveyron or Rouergue in the second half of the eighteenth century), they could account for more than 10 per cent of the population of the average village.

In any case the farmer, the farm-hand and the craftsman are only abstract types. Basically, the peasant lived and worked in a family group. What kind of a family? In England, the Netherlands, Belgium, and northern France, the peasant family was usually of the nuclear type, centred on the couple and their children. They would have lots of babies, but rarely more than two children would survive (a boy and a girl), given the high death rate of traditional societies, especially during the difficult seventeenth century. In general, grandparents, parents and grown-up married sons (if any) did not live under the same roof. Either the grandparents died quite early, or the grandchildren married late, so that there would be only one married couple in the house, that of the generation in between.

In Mediterranean areas (Italy), in the south of France, in Austria, and among the south Slavs, on the other hand, the peasant family in the age of the old agrarian regime was very often an extended one: two or more married couples would live together – the grandparents, the parents and/or a grown-up married son whose role was to carry on the line. The death of one of the spouses would soon break up the oldest couple. This 'polynuclear' household was therefore of limited duration and only involved a minority of families at any one time. But it was enough to give a colouring of its own to the Mediterranean societies which produced these family structures, with a sizeable minority of extended families but a majority, nevertheless, of nuclear ones.

In these southern countries one quite often comes across a developmental cycle in these extended families. Two individuals, male and female (M and F) get married. They have children, boys and girls (B and G); let us call them B1, B2, G1, G2, and so on. It has to bring in outsiders, a farmhand, a maid, since the children are still too young to help their parents in the fields and at home. When the sons grow up, the family no longer needs to employ servants, since it can now muster an adequate workforce from within its own ranks. However, the eldest son B1 gets married. He and his wife W form a young couple, soon surrounded by young children; they all live with the couple M and F, who are now old. The family has thus become extended ('bi-nuclear'). It becomes nuclear again when M and F die one after another, and leave B1 and W alone with their own children. Then these children marry in their turn; one of the couples that they have made will live with B1 and W. The family is now extended again, and so on.

The more or less extended family with its corresponding family cycle found its *raison d'être* and its justification in certain countries of southern Europe in the idea of 'the house'. The family, made up of individuals of flesh and blood, identifies itself with the hearth, the source of physical warmth in the home; with the kitchen itself, that 'house within a house', which was at once living-room, dining-room and place for preparing food; with the kitchen ceiling or 'sky of the house' (*ciel d'ostal*); with the whole house or farm (in occitan, *ostal* means both a house made of wood or stone and a family). The family also identifies itself more widely with the fields and even with the flocks and herds of domestic animals involved in the farm which was centred on the house. Of course these solid peasant houses, based on the trinity of men, walls and lands, were not eternal. But they could last for three or four generations or more, and they linked the name of the family to that of the place. They gave their members a strong sense of continuity, pride, and of an existence which transcended the individual.

It is impossible to understand these different types of family or 'house' without taking into account the basic rules of inheritance. As far as this was concerned, peasant societies had several solutions open to them, along a spectrum of possibilities from primogeniture to the equal division of the parents' property among the children. Jean Yver, the Lévi-Strauss of Normandy, has thrown much light on this network of systems of inheritance by subjecting it to structuralist analysis. The first distinction which must be made here is, of course, that between the nobility and the common people. We shall not discuss the clergy, who are, from the legal point of view, immortal. There are therefore no problems of succession so far as their goods are concerned, except when laymen, at a time of politico-religious crisis or demographic pressure, tried to take back the huge 'cake' of church property. This happened in England in the six-teenth century, at the time of the sale of the monastic lands; in France, in 1790; and in Spain, in the nineteenth century.

The nobility, then, with a few variations on this basic theme, practised primogeniture everywhere; the major part of the inheritance (including the family home and the estate surrounding it) went to the eldest son. This custom ensured the survival of the great noble estates for many centuries, until the French Revolution and often beyond. From the point of view of social justice, the existence of these large estates was unfair to the mass of the peasantry, but they had the advantage of providing an agricultural surplus for the market and for the consumption of the towns. This was the case, for example, in the north and the south of France, and even more in England. In that country, where the privileged classes owned more than two-thirds of the arable land, it might be said that agricultural capitalism, so important in the industrial development of the British Isles, sprang ready armed from the aristocratic system of primogeniture.

It is, of course, inheritance among the common people which concerns me here, since the peasants were nearly all commoners (apart from a few nobles, fallen on hard times, who rolled up their sleeves to grab hold of the plough). In several parts of Europe a kind of peasant or commoner primogeniture did exist. In principle, it ensured the indivisibility of the estate in the regions where it applied, and we can say at least that in periods of demographic growth like the sixteenth century, it did some-thing to limit fragmentation of holdings. This peasant primogeniture can be found in most English counties. It seems that initially it was a snobbish imitation of the inheritance customs of the ruling class. In the south of France under the old regime, one can also find a peasant primogeniture *de facto*. It derived, in practice and in theory, from Roman law, which itself legitimated the male and sovereign powers of the head of the family, who alone chose his (sole) heir. This heir was usually, 'as if by chance', the eldest son, but it could also be a younger one, or even, in the absence of any boy, a daughter whose husband would come to play the son-in-law (*faire gendre*) in her father's house. Among the common people in Languedoc as among the nobility in Europe, there were therefore bitter rivalries between the privileged eldest sons and the less favoured younger ones. This was to last until the egalitarian reforms of the French Revolution, or even longer. Eldest sons were murdered by envious younger brothers. A girl might commit suicide because her father, who wanted to keep as much as possible for his heir, had cut her dowry down to the minimum. Even the mother was encouraged to give preferential treatment to her eldest son, the heir apparent who would carry on the line, when she was feeding the children; the younger sons had to make do with milk from wet-nurses or even from goats!

Completely different was the egalitarian system which could be found in the woodlands of the west of France and in certain parts of England before the great 'modern' wave of enclosures. This long-established egalitarianism might even be radical enough to include all the children, boys and girls, as in Anjou and Brittany. In Normandy, where this custom of dividing the inheritance seems to have been strengthened, from the start, by certain influences from Scandinavia, it only affected the sons, the group of brothers. The authority of the paterfamilias (so powerful both before and after his death, as we have seen, in the Roman law regions of the Mediterranean), was therefore completely undermined in Normandy, to such an extent that wills did not exist. There was no need for them, since the wishes of the father ceased to have any force after he was dead.

In this way the woodlanders in general and the Normans in particular practised a 'compulsory return' (*rapport forcé*); once orphaned, each child had to return to the common fund whatever advantage he had received from the father during the latter's lifetime. This return became necessary when the custom of western France imposed a strictly equal division of the inheritance, whether among the brothers (Normandy) or among the brothers and sisters (the Loire region). Moreover, these customs, especially in Normandy, gave rise to a fierce individualism among the heirs: 'It's my right and I'm sticking to it' (*C'est mon droit et moi j'y tiens*). There was no question here of what sometimes happened in Languedoc, of a generous, disinterested younger brother standing aside for his elder brother, voluntarily but at the same time according to custom. The egalitarian customs of the Norman or Flemish type are at once extremely archaic, (sprung from the depths of the race, from Scandinavia for example), and very modern; indeed, they prefigured the egalitarianism which was to emerge from the French Revolution.

There was, therefore, an inegalitarian patriarchal system of inheritance in Occitania, and an egalitarian fraternal system in certain woodlands. Intermediate between these two extremes there was also the system of the married couple, that of the father and mother. It can be found in the Paris basin, in Germany, in Switzerland and in Poland. This was inegalitarian at first but became more egalitarian later. It was based on the joint decision of the father and mother. It was in keeping with the spirit of Christianity, even if it preceded (who can tell?) the coming of Christianity in the West. In accordance with the teaching of the New Testament it favoured the union of husband and wife 'who are one flesh' and prove it by producing together the single body of the baby. (The occitan paterfamilias, on the other hand, who retained his earthly omnipotence after his death by virtue of a kind of ancestor worship, remained largely Roman, and so pagan.)

What would a couple from the Paris region do with this joint power of decision, when it came to passing on their inheritance? Basically the two villagers, father and mother, left their goods to those of their children who agreed to live with their parents during the latter's lifetime and share their arduous and disciplined existence on the family plot; these obedient children would thus prove that they were qualified to take over the management and the ownership of that plot on the death of their parents. The Flemish or Norman rules of succession exalted the lineage; they tried to ensure that each child of the lineage received its fair and equal share of the family property. The custom of the Paris countryside and the old Capetian lands, on the other hand, favoured the household, the union of spouses who were by definition descended from two different lineages.

Household (*ménage*, etymologically *manse*); the basic peasant holding of a single family, with its house. Under this household system, whereby the right to inherit was restricted to the child who lived at home, forming part of the 'trunk' of the family tree, it follows logically that the other children, who had set up home elsewhere, were excluded. They had detached themselves from the parent stock and from the farm. They had renounced their claim to this farm because they had ceased to make it fertile with their sweat and labour. They had left, emigrated, gone to be hanged elsewhere; or else, as far as girls were concerned, they had married into an alien family which by definition was not their own. This law of the household was originally (in the Middle Ages) inegalitarian. It was outrageously biased in favour of children living at home, it disinherited those who left, who had only the right to take with them, under their arms, in their baggage or in their wake, some small material or financial token, a cow or (for girls) a dowry. In old legal terms, this arrangement was known as 'the exclusion of the endowed child' (*l'exclusion de l'enfant doté*)!

This irritating inegalitarianism of the Paris region decreased in the modern period, however. After 1510 a special clause, called 'option' or 'return' (*rapport*), allowed the children who had left home or received dowries to 'return' to the estate the benefits they had received in return for disinheritance. They then regained all their rights to the estate, so that the system became egalitarian. On the Continent at least, the great wind of egalitarianism was felt, so far as inheritance was concerned, nearly three centuries before the French Revolution.

II

In spite of these tendencies towards egalitarianism, the overall structure of rural economy and society remained for a long time extremely hierarchical. This reflected the fact that the manor, the fundamental unit of power and property, remained for many centuries the 'vertical' axis of the agrarian world. The horizontal axis was at the level of the peasant community. The manor of early modern Europe was in decline relative to its medieval splendour, but it remained extremely vigorous. It linked extremely diverse elements and sectors with a strong logic of its own, and it deserves an important place in this essay.

First, a brief historical survey of the long phase preceding the period considered in this book. From the bronze age, and more particularly from the iron age onwards (first millennium before Christ), rural chieftains had separated themselves from the mass of peasants, as a result both of a process of social differentiation and of conquest by new rulers thrown up by the Celtic invasions. This landed aristocracy lived off a levy on the peasants; it was made up of cavalry, or knights (*equites*), who used the horse as an engine of war. In the first century B.C., Caesar discovered that the mass of the rural population was indebted to or otherwise dependent on a group of *equites* and landlords. The texts of Greek geographers and the finds of archaeologists (including the treasure of the Lady of Vix), confirm that the situation described by Caesar was in fact much older. Later on there would be considerable variations in the way in which the local lord exercised his power. The heavily moustached patron manipulating his clientèle in Celtic and pre-Roman times was very different from the Gallo-Roman master of the villa and its slaves. As for the *colonat*, though long established, it is only documented fully from the fourth century A.D. onwards. It already implies a well-organised form of manor: the *colon*, in other words, the peasant, was indeed 'bound to the soil' by legal and cultural, even mystical ties which made him quasi-dependent on his noble masters. The *colon*, according to the texts, was 'like a part of the earth'. Other forms of control over the land arose during the following centuries, or rather, during the following millennium: the manor of the early Middle Ages (ninth century), with its serfdom and forced labour, the classical medieval manor, more liberal than its predecessor; and in spite of important differences between them, these latter two types of manorial power both imply a triangular relationship between P (peasant), E (earth) and L (lord of the manor).

P is more or less attached to E.

P is subject to L, to whom he owes respect, labour and/or other dues.

L has some kind of property rights over E, and sometimes over P as well.

May we therefore suggest that there was a long history of more than a thousand years behind the manor as it was still working between 1500 and 1789, and even beyond, in several countries in eastern, and even in western Europe.

In the remarkable chapter which he wrote in 1941 for the *Cambridge Economic History*, and which stands as his intellectual testament, Marc Bloch insisted on a continuity which cannot be denied: a chain of institutions without a break joins the local chieftains of Gaul to the feudal lords of the Middle Ages and even those of the modern period. They all enjoyed political and economic (not to mention sexual) rights, which they long enjoyed at the peasants' expense! After 1500, the *ius primae noctis* only existed here and there *de facto*. Its more or less willing acceptance by the peasant girls amounted to an acknowledgement of alienation, of sexual oppression and/or seduction on the part of the lord. But it could also represent a homage to the genetic superiority which the lower classes had for a long time attributed to the seed of the aristocracy. The supposed excellence of the breed conferred a certain prestige, even if the grounds were fallacious! It was all part of the idea of nobility, and the majority of manors were held by nobles.

Until the eighteenth century, the lords of the manor claimed only limited rights over the land, over the peasant plots. A farm could easily belong, in practice, to the farmer himself. Except in cases where the land was totally freehold (*allod*), it was held in leasehold or copyhold. An annual payment in kind, often small, was then due to the lord (known in French as the *cens*). A transfer tax, *lods et vente* or 'heriot', was also due on each change of tenant, whether by death or by sale. The *cens* was often commuted to a fixed annual sum of money. This commutation was particularly common in the seventeenth and eighteenth centuries in the more monetarised areas of the West. In these cases, the feudal dues became the victim of 'monetary euthanasia'; in other words, their real value was eroded by inflation over the centuries, and they ended up worth next to nothing. More burdensome but less common than these dues were the payments in kind; a part of the crop, given by the peasant to the lord each year, at harvest time; a quarter, a third, an eighth of the grain. This was the *champart*, *terrage*, *tasque*, or *agrière*. This recurrent *champart* must not be confused with the short-term arrangements of the *métayage* or share-cropping system.

In addition to the peasants' holdings, the lord also had his own demesne, whose area could vary from tens of acres (on the Continent) to hundreds

(England). In eastern Europe, where the effects of the 'second serfdom' were widely felt in the seventeenth and eighteenth centuries, the lord's demesne was cultivated with the help of forced labour under the supervision of a bailiff. The serfs who rented the neighbouring plots had – under threat – agreed to this. The almost incredible archaism of this system of forced labour did not prevent the great estates in question, in Poland for example, from being oriented, from the sixteenth century on, towards the most dynamic of markets, that of Baltic grain, above all rye, exported by sea to Amsterdam and to the western consumers along the shores of the North Sea. The great Polish estates with their forced labour were thus linked, as Braudel and Wallerstein have shown, to the developing capitalist world-economy (just like the slave-worked sugar and cotton plantations of the New World).

In the West, however, serfdom and forced labour had more or less disappeared by the sixteenth century, and more often than not much earlier, except in a few provinces which were (in this respect) backward: Burgundy and Franche-Comté for instance. In the West, then, the demesne was cultivated by methods other than forced labour, which gave rise to social relationships of a new kind. In some cases the lord could himself, with the help of a bailiff, direct agricultural work on his own demesne. This was the case, for example, in fifteenth-century Languedoc, because the ground rents were very low at that time: the canons of Narbonne, great noble landowners in the area around their town, managed their lands themselves because the rent was too low in that period of crisis, so that putting in a tenant-farmer would not have been profitable from the landowner's point of view. This was also the case in certain parts of England and France in the eighteenth and nineteenth centuries. Landlords first north and then south of the Channel became agronomists; they raised the productivity of their estates by skilful management. These examples were in the minority, however. As a general rule the landowners did not want to lose status by handling the ploughs themselves. Their demesnes were therefore worked and managed by share-croppers or tenant-farmers. These two ways of exploiting an estate, leasing and share-cropping, had been known in the Mediterranean world since antiquity (see the letters of the younger Pliny). In the sixteenth century and later, they were practised not only by lords of the manor on their demesne but also by middle-class and lower middle-class landowners. Under the share-cropping system, the tenant, who was often poor, took a short-term lease of the land (for four, six or eight years). He gave half or a third of the produce to the landowner, and received from him half or a third of the seed or livestock. Share-cropping (in Italian, *mezzadria*), made it possible to cultivate vast areas in the south-west of France, in Tuscany, and so on. It ended up, in the nineteenth century, by becoming synonymous, often unjustly, with backwardness and under-development.

The main method of cultivating the lord's demesne and the land owned by the middle class was by means of tenant-farmers. For a long time the tenant farmers continued to work on a family basis, but they began to take on farm hands and showed capitalist tendencies. These farmers appeared from the thirteenth century onwards around Paris and in England. In exchange for the use of the land which they cultivated, they paid the lord of the manor or the landowner a rent which was fixed for a short-term on the basis of a lease of three, six or nine years.

The manor was therefore primarily a piece of land, composed of peasant holdings and the lord's demesne. It will be noticed that this form of social and economic organisation, with its dual system (demesne/holdings), had very great strength; it could re-establish itself after a period of eclipse. When Stalin, from 1930 onwards, had crushed the Russian peasants under the weight of terror, genocide, and oppression, the collective farms he had organised reverted almost immediately – apart from a few tractors – to the structure of the great landed estates which had characterised eastern Europe under the second serfdom and the West in Carolingian times. Side by side with the collective fields of the *kolkhoz*, carelessly cultivated by the semi-forced labour of badly-paid peasants, there were the individual plots, lovingly tended by each family, in the small surviving private sector.

The European manor of the sixteenth and seventeenth centuries was not only an agricultural unit, but a legal and political one as well. It implied monopolies – the lord's oven, the lord's mill, the lord's right to hunt, and so on. It represented power, or a collection of powers. Religious power, financed by the tithe, on ecclesiastical estates. Lay power, on secular estates; the man who exercised it was the judge of the manor court, the *bailli* or *lieutenant* of the north of France, the *bayle* in Occitania. This judge embodied an undeniable if crude division of power which Montesquieu would not have rejected. The lord himself corresponded to the executive power, which was a distant one when the noble master was an absentee, as was often the case in eighteenth-century France. The little judge of the manor court corresponded to the judiciary, by definition; he was under his master's orders, but he was relatively autonomous. These judges were commoners, and often peasants; and there were probably tens of thousands of them in the area covered by present-day France. They had always been the real links between the state, cr society as a whole, and the peasant communities. They declined to some extent as the state grew in the seventeenth and eighteenth centuries, but remained important as go-betweens all the same until the Revolution suppressed them and replaced them by magistrates who would in future receive a salary from the state.

Between the sixteenth and the eighteenth centuries, the European manor developed at very different rates, much more slowly in the East than in the West. To some extent it shed its fragmented structure (the smallholdings), and its political and legal function (manorial justice). It moved towards a more specialised, capitalist structure based on the demesne, just as the physiocrats wanted. It was centred (though by no means exclusively) on the demesne itself, as the source of ground rent; on the person of the tenant-farmer (essential, whether because or in spite of his subordination to the landlord); and on the production, by the demesne and by the tenant-farmer, of rent for the landowner and of an agricultural surplus destined for the market and the towns. The manor was thus, paradoxically, an essential part of the structure of agricultural capitalism.

It is true that from ancient times there have been free, rural societies living together without lords. France found itself in this situation, but only after the Revolution. In Switzerland, the central cantons were liberated, from the end of the thirteenth century, from outside overlordship. They often did no more than change masters, falling under the yoke of towns such as Zürich and Bern. The model, ancient but for a long time affecting only a small minority, of a peasantry independent of overlords, raises all kinds of problems concerning peasant wars and revolts; problems to which I shall return.

III

In one sense, the manor and the forms of land tenure associated with it are only a kind of superstructure – often quite a thick one! – on top of peasant society. As for the deep structures, described in the first section of this chapter (farmers versus farm-hands), we need to make them dynamic, to show them developing, in order to have a complete view of rural society as a historical phenomenon.

This development, in some extremely important and representative cases, is related to forms of history which are at once fluctuating and immobile, oscillating and stationary. The development is a non-development. It turns out that neo-Malthusian models (which are taken from the work of M. M. Postan in England and W. Abel in Germany, as well as from French research on Languedoc and Normandy), can be extremely useful. They give shape, not only to economic and demographic history, but also to changes in the social structure of the peasant world.

We must start from demography. It is not the queen of the sciences, but it does provide us with basic figures from which we can build up our concepts. In the first half of the fourteenth century, around 1320–30 (say), if we look at the area known as 'France' today, we find that in Provence, Dauphiné, Savoy, the Paris region, Picardy, Normandy, Cambrèsis, Brittany, Languedoc, Rouergue (and also overall, according to the tax records, the *Etat des feux* of 1328), the population was thick on the ground, and not so very different from what it would be again at the end of the seventeenth century, at the time of the first great censuses and parish registers. In other words, 17 or 18 million inhabitants around 1330, and perhaps 20 millions in 1700. In 370 years, then, there was hardly more than zero growth. We might long for a similar 'progress', which is equivalent to long-term stagnation, in the Third World today, where the population is increasing at an alarming rate. We might long for it, if only the factors which assured this stagnation in the late medieval and early modern period were not, from our point of view, barbaric and intolerable: plagues, epidemics, wars and famine.

The other discovery, recently made by several historians, concerns the stability of agricultural techniques and grain yields in France, between the first agricultural revolution (eleventh to thirteenth centuries), and the second, which stemmed from the agronomy of the Enlightenment. Without going into the rather ambiguous case of the eighteenth century, we can at least say that in France, unlike the Netherlands and England, food production and above all grain production kept more or less to stable yield ratios between 1300 and 1720. This shows an extraordinary equilibrium. There were, of course, upheavals and unfavourable, possibly monstrous fluctuations, but these were always temporary. This general equilibrium, as susceptible to changes of mood and to adjustments as that of the economists, can be reduced to a sketch for a landscape: within the limits of a 'green belt' of surviving forests, reduced by the great clearances of the eleventh to thirteenth centuries, twelve or thirteen generations of peasants between 1300 and 1700–20 lived and reproduced themselves within the inexorable constraints of a certain range of numerical possibilities. Although these constraints weakened later, after 1720, they did not disappear as soon as all that. To stick to the crucial period 1300–1720, the long-term quasi-stability of demographic and agricultural parameters brings us right back to the old idea of the potentialities of a more or less steady state. There was economic, social and demographic *standardisation* over the long-term.

Standardisation was by the plague, of course, and by other epidemics (dysentery, typhus, etc.). From the fourteenth century to the sixteenth, and beyond, there were more and more frequent contacts between continents by land (across Asia) and by sea (across the Atlantic); this meant that microbes were spread throughout the world, a sort of 'common market' of germs. This was enough to prevent any real demographic growth (which would have, by definition, to be more than simply recovery from a previous disaster), among the mainly peasant population of western Europe (exception being made for the Netherlands and for England, which were much more dynamic). It was also enough to produce general slumps over the long-term, like the reduction by half of the German population over the period 1630–50, or, above all, the reduction of the French population from 17 or 18 millions around 1330, to 7 or 8 millions at the most around 1450 – the pendulum then swung back till the population reached 18 or 19 millions around 1550–60, remaining at this level till about 1715.

In both these cases, French and German, the plague and other pandemics were not, of course, the only factors. War also played a part: the Thirty Years War in Germany, and the Hundred Years War between the Vosges and the Pyrenees. War: that means, ultimately, the system of large states (the kingdoms of England and France, the house of Austria). They became entangled in armed conflicts which they could not finish and which might drag on for a generation or even a century. In other words, the social history of the peasants turns out to be dependent on the biological history of microbes and the superstructural history of the international state system. The factor of famine must also be added to the plague–war duo. Famine was, of course, closely linked with climatic conditions, but it was aggravated by the debilitating effect of war on the agricultural economy, and in its turn engendered favourable conditions for the outbreak of epidemics. The three scourges, plague, war and famine thus worked together, and between them they caused massive slumps in the rural population over the long-term (the Thirty Years War) or very long-term (the Hundred Years War).

Death, however, is not the only factor to be considered in relation to the stabilisation or reduction of the peasant population. Other demographic restraints were in operation, derived from social institutions and the deliberate control of humanity over itself. I am referring to late marriage (between the ages of 24 and 25 for women; a year or two more for men). This custom, in a society with little or no contraception, meant that the woman did not give birth to the extra two or three babies she would undoubtedly have produced if she had married at 16 instead of 24. In the absence of true contraception, this method represented 'the favourite weapon of birth control in classical Europe' (P. Chaunu). It spread gradually through western Europe between the fifteenth century and the eighteenth (in Normandy, for example, the average age of marriage for girls was 21 years around 1550, but 24 years around 1700). It was not, however, the custom in eastern Europe, where, as in traditional Asia, girls were married just a few years after puberty. The development of late marriage as a sophisticated Western method of stabilising the population suggests that people had a sense of an optimum family size and an understanding of the social and moral aspects of sex. This makes the average peasant of former times quite a different figure from the breast-beating gorilla who emerges from the unflattering and in fact defamatory portraits of the villager offered by writers like Balzac and Maupassant.

A steady state over the really long-term does not imply absolute stability – on the contrary! The vast demographic ebb and flow which I have described for France in the fourteenth, fifteenth and sixteenth centuries was accompanied by smaller fluctuations which themselves had an extraordinary influence on the economic and social structures of the agrarian world.

Between 1330 or 1348 and 1450, at the same time as the French population was falling, prices, agricultural production, the improvement of land, the relative number of poor peasants, and ground rents all declined. Real wages, however, rose, and the average size of farms increased, as a result of the reduction in population. People had a higher standard of living, or let us say that the survivors had a higher standard of living, since for those who died of the plague it was a different matter! The prices of manufactures (kept up by the shortage of labour), fell, but not as much as agricultural prices, which were kept down more than others by the abundance of land, now available for anyone who wanted it.

Between 1450 and 1560, it was exactly the opposite. The see-saw tipped the other way – in all areas. Demographic growth or recovery brought with it, in the upward direction this time, the factors already mentioned: prices, agricultural production, the improvement of the land, the relative number of poor peasants, and ground rents. There was also a marked long-term decrease in the real buying power of wage-earners, and a further fragmentation of smallholdings. Agricultural prices rose again, and to a greater extent than the prices of manufactures, the inverse, as one might expect, of what had happened during the previous period of long-term slump.

The reality behind these abstract indices was of course the changing destiny of different social groups. There is little point in stressing the well-known fate of agricultural (and urban) wage-earners. During the second-third and the third-quarter of the fifteenth century, they reached the height of their consumption of wine and meat, the peak of their real buying-power. Throughout the sixteenth century, however, they became poorer and poorer, because of the over-rapid increase in their numbers which meant that the supply of labour exceeded the demand for it. Around 1550–60, as the downward trend became firmly established, they tightened their belts to the maximum and went on to black bread and water – themselves, their children, their grandchildren, and so on until at least the eighteenth century. This immense inflation and deflation of the social structure did not affect wages alone. The great landowners – nobles and others – had not made much profit from rent, which had fallen around 1450–60. But during the century or more which followed, they gradually got their own back. They took advantage of the keen demand for land amongst a farming class which was in a state of demographic and/or economic expansion. They were now at last able to increase the payments they demanded for making or renewing leases. They thus increased and then consolidated their income from the land and their dominance over rural society from 1500–50 to 1700–50.

The peasant farmers themselves had quite large holdings around 1460. But in the course of the following generations, and especially after 1500, they became victims, on the one hand, of a rapidly increasing fragmentation of holdings, owing to increased demographic pressure. On the other hand, they suffered from a capitalist offensive on the part of those who were laying acre to acre.

A minority of wealthy yeomen and rich farmers did, however, come out on top in the sixteenth century, thanks to precisely this capitalist process, and thanks also to the process of natural selection set in motion by the population explosion; the fittest survived, while the weak became weaker and poorer still. The wealthy yeomen, thus selected, established a position of relative dominance in the village. But however high they climbed, they were distinctly lower on the social scale than the great landowners, who were often the people who leased the land to these yeomen farmers.

The majority of the rural population around 1460, however, was made up of a middle peasantry. They experienced a modest but undeniable affluence in this period. A century later, in 1560, the majority of the rural population were farm-hands, *de facto* if not always *de iure*, impoverished by the huge increase of population between these two dates. Yeomen, especially if they were wealthy, were in the minority from now on.

From the mid-fifteenth to the mid-sixteenth century, agricultural production was on the increase; but it seems, especially after 1500, to have increased less rapidly than the population. The notorious Malthusian 'scissors' of economic and demographic growth thus tended to open out during the first half or the first two-thirds of the sixteenth century. This situation led to quite serious subsistence problems for the poor, and even for the 'non-rich' as a whole. They took the form of periods of scarcity (or sometimes famines), which recurred at regular intervals every twenty or thirty years, and sometimes even more rapidly after 1520. They did not disappear in France until after 1710, and perhaps only after 1741.

The rise in cereal prices after 1460, and especially after 1500, was sharper than the rise in non-cereal and industrial prices, so this tended to benefit the grain producers (the great landowners and the bigger farmers), at the expense of the craftsmen, whose products were depreciating more and more in relation to wheat or rye. This change in the 'terms of exchange' between industrial and agricultural products was in exactly the opposite direction to what had happened in the period 1330–1450.

The whole system, we could even say the whole agricultural ecosystem, functioned according to strict relationships between extremely diverse variables; variables affected by the great movements of ebb and flow across the centuries; variables including the central forces of social history.

One can say that on the whole, between 1300 and about 1720 (a little earlier or later according to the region), the agricultural system in France (and also in Germany, Italy and so on), operated along Malthusian, or rather neo-Malthusian lines. The food supplies available (which were limited), and, more important, the effect of epidemics, not to mention wars, with late marriage thrown in as a minor form of demographic restraint, meant that the overall population figures, however they might fluctuate, scarcely exceeded the levels they had once reached around 1300–20, during the first long period of growth in the Middle Ages. Given these conditions, the social and rural history of the four centuries which concern us (1320–1720) was not liable to real population increases that would have broken all records. It was simply disturbed by large fluctuations: I am not just thinking of the 'Hundred Years War' in France, or the 'Thirty Years War' in Germany (convenient labels which in fact cover a much wider range of phenomena, connected and unconnected with war). I am also thinking of an event like the plague of 1656 in certain areas round Naples; it destroyed more than half the local population, and was followed by a long phase of reconstruction, which was not just the straightforward reconstruction of the social and demographic structure as it had been before the catastrophe of 1656.

This example illustrates a general point. The system, or ecosystem, did not operate by merely making a 'photocopy' of its former self when it emerged from one of these periods of what was sometimes violent fluctuation. It was also subject to a kind of 'drift'. This was noticeable, for example, in France and northern Italy, and it introduced various elements of capitalist or, one might say, 'physiocratic' organisation into our traditional rural societies from the sixteenth century – or even earlier – onwards. It must not be forgotten that throughout this period, sectors such as the state, elementary and higher education, industry, towns, the urban market, élites, and trade did experience that famous period of growth unknown to the world of the peasantry. Even if this long-term expansion in non-agricultural sectors was interrupted, at irregular intervals, by 'pauses' of various lengths, it remained, all the same, a lasting *fact*. And this 'fact' could not fail to have small but undeniable consequences, disturbances on certain fringes of rural society between the sixteenth and the eighteenth centuries. Around Paris, for example, and around the towns of northern France, large farms with 'capitalist' tendencies developed in the sixteenth and seventeenth centuries, right in the middle of the 'crisis' period. They were formed from old noble estates which had been bought up and reorganised, often around a manorial demesne, by influential citizens who accumulated pieces of land. (These citizens could be nobles, office-holders, or even merchants.) These large farms were therefore under the control of great urban landowners; their surplus produce was sent to the towns in which their owners lived, which provided them with a ready market. The wealthy tenant-farmers who ran these estates did so partly on family and partly on capitalist lines. This class of large farmers, who were relatives, friends and guarantors of one another, continued to consolidate its power between the sixteenth and the nineteenth centuries. In Italy and in the south of France, the shift of quite large areas round important towns to a share-cropping system also marked a stage – paradoxical only in appearance – in the suburban modernisation of agriculture. This stage broke down the old system by bringing numerous large farms into a relationship with the market; they now sent their produce to the towns. It is an over-simplification to present share-cropping, or *mezzadria*, as a feudal archaism, although, by contemporary standards, it has undoubtedly become one; it is a question of historical relativity.

Moreover, the French model, with its long period of non-growth at the peasant level, was not unique. It was, no doubt, valid far beyond the borders of France, in vast areas of western continental Europe (Germany, Italy, etc.); there too the rural economy and society continued to reproduce itself, its functioning possibly being disturbed or interrupted by major fluctuations, followed by a period of recovery, but without any irreversible expansion. However, certain countries extricated themselves from the Malthusian, or neo-Malthusian model from the seventeenth century or even earlier; this was the case, for example, in the area inhabited by the Flemish, the Dutch' and the Walloons, the latter being influenced by good Flemish habits. The Netherlands, indeed, offer an example, rare elsewhere, of an intensive, 'Chinese' style of farming, which was gradually established between the thirteenth and the sixteenth centuries. No danger here of coming up against the barrier of diminishing returns, since they followed an efficient system of cultivation, developed by the small-scale tenant-farmers of Flanders. In this example of undeniable modernisation we are still, however, a long way from capitalist agriculture as it was practised in the Paris or London basins at the same period. In the Netherlands small-scale farming demonstrated its remarkable capacity for producing a food surplus for the market, despite the scorn poured on it from the eighteenth century to the twentieth by armchair economists and agronomists, seduced by English methods. The Flemish system depended on extraordinarily productive small-scale farming. Fallow had been abolished centuries before. The system was based on cereals, of course (wheat, rye, barley, oats); but also on greens (colza for oil; and a kind of cabbage the leaves of which were given to the cows, while the stems were used for heating the oven). In the third place, it was based on vegetables, and legumes such as beans, clover and vetches, because these nourished the soil and fed men and animals. Finally, there were the root-crops, for human food and cattle fodder (turnips, carrots, beetroots, and finally potatoes). All this was seasoned later on with a few variations, such as tobacco, and generously sprinkled with dung, pigeon droppings, ashes, urine and human excrement.

The Flemish system was rounded off, in a far from Chinese style this time, by stock-breeding in small herds, some kept permanently under cover. Cattle and piglets were raised for the market. The food for these animals consisted of oil-cakes (made from colza), of peas, vetches and beans, grown on the old fallow fields, and of winter fodder (rye, peas and vetches, clover, with lucerne and sainfoin in addition). All these raw materials for intensive animal farming were produced by intensive crop farming. This system worked to full capacity near towns; they provided the necessary manure, especially horse manure. And there were of course towns all over the Netherlands. Finally, the farmer, his labourers, maids, wife and children earned an extra income at home by spinning (women), and by weaving (men); they both brought in something to eke out the budget and pay rent, tithes and taxes. Taxes, moreover, were not too crushing in the Netherlands, which was partly affected by good Spanish habits of fiscal administration.

Such an extraordinary increase in productivity per head or per family presupposed not only technical and biological innovations but also an enormous amount of human effort, together with a strong sense of economy and sometimes a miserable stinginess. In the eighteenth century, however, the furnishings of farmhouses improved in quality all over the Netherlands. Earthenware bowls and wooden dishes were replaced by finer pottery and by pewter. Firedogs, casseroles, kettles and frying-pans indicated an increased desire for consumption.

In England, too, rural society – and society as a whole – escaped the constraints of the continental neo-Malthusian model. This 'escape' into modernity took place, as Brenner suggests, in the seventeenth century or even in Elizabethan times. The population of Britain was 4 millions at the time of its medieval maximum in 1300–47; but it had already reached 5 millions in 1600, and 5.8 millions in 1650–1700. Let us imagine a France of 18 million inhabitants in 1300–47 (which was the case), but also one which (as was not the case) would reach 22.5 millions in 1660, and 26.1 millions in 1650–1700; almost as many as in 1789, when the census in fact recorded 27 million Frenchmen. And all that instead of the actual 20 millions who lived, in the period 1650–1700, in the kingdom of Louis XIV. It makes one shudder to think of the famines which would have occurred as a result in the dreadfully over-populated hexagon – unless a real economic expansion, and particularly an agrarian expansion had taken place to enable these human masses to be fed.

In Great Britain, in any case, the demographic ceiling of the early fourteenth century was well and truly raised in the seventeenth century. However, this increase in both the rural and the urban population did not mean that poverty was increasing too; far from it. From the end of the seventeenth century on, 40 per cent of the working population had left the agricultural sector for crafts or the service industries. It was precisely the high agricultural productivity which enabled the extra population to be fed; it lived thanks to the food surplus produced by the narrow majority (60 per cent) who worked the land. This high agricultural productivity north of the Channel was achieved by a judicious imitation of Flemish methods (partial abolition of fallow fields, the use of manure, the cultivation of fodder, turnips, and so on). Remember that during early modern and modern times these 'Flemish methods' spread through the West in an anti-clockwise direction. First, the Netherlands (thirteenth to seventeenth centuries); then Great Britain (seventeenth and eighteenth centuries), and finally France (eighteenth and especially nineteenth centuries). Thanks to this process, Malthus was knocked out of the game in his native country before he had even been born. In England, however, this process did not take the form of small, super-efficient family holdings. The structure of English society, as revealed by the distribution of land, was characterised by the predominance of great estates (the aristocracy and gentry owned 70 to 75 per cent of the land at the end of the seventeenth century, compared to less than 50 per cent in France); by the maintenance and the strengthening of their dominant position, thanks to primogeniture, enclosures, etc.; and by the relative insignificance of peasant communities and peasant property. These different factors permitted a *capitalist* agricultural economy to spring ready armed from the great manorial aristocratic system. (Such a connection, of course, goes right against one of the theses of vulgar Marxism – as opposed to Marx's own ideas – the proposition that claims that 'capitalism' is necessarily opposed to 'feudalism'.) The substantial English farmers leased the land from the aristocracy and gentry; they worked estates of more than 250 acres with efficiency; they opened a new chapter in the history of the (rural) world; they invented large-scale agriculture, oriented towards profit and the market; the very kind of farming that the physiocrats later sought to introduce or develop in France.

In their different ways the great English farmer and the small Flemish peasant both broke away in the seventeenth century from the static agriculture of the past, fundamentally static despite huge fluctuations. The French, followed by the rest of Europe, did not disentangle themselves from this neo-Malthusian immobility for another century or two, in 1720 or in 1820, according to the region.

IV

Apart from these social mechanisms, the peasantry from 1500 to 1720 can also be defined as a cluster of attitudes, mentalities and institutions – as a 'collective mind'. The peasant community embodied in each village, at once an image and a social reality, first springs to mind. In the Mediterranean region (Italy, Provence, Languedoc), the community, however tiny, took on the appearance of a small town. In western Europe it was generally quite powerful. On Sundays after mass it held formal or informal meetings of the heads of families, joined here and there by widows. It served the king, or whatever took the place of the state in the locality (supervising the payment of taxes); it served God (the upkeep of the parish church, the election or appointment of churchwardens); finally it served the inhabitants (by supervision of the standing crops, and, sometimes, by the protection of the common herd). It often elected its officers, mayors, consuls; it was linked to the authority of the lord and the state. In England, the village community was much weaker. Its disintegration was due to the same forces as the eviction of the independent peasantry, to the profit of an agricultural capitalism under the control of the landlords and the large farmers. The enclosures put an end to collective obligations; and the English parishes were placed under the close control of the local gentry as Justices of the Peace.

Religion was even more essential to peasant life than community politics. Even in Protestant countries which had adopted a 'purified' Christianity in the sixteenth century, the peasants were often urgently preoccupied with a religious magic concerned with the immediate future. Its purpose was to ensure rain (when necessary), a good harvest, or the health of the cattle. These practical concerns, on which Keith Thomas places so much stress, did not, however, exclude other ideas. Peasant religion was not 'terrestrial' and nothing more. True, it made considerable use of the cult of the saints with their undeniably pagan associations. But it was also concerned with the essential problems of the after-life. These spiritual problems clearly had little to do with the amount of the harvest or the prosperity of the farm. What would happen to the soul after death? That was the other real question. Would it move horizontally and wander with the ghosts? If so, we remain in the realm of Celtic, and particularly Breton folklore. In the Breton peninsula, ghosts behaved in an almost intolerable fashion. They were constantly coming back, especially at night, to pester the living, near the dolmen or menhir, in the buckwheat field, or in the kitchen. Irritating visitors, and not only in Brittany. To put an end to them, or to limit the damage they caused, the villagers of Languedoc appointed a special official, the *armier* (from *arma*, i.e. *âme*, soul), or messenger of souls. He was the only one in the village to have dealings with the dead, and he thus spared the mass of the living the possibly painful meetings with their departed relatives. The *armier* of Languedoc was close to the Spanish *animero*, who specialised in collecting alms for the souls in Purgatory.

However, the 'horizontal' wandering of the souls of the dead only lasted for a time. After a while, if all went well, the question of their 'vertical' journey arose, their ascent into heaven after death or later, at the Last Judgement. The countryside of Europe was not exempt from explosive quests for salvation, incarnated in the great Protestant revivals, of which one of the earliest – a hysterical and bloody one – took place outside the British Isles, in the south of France, in the Cevennes of the Camisards. And what, in the end, was the Protestant Reformation, which won over a large part of the German, English and Scandinavian peasantry from the sixteenth century on, if not the pursuit of salvation by means of the conversion of the peasants. Rightly or wrongly, they were considered by the Protestants as idolaters, virtually pagans (i.e. *pagani* which means 'peasants').

This preoccupation with magic and salvation was obsessive, and justified extremely heavy investments, in parish churches, for example, which were of medieval foundation but constantly patched up and rebuilt, even during the seventeenth-century crisis. The same preoccupation motivated the payment of heavy tithes. The Protestant Reformation, when it triumphed, simply transferred these to the new clergy. Both the Catholic and the Protestant churches had long understood, well before psychoanalysis and the great restaurants, that in order to be taken seriously, you must make yourself expensive – and too bad for lay resistance. These good Christians but bad payers were in a state of semi-strike against the tithes at different periods (in the sixteenth century, during the Protestant expansion; in the questioning eighteenth century, before the French Revolution).

Was the religious history of the peasantry fundamentally unchanging, in spite of these agitations? This suggestion has some truth in it so far as the Catholic countries are concerned. There was no change of allegiance between the fourteenth and the eighteenth centuries. The Reformation had been rejected like a foreign body. But in fact, even in the case of the regions which remained 'papist', things changed a little from the seventeenth century onwards. In its original baroque or later Jansenist form, depending on the region, the Catholic Counter-Reformation, which had started in the towns, ended up in the classical period by bearing down directly on the countryside. It installed a network of purer harsher parish priests, who were trained, from the reign of Louis XIV onwards, in seminaries. These relatively zealous pastors guarded their flocks more efficiently than the concubine-keeping, truculent village priests of the Renaissance, denounced by the Huguenots.

These new-style priests, who kept a close watch over the activities of their flock, were partly responsible for a certain sobering down of peasant behaviour (other factors in this sobriety included the school, the family, etc.). A considerable measure of primitive violence was still to be found in the countryside. All the same, despite terrible exceptions at the time of the Thirty Years War, it may be suggested that rural delinquency tended, if not to decrease, at least to change its nature between the sixteenth and eighteenth centuries. Violent crime became a little less common, while theft and pilfering increased. This development did not take place in a day or even in a century; the 'lions' (murderers) did not all turn into 'foxes' (thieves). But the trend away from violence is unmistakable all the same.

This did not mean that the peasants now behaved like choirboys – on the contrary. It is time to say something about the peasant revolts of the period.

These revolts, which could attain the bloody dignity of rustic wars, did not necessarily involve all the peasants in a given region. In a particular village, the dominant faction might start a rebellion against the local landowner, but another faction in the same area might for one reason or another remain faithful to the lord of the manor (Provence, Varoise, 1579–80). All the same, if the revolt spread, it would involve the whole peasant community. It was the same with a peasant revolt as with the French atomic bomb during the presidency of General de Gaulle. It could if necessary be directed against all possible enemies; enemies, in this case, of the rural community. These potential enemies included the landowners, the state, the towns, and so on.

A solid tradition of historians and theoreticians (Marx and Porshnev, among others) maintains that peasant revolts were essentially anti-manorial, 'anti-feudal'. A number of risings do indeed come into this category, such as the Swiss rebellions at the end of the thirteenth century ('William Tell'), and the Jacquerie of 1358 in France. There was also the war of the German, Alsatian and Swiss peasants in 1525, a 'war' which was, moreover, influenced by the egalitarian gospel brought to the notice of the villagers by the recent diffusion of the ideas of the Lutheran reformation. The peasants turned this 'gospel' to their own advantage by using it as an extremely 'striking' argument against the manorial system in general and ecclesiastical lords in particular. Generally speaking, specifically anti-manorial revolts were numerous in the West in the sixteenth century; for example, in Germany, Switzerland, France (Dauphiné, 1580), and even in England. In the seventeenth century, they went underground. In the eighteenth century they gradually rose to the surface, and after 1789, turned into a torrent which swept all before it. It was no longer a revolt but a revolution. It was then that the peasants won the decisive victory; the manorial system was finally destroyed.

Revolts against the state (and especially against taxes) were, however, almost as common and as serious as revolts against the seigneurial system. In seventeenth-century France, this was the main kind of revolt, to such an extent that between 1620 and 1707 the royal bureaucracy and treasury became the scapegoats. As for the lord of the manor, he was rubbing his hands; he appeared to be unassailable! The popular risings of the period 1624–47, just before the Fronde, included a long series of violent peasant protests against Richelieu's and Mazarin's turns of the fiscal screw.

Were there risings against the town? They did happen. The revolt of the first *croquants* of 1593, for example, against the little towns of the Périgord who were exploiting the peasants; and that of the *Chouans* of the woodlands of the Sarthe in 1793, against the Republican Blues and other bourgeois and petty-bourgeois supporters of the Revolution, in Le Mans and elsewhere. Do the peasant revolts stand for a bright, progressive *future*, as opposed to a feudal and reactionary *past*? (B. Porshnev's thesis.) Or were they defending an old-fashioned or mythical golden age of rural bliss against the legitimate onslaught of state, nation, and modernisation? (R. Mousnier's thesis.) This antithesis between past and future (in whatever sense) often seems questionable. What happened was that the peasantry defended itself in the name of a style of life and a system of farming which was based on the family. This system can be considered old-fashioned, but it had its points; it was capable of development, efficiency and adaptation, not only in the area of subsistence agriculture but also in order to satisfy the demands of the market. In France, the interesting peasant culture of the nineteenth century is worth noting; less productive than that of the English farmers, but quite viable all the same. On the Continent, this culture based on the smallholding emerged from the conquests of the French Revolution, itself the daughter of peasant revolts.

Conversely, the forces attacked by the rebellious peasantry might be extremely oppressive (Richelieu's government), but they were not necessarily behind the times. In the eighteenth century, at the very time when it was to be overthrown by peasant revolts, carriers of modernisation from *below*, the French manorial system was in the process of modernisation from *above*. The aristocracy and the large tenant-farmers were just welcoming physiocratic and even capitalist developments, stamped with the mark of agricultural revolution.

From Switzerland in the 1290s to France in 1788, the rebellious peasants and their various adversaries opposed to one another two models of society, quite different but equally feasible (for example, the small-scale agriculture of the peasants of 1789, and the great estates of the physiocrat-minded landlords). Both sides shot bold arrows into the future; each was capable of winning the struggle until the moment of violent decision. The peasant revolt was doomed to failure by definition. If it was successful, it was no longer a revolt but a revolution; from then on it provided its own justification.

The agricultural revolution, in the strict, technical sense of the term, could have come about intellectually by means of 'agronomy'. This was what in fact happened in the nineteenth and especially in the twentieth centuries. From the sixteenth century, fifteen or so great agronomists, like Olivier de Serres and Conrad Heresbach, flourished in different countries in the West, from Spain to Germany and Poland, and from Italy to England, as C. Beutler has shown. The maximum area of diffusion of this revival of agronomy can be measured, by counting the number of editions published in different towns up to the year 1600 of the works on this subject, whether 'ancient' (Columella) or 'modern' (Heresbach). The privileged area where the number of editions of treatises on agriculture exceeded ten or twenty in the period, was the Europe which read and made progress; it was a sort of vast Lotharingia, but much more extensive in every direction than the original one! It corresponded to an irregular polygon linking Venice, Basel, Frankfurt and even Leipzig, Antwerp, London, Paris and Lyons. The direct influence of the agronomists on individual enlightened landowners who read them and put their good advice into practice on their own estates was no doubt considerable. The major innovations in agriculture in early modern Europe, however, were derived from the daily practice of the Flemish peasants, rather than from the reading of Italian, French or German agronomists.

The cultural revolution in the countryside of the old regime did not – yet – owe very much to agronomy. It owed much more to the more modest enlightenment of elementary education. The parish school provided this for the most advanced young peasants, a small group of yeomen's sons and the occasional girl. From the end of the Middle Ages, a certain number of villages had had schools, and these increased in number in the following centuries, but it was not until the nineteenth century (in France, for example), that every village had its own. The young people who received this minimal education learned at least how to sign their name, and sometimes even to read a bit of the Bible; they could write out a receipt and count their flock of sheep. However basic it may have been, this education gave prestige to the better-off peasants. It enabled the rich farmers to cope better with the basic details of a legal and bookkeeping system which the landlord would otherwise have been easily able to turn against them. The slow but undeniable spread of education in the sixteenth and seventeenth centuries also owed a great deal to religious motives; encouraged among the faithful by the churches and the clergy. The Protestants, Luther at the head, took the initiative. The Bible was available in manuscript and in print, so it was necessary to be able to read it, even in the depths of Saxon villages. The Catholic Church, in turn, threw itself – sporadically – into the education battle, out of a sense of rivalry, and then as a genuine part of the Counter-Reformation. You get to heaven faster if you can read pious books. And besides, in this earthly vale of tears, public morality can only gain from the education of the young. The bureaucratic state, too, got something out of this first stage of acculturation; the simple peasants who collected the king's taxes in the villages were more efficient when they could read and write. Even so, the major states of the sixteenth and seventeenth centuries, apart from Scotland, did not give a penny to the primary schools; the peasant community, the parents and various religious or educational foundations had to finance them.

In the 1680s, 45 per cent of English males, including many country people, were able to sign their names. In France at the same time, the figure was only 29 per cent for men (and 14 per cent for women). Literacy declined from north to south. The same pattern can be found, still in the

1680s, within the kingdom of Louis XIV. The France which could read (partially) was the rich France, or in any case the least poor; it was situated north-east of a line from Saint Malo to Geneva. To the south-west of this line, Brittany and the whole of the south were more or less completely illiterate. Yet even in this huge southern zone, certain mountain regions – which specialised, it is true, in the production and export of primary school teachers to the neighbouring lowlands – had already achieved some remarkable results. In 1686–90, 64 per cent of the present département of the Hautes-Alpes could sign their names! A situation which made this rural sector of the Mediterranean Alps one of the most literate regions in the whole of western Europe in the age of Louis XIV.

v

Starting from various dates around 1720 (let us say, to allow for regional and national variation, between 1710 and 1750), *real* demographic growth (such as England had known for ages), began on the Continent. After four centuries of near-stagnation (in spite of vast fluctuations), the rural population of western Europe burst out and broke through the old constraints. There were probably 16 or 17 million peasants in France around 1700. But there were 22 millions in 1789 (including 18 million agricultural workers) and 27 millions in 1841. The other European countries (Germany and Russia included) also experienced increases, which between 1700 and 1850 or beyond, were even greater than those in France. On the other hand, during the second half of the nineteenth century (in France), and the first half of the twentieth century (everywhere), the rural and particularly the agricultural population first stopped growing and then fell. In absolute terms it is now lower than it has ever been since the Middle Ages. Joan of Arc's France, its numbers drastically reduced by the great plague, boasted considerably more workers on the land than the France of that latter-day Joan of Arc, Charles de Gaulle.

The great modern cycle (eighteenth to twentieth century), with its rise (1720–1850) and its decline (1850–1950) in the peasant population, is not just a matter of demography. Given that the supply of available land was limited, and taking into account improvements in technique and the influence of the market, it was inevitable that friction and conflicts of interest would arise. These factors in turn had an effect, simultaneously or alternately, on the different groups within rural society – wage-earners, tenant-farmers, landowners – throughout these two-and-a-half centuries.

After about 1720–50, the increase in population revealed itself, at least in those continental countries where the peasants had some access to the land, in the rapid multiplication of small-scale farmers, who were often the owners of small or even tiny pieces of land. This group increased at much the same rate as the total number of people living on agricultural land.

They reclaimed heath and waste land. They cut down woods. In the Mediterranean region, they undertook expensive terracing on previously unproductive slopes. They survived somehow or other, thanks to polyculture, market gardening, maize, and vines; their efforts even provoked admiring comments from Arthur Young (who was not easily impressed), in the south of France in 1789. However, the division of land into Lilliputian portions – thanks to the distribution of land among an everincreasing population – brought with it a greater risk of pauperisation, as in the Third World today. The French Revolution has, no doubt, many and often contradictory meanings. As regards the division of holdings, however, which concerns us here, its significance is quite clear; in this case it had very little to do with the abstract triumph of agricultural 'capitalism' over 'feudalism'. On the contrary, it supported a powerful counteroffensive on the part of a frustrated, aggressive, teeming, small-scale family agriculture. This system of farming was suffering from overcrowding. It wanted land, which it was partially to obtain by the takeover of state property and that of émigrés (an acquisition the peasants achieved with difficulty, owing to fierce competition from the wealthy bourgeoisie, who were also after estates). It also wanted to get land by means of the abolition, under the Civil Code, of customs favouring a single heir (like the commoner primogeniture of the south of France, etc.). It tried to grab land from the eldest sons, but also from the powerful, from the dominant figures of the old regime. The old system of the dominance of the great estate and of large-scale, manorial, physiocratic and possibly scientific agriculture was, however, by no means entirely reactionary, since it produced by far the largest part of the food surplus for the towns, for the market, and so for a possible industrialisation.

However, the family-based farming system paid no attention to these fine capitalist prospects; either it hated them or it did not know about them. It continued to forge ahead after the Revolution – at considerable risk to its own standard of living. The process of subdividing holdings continued in France until about 1860 or 1880 – it would not be checked until the end of the nineteenth century, and of course the twentieth, when the exodus from the land and the fall in the rural population finally produced a state of 'decongestion'.

Does the accelerating subdivision of holdings produce pauperisation? If productivity is not increased, then the answer, alas, is yes. The risk of impoverishment was all the more acute in that eighteenth-century demographic growth was often accompanied in France, for example (but not in Catalonia) by a drop in the real, daily income of the agricultural worker. In Occitan (southern) France between the 1720s and the Revolution, this drop in real daily income was around 22 per cent.

We should not feel too sorry, however, for the west European agricultural worker of the eighteenth century, or his relatively poor brother, the smallholder. (Very often these two characters were one and the same person, with two 'hats'. To supplement the inadequate income from their tiny plots and to feed their families, they were often obliged to hire themselves out to a wealthy farmer.) We should not, first, so that we may be more sparing with our pity, because the (theoretical) reduction in real income in the eighteenth century (22 per cent) was much less than that which had occurred between 1460 and 1560 (66 per cent). In the second place, this reduction was only theoretical. The agricultural worker in the eighteenth century could easily make up for the average reduction of about a fifth of his purchasing power, by working more days in the year and by means of the increased work of his wife and children. What is more, an intensification of work, not only on the land of the employer but on the labourer's own plot, enabled him to maintain and sometimes even to increase his family's income. In the seventeenth century our labourer, the victim of famine, often took the road to the cemetery. At the end of the eighteenth century he escaped death and sometimes took the road to, well, revolt. If he did rebel, it was not because he was worse off; on the contrary, because he was living a little bit better, he now had higher expectations. The inventories made after the death of agricultural workers under Louis XVI reveal more material possessions, including some of value, than was the case under Louis XIV. The (purely theoretical) impoverishment contrasts, therefore, with an actual increase in wealth, or, let us say, with a decrease in poverty. There was a larger rural proletariat, in both absolute and relative terms, as a result of the increase in population. But they lived rather less badly, or at least died rather less quickly than in the past.

The French Revolution coincided, more or less, with a political and social offensive on the part of the family-based agricultural system of people working medium-sized farms or small plots. This Revolution freed the peasant from obligations to the lord of the manor as well as from the tithe, and it gave him more access to the land (by means of the sale of state property and other measures). It appears, therefore, to have coincided with some improvements in the standard of living of the peasants, including the poor peasants. It is remarkable that, according to an important survey by the French National Institute for Demographic Studies, it was only in the decade 1789–99 that infant mortality in France began to decrease. Since vaccination against smallpox was virtually unknown, this decrease must be attributed to non-medical factors like improvements in diet, housing and in living conditions.

In the nineteenth century, the ghost of the impoverishment of the agricultural proletariat was finally laid. The rise in agricultural productivity and, after 1850, the exodus from the land (which affected above all the proletariat, who had scarcely anything to lose), meant that the wages of those who remained on the land were assured. The supply of agricultural labour decreased, and its productivity increased; wages were thus doubly improved, and the wage-earners lived in more decent conditions – but they were soon to be very few in number. In 1750, the majority of the rural population was proletarian or semi-proletarian, and very poor. In 1950 it was no more than the minority of a minority, since there were fewer agricultural labourers in the countryside, and fewer country people in society as a whole.

At the other end of the social scale, right at the top of the pecking order, the great landowners improved their position during the new period of expansion in the eighteenth century. This was not really the result of landlord imperialism (the crucial period of the conquest of the land by local élites, nobles or commoners, at the expense of the peasants co-incided with the great agrarian crisis of the seventeenth century). How-ever, the income of the great landowners rose in the eighteenth century, even when their estates had stopped expanding. Rents increased at the same time as the demand for land, stimulated by the rise in the population. It is worth distinguishing different components of this income from the land, from the social point of view. If we set aside the tithe, which re-mained very substantial almost everywhere, the strictly manorial part of the landlord's income (feudal dues and the profits of justice), was now very low indeed (sometimes as little as 2 per cent or 3 per cent of the total, in the Toulouse area). What was much more important was the rent; a modern type of rent, derived from short-term leases (three, six or nine years), paid by the tenant-farmer to the landowner. The real value of this rent increased by 51 per cent in France between 1730 and 1789. This enabled the landowners – nobles and prominent citizens – to keep up their life-style of absentee rentiers. They were thus cut off from the rural lower class, whose increase in prosperity was considerably less, by a widening gap of arrogance and bitterness. In the north-east of France, it was often more than half the land which was in the hands of the wealthy rentiers (nobles, clergy and bourgeoisie). The increase in rents therefore enriched a social group which was already well endowed. This point was even more true of England, where the landlords controlled more than three-quarters of the arable land at the end of the eighteenth century. At their encourage-ment, or spontaneously, the English tenant-farmers increased their productivity, thus increasing (even more than in France) the wealth of their noble masters, as well as their own.

Then came 1789 and its wake. On the Continent the French Revolution seemed to herald a set-back to the prosperity of the class of great land-owners. Feudal dues were abolished. With them went, as a result, all the strictly 'manorial' (and so relatively unimportant) part of the income from the land. For clerical landowners the heaviest loss was the tithe, abolished shortly before the estates of the church were themselves sold for the benefit of the 'nation'. (The tithe, however, was to survive, in part and in secret; it fell into lay hands insofar as it was surreptitiously incorporated by the landlords into the terms of their tenancy agreements.)

And yet, as is well known, the French Revolution did not by any means lead to the destruction of the class of (great) landowners, despite a few guillotinings. This class was simply subjected, by a reasonable turn of events, to a few temporary restrictions. It had to 'move over a bit' in order to make a fairer and more generous provision for the small-scale farming of the independent peasants. Paradoxically, we can even speak of a revolutionary 'modernisation' of this group of great landowners; it lost the last vestiges of its feudal structure, while the distinction between the two types of landowner, noble and bourgeois, was largely obliterated. It was therefore more united, and it was also held together by a common Roman and physiocratic conception of the great estate, completely leased out and freed, by force, from feudal survivals.

In the first half of the nineteenth century, the class of great landowners, now unified and de-feudalised, retaliated. Rents increased in real terms by 20 to 25 per cent in France between 1815 and 1851. This was due to two factors: demographic pressure, which was continuing, and agricultural progress, which was becoming serious and real. In any case, the great landowners were still extremely well off; the 100,000 'electors' of the period before 1830, who represented the upper crust of the French ruling classes, owned a third of the country's arable land. Relations between noble landowners and villagers were still, in 1830, extremely authoritarian and hierarchical. 'The peasants', said the Count of Comminges later, 'were very devoted to my father, even though he treated them like niggers. Woe betide anyone who spoke to him without raising his hat. A back-handed stroke of his cane soon sent the offending headgear flying...' In the same region, the great noble landowners and even their children used the familiar form of address when talking to the peasants, which is also quite significant.

The age-old dominance of the class of great landowners was, however, undermined on the Continent by the abolition of primogeniture. This did not prevent rents from reaching their ultimate peak at the end of the 1860s and the beginning of the 1870s, during the great wave of prosperity which swept over Europe at the time of the French 'Second Empire'. After this, the economic crisis of the last quarter of the nineteenth century produced a complete reversal of the situation, the results of which can still be felt. From 1880 onwards, the drop in rent was quite clear. It fell by 30 to 45 per cent during the last two decades of the nineteenth century. It thus lost part of the ground it had slowly but triumphantly gained between 1720 and 1880. Marcel Proust's aristocrats of the Faubourg Saint-Germain, who lived off rents and the produce of their land, were by then no more than pale shadows, however fascinating, of their ancestors. In the long run the effects of the system of equal inheritance, a product of the Revolution, made themselves strongly felt. The great landowners lost not only income but capital as well. They shared, sold, and divided up the estates of their grandfathers, and, if it came to the worst, became farmers themselves...in the second half of the twentieth century one might sometimes see viscounts or even dukes with calloused hands, driving tractors over their own lands, surviving, somehow or other, as the – somewhat chipped – figureheads of the rural world. After the Second World War, various laws, of which the French *Statut de Fermage* is one example, confirmed the new relationship between landlord and tenant-farmer. In future, where he still existed, he was reduced to playing second fiddle.

VI

There was, then, a decline of the class of great landowners who had previously controlled or manipulated the villagers from their country houses or their town residences. (This decline must not be exaggerated. In Normandy in 1975, rents could still amount to a fifth or a quarter of the gross product of an average quality holding.) There was a decline, too, in the number of agricultural workers, although there was an improvement in the individual worker's standard of living. Given these facts, we have to ask whether we can talk about the persistence and even the strengthening of a certain kind of authentically peasant and family-based agriculture. The answer is yes, provided, of course, that the meaning of these terms is clear.

Family-based agriculture in the strict sense, as described by Chayanov, only took on extra hands 'cyclically' (during the phase in the family cycle when the children were too young to help on the farm). It was not a profit-making system, but rather aimed at the continuity or slight enlargement of the domestic unit; this unit or 'cell' being made up of the family, the house, the land and even, possibly, certain craft activities as a sort of 'appendix'. This kind of peasant, family-based enterprise would manage to operate 'at a loss' (the loss being calculated according to strictly capitalist norms). This was because the members of the family did not draw wages but were simply fed, housed, and allocated an often minimal amount of pocket money, which varied according to circumstances.

This is the family-based agricultural system as defined in a strict sense. In a wider sense, however, it must be recognised that before (and even after) 1950, the agriculture of continental western Europe knew little of the more or less total divorce (in European industry and banking, and also in American capitalist agriculture) between technocratic and old-style family management. (We are not, for the moment, considering Russian collective farms or their more or less close imitations in certain parts of eastern Europe. In Russia, the *kolkhoz* was not particularly productive, but it did manage to give Soviet agriculture a bureaucratic-technocratic rather than a family character. The process by which this came about included the great peasant genocide, the destruction of the *kulaks* around 1930. It should also be pointed out that the individual holdings of the *kolkhoz* farmers, the yield from which was quite considerable, retained their traditional family management.)

In western Europe the family remained inseparable from the farm, however big. In this particular case, the analysis of Chayanov is too narrow. Even when the farm employed permanent wage-workers, which introduces a 'capitalist' element not included in Chayanov's model, its management still centred on a family of peasants living on the spot; the head of this family organised all the work on the farm; his wife specialised in dairy farming, for example, and took more of an interest, in the twentieth century, in the accounts; the children, especially the son who would if possible succeed his father one day, took part in the farm work just like the hired hands (although the spread of education, especially secondary and higher education, after 1950 would reduce the importance of child labour).

In 1906, there were between 2 and 2.5 million genuine family-based farms in France. At a slightly higher level, there were 1.5 million farms employing up to five hired hands (this figure shows the low productivity of labour at the time); and then there were 45,000 farms with between six and fifty workers, and 250 great estates (producing cereals, beets, and even wine), employing more than fifty workers each. These tens of thousands of (relatively) large farms obviously corresponded to the demesnes of the eighteenth century. What is remarkable is that, with a few exceptions (amongst the 'giant' estates in particular), almost all these units, from small to large, maintained a style of management which was family-based, according to the model already described. This style of management had little to do with the methods of a capitalist firm or a limited company. Between 1906 and 1950 the family character of agriculture was maintained and even, paradoxically, reinforced insofar as mechanisation reduced the number of both seasonal and permanent workers living on the farm – relative to the size of the farmer's family. This family management was capable of a high degree of modernisation (despite the technocratic myths which, according to ideological preference, do not admit any real progress outside the Soviet agro-town or American capitalist agriculture). It may not be widely known that in France in the thirty years since the Second World War, it is agriculture (starting from a very low level, it is true) that has shown the greatest gains in productivity, higher even than those in industry. The traditional farm was infiltrated by modern technology; chemical fertilisers after 1880, and especially after 1900, and on the Continent, threshing-machines before 1940, tractors and combine-harvesters after 1945. It was also infiltrated, especially after 1950, by more sophisticated methods of bookkeeping and management.

At the same time, there took place a rise in the social status of the peasant and a levelling of the peasant hierarchy. The disappearance of the great landowners, who had previously dominated the countryside (except in a few mountain regions like Switzerland), was reflected in more than the sharp fall in the percentage of the gross national product accounted for by rent. Things had often reached the point where the peasant bought the land from the nobleman, the bourgeois, the priest or the distinguished absentee. This had happened before, during the sale of church lands at the time of the French Revolution. It was to recur on a considerable scale during the long crisis of 1880 onwards, which deflected urban capital from agriculture and encouraged the farmer to buy the land which had dropped in price.

Abandoned by its day-labourers (who had emigrated to the towns), its artisans and its great landowners (who had become absentees, or sold their land), the village became more strictly and authentically peasant – especially because the farmers themselves had, since the early or mid-nineteenth century, abandoned the non-agricultural activities (spinning, weaving, etc.) which had brought them in a supplementary income.

And yet, ironically enough, this peasant, who was more and more authentically himself, was becoming less and less what he had been in the past. Primarily, not to mention secondary education put an end to patois; I shall come back to this in the next section, on attitudes between the eighteenth and the twentieth century. As they grew richer and had more contact with urban civilisation, a certain number of peasants rose into the lower middle class or even higher. Access to property was clearly fundamental, whether it was a case of the farmer taking full possession of his land, or a case of semi-ownership, by which the tenant-farmer, thanks to the 'droit de marché' (in Cambrésis, for example), could acquire security of tenure for himself and his descendants over several generations, though the land still belonged in principle to the proprietor.

From this point of view, the outer signs of ownership, which are to it what a beard, whiskers and other secondary sexual characteristics are to virility, became particularly important; the spread of hedges and then, from the end of the nineteenth century, of barbed-wire fences, did not necessarily mark a vital stage in agricultural progress, whatever the ardent anglomanes may think. In the great Paris plains, where arable farming was predominant, while cattle-raising was much less important than in Great Britain, the need for fences was much less urgent than it was to the north of the Channel. These plains round Paris had managed very well, from the agricultural point of view, with very few hedges and barbed-wire. The fact of enclosing property, and doing the job well and aesthetically, was a material expression of the pride of the working, resident proprietor; and it could also express the honour and pride of the tenant, whose claim to the land is often scarcely contested in the twentieth century.

VII

As far as rural attitudes are concerned, the period from the eighteenth to the twentieth centuries coincided with the final elimination of illiteracy in the countryside. In countries like France and England, the literacy rate in 1780 was between 47 per cent and 60 per cent (compared with 88 per cent in 'enlightened' Scotland). There had been rapid progress since the end of the seventeenth century. France, in particular, had begun to catch up with Great Britain. By about 1900, the figures had increased to 95 per cent (France), 98 per cent (Scotland), 97 per cent (England and Wales). The real problem for the rural population in the twentieth century, especially after 1950, was no longer primary education, now established once and for all, but secondary and further education. At the same time as this astounding improvement, structural changes were taking place. The primary schools in the French countryside in the eighteenth century were still run on Catholic lines, and offered a way to heaven via a better knowledge of religion. During the nineteenth century, they became at least partly secularised. The state and even, after 1880, the anticlericals took over the primary schools in order to snatch the rural masses from the influence of the church. The primary school teacher had previously been the priest's right hand; he became, around 1900, his enemy number one. What is more, the rise towards the critical threshold of literate males coincided, according to Lawrence Stone, with a difficult moment, accompanied by a 'qualitative leap' in the development of society. It was just below the 50 per cent threshold that the three great European revolutions occurred; the English in the middle of the seventeenth century, the French at the end of the eighteenth century, and the Russian in 1905 and 1917. Revolution does not prevent the relentless advance of elementary education – but perhaps this diffusion of enlightenment itself encourages revolution.

The spread of literacy amongst the peasants eventually became a sort of autonomous factor, a pure fact of 'cultural revolution', independent of the underlying 'base'. This had not always been the case. Between 1680 and 1840, at least, the literate areas of France coincided with the wealthier villages who had been able to afford the 'luxury' of paying for a primary school teacher. These villages were to be found in north-east France, where the people were relatively well fed and well built. The zone of literacy was roughly north-east of a line from Saint-Malo to Geneva. After 1880, when the steam-roller of literacy, pushed forward by the government of Jules Ferry, had crushed ignorance throughout France, all regions became literate, whatever their degree of economic development or underdevelopment. The 'superstructure' was emancipated from the 'base'.

Scientific agriculture did not spread at the same rate as literacy. It went through two stages in any case. The first was the period when the essential contribution, not widely known as yet, came from specialist agronomists (who were intermediaries between the practising farmers and the real scientists). I am thinking, for example, of Duhamel du Monceau and François de Neufchâteau, for the period between Louis XV and Napoleon. Then, after 1830–50, came the second period, that of the great breakthrough; Liebig, Pasteur and other real, first-class scientists renewed agricultural theory from the outside and by this means changed the practice of the farmers themselves.

The necessary and sufficient conditions for the acceptance of this intellectual and social progress still had to develop on the spot. Among these conditions was the improvement of communications. Railways were necessary to put the new chemical fertilisers within reach of customers living in the depths of the country. They were also needed to transport the bearers of ideas about the benefits of the said fertilisers. Another factor in the 'agronomisation' of the countryside (and of rural minds in western Europe, from north to south), was the levelling out of the differences between the backward (southern) and the developed (northern) zones. In France, for example, the area to the south of the Loire began to catch up with the north. This was a gradual process, but already noticeable in terms of income and techniques between 1850 and 1880. The growing specialisation of the peasants made them less allergic to a scientific agriculture. Instead of the old type of farmer, more or less self-sufficient, like Robinson Crusoe, there appeared, between 1830 and 1880, wine-growers (in Languedoc), beet-producers (in Belgium), stock-breeder and dairy farmers (in Normandy, Ireland, etc.). These specialist farmers worked with the market, not to say profit, in mind. They were distinctly more willing to experiment with sophisticated new techniques than their all-round self-sufficient ancestors had been, provided that these methods met their exact needs and took into account their particular problems. Between 1850 and 1900, a half-century during which the peasants were generally thought to be creatures of routine, the specialist wine-growers of Languedoc, for example (helped by the School of Agriculture at Montpellier), were quick to deal with the successive diseases that attacked their vines. These winegrowers (who did not think of themselves as peasants, it is true), used chemistry and botany in their fight against oidium, mildew and phylloxera; in other words, they used sulphur, copper sulphate and the technique of grafting local vines on to American stock.

Last but not least, scientific agriculture could not establish itself without the support of an enlightened élite. This élite, around 1780–1830, was primarily made up of great noble proprietors flanked by a few wealthy, landowning bourgeois. A century or a century-and-a-half later, the élite in question was no longer exclusively or even essentially noble, but rather bourgeois and to some extent peasant. It was an élite trained in part in the schools of agriculture, which multiplied after the period 1850–80. It was also receiving government support, since the nineteenth-century state ceased to consider the peasantry as nothing but a reservoir of taxes and troops. In Ireland (1832), in England, in Sweden, in Prussia, in Alsace-Lorraine (after 1871), in France (1903), the government organised improvements, drainage, and 'rural engineering' (the French *Génie Rural*). These useful services did not prevent the rural population from considering civil servants, even those concerned with agriculture, as a race apart; they were despised by the great landowners because of their low social status, and they were envied by the ordinary peasants because of their retirement prospects, their job security, their monthly salary, and so on. All the same these hated civil servants contributed (to a certain extent) to the economic growth of an agricultural world in a state of demographic decline.

In theory and in practice, scientific agriculture advanced on four fronts, which sometimes but not always corresponded to four successive phases.

First, the 'mechanical' front: the agronomist Mathieu de Dombasle's plough was known in Lorraine from 1820; it spread far south in the following two or three decades. The steam-thresher, surrounded by a whole folklore, first appeared between 1850 and 1880.

The 'chemical' front: a practical offshoot of Liebig's research was the development of pesticides to guard against vine diseases, and above all the production of artificial fertilisers. In 1914, the consumption of superphosphates in western Europe was nearly a hundredweight for every two-and-a-half acres.

The 'biological' front: thanks to Pasteur, sheep were vaccinated against anthrax and improvements were made in the fermentation processes of wine and beer.

Finally, the 'genetic' front: dogs and horses had been bred selectively for the pleasure of the lord of the manor since the Middle Ages, and the already widespread notion of a hereditary 'taint', to be found in human families too – commoners or nobles – showed a crude awareness of genetics. This notion could of course give rise to the absurdities of racism. From the eighteenth century in England, and the early nineteenth century in France, stock-breeders, who were often ordinary farmers, selectively bred cattle and sheep for the meat and wool markets. Darwin (among others) was inspired by their empirical research. Great seed merchants, like the Vilmorin family in Paris, did the same in developing seed corn in the first third of the nineteenth century. From this point of view, however, the West was considerably behind China. In the tenth century, the Chinese empire was sending leaflets to the provinces popularising new early ripening rice seeds. Imagine Hugues Capet doing that! The fact remains that beyond Darwin and Mendel, the green revolutions which have sprung from modern genetics, allied to fertilisers, pesticides and machines, have completely transformed the farmer's thinking and the way he does his job. Hybrid maize has spread across northern Europe; wheat yields can be as high as twenty-four hundredweights an acre (six times as great as in the eighteenth century); in the West, armies of combine-harvesters cut the crops in an instant. All this has not put an end to family-based farming, but it has completely changed it. It has changed the role of the farmer, for example; his concern with machinery is assimilating him to...a garage mechanic.

The peasants now go in for scientific agriculture, after a fashion. To what extent do they also go in for politics?

To achieve this other step forward, they did not always have to go very far. The good old style of banditry, in the Carpathians and in Sicily from the eighteenth to the twentieth centuries, and in the Dauphiné of Louis Mandrin (executed in 1755), as well as in the medieval England of Robin Hood, could easily embody for a time the various aspirations of the popular struggle against oppression. In a famous book, Eric Hobsbawm has well described the primitive rebels of the most recent Mediterranean peasant communities, up to the period 1900–10; millenarians in Tuscany; old-style *mafiosi* and *fasci* amongst the peasants of Sicily; anarchists in Andalusia. In varying degrees, they all tried to limit, oppose or even destroy the power of the ruling classes; to reduce the amount of rent paid under the share-cropping system; and to achieve a fairer distribution of arable land. At the same time, their hopes often crystallised around the idea of a kind of Last Judgement on Earth. This would finally establish equality, distributive justice and even mutual love, communism or anarchy, all rather vaguely defined. Even more primitive or more basic impulses – straightforward panic, for example – could also contribute to the politicisation of the struggle. The Great Fear of 1789 was a prelude to anti-manorial rebellions which (along with other warning bells) sounded the knell of the old regime.

This nineteenth- and twentieth-century 'primitivism' was, however, no longer characteristic of the more developed peasant communities, whether economically developed (England) or socio-politically (France). Are the concepts of 'Violence' and 'Revolution' any more enlightening? In France (certain country areas included), the Revolution of 1830, with its symbols (the national maypole, and the Gallic cock in place of the fleur-de-lis), was another 1789 on a small scale. The cycles of specifically peasant violence are at once far apart and heterogeneous. To continue with French examples, there were the *Chouan* revolts of 1793–4; the armed resistance to Louis Bonaparte's *coup d'état* in 1851; Catholic riots against anti-clerical governments in 1902–5; an uprising of the wine-growers in the South in 1907; the underground in 1943.

To return to the various categories of peasant revolt which have already been discussed. First of all, the fight against the lord of the manor. This continued under new forms in the nineteenth and twentieth centuries, and could be extended into a straightforward struggle against great land-owners; rent strikes by tenant-farmers (in France after 1870); occupations of great estates by the villagers (in Spain and southern Italy). In Russia, the 1917 Revolution gave the peasants the land seized from the great proprietors, thus concluding the movement begun in 1861 with the abolition of serfdom. The Russian Revolution has inspired bloody but fruitful peasant wars throughout the twentieth-century world. In 1930, though, the wheel turned full circle with Stalin's oppression of the peasants, an oppression which took a new, and even a 'socialist' form.

In Western countries, where the manorial system as such had been destroyed (France, the Rhineland), a sporadic fight continued against its surviving symbols (there were a few attacks on country houses in 1830 and in 1848). Or else the object of attack changed: the state, as master of the Forestry Commission, took the place of the old landowners, and became the target of peasants struggling to preserve their traditional grazing and foraging rights in woodland areas ('guerre des demoiselles', in which the rebels dressed as women, in the Pyrenees in 1829; this rebellion followed the introduction in 1827 of new forestry laws which protected the interests of the state, the preservation of trees for example, at the expense of the peasants).

However, all this was beginning to turn into folklore. Other forms of protest also declined in the nineteenth century; they had had their day (often a bloody one) in the peasant (and urban) revolts of the seventeenth and eighteenth centuries. Protests against the state, for example, led, during the French Revolution and the First Empire, to the boycotting of conscription, that thorn in the side of French peasant youth. The anti-conscription movement declined after 1815, for obvious reasons; after this it would only recur in the form of sporadic passive protests in the Massif Central, the rural population of this area having less to do with the slowly rising tide of nationalism than 'our valiant people of the East'. In 1914, the peasants all over Europe went as one man to the front. If only (impossible ideal) they had refused en bloc and in every country, Europe in general, and the peasantry in particular, would have been spared a few disasters.

As for the protests against the tax authorities, these had given rise to the famous revolts of the seventeenth century, dear to Porshnev and Mousnier. They flared up once more in 1848, in central France, with the sometimes violent resistance to the new '45 centime tax'. Poujadism in France in the 1950s was also a fiercely anti-fiscal movement, but it involved shopkeepers and craftsmen rather than peasants.

Food riots, too, were gradually becoming less common. They united the semi-proletariat of the countryside with the craftsmen of the towns. They were opposed to the profiteers who bought up stocks of grain during periods of dearth. This alliance of the lower classes was extremely marked in the 'flour war' which took place in the Paris region in 1775. This 'war' illustrated what E. P. Thompson has called 'the moral economy of the crowd', in other words a claim for justice and fair prices within the framework of an archaic or traditional economic system, a system in opposition to the boldness of *laissez-faire*. It was not exactly a revolutionary demand. A little later, food riots were involved in the battles of the French Revolution, in Paris and in the provinces. This sort of *mêlée* took place when Simoneau, the mayor of Etampes, was murdered in March 1792, in the middle of the rising of the labourers of Maine and Perche, outraged by the shortage of corn and the price of bread. There was a further outbreak of food riots – one of the last – in 1817, at the time of a west European subsistence crisis.

These forms of action belonged to the past. What was, more or less, new in the nineteenth century was the politicisation of the peasant. This politicisation became more acute with the new practice of regular elections. The attitudes of the peasants varied according to the region. The dividing lines were often much older than universal suffrage and they were to prove astonishingly long-lived.

An example of these long-lived divisions is that between the Whites of the Vendée and the Sarthe (formerly *Chouans* and royalists) and the Republican Blues of the towns in 1793; this opposition was to continue in different forms until about 1950! There was more to this long and savage hostility to the towns than conservative ideas of property, religion and the family.

The Carlists of Spain and the monarchist peasants of southern Italy would no doubt reveal similar long-standing attitudes which became part of the peasant identity and expressed themselves in deference to the local hierarchy. On the other hand, the Romagna, the south of France, Catalonia, Andalusia, and wine-growing districts in many parts had their hearts on the left and supported the great values of Justice and universal suffrage. These 'radical' attitudes are often to be explained in terms of the influence of urban (democratic and petty bourgeois) values in the case of the large wine-growing villages, villages which, in Provence for example, were, from the cultural point of view, really small towns.

Peasant politics were not concerned exclusively with the opposition between White and Red, or Right and Left. In the French countryside in the time of Napoleon and Napoleon III, and again in the period of nostalgia after their reigns, Bonapartism was a complicated and sometimes explosive mixture. Among the ingredients were the imperial cult of order and prosperity, which benefited the countryside; the attraction and prestige of wearing the uniform of an emperor who led the French peasants as far as Moscow; and the desire to challenge traditional élites (here a certain left-wing element, sprung from the Revolution, showed the tip of its ear under Napoleon's cocked hat). The 'legitimist' élites who had crushed the villagers with their arrogance did not welcome the charismatic upstart Bonaparte, symbol in himself of the national community of the peasant masses. In the twentieth century, the Fascists and even the Nazis have been able to turn to their advantage – with unfortunate results – certain aspects of this peasant Bonapartism, which was not confined to France.

Bonapartism and Fascism were essentially short-term temptations. In the liberal countries of the West, where feudalism had been swept away, the peasantry was by no means a natural breeding ground for authoritarian ideologies. Indeed, a new social stratum emerged composed of leading citizens of peasant origin, who respected the institutions of the republic or constitutional monarchy (depending on the country). It included genuine farmers whose economic and social status was sufficiently high, and also local leaders (merchants, small manufacturers, teachers) who were of peasant, rather than of noble or upper bourgeois stock. This new social stratum, precociously established in France, revealed itself in an institution like the Senate (the 'great council of the French communes'), or at the banquet held in Paris in 1900 for 20,000 rural mayors, all wearing dark suits and tricolour sashes.

Mediated by the politicians elected at a national level (who were not normally peasants), the electoral influence of the peasantry on the destiny of the nations of continental Europe probably reached its maximum during the first half of the twentieth century; in other words, at a time when there was still a high proportion of agricultural workers in the total population, before the recent exodus from the countryside. Between the wars this enormous influence was reflected in the often considerable activity of genuine 'peasant parties', which were usually conservative. They were especially common in eastern Europe, which was not yet Communist. During the 1950s, the 'independents and peasants', a conservative but not authoritarian party with strong rural support, had a certain political influence in France.

The great 'isms' of the long twentieth century (1880–1980) have had an important effect on peasant life. For example, peasant trade unionism, originally inspired by militants of noble, conservative, or Christian-conservative origin. This political traditionalism of the founding fathers of the great era of the first agricultural trade unions (1880–1940) did not, however, mean that there was no economic, social or technical progress. The first unions were shops offering fertiliser, seed, ideas and agricultural publicity. Left-wing peasant unions did exist, but in spite of their importance among the wine-growers, they were in a minority in the movement as a whole. The extreme left asserted itself in the organisations of agricultural workers, woodcutters, etc., especially after 1900. Red trade unionism, derived from socialist and Marxist tendencies in the towns, thus infiltrated and inspired the agricultural proletariat. It multiplied the strikes of the *braccianti* (labourers), especially in northern Italy and in Languedoc in the first decades of the twentieth century.

This working-class trade union movement, though clearly political, is not to be confused with socialism or communism. The rise of 'socialism' or collective farms in Russia, East Germany, Bulgaria, etc., was one thing. The infiltration of socialist and later of communist ideas into the peasant communities of southern France or northern Italy was another. These urban collectivist ideas eventually fused into a curious and often useful synthesis with the dominant ideology of the smallholders. 'Marx' and 'Lenin' were thus converted posthumously into wine-growers and peasants.

Regionalism sometimes turned into nationalism (Flemish, Breton, Occitan, Basque, Catalan, etc.). At the beginning of the twentieth century it often had agrarian and conservative overtones insofar as it relied on certain rural élites or exalted the patois-speaking, right-minded rural masses. It was to be revived in the years 1960–70, but its inspiration had shifted from the extreme right to the extreme left, and it had been transplanted from its rural base to the campuses and the student youth of the towns.

Regionalism brings us to the problem of what we might call 'rural civilisation'. This seems to have reached its peak on the Continent between 1850 and 1914, up to the very eve of the great massacre of the peasants. In France, where the exodus from the land and the fall in the birth rate began relatively early, the dates were closer to 1840–1900. This peak came at the intersection of two trends which are only apparently contradictory. On the one hand, economic growth, which meant a modest but undeniable increase in wealth among the farmers, and hence a blossoming of their authentic original life-style, an increase in consumption, and the spreading of rural fashions in clothes, furniture, food. On the other hand, the birth rate was beginning to decline. Until 1900 or 1914 this was only just getting under way and did not threaten the very existence of the village community, as it was to do thirty years later. Until the First World War, this community, though slightly reduced, still retained its solid age pyramid, well weighted with young people at the base. It also retained a strong core of farmers, who stood out all the more because the group below them, the rural proletariat, had partly disappeared as a result of the first exodus from the land. The second exodus, after 1920 and more particularly after 1950, struck much more deeply. It emptied the countryside of the farmers themselves and sapped the strength of the community through a kind of demographic anaemia.

To return to the 'triumphant' rural civilisation of the second half of the nineteenth and the early years of the twentieth century. There is no question of presenting it in a rosy light. There was a fair amount of serious or at least residual poverty among the lower strata – which were not always in the minority – of the rural population. This civilisation's greatest achievement (which unfortunately did not last) was to have breathed into the traditional peasant community a new, wider kind of existence, technologically, socially and in other ways typical of the late nineteenth century. At this time the peasant community had certainly lost some of its most characteristic medieval and early modern features; common fields, collective grazing rights on fallow fields, and so on. (It is these losses which lead many historians to talk, ritually, of the decline of the community, just as they talk, again ritually, of the interminable rise and fall of the bourgeoisie, and so on.) This so-called decline, however, conceals a positive transformation and adaptation. In the second half of the nineteenth century the community acquired or preserved certain elements of collective life which encouraged social intercourse of conviviality, while respecting the autonomy of the family and the household. Among these elements was of course the church (often done up in neo-Gothic style), but also the mayor's office, which was sometimes inflated into an imposing townhall – *Monsieur le Maire* now had his place alongside *Monsieur le Curé*. There was also the post office, from which emerged that popular figure characteristic of the new peasant literacy, the postman on his bicycle. There was the café or *bistrot* (a centre of male social activity and sometimes in woodland regions such as Normandy and Ireland, the privileged scene of an alcoholic subculture). There was, too, the local railway station; the public washhouse and the communal fountain, sometimes in monumental form, both of which offered new places for the village women to chatter and pass on information. There were the new local shopkeepers, who marked the beginning of a 'consumer society' (the butcher, baker, etc.); and of course there was the school for boys and girls, under the anticlerical care of that august pair, the primary school teachers, married to one another for better or for worse.

The 1920s would only add one more to these symbols of communal life: the memorial to the dead of the First World War; and one might wonder whether the circumstances which gave rise to this were indispensable to the development of community consciousness.

Apart from this forest of symbols (*bistrot*, church and townhall), rural civilisation was above all preoccupied with its daily bread, with a certain way of preparing and eating soup or pancakes or bacon – a way which varied, of course, with the country and, even more, with the region. The Bretons ate buckwheat pancakes; the northern Italians and the people of Aquitaine, *polenta* or maize gruel. The history of these rural eating habits in the nineteenth and twentieth centuries can be summed up in two points. In the first place, food shortages came to an end. The peasants went from empty stomachs to full ones, relatively speaking, of course. (The last great food shortage in western Europe, which turned into a lethal famine in Ireland, was in 1846–7; as for the serious food rationing of the Second World War, this affected the towns more than the countryside, which even – let it be said without shocking anyone – enjoyed a brief period of prosperity between 1940 and 1945, thanks to the high price of foodstuffs, not to mention the black market.) The end of food shortages after 1850 did not by any means lead to the uniformity of regional eating habits. Under the Second Empire the people of Dauphiné were to keep their cabbage sausages, and those of Picardy their leek flans.

A second, distinctly later stage involved the standardisation of eating habits and the disappearance of differences between regions and also between town and country. As far as France is concerned, the typical meal became steak and chips, camembert, red wine and white bread. This change took place very slowly between 1850 and 1950 and it was completed only after the latter date. It was a result of the influence of the towns on the countryside, but it did not necessarily represent 'progress'.

Real 'progress' is of course to be measured in terms of calories, vitamins and mineral salts. The proof of the improvement in the diet of the country people emerged only gradually; it was reflected in the distribution of tall people (over 1.7 metres, let us say). These people, whose height is the result (amongst other factors) of a balanced diet, are no longer to be found only in northern France and, in general, in northern Europe, as was the case in the eighteenth and early nineteenth centuries. (This temporary northern advantage was later to be used as justification for the dangerous racist idiocy about the superiority of the tall blond Aryans.) In 1830, a Provençal villager was distinctly smaller than a Flemish farmer. In 1950, the man south of the line from Saint-Malo to Geneva had caught up with his northern brother. Only the Bretons lagged behind, as a result of the underdevelopment of the Armorican peninsula. In the middle of the twentieth century, they still had a high percentage of small men.

Although they were small they were well dressed – at least on Sundays. The peak of rural civilisation in the nineteenth century (till about 1880), coincided with a flourishing of folk costume. The villagers' Sunday best was quite different from the fashions of the town, as it was modelled on old-fashioned town or even court costumes. In 1830, for example, Breton women would dress, on holidays, like Catherine de' Medici. This extravagance in appearance was part of a certain conception of peasant family honour, the external signs of which were to be seen in the Sunday-best parade. This concern for honour, as well as the desire for comfort, is also reflected in the nineteenth-century expansion northwards of the Mediterranean house, built of stone, with a roof of tile or slate. The use of thatch, which was a fire hazard, decreased dramatically at this period, as it was blacklisted by the first insurance companies. Houses built of wood, or half-timbered, sometimes painted, still held their own despite an increase in those built of stone: many fine examples are still to be found in Germany, England, Alsace, Normandy and in the Basque region.

Rural civilisation was not constant over time. As Maurice Agulhon has suggested, it went through cycles in which some elements disappeared and others came to the fore. Witchcraft, for example, in its benign form, was an integral part of the cultural life of the villagers; it included, in varying degrees, the bewitching of enemies and other spells, the popular medicine of the bone-setters and the fortune-telling of wise women, contact with ghosts and soothsaying. The belief in astrology and the influence of the moon on everything which waxes and wanes was equally fundamental. On the other hand, the more sinister diabolical phase of witchcraft, when the women would go to 'sabbaths' and kiss the rump of a goat, now belonged to a distant past and had virtually disappeared at the end of the seventeenth century. Moreover, it would seem that these dreadful sabbaths were almost always pure invention on the part of the priests and the magistrates, who extorted 'spontaneous' confessions from the wretched 'witches' under torture.

Let us leave these church devilries. On the whole, the traditional peasant culture still flourished in the first half of the nineteenth century. There were *veillées*, social evenings for work and pleasure at which the women span, the young people flirted, and the men told jokes and mended their tools, or when everyone might perhaps be busy shelling nuts. There were outdoor games on the common (football in England, skittles or bowls on the Continent). A specifically popular literature also developed and spread. This was aimed at those who could now read and also at those who could not, but who could listen to someone else stumble through the book at the evening gatherings. It was made up for the most part of almanacs, gardening and cookery books, handbooks of etiquette, medieval romances, and so on. In France it was known as the 'blue library' (*la bibliothèque bleue*), and it was spread by pedlars. It first developed in Champagne, at the printing presses of Troyes, in the seventeenth century; between 1700 and 1850 it simply grew in size and variety. This 'blue library', which virtually disappeared a century ago, was superimposed on to the old, purely oral stratum of folktales which had been transmitted for centuries from the Urals to Gibraltar and vice versa.

About 1850, roughly speaking, a new pattern of leisure and culture was established. For the men, the café and the discussion of the (possibly 'red') newspaper replaced the more traditional *veillée* (which could have a royalist, or even Bonapartist flavour). Urban games (cards, lotto, billiards, dominoes) were established in the countryside under the male auspices of the café. The 'republican neo-folklore' (as Maurice Agulhon calls it) of the drum and the bugle replaced the hurdy-gurdy and the bagpipes, so popular in the old Celtic regions. These changes took place according to the same rhythm as changes in transport; the light cart and the local railway were replacing the ox wagon and the pack mule. Nowadays, a third pattern has taken over: television, tarred roads and cars have relegated to the museum those comparatively recent improvements in communications, the train and the *bistrot*. Suddenly, the railways and the café on the main square, previously considered dangerous disseminators of speed and new ideas, have come to be bathed in nostalgia and regrets for a 'golden age', real or imagined.

In the eighteenth and nineteenth centuries popular culture was even more flamboyant and had greater resources than in the past, exalting, expressing (or inverting) itself in the regular festivals of the year. Although pagan associations are not to be excluded, calendar festivals were linked with different saints' days and with the various stages in the life of Christ (Christmas, Easter, Pentecost, and so on). Each village had its patron saint, whose feast was celebrated annually with a fair and with secular games involving the young people. On the shortest and longest days of the year, there were bonfires symbolising fertility (the Yule log and the fires over which young people jumped on St John's Eve). The Roman Saturnalia and the annual return of the dead were marked, according to the region, by the celebration of the end of winter (Carnival) or the beginning of winter (Hallowe'en, All Saints, All Souls). Republican or national festivals were celebrated locally with drums, bugles, flags and parades (as in the case of the French 14 July, the anniversary of the taking of the Bastille).

The different stages in the life cycle ('from the cradle to the grave') were marked by another series of celebrations, starting with the christening and ending with the great feast which followed a funeral. This second series of celebrations also included the various 'rites of passage' of young adulthood (for example the festival of the 'conscripts', the age group liable to be called up for military service), especially the wedding celebration, which was extraordinarily lavish; it consecrated the reproduction of the household over the generations as well as the entry of the young man and woman into their new, wedded, fertile state. Hence the gastronomic excesses illustrated in the 'Normandy wedding' in *Madame Bovary*; and also the demonstrations of hostility, by means of 'charivari' or 'rough music', in the event of a marriage contracted by elderly people, widowers or strangers to the village. In the general decline of village festivals in the twentieth century, thanks to the exodus from the land and the spread of mass culture, wedding celebrations have survived rather better than calendar festivals.

These festivals suggest that the peasants were extremely religious (in both a Christian and a pagan sense). The traditional infrastructure of their attitudes was a kind of pantheism or untutored 'Spinozism', in which divine forces were mingled inseparably with those of nature, of the woods, lakes, fountains and crops. In this complex situation, the important question is to determine when the process of 'dechristianisation' began. Dechristianisation in two senses; both rationalist secularisation and the revival of traditional naturalistic paganism. On this point, Michel Vovelle's answer (weighed and measured) is one of the clearest; it was around 1750–60 that the insidious destruction of baroque and/or Jansenist Catholicism began, very slowly, in rural France – a pioneer in this respect. This Catholicism had a very strong hold over the countryside, thanks to the network of seminaries and other breeding-grounds for clerical shock troops. Its hold had been strongest at the end of the seventeenth century and even during the first four decades of the eighteenth century. However, the first half of the eighteenth century was the time when the Enlightenment, in the towns, under the auspices of the young Voltaire, pointed the way to quite another intellectual development, which had nothing more to do with the clergy. The separation from the church was at first minimal; it coincided with the slight dechristianisation of the countryside after 1750; but during the following long nineteenth century, from 1789 to 1914, it was gradually to become a destructive torrent. This was first due to the influence of the French Revolution; and later to the 'school without God', established by the left-wing politicians of the Third Republic. In Europe as a whole, however, rural islands or bastions of Christianity with a high density of faithful and a good record for the production of priests survived for a long time. This was the case, for example, in the Armorican peninsula, in the southern Massif Central, in Ireland, Bavaria, Sicily, Poland, etc.

The process of dechristianisation which took place between 1770 and 1914 was at least partly responsible for the change in rural attitudes towards sex. The church had long banned contraception, but rural couples had scarcely thought of it till then. In the eighteenth century, rural society was ready for contraception, even if it did not yet practise it. From 1770–80 onwards, peasants in several regions of France (the Paris basin, Normandy, Aquitaine) began to imitate the distinctly older practices of certain urban élites (the bourgeoisie of Geneva, the peerage, etc.). They were thus initiated into the 'deadly secret' of birth control, 'that deadly secret unknown to any other animal but man'. They began, hesitantly, to practice *coitus interruptus*. Conscription into the revolutionary and imperial armies also contributed to the loss of innocence among the young peasants turned soldiers by bringing them into contact with the world of prostitutes. The new laws of succession at the end of the eighteenth century and Napoleon's Civil Code strengthened this tendency towards the use of contraception. Obliged now more than in the past to share his estate among all his children, the rural landowner of peasant or bourgeois stock could only be encouraged by this Code to limit the number of his offspring. 'No more than one calf out to grass' (*Pas plus d'un veau à l'herbage*), as the Norman peasants would say in the nineteenth century, expressing their desire, not always achieved, to produce no more than one son. From 1860 on, the whole of western Europe, headed by England, together with certain east European countries (like Hungary), were moving very slowly towards the practice of birth control; including the peasants of Germany, north Italy and Scandinavia, though to a lesser extent than the town-dwellers. It took the communist revolutions of Russia and Poland to persuade the peasants of these Slav nations (the Czechs were more precocious) to follow, with some misgivings at first, the 'bad example' of the West.

The secularisation of values was not synonymous with a weakening of morality or an increase in violence. Quite the contrary. The traditional concept of 'honour' was widespread in the countryside, and not only among the nobility. It was particularly strong in Mediterranean regions. In the seventeenth and even in the eighteenth centuries, much bloodshed was caused by vendettas between families. Corsica, for example, broke all records between 1680 and 1720 – in that shepherd culture, homicide, for the sake of honour or any other reason, had a marked effect on demographic trends. On that island, arquebuses went off as easily as fireworks. The rate of violent death in Corsica in peacetime around 1700 was not far below that in Europe during the horrors of the First World War! During the eighteenth and especially the nineteenth century, a gradual and partial change of attitudes took place. The implacable and bloody concept of honour gave way to the more benign and relaxed notion of decency (honnêteté), spread by the primary schools, the family and the church. All this reinforced the trend towards more peaceable behaviour already noticeable during the old regime. It was to take the vicious urbanisation of the Common Market era, the new models of extreme violence offered by the mass media, and the rampant Americanisation of European society, to reverse this long-term trend and bring in a new wave of murder, rape, muggings and hold-ups. This wave has affected above all the great urban agglomerations and has so far barely made itself felt in the little that remains of the rural world.

Is this 'little that remains' (still less in 1975 than in 1950) destined to disappear? If the question is put like that, it is outside the scope of this study, which is not aimed at telling the future. Let us not shed too many tears over the final demise of rural civilisation. Those who have fled the countryside, once overcrowded, now underpopulated, to settle in towns have found there a higher standard of living and a more varied existence than they left behind.

Yet in spite of the undeniable poverty which prevents us regretting its passing too much, rural civilisation at its height, around 1870 and again around 1900, was successfully integrated at a local, regional and national level. It is this rich rural synthesis which the creeping urbanisation of the twentieth century has been determined to destroy, without always knowing why, or how to replace it.

SELECT BIBLIOGRAPHY

Abel, W. *Agrarkrisen und Agrarkonjunktur* (second ed., Hamburg, 1966)

Agulhon, M. *La République au Village* (Paris, 1970)

Bercé, Y-M. *Histoire des Croquants* (Paris–Geneva, 1974)

(ed.). *Croquants et Nu-Pieds* (Paris, 1974)

Berkner, L. K. 'The Stem Family and the Developmental Cycle of the Peasant Household: an 18th-Century Austrian Example', in *American Historical Review*, 77, 1972, 398–418

Blickle, P. *Die Revolution von 1525* (Vienna–Munich, 1975)

Bloch, M. *French Rural History: an Essay on its Basic Characteristics* (London, 1966)

'The Rise of Dependent Cultivation and Seignorial Institutions', in M. M. Postan (ed.), *Cambridge Economic History of Europe*, I (second ed., Cambridge, 1966)

Blum, J. *Lord and Peasant in Russia from the 9th to the 19th Century* (Princeton, 1961)

'The Rise of Serfdom in Eastern Europe', in *American Historical Review*, 62, 1956–7, 807–36

'The Internal Structure and Polity of the European Village Community', in *Journal of Modern History*, 43, 1971, 541–76

Bois, G. *Crise du Féodalisme* (Paris, 1976)

Bois, P. *Paysans de l'Ouest* (Le Mans, 1960)

Bouchard, G. *Le Village Immobile: Sennely-en-Sologne au 18e Siècle* (Paris, 1972)

Braudel, F. and Labrousse, E. (eds.), *Histoire Economique et Sociale de la France*, 3 vols (Paris, 1971–6)

Brenner, R. 'Agrarian Class Structure and Economic Development in Preindustrial Europe', in *Past and Present*, 70, 1976, 30–75

Campbell, M. *The English Yeoman under Elizabeth and the Early Stuarts* (New Haven, 1942)

Chayanov, A. V. *The Theory of Peasant Economy* (Homewood, 1966)

Duby, G. and Wallon, A. (eds.), *Histoire de la France Rurale*, 4 vols (Paris, 1975–6)

Dunbabin, J. (ed.), *Rural Discontent in 19th-Century Britain* (London, 1974)

Evans, G. E. *Ask the Fellows who cut the Hay* (London, 1956)

The Pattern under the Plough (London, 1966)

Flandrin, J-L. (ed.). *Les Amours Paysannes (16e–19e Siècles)* (Paris, 1975)

Giorgetti, G. *Contadini e Proprietari nell'Italia Moderna* (Turin, 1974)

Goody, J. *et al.* (eds.). *Family and Inheritance: Rural Society in Western Europe, 1200–1800* (Cambridge, 1976)

Goubert, P. *Beauvais et le Beauvaisis de 1600 à 1730* (Paris, 1960)

'The French Peasantry of the Seventeenth Century: a Regional Example', in *Past and Present*, 10, 1956, 55–75

Hilton, R. H. *The English Peasantry in the later Middle Ages* (London, 1975)

Hobsbawm, E. J. *Primitive Rebels* (second ed., Manchester, 1975)

Hoskins, W. G. *The Midland Peasant: the Economic and Social History of a Leicestershire Village* (London, 1957)

Jones, E. L. *Agriculture and the Industrial Revolution* (Oxford, 1974)

Kula, W. *An Economic Theory of the Feudal System: Towards a Model of the Polish Economy, 1500–1800* (London, 1976)

Laslett, P. *The World We have Lost* (second ed., London, 1971)

Lefèbvre, G. *Les Paysans du Nord pendant la Révolution Française* (second ed., Bari, 1959)
'La Révolution Française et les Paysans', in his *Études sur la Révolution Française* (Paris, 1954)
Ladurie, E. Le Roy. *The Peasants of Languedoc* (Urbana, 1974)
Lütge, F. *Die Bayerische Grundherrschaft* (Stuttgart, 1949)
Maddalena, A. da. 'Rural Europe 1500–1750', in C. Cipolla (ed.), *The Fontana Economic History of Europe*, 2 (London, 1974)
Mousnier, R. *Peasant Uprisings in 17th-century France, Russia and China* (London, 1971)
Parker, W. N. and Jones, E. L. (eds.), *European Peasants and their Markets* (Princeton, 1975)
Porshnev, B. *Les Soulèvements Populaires en France de 1623 à 1648* (Paris, 1963)
Postan, M. M. 'England', in M. M. Postan (ed.), *Cambridge Economic History of Europe*, 1 (second ed., Cambridge, 1966)
Saint Jacob, P. de. *Les Paysans de la Bourgogne du Nord au dernier Siècle de l'Ancien Régime* (Paris, 1960)
Salomon, N. *La Campagne de Nouvelle Castille à la Fin du 16e Siècle* (Paris, 1964)
Samuel, R. (ed.), *Village Life and Labour* (London, 1975)
Sereni, E. *Il Capitalismo nelle Campagne, 1860–1900* (second ed., Turin, 1968)
Shanin, T. *The Awkward Class: Political Sociology of Peasantry in a developing Society, Russia 1910–25* (London, 1972)
(ed.), *Peasants and Peasant Societies* (Harmondsworth, 1971)
Slicher van Bath, B. H. *The Agrarian History of Western Europe, 500–1850* (London, 1963)
'The Rise of Intensive Husbandry in the Low Countries', in J. S. Bromley and E. H. Kossmann (eds.), *Britain and the Netherlands* (London, 1960), pp. 130–53
Soom, A. *Der Herrenhof in Estland im 17. Jahrhundert* (Lund, 1954)
Spufford, M. *Contrasting Communities: English Villagers in the Sixteenth and Seventeenth Centuries* (Cambridge, 1974)
Stone, L., 'Literacy and education in England, 1640–1900', in *Past and Present*, 42, 1969, 69–139
Thirsk, J. *English Peasant Farming* (London, 1957)
(ed.), *Agrarian History of England and Wales*, IV, *1500–1640* (Cambridge, 1967)
Thomas, K. V. *Religion and the Decline of Magic* (London, 1971)
Thompson, E. P. 'The Moral Economy of the English Crowd in the Eighteenth Century', in *Past and Present*, 50, 1971, 76–136
Vries, J. de. *The Dutch Rural Economy in the Golden Age, 1500–1700* (New Haven, 1974)
Wallerstein, I. *The Modern World-System* (New York and London, 1974)
Weber, E. *Peasants into Frenchmen: the Modernisation of Rural France, 1870–1914* (London, 1977)
Wolf, E. *Peasants* (Englewood Cliffs, 1966)
Peasant Wars of the Twentieth Century (London, 1971)
Wright, W. E. *Serf, Seigneur and Sovereign: Agrarian Reform in 18th-Century Bohemia* (Minneapolis, 1966)
Yver, J. *Essai de Géographie Coutumière* (Paris, 1966)

CHAPTER VI

BUREAUCRACY

1. *Definitions*

BUREAUCRACY is a word in constant everyday use. Over the last generation or so, its use has become far more common among historians, as well as social scientists, political commentators, journalists, politicians, and the public at large. Perhaps inevitably, its meanings have multiplied to the point where clarity and agreed definitions often seem to have been lost, and more heat than light is generated. For the purpose of historical discussion, there are three principal meanings of the word which need to be distinguished before proceeding any further.

(1) Bureaucracy as administration, either public or private, by full-time salaried officials, who are professionals, graded and organised hierarchically, with regular procedures and formalised record-keeping, and recruited for the tasks in hand. This is essentially the definition established by the great German sociologist of the late nineteenth–early twentieth century, Max Weber; the word has most often been used in this sense by historians and social scientists since then.

(2) Bureaucracy as a political system or other institution where power resides in the hands of such officials. Logically this meaning is impossible without (1), but it is often used independently without strict adherence to (1). *The Oxford English Dictionary* and political theorists of the nineteenth and twentieth centuries in particular have used this meaning, where the word is an amalgam of classical Greek and modern French – an addition to terms like aristocracy and democracy.

(3) Bureaucracy as a pejorative description of (1), and/or (2), signifying: 'form-filling'; 'red-tape'; procrastination and frustration; a waste of time, money and resources; the stifling of enterprise and initiative; the rule of 'jacks in office'. In recent years, this heavily political or 'ideological' meaning has come to be shared by the neo-*laissez-faire*, individualist Right and by some sections of the revolutionary Marxist as well as anarchist Left; but it is frequently used by people of all political persuasions or none in particular, to describe something they instinctively dislike and cannot otherwise define.

A point of particular controversy is whether bureaucracy, in any of its meanings, can only refer to public, and governmental institutions, or whether it is also applicable to private ones – in commerce, finance and industry, and in other areas of life. A possible compromise is to argue that bureaucracy, in its fullest sense, should be limited to the public sector, although the adjective bureaucratic and the noun bureaucrat(s) may be applied with equal fitness elsewhere. Weber himself clearly envisaged bureaucracy in private industrial corporations as well as in state administration; indeed he specifically commended a system of checks and balances between the two, and pointed out that under complete state socialism this would inevitably be lost, leaving the individual in the shadow of a single vast hierarchy. A recent American study suggests, on the contrary, that a bureau, as opposed to any other form of organisation, is partly defined by its main output – of goods, services, or other activities – not being subject to market-evaluation. Amongst other things, a bureaucrat is one whose output, the quality and quantity of whose work, cannot be calculated on a market basis. On this definition, some government departments and officials might not be bureaucratic, while even within the private sector certain institutions and their staffs would be.[1] In a mixed economy, such as that of the later twentieth-century United Kingdom, this produces some rather paradoxical distinctions. For example, did the British Post Office cease to be a bureau when it was transformed from being a government department into a nationalised industry in 1969–70? And was the size of the British civil service correspondingly reduced at a stroke by the total number of full-time postal and telecommunications employees? Since in the 1930s an absolute majority of all non-industrial civil servants in Britain were employed by the Post Office, and since as late as 1951 they comprised over 40 per cent, this would indeed have represented a 'de-bureaucratisation' beyond the wildest dreams of the protagonists of *laissez-faire*. Clearly there is an 'Alice-in-Wonderland', or 'Through-the-looking-glass' danger here, if we let our worries about definitions obscure our perception of historical realities. And any historian whose ideal remains that of Leopold von Ranke, to see and understand the past *wie es eigentlich gewesen*, is tempted to prefer more neutral terms like office-holding and civil service to bureaucracy, although on reflection this will be seen merely to evade or disguise some of the difficulties, not to overcome them.

The same author who proposes the criterion of exemption from market forces rejects Weber's famous definition in terms of hierarchy and rationality, retaining only the criteria of the size of the organisation, and the fact of its staff being full-time and professional. The recruitment and

[1] A. Downs, *Inside Bureaucracy* (Rand Corporation Research Studies, Boston, 1966, 67), esp. ch. III; contrast with *From Max Weber: Essays in Sociology*, transl. H. H. Gerth and C. W. Mills (London, 1948). The article, 'Bureaucracy' by R. Bendix in the *International Encyclopaedia of the Social Sciences*, vol. 2 (New York, 1968) is a judicious and helpful introduction. The expository literature, both on Weber's theories and on the sociology of bureaucracy, is now extensive. See Max Weber, *Economy and Society: An Outline of Interpretative Sociology*, ed. G. Roth and C. Wittich (3 vols. New York, 1968), vol. 3, chs. xi–xiv; also M. Albrow, *Bureaucracy* (Key Concepts series. London, 1970); D. Beetham, *Max Weber and the Theory of Modern Politics* (London, 1974); P. M. Blau, *Bureaucracy in Modern Society* (Studies in Sociology series. New York, 1956); T. B. Bottomore, *Elites and Society* (The New Thinker's Library series. London, 1964); M. T. Dalby and M. S. Werthman, eds.), *Bureaucracy in Historical Perspective* (Topics in Comparative History series. Glenview, Ill., and London, 1971); R. K. Merton and others (eds.), *Reader in Bureaucracy* (New York and London, 1952); W. J. Mommsen, *The Age of Bureaucracy: Perspectives on the Political Sociology of Max Weber* (Oxford, 1974); D. Warwick, *Bureaucracy* (Aspects of modern sociology series: Social Processes. London, 1974).

promotion of personnel are related to their role in the bureau and its functions. Interestingly these definitions, just as much as Weber's, would – if strictly applied – rule out most pre-nineteenth-century governments. Vital sectors of central administration, for instance in seventeenth- and eighteenth-century England, were still numerically tiny, so that there could still be 'face-to-face' personal relations at all levels. Moreover many of their personnel were either courtiers or parliamentary politicians, or simply part-time amateurs (especially members of royal commissions and parliamentary and other committees). Many were recruited, perhaps it would be safer to say, gained admission, on grounds far removed from their ability and their technical or educational qualifications.[1]

As for the private sector, one serious difficulty is lack of source material. With very few exceptions, the best studies of industrial and commercial bureaucracy in the United States of America and France are in fact taken from the public, or semi-public sector. In Britain only a few historians of private industry and finance have shown any awareness of the problem at all.[2] Some institutions which are neither governmental nor economic (industrial, commercial, financial) in purpose and function are relatively well documented, and have been much studied. Pre-eminent among these is the Roman Catholic Church and in particular the central administration of the Papacy itself. The same applies to the church in England before the Reformation and the Church of England since then. Similar studies either have been made, or would be feasible, for other large religious organisations and for other Christian denominations.[3]

Before attempting any historical assessment of bureaucracy, either as a system of power, or as the abuse of power, we must try to see what can be established about it in the first, more descriptive, sense, as a type of administration.

[1] One of the most ambitious but also most persuasive of recent general works, while it distinguishes between public or governmental, and private or industrial bureaucracy, has no doubt of the latter's existence: Henry Jacoby, *The Bureaucratization of the World* (Berkeley, Cal., 1973; original German edn *Soziologische Texte* series, no. 64. Neuwied and Berlin, 1969).

[2] See for example P. M. Blau, *The Dynamics of Bureaucracy* (Chicago, 1955); M. Crozier, *The Bureaucratic Phenomenon* (Chicago, 1964); P. Selznick, *Leadership in Administration* (Evanston, Ill, 1957). The clearest exception known to me is A. W. Gouldner, *Patterns of Bureaucracy* (Glencoe, Ill, 1954). Among the large, specially commissioned 'company histories' of recent years, few devote any attention to this; but note brief references in D. C. Coleman, *Courtaulds: An economic and social history*, II Rayon (Oxford, 1969), ch. xiv; and C. Wilson, *Unilever 1945–1965* (London, 1968), chs. 2 and 3. See further discussion in the last section of this chapter.

[3] For a brief outline, see R. W. Southern, *Western Society and the Church in the Middle Ages* (*Pelican History of the Church*, vol. 2. Harmondsworth, Middlesex, 1970), ch. 4; and in more detail for one period, Bernard Guillemain, *La Cour Pontificale d'Avignon 1309–1378, Étude d'une société* (Paris, 1966; 1st edn. Bibliothèque des Écoles Françaises d'Athènes et de Rome, fasc. no. 201, 1962). Of numerous works on English ecclesiastical administration, few deal specifically with the bureaucracy; see, however, Rosemary O'Day and Felicity Heal (eds.), *Continuity and Change. Personnel and administration of the Church in England 1500–1642* (Leicester, 1976), esp. ch. 3.

2. *Chronology: the sixteenth to eighteenth centuries*

The New Cambridge Modern History covers the period from the Renaissance (the mid-, or later-fifteenth century) to the Second World War (the mid-twentieth century). However, the history of western and central Europe, in this as in other respects, displays much essential unity over a longer time-span from about the eleventh, twelfth or thirteenth centuries to around the middle or later eighteenth century. Naturally there were great changes in government and administration during the course of between 500 and 700 years. And those who still favour the idea of a transition from medieval to modern history around 1450–1500, or of a transformation of feudalism into capitalism at whatever date within this chronological framework, will be reluctant to accept the arguments for continuity. The case for this is partly that of the general historical context: the obvious fact that Europe remained primarily agricultural and rural, however important the commercial and urban sectors of society and the economy may have been. Politically the surviving republics were few, small and decentralised; monarchy and aristocracy were still politically and socially predominant. Technological and scientific changes had not yet begun to transform the whole material basis of life at the rate they have done during the past two centuries. It is surely likely that changes in administration will be limited by the general stage of historical development: it is not necessary to subscribe to economic or any other kind of historical determinism to accept this. For instance, bureaucracy in any sense is hard to imagine in a non-literate society, although alphabetic writing is not of course a prerequisite; nor among nomads, or those whose effective political units are no larger than an extended family. Until very recently these criteria would have excluded the possibility of its existence in the Arctic regions of North America and North Asia, Australasia and the Pacific islands, extensive areas of sub-Saharan Africa, and the upper Amazon region of South America. It is tempting to go further than this, and to say that bureaucracy is impossible without an established urban sector, and a sizeable middle class, or at least without enough people who are neither priest kings, leisured aristocrats or warriors, nor mere manual-working drudges. But here and there exceptions could certainly be produced to confound even these broad generalisations, while even some of the relatively developed states of early modern Europe were heavily dependent on foreigners to staff their administrations: the bureaucratic equivalent of mercenary soldiers. None the less, a measure of political as well as geographical stability, political units of above a minimum size, organised town life, and a middle class are prerequisites: in philosophic terms, necessary but not sufficient causes of the development of bureaucracy.

In no state, not even in Prussia, could there be said to have been a fully professional civil service before the end of the eighteenth century. In all the monarchical countries of Europe, many administrators were still the personal servants of the monarch; many subordinate officials were appointed by their seniors and not by the state, indeed many were the employees of their superiors, entering and leaving the public service with them. For many their offices were still a species of property, to be acquired, exploited and disposed of like other kinds of property. In several countries the tenure of many offices was still semi-hereditary. Officials were remunerated, and recouped themselves, in a variety of ways, but it was still the exception for them to be wholly dependent on fixed salaries from the state; very many depended on a combination of fee or salary payments from the crown or the public purse, perquisites in money and in kind, fees and gratuities from other officials and from members of the public who needed to make use of their services, and what we should call downright plunder of royal or public resources and the acceptance of bribes over and above gratuities and presents. Only in a minority of cases was there yet any adequate regular provision for pensioned retirement. The criteria for appointment, promotion and dismissal were varied and often unclear. Usually, birth and family connections, political, regional or family patronage, and wealth (making possible the purchase of office or at least of favour) were more important factors in entry to office than technical qualifications or general ability, let alone success in open competitive examinations. In many cases, once appointed, officials were all but irremovable.

Granted that the system of office-holding had some similar features in most of the European states, it should be possible to make some comparisons of its relative importance. If the number of officials employed under the Crown is taken as the decisive element, then office-holding must have been a much more important influence in France than in England. Throughout the period from the sixteenth to the late eighteenth century, the number of office-holders was vastly greater in France (see Table 2). This is not to say that proportionately more people took part in government; indeed at the local level, the number involved on a part-time basis in the government and legal institutions of counties, cities, boroughs, manors and parishes, may have been larger in England than the corresponding total in France. But if office-holding, as a profession affecting economic and social structure, and affording opportunities for upward social movement, is to be correlated with numbers, then it must have been proportionately more important in France – and in several other states of continental Europe – than it was in England. Notwithstanding this, some branches of government were at least as large in England as elsewhere: for example the royal household under the Tudors and early Stuarts was probably larger, and proportionately costlier, than in France under the last Valois and the Bourbon kings. Despite the massive takings of many

English officials in fees and gratuities – far in excess of what they were paid by the crown – the total burden of the state on society was heavier in France; the level of taxation per head of the population was higher in France than in England or the Netherlands until the very late seventeenth century. Then the costs of war and the extension of the fiscal system that accompanied and provided essential support for it, began to change this; so that by the time of the great wars from 1689 to 1713, the tax burden may have been as heavy in England as it was in France, and was perhaps even heavier in the United Provinces. However, while the French system of office-holding was more rigid, with a stronger hereditary element in it, in England and other states where the civil service was numerically smaller but more open to outsiders, royal and later public service may have provided a better way for people to make their way up the economic and social ladders.

If we think of taxation as comprising the total burden of the state upon society, it must be extended to include the amount taken by officials and others direct from members of the public in fees, gratuities, and so on. But apart from this, we may think of taxation as operating in three possible ways, each of which may in turn have been either intended or unintended: the tax system may have been 'progressive' in the sense of bearing more heavily on the rich than on the poor, the few than the many, and so tending to redistribute wealth in that direction; alternatively, it may have been 'regressive', and have operated in the opposite way, making the rich richer and the poor poorer; or it may have acted to preserve equilibrium, not effecting a redistribution either way. A variant form of regressive taxation is to effect redistribution from the population at large – of all levels and classes – to those in office – rulers and petty functionaries alike. For convenience, this may be called the 'Court-Country' model. If all the material advantages of office-holding are included, as well as taxes in the narrower sense, then the 'Court-Country' fiscal hypothesis may seem to fit the facts more closely than any other, at least for sixteenth- and seventeenth-century Europe and perhaps for parts of the Third World today. But it is well to remember our ignorance of basic population and income data before the nineteenth century. In the absence of reliable quantitative evidence, the economic effects of office-holding and taxation in the early modern period must remain largely conjectural. The kinds of taxes that could be levied depended on the constitutional position in each country, but also on the nature of its economy. A large volume of overseas trade, as in England and Holland, meant that customs duties on exports and imports, could play a more important part in the fiscal system than elsewhere. A large middle class, or rather a relatively large number of people of middling wealth, would make certain kinds of commodity or sales taxes possible without these bearing excessively on the masses of the poorest people as they would if levied mainly on necessities. Up to a point there is a contrast here between France and the Castilian parts of the Spanish Empire on the one hand and the United Provinces and England on the other. Sweden under Gustavus Adolphus and again under Charles XII is an example of a fairly heavily taxed but not very rich country, where the monarchy's prestige and popularity and its apparent readiness – up to a point – to side with the people against the nobles enabled it to get away with more than elsewhere, and more than at other junctures in Swedish history, for example under Christina and in the minority of Charles XI. Generally speaking, it seems unlikely that taxation acted progressively in any state before the later nineteenth century, though there may have been temporary, local unintended exceptions to this. The relative share borne by the wealthiest sections of society, the middling and the masses, probably varied more with constitutional and economic factors than according to the deliberate intentions of governments.

What are often thought of as the most characteristic features of the old administrative system were not all equally fully developed in the same states. For instance, venality was sometimes deliberately used by the crown or other agencies of government as an additional source of revenue, sometimes by the office-holders themselves as a part of the material rewards for their services. In the seventeenth century (but this is also broadly true for the longer time-span from the sixteenth to later eighteenth centuries), it was most widespread in Castile, Italy (except Florence), France and south-west Germany, next most in England; less so, on the whole, in the northern and eastern parts of Europe. Tax-farming, the handing over of whole sections of the revenue system to individuals or syndicates of financiers (who might or might not technically be office-holders themselves) came and went in England, Sweden, Brandenburg-Prussia, was most widespread and longest lasting in France. Dependence of officials on fee payments, or at any rate on payments other than fixed salaries from the state, was all but universal with temporary exceptions in England during the Interregnum and Republic (1642–60) and permanent ones elsewhere, especially by the eighteenth century in Prussia. By twentieth-century standards what would be considered as corruption on the part of officials was likewise virtually universal, though again there were important variations between different states and at different times in the same countries. The attitude of absolute or would-be absolute governments (which in this period means monarchies) was ambivalent. They had to accept venality, tax-farming, fee-payments, and tolerate corrupt practices because of their own financial needs and the limits of their effective power, yet the traditional office-holding system often gave its members some security of tenure and ability successfully to oppose royal policies of which they disapproved from within the administration. The role of the *officiers* during the Fronde (1648–53) and their resistance to the French crown's use of *commissaires* (especially the famous *Intendants*) is only the most obvious and dramatic example of this. Again, this might operate to preserve social and political immobility in some cases, to affect change in others. If such a broad generalisation has any value, the old administrative system may be seen as part of a society of estates, or orders, a *Ständestaat*, which by the nineteenth century was being replaced by a society divided into social classes, defined by their economic position, and for which another type of administration had become appropriate.[1]

In several countries institutions were organised on the 'collegiate' principle. In this way a group of office-holders, often with an internal order of seniority, but sharing collective duties, privileges and responsibilities, did the job that would otherwise have been done by one, or by a vertical hierarchy of officials. The seventeenth–eighteenth century English, then British equivalents were called 'boards' or commissions. As with venality, tax-farming and payment by fees and gratuities, the collegiate system certainly had medieval origins, but it too reached its apogee in seventeenth-century France. There the system of office-holding was at once so necessary to the crown as a major source of revenue and so inefficient and unresponsive to royal and ministerial requirements, that the system of *commissaires* had been developed alongside it. From being temporary, *ad hoc* and extraordinary, the commissaries in turn became institutionalised as the intendants who came to have their own subordinate staffs, creating a new hierarchy between the king and his ministers at the centre and government action in the localities. Several of the

---

[1] K. R. Swart, *Sale of Offices in the Seventeenth Century* (The Hague, 1949) is the most ambitious attempt at a general, comparative study, with valuable bibliography to that date; see also O. Hintze, *Historical Essays*, ed. F. Gilbert (New York, 1975), esp. chs. 6 and 7. On western Europe in general, see also T. Aston (ed.), *Crisis in Europe 1560–1660* (London, 1965), ch. by H. R. Trevor-Roper and comments by R. Mousnier and others (also available, with additional comments in *Past and Present*, nos. 16 and 18 (1959–60); C. Wilson, *Economic History and the Historian* (London, 1969), ch. on 'The Over-Taxation of Empires'. For France, see particularly Roland Mousnier, *La Vénalité des Offices sous Henri IV et Louis XIII* (Rouen, 1948; repr. Paris, 1971), and his collected articles in *La Plume, La Faucille et le Marteau* (Paris, 1970); also *Dix-Septième Siècle*, nos. 42–3 (1959). 'Serviteurs du Roi', by Mousnier and others; Edmond Esmonin, *Études sur la France des XVII⁰ et XVIII⁰ Siècles* (Univ. de Grenoble, Publications de la Faculté des Lettres et Sciences Humaines, no. 32. Paris, 1964), esp. Pts. I and 3; for the eighteenth century, F. L. Ford, *Robe and Sword: The Regrouping of the French Aristocracy after Louis XIV* (Cambridge, Mass., 1953). For England, see G. E. Aylmer, *The King's Servants: the Civil Service of Charles I, 1625–1642* (London, 1961; rev. edn, 1974), and *The State's Servants: the Civil Service of the English Republic, 1649–1660* (London, 1973); G. R. Elton, *The Tudor Revolution in Government* (Cambridge, 1953); J. Hurstfield, *The Queen's Wards* (London, 1958), and *Freedom, Corruption and Government*, reprinted articles and essays (London, 1974), chs. 5–7; J. E. Neale, 'The Elizabethan Political Scene', in *Procs. Brit. Acad.*, 34 (1948), and in Neale, *Essays in Elizabethan History* (London, 1958); L. Stone, *The Crisis of the Aristocracy 1558–1641* (Oxford, 1965), ch. VIII; H. R. Trevor-Roper, *The Gentry 1540–1640* (Econ. Hist. Rev. Supplements no. 1. Cambridge, 1953). On Sweden, in English, see R. Hatton, *Charles XII of Sweden* (London, 1968), Index entry 'Sweden, administration'; M. Roberts, *Gustavus Adolphus* (2 vols. London, 1953–8), vol. I, ch. VI and ch. VII, sections vii and viii; vol. II, ch. II, sections ii and v, ch. III, section iii, and book review in *Eng. Hist. Rev.*, XCI (1976), 642–3.

reforms by the rulers of Sweden, Brandenburg-Prussia and Russia in the seventeenth and early eighteenth centuries were derived directly or indirectly from French models, or from what were presumably believed to be the desirable features of French government under the two great Cardinals and then Louis XIV. By the eighteenth century Prussia was itself becoming a model for other states, especially in central and eastern Europe. In western Europe, Castile had developed in the sixteenth century the first great 'imperial' administrative system of modern times, exhibiting on a larger scale many of the same features which were to be found in France and England; in parts of Central and South America, Spanish rule was superimposed on the existing Indian culture and institutions, along lines which with various modifications were to be followed by the Portuguese, the Dutch, the French and the British in different parts of the non-European world.[1] Yet the decline of Spanish power and in the vitality of Spanish government was so precipitous during the seventeenth century that by the time of the new dynasty of Bourbon kings in the eighteenth century, effective reform in Spain involved eclectic borrowing from France and elsewhere. In Italy, the major city states, notably Milan, Florence and Venice, had by the fifteenth century developed techniques of administration which put them in this, as in most other respects, ahead of the rest of Europe; and especially in the methods of inter-state diplomacy. But the process of borrowing was to a large extent also part of the process of swallowing up. And as the Habsburgs gained control of much of central and northern Italy, the republican city states ceased to have much influence, except in the case of Venice as a rather abstract constitutional model. As for the first new republic, indeed the first new 'nation' of the Western world, in the United States of America there was at first an attempt to keep central administration to an absolute minimum. In so far as the new federal executive under the Constitution (1788-9) required some officials and departments, the Americans borrowed ideas and techniques from their erstwhile imperial rulers the British but also improvised, and generally sought to avoid what they (rightly) saw as the excesses and corruptions of the Old World – in this case of the old administrative system whether in France under Louis XVI or in Britain under George III.

Perhaps the clearest long-term change in western Europe between the twelfth and the seventeenth centuries is the extent to which the institutions of central government had become distinct from the household and personal *ménage* of the monarch. This process, which the early twentieth-

[1] See R. Morse, 'The Heritage of Latin America', in L. Hartz (ed.), *The Founding of New Societies* (New York, 1964); J. H. Parry, *The Sale of Public Offices in the Spanish Indies under the Habsburgs* (Berkeley and Los Angeles, Cal., 1963); J. L. Phelan, *The Kingdom of Quito in the Seventeenth Century: Bureaucratic Politics in the Spanish Empire* (Madison and Milwaukee, Wisc., and London, 1967), esp. ch. 17; M. Sarfatti, *Spanish Bureaucratic Patrimonialism in America* (Inst. of International Studies, Politics of Modernisation ser., no. 1. Berkeley, Cal., 1966).

century British historian T. F. Tout described as 'going out of court', involved a series of progressive formalisations, physical as well as institutional separation or 'hiving-off', and often the creation of new informal 'inner rings' to replace those which had become too large and cumbrous, too physically distant and impersonal, to serve the needs of effective policy-making and the quick carrying out of decisions once taken. Nor did this process come to an end in 1800; in a sense it is still with us. The establishment of the Office of the President in the United States (1939) may well be regarded as a latter-day equivalent to the French administrative changes of the 1520s or those in England during the 1530s. Likewise Hitler's use of the *Schutzstaffel* (or SS) against the *Sturmabteilungen* (or SA) in 1934 has earlier parallels in Peter the Great's action against the Streltsi in 1696, and even in the conflicts between praetorians and legionaries from the provinces in the later Roman Empire. No American President, however hard-working, can retain direct personal supervision and control over the whole federal executive merely by having a bigger and better personal office, whether inside or outside the White House itself. Not even Frederick the Great, the very archetype of the 'bureaucrat king', could by his latter years maintain total oversight and domination of his entire administration. His successors lacked both the desire and the ability even to attempt it. Yet in a small country with a relatively simple structure of government this may still be possible for brief periods. By all accounts the regime of Dr Salazar in Portugal during the 1930s and 40s came very near to the ideal of complete personal oversight. But most modern dictators, regardless of their political colouring, have no more been able to achieve such total direct control than have the leaders of parliamentary or other constitutional governments. It is, for example, sometimes said that Peel in the 1840s, Gladstone in his first ministry (1868–74) and Wilson in his early years as Prime Minister (1964–6) so succeeded. A moment's reflection tells us that while each may have enjoyed a remarkable personal dominance over his respective cabinet colleagues and have had an unusually good grasp of what was going on in the main departments of government, this cannot even in the nineteenth century have extended below ministerial level, and by the later twentieth century must have been a physical impossibility there too.

To be able to generalise in a meaningful way, it may be better to look at what early modern European governments were trying to do, rather than seeking to characterise their civil services in the abstract. First and foremost came the safety, well-being and splendour of the state itself, which usually meant that of the sovereign and his or her court and entourage. Here, in the relationship between royal courts and government as a whole, there had been the most marked changes, going further in some countries than in others, between (say) the fifteenth and eighteenth centuries. By far and away the biggest preoccupation of all states was with the preparations for and the effective waging of war. Military expenditure, and all the by-products of military preparations, would seem to have constituted a proportionately bigger drain on national wealth and financial resources for many countries in the sixteenth and seventeenth centuries than they were to do in the nineteenth century. As a proportion of total governmental activity and expenditure, war may even have been more important than in the twentieth century, although we lack the necessary information to make exact comparisons. Internal security, the enforcement of law and order, the exercise of justice, like defence against external enemies, are pre-occupations of all governments at all times in recorded history. But here too this role bulked larger, relatively speaking, than it has come to do in the last two centuries or so. Taxation, which took many forms and was administered in varying ways, was designed mainly to provide for the maintenance of royal courts and the establishments of government themselves, for armies, navies, buildings, fortifications and diplomacy, and for a few other, strictly limited purposes. This can be related to the last area of governmental activity, what we may call general administrative control, especially in the three areas of economic regulation, particularly for foreign and colonial trade, of poor relief, and of education. Only in a few states was expenditure on the last of these more than a minute proportion of the whole; in general expenditure on social welfare was only a small fraction of the total anywhere. The best brief, general account of the development of public administration in western Europe since 1660, written a generation ago, concentrated on the fields of general administration (including the reform of civil services themselves), conscription for military service, taxation, social services, and education.[1] But in all cases, most of what Ernest Barker had to say related to the period after 1789, much of it to the last hundred years with which he was concerned.

How successful were the countries of early modern Europe and their governments at discharging the tasks which they set themselves? Although boundaries changed with war and dynastic accident, few states ceased to exist, and in so far as there were no successful popular and permanent revolutions from below, they avoided disaster. But measured by any more positive and exacting standards than this, the success which they achieved obviously varied very widely indeed, not only from country to country but also from one epoch to another within the same countries. It might be possible to take a series of strong, reasonably efficient administrations by early modern standards. as one archetype: the Spanish-Habsburg Empire under Charles V and Philip II; England under Thomas

---

[1] (Sir) Ernest Barker, *The Development of Public Services in Western Europe 1660–1930* (London, 1944), originally published as a chapter in E. Eyre (ed.), *European Civilisation: its origins and development*, vol. v (Oxford, 1937). Although limited to a comparison of England, France and Germany, this is still very well worth reading.

Cromwell and then again under William Cecil; France under Richelieu and Louis XIV, Sweden under Gustavus Adolphus and Chancellor Oxenstierna and then Charles XI; Russia under Peter the Great; Brandenburg-Prussia under the Great Elector and again under Frederick William I and his son, Frederick the Great. One might contrast with these the situation of countries under weak, corrupt, or otherwise inadequate rulers, or in chronic conditions of ineffectiveness and disarray: France from the 1560s to 90s; Spain under Philip III and again under Charles II; Russia during the Time of Troubles in the immediate pre-Romanov era; Poland almost throughout; the Ottoman Turkish Empire between the great Sultans of the fifteenth and early sixteenth century and the Kiuprili revival of the seventeenth century; England under James I and perhaps at times under Charles II. This is not to argue that the quality of rulers and of their favourites or chief ministers made all the difference; only to suggest that it may be instructive to consider how much they did in fact count for in relation to the tasks which governments set themselves and the means at their disposal to achieve these. The reader who wishes to pursue this line of thought will find ample materials for doing so in many chapters of the *New Cambridge Modern History* from volumes I to VIII. It would be plausible to conclude that, by twentieth-century standards, the differences between the most and the least successful early modern governments are less striking than their similarities. Nor is it easy to estimate how much difference the variations in tone and quality at the top made to ordinary people at the receiving end. The collectors, billeting officers, recruiting sergeants, constables and magistrates or their equivalents may sometimes have behaved better because of a particular ruler or minister of state, but only sometimes and most often only within narrow limits. Indeed the quality of the harvest and the character of the local landlord or town governors may very often have mattered more to ordinary people than the differences between 'good' and 'bad' kings and ministers. For example, even if there were less waste and dishonesty and sheer incompetence, the military and fiscal burdens of the state on society might well be heavier under an effective than under an incompetent ruler. Many governments of the utmost reputability by the standards of their own time relied on tax-farmers for key sectors of revenue collection – a system that, by twentieth-century standards, seems inherently unsatisfactory, being all too likely to lead to extortion and exploitation. Nor should we forget that even Jeremy Bentham – founding father of utilitarianism in Britain and so indirectly a decisive influence on governmental reformers from the 1830s to 70s – defended venality, on the grounds that a state would get better officials from the classes with enough money to buy their way in than it did from those who entered via aristocratic patronage and family connections.[1] On

[1] Besides the works cited in n. 1, p. 171 above, see J. van Klaveren, 'Die Historische Erscheinung der Korruption...', *Vierteljahrschrift für Sozial- und Wirtschaftsgeschichte*,

the other hand, tax-farming had disappeared in Britain before the end of the seventeenth century, and by the end of Bentham's lifetime substantial advances had been made towards a salaried civil service, whose members were distinct from office-holding politicians. This is a reminder that, within individual countries, developments could be very uneven as between different sectors or branches of administration: some revenue services and some military supply departments often being among the most advanced, royal households and law courts often among the least.

Where the other differences in historical circumstances and context are too marked, it may be misleading to press any such comparisons too far. And the rest of this chapter will be largely devoted to testing out the hypothesis that nineteenth- and twentieth-century administration, and so bureaucracy, is substantially unique, with only the loosest and most limited earlier parallels. The reasons for this may seem shatteringly obvious. Yet the very fact of giving the reasons for this transformation may well be to beg the question of the connection between administrative changes and those in the economy and society to which that administration belongs. That is to say, is modern bureaucracy simply a uniform response to, or a product of, industrialisation, urbanisation, and democracy or 'mass politics'?

3. *Chronology: the nineteenth and twentieth centuries*

Looking at the history of the last two hundred years or so, the main problems relate to numerical growth and the reasons for it, to the nature or quality of modern bureaucracy, and to its social and political role. If growth in the numbers of public officials or civil servants has not simply been continuous and uniform, in proportion to total populations and to the level of economic development, what other influences have caused it to vary between different countries and in the same countries at different times? Secondly, how far can the rate of growth be related to other factors such as wars and revolutions, as well as to levels of wealth, complexity and technological development? How far are the scope and functions of government – notably in the fields of social welfare and direct economic management – decided on political grounds and then found to be reflected in the size and scale of the bureaucracy? How far is there, and has there been, a meretricious, 'Parkinsonian' growth of bureaucracy and the number of bureaucrats in the third, pejorative sense of the word? Has this trend been accelerating in the twentieth century, and, if in some countries

---

vols. 44–6 (1957–9), and J. Vicens Vives, 'The structure of the administrative state in the 16th and 17th centuries', *Rapports IV, Histoire Moderne* (XIth International Congress of Historical Sciences. Stockholm, 1960). For corruption in the twentieth century, see below, pp. 191–2 and 192 n. 1. The most recent discussion is in Betty Behrens, 'Government and Society', ch. viii of *The Cambridge Economic History of Europe*, vol. v, *The Economic Organisation of Early Modern Europe*, ed. E. E. Rich and C. H. Wilson (Cambridge, 1977), pp. 549–620.

more so than in others, why? Then there is the whole Weberian notion of a change from a patrimonial to a rational bureaucratic system, and how far outside Weber's 'ideal types' this has or can ever be expected to have come about. It may be helpful to take the transition in Prussia and then in modern Germany between the eighteenth and the twentieth century as a kind of *locus classicus* or testing ground. Finally, what of the existence of a distinct bureaucratic class, and its relation to the ruling class in different kinds of state and society? Has the growth of bureaucracy in the last century or so tended in more cases to impede social mobility and accentuate social stratification or – vice versa – to accelerate mobility and reduce stratification? Does this in turn depend upon the presence or absence of private ownership; and at that point do we move out of the realm of historical study into that of political debate between Marxists and non-Marxists? Unfortunately for the purposes of easy definition, Marx's own most extended discussion of bureaucracy occurs in one of his earliest writings, his *Critique of Hegel's 'Philosophy of Right'*. This was written in 1843, but remained unpublished until the 1920s. The relevant passages are of remarkable interest for the intellectual history of the nineteenth century as well as for the development of Marx's own thought. He effectively rebuts Hegel's claim that civil servants constitute a 'universal class' or a 'class above classes'; yet the style and the form of the argument are still markedly neo-Hegelian. Whatever may have been the case later in his career, at this stage Marx was emphatically not a Marxist.[1] In the twentieth century, as we shall see, heterodoxies and cross-currents may be found both among Marxists and their opponents in this debate. For example Djilas and Hegedus argue that there can be a bureaucratic class even in a socialist state; non-Marxist Western social scientists disagree on the contrary point, as to whether bureaucracy can exist in the private, profit-making sector. This is not meant to be a definitive list of themes or problems, only to indicate possible lines of thought.

In the development of public administration since about 1800, no two countries present an identical pattern. Yet in almost all the general trend has been in the same direction. How is this to be explained?

By the eighteenth century some countries had moved a good deal further than others towards having what we should recognise as a modern civil service, or indeed a rational 'Weberian' bureaucracy – by almost any standards, Prussia probably the furthest of all. Not that we should think of the three great Hohenzollern rulers: Frederick William, the Great Elector (1640–88); King Frederick William I (1713–40); Frederick II, 'Frederick the Great' (1740–86) as having consciously decided to create a modern civil service. Identifying monarch and state to an unusual extent, they simply wanted the most efficient and obedient administration that they

[1] Karl Marx, *Critique of Hegel's 'Philosophy of Right'*, ed. Joseph O'Malley, transl. Annette Jolin and J. O'Malley (Cambridge, 1970), esp. pp. 41-54, 80.

could get. There are several good accounts of Prussian administration during this period.[1] For our purposes, the decisive question is: how nearly had this system come to being a bureaucracy in the modern, or 'Weberian' sense? For instance, centrally administered examinations for entry into office were introduced in 1770, conceivably influenced by knowledge of their use in China. But too much should not be made, here or elsewhere, of examinations in themselves. There is a distinction between qualifying tests of numeracy or literacy (see the famous description in Anthony Trollope's novel *The Three Clerks*, which he tells us in his *Autobiography* was founded on his own experience!), and entry to office by competitive examination. More important, however, even the latter may make little difference to the kind of people who get in, if the social, educational and other circumstances continue to favour candidates from a particular background. Thus in Prussia there was apparently little to show for the examinations system until into the 1800s. Under Frederick the Great himself promotion within the administration may well have depended on merit (that is ability and achievement) more than anywhere else at the time. Yet members of the nobility still predominated at the top, probably to a greater extent than under his more austere and – in a perverse way – more egalitarian father. Despite some imitative moves in Saxony and Austria, the superiority of Prussian administration stands out unmistakably. Comparable reforms and rationalisation in Bavaria came, under French influence, in the 1790s–1800s. Already in Prussia the notion of all, from the monarch and his ministers down to the most junior royal officials, as servants of the state was more than a mere propaganda slogan. As with the development of public administration and modern bureaucracy in general, it is an ideal which has carried its own dangers as well as benefits for humanity. The extent to which the effectiveness of Prussian government depended on the ability and hard-work of its rulers appeared after Frederick II's death under his mediocre successors, Frederick William II and III. Legal reform, directed by the great cameralist Cocceji, had been amongst Frederick's earliest concerns; the King and his advisers returned to this aspect of government towards the end of his reign. A revised general law code was in active preparation under the direction of Carmer, a younger jurist also influenced by the cameralists, when Frederick died. It was partly their dislike of the rule of court favourites and cabinet secretaries – the equiva-

---

[1] These include: H. Brunschwig, *Enlightenment and Romanticism in 18th-century Prussia* (Chicago and London, 1974); F. L. Carsten, *The Origins of Prussia* (Oxford, 1954); R. A. Dorwart, *The Administrative Reforms of Frederick William I of Prussia* (Cambridge, Mass, 1953), and *The Prussian Welfare State before 1740* (Cambridge, Mass, 1971); J. R. Gillis, *The Prussian Bureaucracy in Crisis 1840–1860* (Stanford, Cal., 1971); C. Hinrichs, *Preussen als historisches problem*, ed. G. Oestreich (Berlin, 1964); O. Hintze, *Historical Essays*, chs. 1 and 2; W. Hubatsch, *Frederick the Great Absolutism and Administration* (London, 1973 and 75); H. C. Johnson, *Frederick the Great and his Officials* (New Haven, Conn. and London, 1975); H. Rosenberg, *Bureaucracy, Aristocracy and Autocracy: The Prussian Experience 1660–1815* (Cambridge, Mass, 1958).

lent of thirteenth-century *curiales* or *familiares*, and of twentieth-century political advisers or members of a 'kitchen cabinet' – that led the senior bureaucrats to insist on its being revised before its promulgation in 1794. The *Allgemeines Landrecht* (1794) is perhaps most important in Prussian history for its assimilation of all the Hohenzollern territories, stretching right across northern Germany, thereby laying the legal basis for a unitary state. For our purposes it reflected the tensions between the court camarilla and the established departmental hierarchy. The code recognised the traditional social classes or estates of birth (*Geburtstände*), but also the estates defined by profession or occupation (*Berufstände*); and these included the administrative class or 'bureaucracy' (*Beamtenstand*), which was accorded special rights and privileges, even protection against the monarch himself. It is still debatable how far an ossifying administrative system, without Frederick the Great's capacity to stimulate as well as merely to supervise, was responsible for Prussia's disastrous defeats by the Napoleonic armies in 1806–7; inept political and military leadership and out-dated military methods would seem to have been more to blame. Be that as it may, a leading role in the Prussian reform movement of 1806–13 was assumed by members of the *Beamtenstand*, albeit (and perhaps significantly) in the case of Stein and Hardenburg by officials of non-Prussian origin. So far was the personal role of the monarch eclipsed, that the period of nominally monarchical reaction which followed the Napoleonic Wars and the subsequent reconstruction of Germany has sometimes been called 'the age of bureaucratic absolutism' (1815–48). Despite its own vulnerability and internal political divisions, the Prussian bureaucracy helped to bring about the defeat of both the liberal and the popular revolutions (1848–50), and then adapted itself to the rapidly industrialising Prussia of the 1850s–60s and after. Despite difficulties in the stormy years of the 1860s, this only partially reformed but considerably altered civil service proved an effective and generally willing instrument for Bismarck's policies. To begin with, the only German imperial administrative bodies after the creation of the Second Reich in 1871 were the Chancellery and its off-shoots including the diplomatic corps, the Army (in some but not all aspects), the Navy (very tiny then), and the Customs (going back to the Zollverein of the 1830s). Gradually from the 1880s on, additional departments of state and ministries were separated from the Chancellor's office. But to a large extent there were still separate administrations in Prussia and in the other German princely states until the First World War. Although Prussian and German administrations remained distinct under the Weimar constitution (1919–33), indeed the old principalities and other states were simply replaced by *Länder* in an almost federal system, a unified German civil service can probably be thought of as having emerged by the 1920s. Despite its shattering loss of independence and self-respect during the Third Reich (1933–45), and the disasters of defeat, occupation and partition which followed (1945–8), the civil service in the Federal Republic of the later twentieth century is thus the heir to a long tradition in what may fairly be called – even if to some this may seem a dubious distinction – the premier bureaucratic state in Europe.[1]

Whether or not Prussia and then Germany was the most bureaucratised country, it by no means had the largest number of civil servants per head of population (see Table 2).

Of all continental European countries, France has the longest continuous history of centralised rule, as a unitary state. While many institutions of the *ancien régime* were casualties of the Revolution, there was considerable continuity of personnel, and even more continuity – it may be argued – in the spirit and style of French administration. Whatever the potential decentralising tendencies of the constitutional regime of 1791–2, under the Jacobins of 1793–4 there was an abrupt return to centralised absolutism, even if this was now bourgeois or popular and not monarchist and aristocratic. Moreover, building on the new territorial units, the *départements* of 1790, which had replaced the old provinces, the republican system was further improved upon during the Consulate of Napoleon Bonaparte (1799–1804). At the departmental level, a new type of central appointee, the *Préfet*, was endowed with powers resembling, but in some respects exceeding those of the old *Intendants*. At the same time a similarity to the Prussian *Beamtenstand-staat* can be seen in the new supreme appellate tribunal for all intra-administrative disputes and cases between individual officials and the state, the *Conseil d'État*. Through all the subsequent political upheavals – of Empire, Restoration, July Revolution, Orleanist Monarchy, 1848 Revolution and Second Republic, Presidency of Louis Napoleon, Second Empire, Third Republic, Vichy, Fourth, and even Fifth Republics, these two institutions have survived, if naturally with changes of role and composition. The prestige and self-esteem of the top French administrators, the *grand corps*, despite a temporary near eclipse under Vichy and the Occupation (1940–4) has remained second to none. Likewise the corporate solidarity of the French civil service as a whole seems to reflect a continuous heritage from the days of Sully, the two great Cardinals and the Sun King. As for the characteristics which are used to define modern, rational bureaucracy, fully professional recruitment was relatively late to emerge; open competitive entrance examinations only being introduced by stages from 1875 to 1900. (In the neighbouring kingdom of Belgium, they came as late as 1939.) One historian of the French civil service sees the crucial stages in the emergence of the modern theory and practice of *la fonction publique* as having been under the First Empire (1804–14), in 1848, and after the Liberation in 1946; a fuller code of statutory safeguards, partly to protect civil servants against political inter-

---

[1] For the period c. 1871–1960, see H. Jacob, *German Administration since Bismarck: Central Authority versus Local Autonomy* (New Haven, Conn., 1963).

ference, was drafted in 1873 but never passed into law. Another recent authority suggests two formative periods in the long-term development of modern French administration: c. 1770–1800 and 1914–44. Perhaps the seeming disagreement depends on whether one is more concerned with agonising reappraisals or with positive reforms.

Only briefly under the Second Republic, in 1848, was there any sustained attempt to recover the early revolutionary ideals of popular accountability and decentralisation, evident in 1789–91 and effectively submerged ever since then. Despite the attempts at regionalisation under de Gaulle and his successors, the French civil service continues to act as a unifying force: bureaucratic in the rational sense at the top, all too often bureaucratic in the pejorative, unpopular sense lower down. Whatever difference may be made by further development towards a 'mixed' economy, so far there seems to be a marked difference between administration in clerical and in industrial situations under state employment. There may well be comparable differences between the personnel of the *Société Nationale des Chemins de Fer Français* (or state railways) and of the French postal services, although both – like the entire teaching profession – are technically *fonctionnaires*. The abortive upheaval of May 1968 can from one angle be seen as an anti-bureaucratic revolt, a bloodless successor to the anti-authoritarian tradition of the Paris Commune nearly a century earlier. The precedent of the Léon Blum Popular Front ministry in 1936 suggests however that even a major leftward electoral shift of power does not necessarily involve fundamental changes in the relationship between the elected government and the civil service, though this is to move unwisely from history to prophecy.[1]

Whereas some of the leading Italian city states had been in the vanguard of administrative progress during the Renaissance, the story of Italian government for a long time after that is one of decline and disintegration or at best of stagnation. Only Venice survived as a genuinely independent republic, after Florence was absorbed into the Grand Duchy of Tuscany, for long a Habsburg client state; in Rome the papal bureaucracy shared with the English monarchy the perhaps dubious distinction of being able to claim the longest continuous institutional history, for example in certain

---

[1] See B. Chapman, *The Prefects and Provincial France* (London, 1955), esp. ch. 1; E. Grégoire, *La Fonction Publique* (Paris, 1954), and 2nd edn *The French Civil Service* (Brussels, 1964); B. Le Clère and V. Wright, *Les Préfets du Second Empire* (Paris, 1973); F. Legendre, *L'Histoire de l'Administration de 1750 à nos jours* (Thémis ser. Paris, 1968), and *L'Administration du XVIIIme siècle à nos jours* (Thèmes et Documents series. Paris, 1969); Nicholas Richardson, *The French Prefectoral Corps 1814–1830* (Cambridge, 1966); J. Siwek-Pouydessau, *Le Corps Préfectoral sous la troisième et la quatrième république* (Paris, 1969); Alan B. Spitzer, 'The Bureaucrat as Proconsul: The Restoration Prefect and the *Police Generale*', *Comparative Studies in Society and History*, VII (The Hague, 1964–5), pp. 371–92; V. Wright, *Le Conseil d'État sous le Second Empire* (Paris, 1972); also art. by C. H. Church, 'The Social Basis of the French central bureaucracy, 1795–1799' in *Past and Present*, no. 36 (1967). And see M. Crozier, *The Bureaucratic Phenomenon* (Chicago, 1964).

unbroken series of records; in the south the Bourbons of Naples–Sicily inherited the remnants of what had been the vigorous Spanish Habsburg administrative system of the sixteenth century.[1] In this, as in other respects, there seems no reason to doubt the traditional view, namely that the French revolutionary and Napoleonic invasions and conquests were the great awakener of modern Italy. If at the political level Italian unification bears strong superficial resemblance to that of Germany, the administrative outcome was very different. This arose from the absorption first of the north, then of all Italy by the ancient mountain kingdom of Savoy. Piedmont, as it had come to be known, thus formed the nucleus of what was on paper a much more centralised state than the Second Reich of Bismarck and Wilhelm II. Historians agree that the beginnings of a national administration in the 1860s saw a process of 'Piedmontisation' in the rest of Italy.[2] Paradoxically, but in a way which has parallels with underprivileged regions elsewhere, by the twentieth century a much higher than random proportion of all Italian civil servants were southerners by origin. Whether because of the initial superimposition of Piedmontese and other northerners on to the existing personnel of government in the other provinces, or more as a consequence of the repeated political compromises and evasions of the entire period from the 1870s to Mussolini's march on Rome, modern Italy has had one of the largest civil services (proportionate to total population) of any major state. Despite the defeat, division, civil war and occupation of 1943–5, there was no really thorough-going 'de-Fascistification' procedure at the lower levels of the public service, comparable to the 'de-Nazification' attempted in postwar Germany (1945–8). And, unlike Germany, Italy has survived the Second World War as a single state. Administrative malaise, including by all accounts widespread corruption, has probably been more of a brake on economic growth and on a sense of social and geographical unity than in any other Western parliamentary-democratic state.

In one respect Britain's case has been peculiar, some would say fortunate. The great era of civil service reforms, which made possible the development of a rational modern administration, alias a Weberian bureaucracy, was spread over nearly a century (c. 1780–c. 1870); above all it substantially preceded the really massive growth in the numbers of officials and in the complexity of government. Of course there were more government employees (excluding the armed forces of the crown) under Gladstone than there had been under the younger Pitt; moreover, in the

[1] See P. Burke, *Tradition and Innovation in Renaissance Italy: A Sociological Approach* (pb. edn London, 1974), ch. 9; H. G. Koenigsberger, *The Government of Sicily under Philip II of Spain* (London, 1951).

[2] The best general account for the period of Cavour and his immediate successors now appears to be G. Candeloro, *Storia dell'Italia moderna*, v, *La costruzione dello Stato unitario* (Milan, 1968), esp. ch. II, sections 2–4, ch. III, section 3, Ch. IV, section 7, and Nota Bibliografica, pp. 426–9. See also R. C. Fried, *The Italian Prefects, A Study in Administrative Politics* (New Haven, Conn., 1963).

period from about 1830 to 1870, there can now be seen to have been much more positive use of administrative means to implement public policies than a superficial reading of Dicey's famous *Law and Public Opinion in England* (1905), and an equation of that whole epoch with doctrinaire *laissez-faire*, had previously suggested.[1] None the less the growth in the costs of government and in the numbers of those in its employment, both at the national and at the local level, only accelerated dramatically at the end of the nineteenth and in the early twentieth century.[2] To many people living in Britain the rate of growth since then has often seemed not merely fast but portentous and deplorable. Excluding the Post Office and nationalised industries, the great question of the later 1970s is whether the total number of civil servants can be kept below three-quarters of a million and perhaps reduced to 700,000. As regards the quality of administration in modern Britain, there have been relatively few serious scandals, involving either dishonesty or 'bureaucratic' highhandedness, while many more of the cases involving corruption have touched local government than the civil service proper. There has, however, since the 1950s been growing dissatisfaction – closely related to dismay at the decline of British economic strength – with the alleged harm done by 'generalists' in the Treasury and elsewhere, instead of the 'specialists' from whom it is asserted the country would have got better value than it has done from the 'apotheosis of the dilettante'.[3]

Whether or not late twentieth-century Britain is an 'over-governed', excessively bureaucratised country, the proportionate growth in numbers of officials and state employees during the last hundred years or so has

[1] The best general account is now H. Parris, *Constitutional Bureaucracy* (London, 1969), esp. chs. VIII and IX; see also G. Sutherland (ed.), *Studies in the growth of nineteenth-century government* (London, 1972), esp. Introduction and chs. I–III; J. R. Torrance, 'Sir George Harrison and the growth of Bureaucracy in the early nineteenth century', *Eng. Hist. Rev.*, vol. 83 (1968); C. R. Middleton, 'The Emergence of Constitutional Bureaucracy in the British Foreign Office', *Public Administration*, vol. 53 (1975); W. L. Guttsman, *The British Political Elite* (Studies in Society, 1st edn, 1963; rev. edns, 1965, 1968), esp. ch. 11. Older works should not be neglected, especially E. W. Cohen, *The Growth of the British Civil Service, 1780–1939* (London, 1941). On a more general level, note Sir Edward Bridges, *Portrait of a Profession* (The Rede Lecture, Cambridge, 1950) and K. C. Wheare, *The Civil Service in the Constitution* (Centenary Lecture. London, 1954).

[2] M. Abramovitz and V. F. Eliasberg, *The Growth of Public Employment in Great Britain* (National Bureau of Economic Research, general series, no. 60. Princeton, New Jersey, 1957); A. T. Peacock and J. Wiseman, *The Growth of Public Expenditure in the United Kingdom* (London, 1961 and later edns); J. Veverka, 'The Growth of Government Expenditure in the United Kingdom since 1790', in *Scottish Jnl. of Pol. Econ.*, vol. I (1963).

[3] See the notorious 'Fulton Report': Report of the Committee, 1966–8, *The Civil Service* (Command 3638, 1968), in which the hand of Sir Harold Wilson's academic protégé, Dr Norman Hunt (now Lord Crowther-Hunt), has been discerned, esp. ch. 1, but note also the admirable reservation by Lord Simey, pp. 101–3; see also Thomas (now Lord) Balogh, 'The Apotheosis of the Dilettante: The Establishment of Mandarins', in H. Thomas (ed.), *The Establishment* (1959) and in Thomas (ed.), *Crisis in the Civil Service* (The Great Society ser., no. 7, 1968). For a balanced response, see Parris, *Constitutional Bureaucracy*, ch. x. On personnel, besides the Fulton Report, vol. 3, see R. K. Kelsall, *Higher Civil Servants in Britain From 1870 to the Present Day* (London, 1955 and 66).

been greater than in most comparable states. But it might well be argued that, compared to Bismarckian Germany, the Third French Republic, even post-Cavourian Italy, later nineteenth-century Britain was distinctly 'under-governed'.

It will hardly be thought that the same could be said of Britain's great rival for empire and influence in Asia during the nineteenth century. The pre-1917 Tsarist empire in Russia is often portrayed as the epitome of a bureaucratic autocracy. Some characteristic features of Western admini- stration had been deliberately imported by Russia's rulers during the seventeenth and eighteenth centuries, especially by Peter the Great (1682– 1725) and Catherine the Great (1762–96). In theory the Russian aristo- cracy, more so even than that of Brandenburg-Prussia under Frederick William I, was a 'service nobility', in which social rank depended on position in the royal administration. But by the nineteenth century it has been shown that there were huge numbers of nobles who at no time had any regular connection with the imperial civil service. Indeed for a country of such vast area and population the Tsarist administration was by no means so enormous as to be totally out of scale with that of other states. Furthermore, the highly unfavourable image of the Russian nineteenth- century bureaucracy is largely the product of novelists and other writers, often *émigrés* critics of the regime. While the Russian government was unquestionably an autocracy, and there was – if only in a semi-Weberian sense – a large bureaucracy, there is more than a touch of propaganda and caricature in the accepted version. More interesting and less easy to answer is the question whether the combination of political and intel- lectual repression with faster economic development, under Stolypin and others in the last phase before 1914, also involved any significant moves towards a more modern, 'rational' bureaucracy. For the Russian empire to have survived as long as it did, and to have endured two major wars and a revolution before its collapse, may suggest that some at least of its administrators were not wholly incompetent and unprofessional.[1]

At first sight 1917 appears to mark a more abrupt and fundamental dis- continuity in the history of Russian administration than 1940–4 does in France, 1943–5 in Italy, or even 1945–8 in Germany. The Marxist- Leninist regime which came to power through the Bolshevik Revolution displayed a marked ambivalence towards professional administration and bureaucracy: almost an example of that 'love–hate' relationship charac- teristic of the whole revolutionary Left in modern times. According to the orthodox Marxist interpretation, all existing administrative systems, and above all that of imperial Russia itself, were part of the political and ideological superstructure of the old order, be that bourgeois capitalist or feudal-autocratic in terms of its economic basis. Whether the pre-

---

[1] H. Seton-Watson, *The Russian Empire 1801–1917* (Oxford History of Modern Europe series. Oxford, 1967) has a useful index entry under 'Bureaucracy'.

revolutionary state was to be destroyed and then recreated, or seized more or less intact and then transformed, proved – once the Revolution has happened – to be a theoretical more than a practical problem.[1] There was a strong libertarian–anarchist element in the early phase of the Revolution. The Anarchists and the Left Social Revolutionaries were a considerable force from 1918 to 1920, and they opposed as étatist and reactionary any tendency towards a centralised administration or a professional civil service in the new socialist commonwealth. Yet at the same time, in the face of attempted White counter-revolution, western intervention in support of this, the chaos and near collapse of agricultural as well as industrial production and of all public services during the Revolution and its aftermath, only strong and often centralising measures could ensure the survival of the regime, indeed of Russia itself as a territorial entity. It remains debatable, but in any case seems of little importance outside left-wing sectarian circles, whether there were substantial differences as to ends first between Trotsky and Lenin, next between Trotsky and the Triumvirs (Stalin and his then allies), or only as to tactics and timing. Certainly in his last years of active life, and particularly in his final speeches, Lenin showed a simultaneous awareness that professional administration was absolutely indispensable, during the stage of socialism that had then been reached and for the foreseeable future, and that there was a real danger of bureaucracy in the pejorative sense, or 'bureaucratism', developing even in a socialist state under the dictatorship of the proletariat (alias the rule of the Communist Party). Ruthless and pragmatic as Lenin was, in this he surely showed himself a constructive statesman, not merely an opportunist trimmer between Mensheviks and Anarchists, or between the different factions within his own Bolshevik party. It remains a matter of biographical and political speculation more than of historical analysis whether, if he had enjoyed another five or ten years of active life, Lenin would have significantly altered the trend of subsequent developments, including that towards increasing bureaucratisation of both state and party. And this is even truer of speculation as to the consequences if, *per impossibile*, Trotsky had defeated Stalin.

As it was, by the late 1920s the development of Soviet bureaucracy is inseparable from the political hegemony of Stalin and his henchmen. By then we can hardly dignify them with the name of allies. Not that we should naively assume a pattern of continuous uninterrupted growth either at this time, or later. Already by the mid-1920s it is possible to discern a large number of survivors from the Tsarist administrative system in office, especially at provincial and technical levels; and the criticisms of bureaucracy, voiced by Lenin and repeated by many others, seem often to have been motivated by dislike of this unavoidable fact and

---

[1] The classic text is of course V. I. Lenin, *State and Revolution*.

fear of its implications. In the later 1920s demands for economies in public spending actually produced temporary reductions in numbers in certain sectors of state employment and administration. After 1929 there is a dearth of easily available, reliable figures.[1] According to official published statistics, there were 1.85 million government personnel in 1925 and only 1.743 million people working in government establishments in 1937. On the other hand, using Molotov's report to the 18th Party Congress in 1939, one Western author arrived at a figure of about 10 million in all branches of the Soviet bureaucracy. But this seems to include virtually all privileged non-manual-working groups in Russian society, and must surely be set aside if the category of bureaucrats is to retain enough precision to be of any use. The fact that proportionately many more of the population are directly dependent on state employment in Russia and other communist states than in the West must be clearly distinguished from the question of whether or not there are proportionately more civil servants or bureaucrats, even if for the communist states we include full-time Trade Union and Party officials among these. Furthermore there is evidence of some reduction in the numbers of administrators having been achieved during the years of Khruschev's supremacy (from the mid-1950s to 1964). Once again the inaccessibility of unpublished archive sources makes western scholars reluctant to accept official Soviet figures at their face values.[2] Indeed until Khruschev's extraordinary anti-Stalinist revelations in his speech at the 20th Party Congress in 1956, the nature, extent and role of bureaucracy was hardly a subject for discussion within the Soviet Union apart from lively criticism of its minor abuses. And, except for the capture of the 'Smolensk archive' by the Germans in 1941 and its consequent transfer to American hands (in 1945) Western scholars have had very little insight into the workings of the administrative system, either centrally or locally. Western studies of the Soviet Union from the 1950s on have mostly been focussed on the Communist Party, the armed force and defence industries, or other sectors of the economy; below the top level there is little about the Soviet civil service, though no one seems to doubt that it is large and influential. The trend during the 1960s and 70s in the Soviet Union itself and in the communist states of eastern Europe, towards greater managerial autonomy, and something nearer to 'market' pricing, may well have altered the balance of power between central

[1] E. H. Carr, *A History of Soviet Russia*, vol. 5, *Socialism in One Country 1924–1926*, vol. 1 (London, 1958), ch. 3; vol. 9 (with D. W. Davies), *Foundations of a Planned Economy 1926–1929*, vol. 2 (London, 1971), ch. 51 and Table 66.

[2] For the period since that covered by Carr's great work, see J. A. Armstrong, *The Soviet Bureaucratic Elite: A Case Study of the Ukrainian Apparatus* (1959); L. G. Churchward, 'Soviet Local Government Today', *Soviet Studies*, XVII (1965–6), pp. 431–52; M. Fainsod, *Smolensk under Soviet Rule* (Cambridge, Mass, 1958), and *How Russia is Ruled* (Russian Research Center Studies, no. 11. Cambridge, Mass.; rev. edn, 1963), esp. ch. 12; Barrington Moore, Jr., *Soviet Politics – The Dilemma of Power: The Role of Ideas in Social Change* (Cambridge, Mass., 1950; rev. pb. edn, New York, 1965), esp. chs. 8 and 12.

planning officials and local or regional planners and managers. Whether there has been any over-all reduction in the size or power of the civil services is less clear. The crucial factor remains that of the role of the Party. As was the case in Nazi Germany, the question is how many administrators, at what levels of seniority and in which branches of the government, are party members; how many are so out of real conviction and commitment, how many more from motives of careerism and conformity? To this extent, studies of the recruitment and composition of the Communist Parties in Russia and eastern Europe are indirectly relevant to a better understanding of the administrative systems and their personnel.

Meanwhile eastern Europe has made one distinctive contribution to communist administration, in the form of the Yugoslav system of self-management. Yugoslavia has also produced the most blistering as well as far-reaching critique of communist bureaucracy, in Milovan Djilas's *The New Class*. Experiment and critique can also be seen abortively in the Czech experiment of 1968, and intermittently in Hungary since 1956, notably in the writings of the repentant Stalinist, latterly in political disgrace, Andras Hegedus. His criticisms of bureaucracy are more in the tradition of Lenin's than are those of Djilas.[1] The central intellectual problem, by no means only of interest to Marxists, is whether social classes can exist without the private ownership of the means of production. If power, control and privilege can define a distinctive class, then it may be thought that the top administrators together with the top party functionaries, the senior managers and officers of the police and armed forces, plus a few privileged intellectuals and publicists can come to constitute what may, according to taste, equally well be called a 'new class' or a 'power élite'. Yet in most modern states, the great majority of administrators at the middle and lower levels, even if they are functionally important, are hardly powerful or privileged. There seems to be some kind of paradox, or misplaced definition here, which political scientists and sociologists have yet to resolve.

By a curious irony, the history of the other super-power of the later twentieth century reveals an ambivalence towards professional administration and bureaucracy comparable to that which can be seen in the case of Soviet Russia. When Britain's American colonies threw off the yoke of British rule in 1775–83, this entailed the destruction of the old, imperial administrative system, although within most of the individual thirteen colonies the Whigs or Patriots captured control of the executive government rather than destroying it. Their revolutionary origins gave the Americans of the early national period (from the 1780s to the 1800s or

[1] Besides M. Djilas, *The New Class: An Analysis of the Communist System* (London, 1957; pb. edn, 1966), see also Djilas, *The Unperfect Society: Beyond the New Class* (London, 1969); Andras Hegedus, *Socialism and Bureaucracy* (London, 1976), and for reference, H. G; Skilling, *The Governments of Communist Eastern Europe* (New York, 1966, and later edns).

1810s) a healthy distaste for established authority and for traditional hierarchy. Under the Articles of Confederation (1777/81–8) the new United States experimented with a constitution almost as decentralised or 'confederal' as that of the United Provinces in the seventeenth century, or of the Swiss cantons until much more recently. Except for *ad hoc* appointments by the Congress (notably that of Robert Morris as wartime Superintendant of Finances, and of course of George Washington as commander-in-chief), the Articles made no provision for an executive arm of government and most categorically not for a civil service; administration was almost exclusively the business of the individual member States. The new federal Constitution, implemented in 1789, altered this decisively, but not at first very obviously or dramatically. The beginnings of an administrative machine, with full-time professional personnel, have rightly been traced back to Washington's Presidency, and ascribed in particular to Alexander Hamilton's tenure of the Treasury Secretaryship. But the federal civil service remained tiny, comparable to that of pre-nineteenth-century Britain or Prussia, until much later; and it was still relatively small for a country of America's size, wealth and population until into the twentieth century. Moreover, until the late nineteenth or even the twentieth century, it was assumed that extensions of the civil service would take the form of additional executive departments under the President and his personally appointed cabinet officers. But in practice much of the most important, and numerically explosive growth, from the 1880s until the 1950s or 1960s, took the form of agencies and commissions created by the Congress, and answerable as much to the legislature as the executive, sometimes more so. The federal character of the US constitution might lead us to expect that proportionately more civil servants would be employed by the individual states, as in Germany under the Weimar constitution (1919–33) and again in West Germany since 1948, with the *Länder* taking this role.

In fact the rate of growth has been much faster at the federal than at the state level, in terms of numbers and expenditure, and comparable to that experienced in other more unitary states during the twentieth century. Parallel to this can be traced the long-drawn out, inconclusive, and perhaps ultimately not very important debate about the 'Spoils System' and the need for civil service reform on the British model, which extended from the 1880s to the 1940s and in a slightly different idiom has been revived more recently. According to the older view, a fairly promising if still 'nascent' federal civil service was debauched and virtually destroyed by the Jacksonians and their successors from 1828 on, through turning the tenure of quite junior as well as senior administrative posts into a political matter dependent on the party ties and obligations of each incoming President. In recent years historians have proved conclusively that a modest element of a spoils system (with some administrative offices changing hands for political reasons after national swings of electoral fortune) went back at least to Jefferson in 1801; that the extent of this was scarcely if at all more sweeping, numerically speaking, under Jackson (in 1829) than it was both earlier and later; furthermore that professionalism, honesty and efficiency were actually strengthened during Jackson's presidency; finally that the campaign for civil service reform from the 1880s involved a strong element of historical myth, and was in part a rationalisation of the nostalgia for a vanished age among Progressives, many of whom belonged to groups whose own status was in decline and and whose admiration for what they conceived to be the superior British system was often misplaced or erroneous. From the 1890s, more especially from the 1910s, and again much more so since 1933, the size, scope and role of the federal civil service has up to a point been an issue between the parties, with first Theodore Roosevelt and latterly the Democrats standing for 'big government' and higher public spending, the orthodox Republicans for economies in public spending, for fewer bureaucrats with less power. Superficially this is analogous with the Labour–Conservative division on the same issue in contemporary Britain. In fact the consequences of two world wars, and almost continuous military preparations since 1945, has probably had more to do with the growth of bureaucracy and public spending in the USA than any nuances of party politics over health, housing, transport, welfare, or communications. Eisenhower's farewell message – surely a conscious imitation of Washington's – in its warning against the possible growth of excessive power in the 'military-industrial complex' – has a prophetic resonance. As elsewhere, adherents of neo-*laissez-faire*, or here the old-fashioned conservative, seem to make common cause with the radical and near Marxist Left, with the obvious likeness to the argument (if this can be so dignified) of C. Wright Mills', *The Power Elite*.[1]

In modern Japan the creation of a Western-style civil service was very much a part of the Meiji Restoration. Ironically, but perhaps not surprisingly, most of its early recruits, like those who moved to the

---

[1] See S. H. Aronson, *Status and Kinship Standards of Selection in the Administrations of John Adams, Thomas Jefferson, and Andrew Jackson* (Cambridge, Mass., 1964); M. A. Crenson, *The Federal Machines Beginnings of Bureaucracy in Jacksonian America* (Baltimore and London, 1975); R. E. Ellis, *The Jeffersonian Crisis Courts and Politics in the Young Republic* (New York, 1971); C. R. Fish, *The Civil Service and the Patronage* (Harvard Historical Studies, XI. Cambridge, Mass, 1904), which is the classic expression of the traditional view; A. Hoogenboom, *Outlawing the Spoils System A History of the Civil Service Reform Movement 1865–1883* (Urbana, Ill., 1961 and 1968); D. H. Rosenbloom, *Federal Service and the Constitution: the Development of the Public Employment Relationship* (Ithaca, New York and London, 1971); L. D. White, *The Federalists* (New York, 1948), *The Jeffersonians* (New York, 1951), and *The Jacksonians* (New York, 1954); P. Wall, *American Bureaucracy* (New York, 1963); J. S. Young, *The Washington Community 1800–1828* (New York, 1966). Even so good a book as R. Kingsley, *Representative Bureaucracy An Interpretation of the British Civil Service* (Yellow Springs, Ohio, 1944) is in parts marred by an uncritical anglophilia, arising from the American civil service reform movement.

commanding heights of the new capitalist industries, were drawn largely from the traditional military, gentry-cum-retainer class, the *samurai*. Japan already had a historic civil service tradition, going back to Chinese influences over a thousand years before. Moreover the successful achievement of isolation from the outside world, combined with relatively peaceful internal conditions (from the mid-seventeenth to the mid-nineteenth century) meant that many *samurai* were already literate; and some had also developed administrative skills in the service of the Tokugawa *shogunate* and the *daimyos* (or major fief-holders). Hence, paradoxically the old order already contained powerful elements favourable to the emergence of the new. Just as Japan has shown far greater capacity for rapid and sustained economic development than any other country of the non-European world, so the Japanese civil service has been less swollen with people for whom there is little or no real work. More specifically, the Japanese adopted a variant of the French prefectural system, which at least until the defeat of 1945 and the consequent American occupation, gave the government of the day a very high degree of control over the localities; a European-style examination system modelled on that of contemporary Germany was instituted in 1887; senior civil servants and politicians were distinguished by legal enforcement in 1899. Yet historians of twentieth-century Japan write of the 'politicisation of the civil service', and of its subsequent role on the whole as a force for moderation, though by no means for radicalism or democracy, from the 1920s to 1940s. It is still too early to say how fundamental a difference in this, as in other vital respects, has been made by the American occupation of 1945–52. The same argument that we find in America and Europe, as to whether bureaucracy can exist in the corporate private sector or only in state employment, is also relevant here.[1]

The administrative history of China in the twentieth century arguably presents the most dramatic and extreme contrasts to be found anywhere in the world. The old imperial system of written, competitive examinations, going back to at least the tenth century A.D. and in some form to before the Christian era, was still operative in the early 1900s. It is true that for a long time before this the recruitment and promotion of the mandarins or 'scholar-gentry' in this manner, to staff the imperial civil service, was little more than a hollow shell. And by 1900 this can scarcely have concealed from anyone the advanced state of social and political decay and

[1] See R. P. Dore, 'Talent and the Social Order in Tokugawa Japan', *Past and Present*, 21 (1962), pp. 60–72; Dore (ed.), *Aspects of Social Change in Modern Japan* (Princeton, 1967); J. K. Fairbank, E. O. Reischauer, A. M. Craig, *East Asia Tradition and Transformation* (London, 1973), chs. 17, 18, 22 and 23; J. A. Harrison (ed.), *Japan: enduring scholarship selected from the Far Eastern Quarterly and the Journal of Asian Studies 1941–1971* (30th anniversary commemoration series, vol. 2. Tucson, Arizona, 1972); E. H. Norman, *Japan's Emergence as a Modern State* (Institute of Pacific Relations, Inquiry series. New York, 1940); E. O. Reischauer, *Japan: Past and Present* (London, 1947); R. Storry, *A History of Modern Japan* (Harmondsworth, Middlesex, 1960), pp. 107–8, 116, 129, 174, 241.

the ever-increasing encroachment of Western administrative influences, as well as of Western technology and imperialist domination. The role of the mandarinate, *alias* the bureaucracy in earlier Chinese history is a compelling topic, regrettably outside the scope of this chapter, but is very properly included in at least one other chapter of the *New Cambridge Modern History*.[1] The period when the Chinese were relatively free to choose for themselves between different Western models and influences was astonishingly brief: in effect only from the first Revolution of 1911 to the Japanese invasion in 1937. It is therefore idle to ask whether or not China's experience could have been more like Japan's, in developing a Western-style civil service and administration. The victory of the Chinese communists over the increasingly corrupt and autocratic version of Western influence found in the last phase of Kuo-min-tang rule, may have been as much a triumph of native 'puritanism' and traditional grass-roots reformism, as a victory of international Marxist–Leninism over Western capitalist imperialism. Facts and figures on developments since 1949 are hard to come by; probably another generation will need to elapse before the kind of questions posed for eastern Europe by such dissident Marxist intellectuals as Djilas and Hegedus can meaningfully be applied in the Chinese context. Since their breach with the Soviet Union in the 1960s one of the claims made by the Chinese and accepted by their Western admirers is that they have succeeded in avoiding the bureaucratic excesses of the Russian system. It has also become something of a cliché to contrast the 'clean' government of China, however hard, not to say harsh and even tyrannical it may be, with the corrupt, or as Gunnar Myrdal calls it the 'soft-state' government of India. Is this a more extreme contrast than those that can be found in the past, for example between the Prussia of Frederick the Great and the France of Louis XV, between the England of James I and the Sweden of Gustavus Adolphus? Finally it may help to understand Mao's motives in the 'cultural revolution', which did so much to dislocate China and to delay its material development, if this is seen as a desperate attempt to prevent the communist party hierarchy from itself developing into a new mandarinate. But such 'instant history' carries many perils, encroaching as it does on journalism and futurology.[2]

In Southern Asia, as in the so-called Third World generally, since independence from European colonial rule patterns of administrative development have emerged which are strongly reminiscent of Europe

[1] J. P. Cooper, ch. I, 'General Introduction', *New Cambridge Modern History*, vol. IV, *The Decline of Spain and the Thirty Years War 1609–48/59* (Cambridge, 1970), pp. 30–4, and refs. given there.

[2] See Fairbank, Reischauer, Craig, *East Asia*, chs. 16, 19, 21, 24–5, 28; C. P. Fitzgerald, *China, A Short Cultural History* (London, 3rd edn, 1961), and *The Birth of Communist China* (Harmondsworth, Middlesex, 1964). My own speculations are based on a study of the imperial bureaucracy from works in Western languages. For a historian who urges the rest of us to abandon the past for the future, see H. Stretton, *Capitalism, Socialism, and the Environment* (Cambridge, 1976).

before the nineteenth century. Not merely the ubiquitous nepotism and corruption but the accelerating proliferation of staff at the lower levels, far in excess of real administrative needs, are strikingly similar to what can be found in the royal courts and central institutions, and among the 'under-officers' of the sixteenth to eighteenth centuries. The 'Euro-centred' historian should be particularly cautious in generalising about the non-European or Third World. We should not assume an undifferentiated sameness everywhere. No doubt there is less corruption, less nepotism, less 'Parkinsonian' growth of numbers, less bureaucratic 'red-tape' in some of the new countries than in others. Whether relative slimness, efficiency and honesty of administration can be correlated either with Japanese-style capitalist development or with the puritanical social ethics of the extreme Left, it is again probably too early to say. Different indigenous conditions and traditions may be as important in producing variations of style and government growth as external factors of ideology and the world economy. Myrdal makes the important point that corruption was reduced to manageable proportions, and defined as criminal, in north-west Europe at a time when the state's functions were minimal by comparison with the mid and later twentieth century. The far more active role of government in economic planning, even in direct management, and every aspect of social welfare, makes this far harder for Third World countries to achieve today. None the less he sees corruption as a pathological symptom, inimical to economic development as to political and social solidarity. In his view reform and the effective eradication of chronic nepotism and corruption must come from initiative at the top and work down. But the effects of a more austere ethic – be it Pietist and Enlightened, as in eighteenth-century Prussia, or Evangelical and Utilitarian as in nineteenth-century Britain, or Puritan and Republican as in mid-seventeenth-century England, or Marxian Communist as in the Soviet Union and the People's Republic of China – can also operate 'upwards' in society, or at least from the middle levels upwards as well as downwards. In the context, chapter 20 of Myrdal's great work should be read in conjunction with Hurstfield's essays and other recent historical works.[1]

[1] For southern Asia, see G. Myrdal, *Asian Drama An Inquiry into the Poverty of Nations* (3 vols, Harmondsworth, Middlesex, 1967), pp. 501–4, 937–58, 1146. For one part of ex-colonial Africa, J.-C. Williame, *Patrimonialism and Political Change in the Congo* (Stanford, Cal., 1972), esp. ch. 7, is suggestive – and cheerfully eclectic in borrowing its theoretical framework from both Marx and Weber. See also J. La Palombara (ed.), *Bureaucracy and Political Development* (Princeton, New Jersey, 1965, 67 and 70). Corruption has produced its own literature. (See (e.g.) Arnold J. Heidenheimer (ed.), *Political Corruption. Readings in Comparative Analysis* (New York, 1970, esp. Pt. 1, ch. 1, nos. 1–7, ch. 2, nos. 8–12, Pt. 2, chs. 4–7, nos. 19–35, Pt. 4, ch. 11, nos. 52, 56; James C. Scott, *Comparative Political Corruption* (Contemporary Comparative Politics ser. Englewood Cliffs, New Jersey, 1972); Ronald Wraith and Edgar Simpkins, *Corruption in Developing Countries* (1963); and for a useful brief exposition, also pre-Myrdal, Colin Leys, 'What is the Problem about Corruption'?, *Journal of Modern African Studies*, vol. 3 (1965), pp. 215–50. For early modern European comparisons, see the works cited in pp. 171–6 above.

4. *The contemporary scene*

The very fact of disagreement as to whether or not bureaucracy can exist in the private sector may seem irrelevant before the twentieth century. It may appear obvious and beyond dispute that only the size and complexity of modern institutions can create the conditions which make bureaucracy possible. Whether the most important distinction is between profit-making, or 'market-orientated', and non-profit-making, or between private and state, or public, institutions, the decisive elements are surely those of numbers, scale and cost of operations, and complexity of organisation.[1] Until at the earliest the later nineteenth century does this not mean, in practice, that we are discussing exclusively governmental institutions, including among these the Roman Catholic and the other larger established Churches? Plausible as this may seem, it is well to consider possible exceptions. The great overseas trading and colonising companies of the seventeenth and eighteenth centuries certainly had central administrative staffs with claims to be called bureaucratic: the English East India Company, the Dutch Vereenigde Oost-Indische Compagnie (the United East India Company), the French *Companie des Indes*, and others, the first-named administering a veritable empire until as late as 1858. The same may well be true of the Bank of Amsterdam and its later equivalents elsewhere; likewise of the Bourse, or stock exchange. The Bank of England is a debatable case, in that it might be classified as an offshoot of the national government, yet one that was still considered to be in need of 'nationalisation' in 1947, and which has often been denounced on the Left for excessive independence of the state since then. By contrast, even the largest universities, colleges, libraries, hospitals, and charitable foundations generally managed their affairs with the minimum of office staff and 'paper-work' until the nineteenth, if not the twentieth century.

In economic activity the decisive change is usually associated with the rise of large industrial and financial corporations and combines. Here, despite England having led the way in the actual process of industrialisation, and despite the Limited Liability Acts of the mid-nineteenth century, the lead was taken by 'big business' in Germany and America during the

---

For a somewhat different view of the relationship between bureaucracy and modernisation, see the immensely stimulating and suggestive work of Barrington Moore, Jr, *Social Origins of Dictatorship and Democracy: Lord and Peasant in the Making of the Modern World* (New York, 1966; pb. edns, Harmondsworth, 1969 and 1973).

[1] That bureaucracy exists in the private as well as in the public sector is assumed by the well-known popularisers, W. H. Whyte, in *The Organisation Man* (New York, 1956), and V. Packard, in *The Status Seekers* (New York, 1959 and London, 1960). In this they follow C. Wright Mills in his *White Collar: The American Middle Classes* (New York, 1951), which despite its somewhat breathless tone is a work of greater intellectual solidity than his later, better-known writings, including *The Power Elite* (New York, 1956). See also the works cited in the first three notes, pp. 165–6 above.

last decades of the century. This in turn may be related to the debate on whether 'ownership' has ceased to count for as much as it did, compared to management and control, in the large modern corporation; whether, regardless of state or private ownership, the managers are now the masters of industry, finance and so of the economy.[1] Whatever the answer to this, it is beyond dispute that the very large private companies, above all the great 'multi-nationals' of the 1960s and after, employ large numbers of office staffs, and proportionately not significantly fewer than are to be found in comparable state-owned industries or public corporations. Comparisons between state and private enterprise can have little meaning unless the industries or other activities concerned involve similar degrees of labour intensity. Such measurements are also difficult when companies have their headquarters in one country and their field operations are spread out over many others. In short, like must be compared with like. And outside the realms of party political propaganda and ideological debate too little of the necessary research has been done and its findings published.

Another area of dramatic administrative growth and alleged bureaucratisation, in the second or Weberian sense, has been that of Trade Unions and professional associations. The American Medical Association has been a sworn enemy of 'socialised medicine' and of public bureaucracy, but it has its own administrative hierarchy just as does the most socialistic European or North American labour union. Political parties too, besides churches and educational and charitable foundations, have developed their corps of professional administrators, supported by secretarial, clerical and other ancillary staffs. Again the student of bureaucracy in modern history must take note of the great theoretical debate about élites and the alleged 'iron law of oligarchies'.[2] To accept this thesis is effectively to assume that bureaucracy in its first sense, as rational, professional, hierarchical administration, necessarily involves bureaucracy in its second, as a system of power, a form of rule, and probably in its

[1] Building on, but also re-interpreting A. A. Berle, Jr, and G. C. Means, *The Modern Corporation and Private Property* (New York, 1932), James Burnham in *The Managerial Revolution* (New York, 1941, and Harmondsworth, Middlesex, 1945) did much to popularise this view. Various of the writings of Thorstein Veblen, Joseph Schumpeter, and Peter Brucker should also be consulted. For balanced modern appraisals, see N. P. Mouzelis, *Organisation and Bureaucracy: An Analysis of Modern Theories* (London, 1967); Crozier, *The Bureaucratic Phenomenon*, and – except for his exclusion of profit-making concerns – Downs, *Inside Bureaucracy* (Boston, 1966 and 1967).

[2] The classic texts include R. Michels, *Political Parties* (English edn, Glencoe, Ill., 1949; pb. edn, New York, 1959); G. Mosca, *The Ruling Class* (New York, 1939); V. Pareto, *The Mind and Society, A Treatise on General Sociology* (4 vols in 2, New York, 1963). Again, the thesis was popularised, as well as rehabilitated by Burnham in *The Machiavellians: Defenders of Freedom* (New York, 1943). Logically, one can of course easily envisage a ruling élite or an oligarchy which is not a bureaucracy; indeed history is full of such groups. But under twentieth-century conditions, it is hard to imagine how such a group could be other than partly bureaucratic, even if it was not composed exclusively or mainly of bureaucrats.

third sense too – at the very least as bumbledom, delay and 'red-tape', at its worst as the downright abuse of power. While rule by officials alone and unchecked is theoretically possible, both in private and in public institutions, as well as in government itself, this seems in its extreme or pure form to be an exceptional phenomenon.

While bureaucratic attitudes, practices and malpractices exist, perhaps more often and on a grander scale in government departments and large state-run enterprises than in smaller private concerns, this must be put into a wider historical context before the student of nineteenth- and twentieth-century history, still more the a-historical social scientist, leaps to general conclusions about oligarchies and élites. Such trends in the modern world must be measured against the extreme inequalities of wealth, privilege, opportunity and power that characterised most human societies, other than the simplest and most primitive, before the eighteenth or nineteenth century. A more optimistic interpretation of modern history is at least equally plausible. For despite the dangers inherent in size, complexity and bureaucratisation, these very developments have been and are a necessary attribute of a richer but also of a freer and a less unequal society than mankind has ever previously known. Those who declaim against the 'establishment' and the old-boy network, against oligarchy and privilege, and simultaneously against organisation and bureaucracy, might be enlightened by a closer study of mankind's pre-industrial past. Of course there were proportionately more self-employed people then, at least in western Europe and North America, than there are today; certainly there was less government, and on balance less bureaucracy, in the public as well as in the private sectors. But to argue from this that our ancestors enjoyed a better life, that they were in any meaningful sense more free, are entirely different propositions, to which negative answers are at least as convincing as positive ones. Moreover, unless it is thought possible for contemporary society to regress to a more primitive and largely mythic past of individualist free enterprise and self-employment, or to advance to an anarcho-communist Utopia, the historian is better employed in describing and analysing bureaucracy as a basic function of modern living than in deploring its advent. In this way, a study of its evolution may help today and in the future, so that it can be refined, reformed, controlled, and where necessary restrained, and put to its proper purposes – of enlarging the opportunities for human choice and self-fulfilment by more people than ever before. Such a functional view of administration is not a complacent one, because by definition it includes the possibility of institutions and their members working badly or – as the sociologists prefer to express it – of their being 'dysfunctional'.

Another area for possible comparisons between different countries and different eras of history relates to the means of investigating and controlling bureaucracy and its real, or supposed abuses. The office of

'Comptroller', found in many branches of English central administration from the later middle ages until the nineteenth century illustrates one method: that of exercising control over officials by internal checks and balances. In theory, if the administration is basically honest, then the office of a Comptroller should become redundant and its holder a sinecurist; alternatively, if the system is fundamentally corrupt, then the appointment of one office-holder to watch over another is – quite literally – no more than 'setting a thief to catch a thief'. Some administrative systems have had distinct and separate institutions to investigate abuses committed by officials, and for dealing both with intra-governmental disputes and with complaints by members of the public against individual officials and government departments. This was true at least under certain Dynasties in the Chinese Empire; a broadly similar machinery existed in the use of the *Residencia* of imperial Spain, and has done in the French *Conseil d'État* of the nineteenth and twentieth centuries; the *Ombudsmen*, or grievances commissioners in twentieth-century Scandinavian states, and since 1969 in Great Britain, play a comparable but more limited role. Elsewhere, the bureaucracy is checked, and when necessary disciplined, through the existence of a separate but parallel party political hierarchy and by the role of party activists in bringing bureaucratic malpractices to book. Such is the case in the Soviet Union, and – presumably – in the People's Republic of China. Special, or *ad hoc* commissions and committees of inquiry, sometimes armed with extraordinary judicial powers have an earlier parallel in the *Visita General* of the Spanish Empire, but have become a particular feature of the Anglo-Saxon countries: Great Britain, the USA, Canada, Australia and New Zealand. Yet the effectiveness of parliamentary or other independent committees and commissions (and latterly of the Ombudsman, alias the Parliamentary Commissioner) may in turn depend on the existence of a free and vigilant press, on the system of parliamentary questions to ministers (or its American equivalent in Congressional Committee hearings), and on the genuine independence of the judiciary. Clearly the effectiveness of any control mechanism which is set in motion from the centre depends on the nature of the constitution. In the United States, corrupt or otherwise unsatisfactory state governments have never to more than a very limited extent been subject to investigation and control from Washington; in this respect, whatever their other differences, centralised states such as Britain and France have more in common with each other, although one profound difference is often said to be that the Anglo-Saxon countries have never known a distinct *droit administratif*, exempting state officials from ordinary legal answerability. To generalise across space and time: no constitutional safeguards, no sets of administrative procedures will provide absolute guarantees against corruption, or the other potential abuses of bureaucracy – high-handedness, delay, indecision, *'paperasserie'* or red-tape, and worse.

History suggests that it has sometimes been the attitude and the intervention of the ruler or rulers and their immediate circle of top advisers and ministers, that are decisive in determining the quality and character of the administration as a whole. Sometimes this has owed more to the ethos of a section of the population, usually an élite, whether one determined by race, class or function, or one defined by ideology (church or party). But most often, particularly in the plural societies of the modern West, more has been due to a widely diffused, if vaguely defined public opinion.

It would be facile, and also for many of the world's inhabitants past, present and future, downright unjust, to say that every society gets the kind of bureaucracy it deserves. Very often a dedicated élite of experts and professionals has known best what has needed to be done. But this is not the same thing as getting it done in the most humane and expeditious way. Nor does it make such an élite exempt from the potentially corrupting effects of unchecked power, or obviate the need for the means of investigation and control. Even if the student of administrative history does not want to go the whole way with Acton, the dictum that all power *tends* to corrupt is – to say the least – not easy to refute.

Is the immensely greater scale of bureaucracy, with the vastly bigger numbers of civil servants or officials throughout the world, therefore to be seen as a temporary phenomenon peculiar to the twentieth century, as the culmination of a much longer-term historical trend, or perhaps only as one stage in such a process?[1] It is tempting to echo the fashionable, fundamentally conservative dictum, *Plus ça change, plus c'est la même chose.* Some would go further and descry a cyclical rhythm in history where swollen, over-inflated bureaucracies are associated with declining states or even civilisations. But it may be well to remember one of the dichotomies or antitheses suggested earlier in this essay: the distinction between the tasks expected of an administration and its members, and its actual social role. On the one hand there are the needs and commitments associated with defence, security, law and order, taxation, production, welfare, education, culture, and so forth. The great expansion of bureaucracy in the nineteenth and twentieth centuries may indeed be seen as a consequence of other changes in modern society: industrialisation, urbanisation, labour-saving technology, and higher living standards, as well as the greater complexity of life. But if the extent of bureaucracy were the simple outcome of these changes, we should expect to find a direct correlation between the proportionate size and cost of administrations and the level of wealth and development in different countries. And plainly this is not so. Other political and social variables must also be involved. In addition to

---

[1] The best general accounts of the recent period that I have found are F. Morstein Marx, *The Administrative State: An Introduction to Bureaucracy* (Chicago, 1957); and Jacoby, *Bureaucratization of the World* (see p. 166, n. 1 above). See too the brief but trenchant remarks of F. H. Hinsley in ch. 1, 'Introduction', *New Cambridge Modern History*, vol. XI, *Material Progress and World-Wide Problems 1870–1898* (Cambridge, 1962), pp. 17–25.

considering the tasks of government, account must be taken of the scope which such employment affords for increasing either social mobility or stratification, for ethnic, territorial and cultural integration or its reverse – racial, regional or social disintegration. A very tentative contrast may be suggested between bureaucracies according to whether their chief historical importance has been positive or negative – for what they did or for what they afforded opportunity for being done; put another way, whether they are to be thought of as having acted upon, or as having been acted upon, in relation to the societies to which they belonged. From this perspective there are at least some points of comparability between the bureaucracies of the period from the Renaissance to the French and Industrial Revolutions and those of the twentieth century. But the differences are at least equally striking and perhaps even more fundamental in character. In so far as comparative history has a chronological as well as a spatial dimension, there is a very real danger in making comparisons, even in drawing contrasts, between phenomena and situations whose historical context as a whole is too dissimilar. Government by bureaus or rather by their members, rational and hierarchical methods of administration by professional, full-time, paid officials, 'red-tape' with all its delays, high-handednesses and other frustrations – each of the three main meanings of the term Bureaucracy can be found to have some applicability at widely differing times in history, indeed far earlier than the starting point of the *New Cambridge Modern History*. Each definition, however, assumes its own distinct significance in different historical contexts. The greater the other differences – technological, economic, social, political, religious, cultural – the more forced any such comparisons are liable to become, even when there appear to be genuine points of likeness through the centuries and across the millenia.

Table 2. *Total population, and numbers of officials, or non-industrial civil servants*
(in different countries at selected dates)

	Date	Population	Officials
Prussia	1750	3 m	3,000
	1786/7	4.75 m (or 5.8 m*)	6–8,000
	1800	6–7 m	23,000
	1815	10–11 m	
	1850/60	18 m	25,000
Germany	1910/11	58.5 m	250,000
France	1665	18 + m	46,000 (*officiers*; may have excluded the lowest levels)
	1871	36.1 m	220,000
	1956	43.3 m	570,000
England and Wales	17th century	5 m	5–10,000
UK	1850	22.3 m	16,000
	1911/12	50.3 m	71,000†
	1950	50.3 m	325,000
	1955	51 m	382,000
	1977	56 m (est.)	746,000
Italy	1857 (8 states)	25.46 m	
	1859 (8 states; teachers excluded)		*c.* 59,000
	1937	*c.* 42 m	484,000
	1954	48 m	833,000
Russian Empire	1897	*c.* 116 m	147,000‡
USSR	1926/7	147 m	2,329,000 or 597,000§
	1937		1.743 m
	1939	170 m	
	1950		1.831 m
	1953		13.8% of workforce engaged in admin.
	1956	200 m	
	1962/3		9% of workforce (1.308 m)
USA	1900	75.9 m	100,000
	1950	150.7 m	2,000,000
Japan	1908/10	*c.* 48 m	72,000
	1938/9	*c.* 70 m	450,000

* The lower figure is for Prussia proper, the higher for all Frederick the Great's territories.
† The twentieth-century British figures exclude Post Office employees. The UK of course includes the whole of Ireland in 1911/12, only Northern Ireland since 1922.
‡ Above a certain grade only; gross total unknown.
§ The larger figure covers all non-military, non-industrial state-employed persons, the lower relates to administrative and judicial personnel only.

All totals, so far as possible, exclude members of the armed forces (but not of the police), and industrial personnel (of state industries, etc.). The extent to which local and provincial officials are included varies unavoidably. Even using a combination of official and unofficial published sources, it is very difficult to arrive at consistent, reliable figures.

Table 3. *Government employees as a percentage of total population* (in different countries at selected dates)

(a) *The UK and the USA compared in the twentieth century*

Government employees, excluding defence, as a percentage of population:

		UK		USA	
1900/1		UK	2.57	USA	1.68
1950			6.53		5.0

Government employees, excluding defence, the Post Office, and teachers, as a percentage of the total employed population:

		UK		USA	
1900/1		UK	1.6	USA	2.00
1950			6.4		5.4

Even here, it is hard to be confident about the strict comparability of the figures.

(b) *France and the USA compared, seventeenth–twentieth centuries*

	France	USA
1665	1 *officier* per 400 inhabitants	
1839	1 *fonctionnaire* per 261 inhabitants	
1870	1 *fonctionnaire* per 165 inhabitants	1 civil servant per 128 inhabitants
1900		1 civil servant per 68 inhabitants
1914	1 *fonctionnaire* per 85 inhabitants	1 civil servant per 54 inhabitants

(Legendre, *L'Histoire de l'A. ninistration* (see p. 181, n. 1), p. 531, no sources given. Are the American proportions higher because of the inclusion of teachers? Otherwise it is hard to believe that the same categories are being measured.)

I am grateful to the following for bibliographical suggestions: the Editor of this volume, Dr Peter Biller, Professors Bernard Crick, Richard Dunn, Norman Hampson, Dr Paul Ginsborg, Professor A. G. Hopkins, Mr H. W. Koch, Professor Paul Streeten; to colleagues and students who took part in the comparative course on 'Bureaucracy and Social Structure' at York from 1966 to 1971; and to British Petroleum Ltd, Esso International Inc., the National Coal Board, Shell Transport and Trading Co. Ltd, and Unilever Ltd, for responding to enquiries and providing information. The notes to this chapter are only meant to indicate some of the works which I have found useful, and are in no way a substitute for a formal bibliography.

CHAPTER VII

WARFARE

1. *The Renaissance, 1450–1530*

PART of the charm of Renaissance writers is their firm conviction that they were living in a 'golden age'. Their world was bigger and better than anything in the past and, they sometimes reflected, the heroes of antiquity would have been miserable failures as Renaissance men, even as Renaissance soldiers. 'We must confesse', wrote Sir Roger Williams, an English general of the later sixteenth century, 'Alexander, Caesar, Scipio, and Haniball, to be the worthiest and famoust warriers that euer were; notwithstanding, assure your selfe, ...they would neuer haue...conquered Countries so easilie, had they been fortified as Germanie, France, and the Low Countries, with others, haue been since their daies.'[1] We may smile at this characteristic Renaissance hyperbole, but in the field of warfare at least it was fully justified: the military realities of the sixteenth century were indeed far more complex and far more daunting than those of the Classical (or any previous) Age.

European warfare was transformed between 1450 and 1530 by a number of basic changes. First came the improved fortifications of which Sir Roger Williams wrote, linked to the introduction of powerful new artillery. An entirely new type of defensive fortification appeared in Italy in the later fifteenth century: the *trace italienne*, a circuit of low, thick walls punctuated by quadrilateral bastions. The development of large siege-cannon – made of cast-iron from the 1380s and of bronze from the 1420s – rendered the high, thin walls of the Middle Ages quite indefensible. A brief cannonade from the 'bombards' brought them crashing down. The reason why the kingdom of Granada fell to the Christians so easily in the 1480s, when it had resisted successfully for seven centuries, lay in the fact that Ferdinand and Isabella were able to bring a train of almost 180 siege-guns against the Moorish strongholds. The English possessions in France were likewise reconquered in the 1430s and 1440s largely by Charles VII's artillery; at Castillon in 1453, the big guns even won a battle. The initiative in warfare now lay with the aggressor, and, not surprisingly, by 1500 every major European state possessed a powerful artillery park for use against its neighbours or against its dissident subjects. Military architects in Italy, where siege-warfare was most common, experimented with new techniques of fortification which might withstand shelling, and the bastion defence evolved there between about 1450 and about 1525. It revolutionised

---

[1] *The works of Sir Roger Williams*, ed. J. X. Evans (Oxford, 1972), p. 33 (from *A briefe discourse of warre*, 1590).

the entire pattern of warfare because it soon became clear that a town protected by the *trace italienne* could not be captured by the traditional methods of artillery battery and mass infantry assault. It had to be laboriously encircled, usually with elaborate siege-works, and starved into surrender. The French military writer Fourquevaux declared in 1548 that towns whose fortifications were more than thirty years old (that is, which were built before the age of bastions) hardly deserved to be called fortifications at all.[1] There was therefore a scramble among the great powers to build the new 'miracle' defences wherever a risk of attack existed: in Lombardy, in Hungary, in the Low Countries and elsewhere. As it happened these areas were all large plains, what Fernand Braudel has called 'continental islands', where a few great towns dominated the countryside. Whoever controlled the towns controlled the countryside; and therefore in all these areas war became a struggle for strongholds, a series of protracted sieges. Battles were often irrelevant in these areas unless they helped to determine the outcome of a siege. Even total victory on the field did not necessarily compel the well-defended towns to surrender: they could continue to resist, as did St. Quentin after the famous battle of 1557, or as the towns of Holland and Zealand were to do after 1572, either until they were starved into submission or until the enemy gave up through exhaustion. Thanks to the bastion, defence became superior to offence in many areas of Europe.

In naval warfare the development of artillery also brought about crucial changes. Heavy bronze guns could deliver a broadside which would smash through the decks, rigging and crew of enemy ships. In the states of Europe which bordered on the Atlantic, specialised warships were built which were designed to include the maximum number of guns. The first purpose-built warship was constructed in England in 1513 and by the 1540s ships were carrying guns as heavy and as powerful as any they would carry until the age of steam. The Spanish Armada of 1588 even carried a train of fifty-pounder bronze guns, as well as a full range of other ordnance. In all, the 130 ships in the Grand Fleet carried 2,431 guns of all sizes. The only surviving warship of this period – the Swedish *Vasa*, which sank shortly after launching in 1628 – had a displacement of around 1,300 tons and carried sixty-four bronze cannon on two gun-decks. In the Mediterranean, too, fighting ships were equipped with increasing quantities of ordnance. Whereas the Venetian galleys of the fifteenth century carried but a single 'bombard', the Christian galleys at the battle of Lepanto (1571) each carried a fifty-pounder, two twelve-pounder, two six-pounder and six lighter cannon. Gradually artillery bombardment replaced ramming and boarding as the standard tactic in European naval warfare.

Other sorts of firearms became important in Europe during the Renais-

[1] *The 'Instructions sur le faict de la guerre' of Raymond de Beccarie de Pavie, sieur de Fourquevaux*, ed. G. Dickinson (London, 1954), p. 85.

sance. Very slowly, hand-guns which fired a smaller shot were developed. The Hussites had used a primitive form of arquebus in the 1420s, but this innovation was not adopted by other armies until the end of the century. From the 1550s a much larger hand-gun, the musket, was introduced: fired from a forked rest, it could kill a man at 300 paces. Such killing power was a great improvement – as the arquebus had not been – on the bow and arrow: the archer still achieved a more rapid rate of fire than the musketeer, but his effective range was less. More important, a good archer required a lifetime of training to produce the required stamina and accuracy whereas the musketeer could be trained in a week. There was therefore no limit upon the number of musketeers who could be recruited at short notice and sent into action. The same was true of the other major type of foot-soldiers in the armies of Renaissance Europe: the pikemen.

For most of the Middle Ages, the principal arm in any military force was the heavy cavalry, made up of fully armed knights on horseback, three hundredweight of mounted metal apiece, moving at speed. The knights were clumsy, expensive, and scarce: but they were capable of winning great victories: Antioch (1098), Bouvines (1214), and Roosbeke (1382), for example. There were also, however, disastrous defeats, especially in the fourteenth and fifteenth centuries, when it was discovered that a heavy cavalry charge could regularly be stopped either by volleys of arrows or by a forest of pikes. Later it was found that pikemen could be used offensively to charge other groups of pikemen, once the mounted knights had been impaled and disposed of. The victories of the Swiss infantry against Charles the Rash of Burgundy in the 1470s wrote the lesson large, and in the Italian wars the infantry component in every army became steadily more numerous and more decisive. Charles VIII's army in 1494 comprised about 18,000 men, half of them cavalry; Francis I's army in 1525 comprised some 30,000 men, one-fifth of them cavalry. The number of horsemen had decreased both absolutely and relatively. This shift in emphasis from horse to foot was crucial for army size. Whereas there was a limit to the number of knights who could manage to equip themselves and their horses ready for a charge, there was none to the number of ordinary men who could be enlisted and issued a pike, sword, and helmet. A pikeman's basic equipment cost little more than his wages for a week, and in some cases even this paltry sum could be deducted from the soldier's pay.

These innovations in warfare by land and sea were deeply significant. In effect they established the parameters of European warfare for almost three centuries: there was to be no further technological advance of comparable magnitude until the nineteenth century. The invention of the mortar (by the Dutch in the 1580s), of the light field-gun (by the Swedes in the 1620s), of the flintlock musket (in the 1630s) and of the socket bayonet (in the 1670s) were merely refinements of the existing art of war. All the major military problems were now concerned with adapting to the new technology and producing the new weapons in sufficient quantities to achieve success. Between 1530 and 1790, the really important military changes in early modern Europe were connected with quantity, not quality. Warfare during this period altered not so much in techniques as in scale.

2. *The Age of 'Military Revolution', 1530–1790*

The dominant feature of warfare in Europe between the early sixteenth and the early eighteenth century was the persistent and substantial increase in the size of armies and navies. Whereas there was only one English warship in 1513 and only forty in 1640, by 1652 there were eighty-five (one carrying 100 guns and eighteen mounting over 40 guns) and in 1665 there were 160 warships (weighing, in all, 100,000 tons and carrying 5,000 guns and 25,000 seamen). The Dutch Republic maintained a fleet which was almost as great and the major encounters of the Anglo-Dutch wars of the later seventeenth century involved two 'grand fleets', stretched out for between five and ten miles in line ahead, pounding each other for days on end until a decision was reached. The French fleet, too, was extremely large and throughout the period 1660–1815 the three Atlantic states of the north-west struggled to increase the tonnage, gun-strength and size of their navies. There was, however, little further increase in the number of ships or in the method of their construction or use.

A parallel development characterised the 'hardware' of land warfare between the sixteenth and the eighteenth centuries. Bastioned fortifications of increasing complexity – concentric rings, star-shape forts with ravelins and hornworks – were erected around the principal strategic targets in response to the steady increase in the use of artillery for sieges. When the Dutch laid siege to 's Hertogenbosch in 1601 they brought with them only twenty-two cannon (the siege failed); in 1629 they collected 116 (the town has been Dutch ever since). At the siege of Grol (Groenlo) in 1595 the Dutch besiegers had only sixteen guns, and only fourteen in 1597, but in 1627 they had eighty. There was a similar increase in the number of musketeers and the number of field-guns attached to every army. The Swedish army of Gustavus Adolphus was victorious in Germany during the Thirty Years War at least in part because it enjoyed unequalled artillery support. Even more, however, the Swedes won because they were more numerous. A shrewd Spanish general, who had spent several years in war-torn Germany, observed in 1632 that:

I have seen by experience in Germany that who ever has the larger army will win. This proved to be the case most recently at the battle of the Breitenfeld where the army of Tilly was composed of veteran troops who did all that was humanly possible; and yet the king of Sweden emerged victorious because he had more men and because he had a battery of 150 field guns.[1]

[1] Bibliothèque royale, Brussels, Manuscrit 16147–8, fos. 103v–4, Marquis of Aytona to Count-Duke of Olivares, 8 February 1632.

Table 4. *European army sizes, 1470–1760*

Date (circa)	Spanish Monarchy	Dutch Republic	France	England	Sweden	Russia
1475	20,000	—	40,000	25,000	—	—
1555	150,000	—	50,000	20,000	—	—
1595	200,000	20,000	80,000	30,000	15,000	—
1635	300,000	50,000	150,000	—	45,000	35,000
1655	100,000	—	100,000	70,000	70,000	—
1675	70,000	110,000	120,000	15,000	63,000	130,000
1705	50,000	100,000	400,000	87,000	100,000	170,000
1760	98,000	36,000	247,000	199,000	85,000	146,000

SOURCE: G. Parker, 'The "Military Revolution, 1560–1660" – a myth?', *Journal of Modern History*, XLVIII (1976), p. 206; and Lloyd's *Lists of the forces of the states of Europe* (London, 1761).

As Table 4 shows, there was a prodigious increase in the number of troops raised in Europe in the two centuries following 1530. What does not appear so clearly is that the number of troops permanently retained by the various European states in peacetime also grew significantly. The standing army was not new in the eighteenth century, when most governments decided to maintain one. Professional standing armies, regularly mustered, organised into small units of standard size with uniform armament and quartered sometimes in specially-constructed barracks, were maintained by many Italian states in the fifteenth century. Other states were not slow to follow. The kings of Spain kept 10,000 trained men as a permanent garrison in their Italian dominions from 1535 onwards, using them to form the core of every military undertaking from the campaigns against the Turks in the Mediterranean to the duke of Alva's march to the Netherlands in 1567 and the intervention in the Bohemian revolt in 1619–20. In the 1570s the Austrian Habsburgs introduced a similar permanent organisation for their armies along the Hungarian and Croatian border with the Ottoman Empire. In the 1660s even England began to support a standing army (of about 6,000 men, with a further 3,000 men in Scotland and 7,000 in Ireland) to guarantee national defence and internal order. Each of these permanent armies, from Sicily to Scotland and from Ireland to Russia, required a separate network of military institutions and ancillary services: military treasuries, judicial courts, medical care (sometimes involving special teaching hospitals and permanent mobile field-surgery units) and a chaplaincy service besides the more obvious secretarial, quartermaster and victualling arrangements. The demand for more intensive military administration was a powerful stimulus to bureaucratic growth in Europe.

The growth in army and navy size came to an end in the eighteenth century. Even military expenditure stabilised – the annual cost of the

Seven Years War (1756–63) to Prussia, for example, was almost the same as the annual cost of fighting the armies of the French Revolution in the 1790s. The explanation for this relative stagnation appears to be that the various European states had reached the limits of their economic and financial capacity. They could neither produce nor maintain more men, more ships or more weapons. The existence of a material threshold of this sort had long been apparent. In 1588, for example, both the Spanish Armada and the English ships opposing them ran out of powder and shot, and England was only saved by the use of fireships which broke up the Spanish fleet; likewise in 1653 a duel between the Dutch and English navies off Portland Bill ended because the Dutch ran out of ammunition. The problem was not technical but economic: sixteenth-century gun-founders knew how to make cannon which were just as effective as those of their eighteenth-century successors, but neither group could call on adequate funds to manufacture sufficient quantities to overwhelm all opposition. Until the Industrial Revolution, ordnance offices were unable to mass-produce even the basic equipment required by all fighting units: most armies contained regiments which had less firearms and fewer pikes than their total combat strength. Stockpiling in years of peace and standardisation of the weapons issued (begun by the Dutch in 1599) went some way towards alleviating the problem, but still there were never enough arms to go round. Raising troops was far cheaper than equipping them – one could maintain two soldiers for a month with the cost of a single musket and a whole regiment could be raised for the cost of founding a cannon – and governments felt safer investing their money in men rather than in munitions. And even recruiting was not easy.

Few early modern states managed to operate a conscription system for long. Russia appears to have been the only country to succeed in creating a permanent draft (in 1705). The earlier Swedish *indelningsverk*, established in the 1620s and creating twenty-three infantry regiments, was only used during wartime. Most states until 1790 chose to rely on a variety of alternatives. First, and most important, came voluntary enlistment: the government offered to employ as soldiers any able-bodied men who chose to join up. When this failed, there was always the press-gang, especially for the navy (in 1653, the crimps in London were ordered to take anyone they could get 'if necessary taking men in bed from the side of their wives'). Armies might be reinforced in the same way, or by drafting in members of the militia (a technique used frequently in France). However, the most common method of supplementing native voluntary levies was to recruit foreigners to serve as mercenaries.

The presence of substantial bodies of foreign troops in the armies of almost every early modern state was perhaps their most distinctive feature. Spanish armies normally contained a majority of non-Spanish soldiers (Netherlanders, Germans and Italians were preferred); French armies throughout early modern times usually included a large contingent, often up to a third, of German and Swiss levies; British forces abroad in the eighteenth century were normally reinforced by Germans. There were several reasons for this cosmopolitanism: sometimes foreign troops were better trained; sometimes they had a better reputation for reliability; sometimes it was considered important to prevent a rival government from making use of them. In 1748, the maréchal de Saxe, Louis XV's general, noted that: 'A German in the army serves us as three soldiers: he spares France one, he deprives our enemies of one, and he serves us as one.'[1] The fact that the army thus produced was a jumble of different nationalities, none of them at home in the theatre of operations, was not considered to be a disadvantage: indeed it was seen as a strength. Experience showed that the military effectiveness of most troops tended to increase as they moved away from their homeland. No one placed a high military value on soldiers recruited locally, since desertion was too easy and the risk of defection greater. 'The principal strength of this army is its foreign troops', wrote the commander-in-chief of the Spanish army of Flanders in 1595. 'There is no surer strength than that of foreign soldiers' echoed his successor in 1630, adding the following year: 'At the moment no war can be fought in these provinces except with the foreign units because the local troops disintegrate at once.'[2]

Troops from abroad, however, were rarely recruited at random. The German troops who fought for Britain after 1714 either came from Hanover, the state ruled by the kings of Britain until 1837, or from states long allied with Hanover. The foreign troops in Spain's armies likewise came either from other dominions of the Spanish Habsburgs or from states ruled by their relatives. Moreover, the troops normally came from families with a tradition of service in a given army, or else they were recruited by a professional troop-raiser (or 'military enterpriser') who was permanently in the pay of a particular state and responsible to it for the quality and loyalty of his men. Governments which failed to control their troop-raising in these ways normally regretted their oversight. In 1573, for example, King John III of Sweden recruited a regiment of 3,500 Scots for service against Russia in Estonia. After less than one year's service they fell out with the German mercenaries who made up the rest of the Swedish army and some 1,500 Scots were massacred. The rest were hastily dismissed and the senior officers were arrested and charged with treason. One of them was executed, another died in prison.[3] As the Thirty Years

---

[1] A. Corvisier, *L'Armée française de la fin du XVIIe siècle au ministère de Choiseul. Le soldat*, I (Paris, 1964), p. 260.

[2] Quotations from G. Parker, *The Army of Flanders and the Spanish Road, 1567–1659: the logistics of Spanish victory and defeat in the Low Countries' Wars* (Cambridge, 1972), p. 30.

[3] For further details see J. Dow, *Ruthven's army in Sweden and Estonia* (Stockholm, 1965). Despite this unfortunate event, there were still some 500 Scots officers in the Swedish army in the 1620s and after.

War was to show, in early modern times the simple employer–employee nexus was an insufficient bond to control the allegiance of fighting men.

The reason for this failure takes us to the central military problem of the early modern state: money. Most states recruited more troops than they could afford, and in a long war the soldiers' wages began to lag months and (in a few cases) years in arrears. The result was mutiny. The Spanish army in the Netherlands, continuously mobilised from 1567 onwards, was paralysed by more than forty-one mutinies between 1589 and 1607, many of them involving several thousand veterans whose total wage arrears might amount to 1 million florins (or £100,000 sterling). The Parliamentary army during the English Civil War, although solid in its support for the 'Good Old Cause', nevertheless mutinied several times in 1647–9 when pay fell some months in arrears. Things improved in the 1650s, but only because the government of the Republic strained every financial muscle to provide funds for the army. In most years, state expenditure on the army and navy reached £2.5 million, while non-military expenditure came to under £200,000. The early modern state was fast becoming a military institution in its own right. Most governments spent 50 per cent of their budgets on military items in wartime, and this figure could occasionally rise to far more. In 1705 Peter the Great of Russia applied 96 per cent of his revenues to war; in subsequent years the average was between 80 and 85 per cent. And still this was not enough. Although Peter's armies defeated the Swedes decisively at Poltava in 1709, they were surrounded in their turn and made to sign a degrading surrender by the Turks (on the banks of the river Prut) in 1711.

The lack of money to pay for unlimited war was undoubtedly the critical restraint on military developments before 1800. In the words of an English adviser to the Dutch Republic during their war with Spain: 'The matter of greatest difficulty [in war]...is in proportioning the charge of the warres and the nombers of the souldiers to be maynteyned with the contribucions and meanes of the countreys.'[1] It was, above all else, the financial resources of a state which held down the size of its armed forces. If too many troops were engaged, or if they were engaged for too long, mutiny and bankruptcy resulted.

There were still wars which could be fought relatively cheaply, however, using small bodies of picked men operating almost independently as guerrilla bands. Indeed small-scale encounters between picked troops had always accompanied the major operations of the great armies. Most of the memorable 'actions' in the Low Countries' wars between 1572 and the 1590s were minor affairs in which courage and experience counted for far more than technology and armament, partly because the terrain (with so many marshes, estuaries and canals) made regular campaigns difficult. In

---

[1] Thomas Wilkes, 'Declaration' of 22 July 1587, in *Correspondentie van Robert Dudley, graaf van Leycester*, ed. H. Brugmans, II (Utrecht, 1931), p. 402.

the north of Europe, too, nature inhibited adoption of the 'new warfare':
in 1656 the entire Swedish army in Finland had to be trained to operate on
skis in order to defend their positions against Russian attack.[1] Outside
Europe, regular troops were hardly used at all until the eighteenth
century. In America, the Spanish conquerors found that after they had
destroyed the established Inca and Aztec empires in pitched battles, the
smaller tribes were unwilling to fight formal engagements (because it was
obvious that they would lose them!). The 'Indian wars' therefore developed into a prolonged guerilla action and one local commander, Don
Bernardo de Vargas Machuca, wrote the first European manual of
guerrilla warfare in 1599 to explain how to control a country with the aid
of bands of twenty-five to thirty men, highly trained in the techniques of
survival and counter-insurgency in jungle conditions. Not for nothing did
one Spanish commentator refer to the war in Chile in the early seventeenth
century as 'the Flanders of the Indies', while another called it 'a chase, a
great chase for deer'.[2] As late as 1775, on the eve of the American War of
Independence, there were some who favoured guerrilla action against the
British, waging a 'popular war of mass resistance' rather than raising
soldiers to be 'servilely kept to the European Plan'. Similar views prevailed
among Europeans in Asia. An officer in the British East India Company
expressed the opinion in 1756 that troops intended for service in the sub-
continent 'require no exercise but to be perfectly acquainted with the use
of their arms, that is to load quick and hit the Mark, and for Military
Discipline but this one rule: if they are attacked by French and Indians to
rush to all parts from where their fire comes'.[3] It was a far cry from the
neat lines and squares of Marlborough or Wellington; but times were
changing. Wars in which a handful of Europeans presided over a conflict
between rival native Asian, African or 'Indian' armies – and reaped the
fruits of victory – were over. In future, battles would be fought by a
European – or European-trained – army on the one hand, armed with
mass-produced effective weapons, and a native horde on the other,
equipped with grossly inferior arms. The first of the 'modern' confronta-
tions was Napoleon's invasion of Egypt in 1798–9. This event also began
Europe's serious cultural penetration of the Arab world: Napoleon
brought with him a printing-press (the first to reach Egypt), a team of
scientists (to study Egyptian history and natural history) and a group of
engineers (to design a canal to link the Mediterranean with the Red Sea).

[1] J. T. Lappalainen, *Elämää Suomen sotaväessä Kaarle X Kustaan aikana* (Life in the
Finnish army in the reign of Charles X: Jyväskylä, 1975), pp. 84 and 211 (French résumé).
[2] A. Jara, *Guerre et société au Chili: essai de sociologie coloniale* (Paris, 1961), pp. 18 and
141; B. de Vargas Machuca, *Milicia de las Indias* (Madrid, 1599).
[3] J. Shy, *A people numerous and armed: reflections on the military struggle for American
independence* (Oxford, 1976), p. 155; P. Paret, 'Colonial experience and European military
reform at the end of the eighteenth century', *Bulletin of the Institute of Historical Research*,
XXXVII (1964), p. 47.

But the Arabs were not impressed by these things: their respect for the New Europe was won by Napoleon's military power alone, based on weight of numbers and above all on superior technology.

3. *The Age of Revolution, 1790–1848*

The size of European armies between 1792 and 1815 dramatically increased over all previous levels. Where Villars had led a French army of 100,000 at the battle of Denain in 1710, and the maréchal de Saxe had commanded 80,000 men in the field during the campaign of 1760, Napoleon invaded Russia with 550,000 men in 1812. Around 2 million men passed through the French army between 1700 and 1763; but almost the same number were called up during the single decade 1805–15 (of whom almost half, 900,000 men, died in service). In order to combat this 'nation in arms', France's enemies were compelled to increase their armed forces: Britain's army, for example, numbered 45,000 in 1793 but 211,276 in 1815 and between these two dates some 793,000 men were recruited (of whom 219,000 died in service).

Curiously, these gargantuan bodies did not fight in ways that were significantly different from those of their immediate predecessors. The armament and tactics of Wellington's troops in the Peninsular War, and even at Waterloo, differed little from those of Marlborough a century before: men with smooth-bore muskets and bayonets, drawn up in thin lines or squares, stood their ground against the charges of cavalry or infantry phalanx alike. Wellington's adversaries, the French, did of course operate in a new way – attacking in columns with bayonets – but it is easy to exaggerate the novelty of French tactics after 1790. The victories of the armies of the Revolution owed far more to simple numerical superiority at the moment of battle, a superiority produced by a better strategic grasp than that of their enemies. The French campaign armies were divided into divisions (and later into army corps) which could operate independently but which could concentrate when need arose. At Jena (1806), for example, Napoleon managed to destroy the Prussian army by concentrating 80,000 men against 43,000 through his superior strategy; his tactics – demoralising the Prussians with his sharpshooters and finally decimating them by column attacks and close artillery support – were of secondary importance once a numerical superiority of almost two-to-one had been achieved. The victory was then maximised by French diplomatic skill which isolated the defeated power and secured a separate peace which left Prussia's allies fatally exposed.

Although not revolutionary in the tactical or strategic sense, the Napoleonic wars nevertheless produced some profound military changes apart from the increases in military size. Above all they established war as a matter which was too serious to be left to the care of non-specialists.

British schoolboys are taught that George II was the last British monarch to lead his troops into battle; it was the same elsewhere. Heads of state who did not, like Napoleon, rise to power through their control of the army, no longer directed battles and campaigns in person in the nineteenth century. Armies and navies became professionalised to an unprecedented degree and strategy, too, became more streamlined and more openly aggressive. Officers now had to submit to a rigorous programme of training at Staff Colleges (Sandhurst for Britain from 1802, St Cyr for France from 1808, Berlin for Prussia from 1810); soldiers were now conscripted into the army by most states and were subjected to prolonged military service before joining the regular army; military policies were now judged by the standard of Napoleonic decisiveness and anything which fell short of total victory was held to be a failure. It was the same in warfare at sea: the 'Nelson touch', which was supposed to bring complete victory in any encounter, became the sole test of success or failure.

The larger countries of nineteenth-century Europe therefore began to build up a large professional army which was kept separate from society in general (mainly by means of the barracks which were constructed in most major towns along the frontiers of each state). Perhaps the new trends in warfare were best exemplified in Prussia. The Prussian state had suffered serious damage at the hands of the French and it was therefore more responsive to the lessons of the revolutionary period. The army law of 1814 created a regular force manned by conscripts serving for three years; after that they spent another two years as part of the militia (*Landwehr*). The officers of the militia were merely local landowners, but the officers of the regular army, although aristocrats, were trained at the *Kriegsakademie* in Berlin. There was, at the centre of the military machine, a General Staff which co-ordinated and directed military operations over the whole state. After 1860 this system was reorganised: the period of conscription was extended (three years with the colours, four with the reserve – which was equal to the seven years now served by French conscripts) and the reserve and the militia were brought under the control of the regular army and the General Staff. The entire state was divided into army corps districts, each responsible for mobilising and equipping its own troops in an emergency, and the General Staff ensured that the various units were deployed according to a single plan.

In 1864, using its new system, the Prussian army defeated Denmark; in 1866 it routed Austria; and in 1870–1, with 1,200,000 men mobilised, it crushed France and occupied Paris. This remarkable performance, which reinforced the myth of 'Napoleonic decisiveness' as the only valid yardstick in warfare, led almost all the other states of Europe to emulate Prussian military organisation. Only Britain hesitated, but her failures in the South African war forced even her to create a General Staff in 1904.

These Prussian victories, however, were not the result of administrative reform alone. The actual battles which her armies won were decided to a large extent by superior technology: by the railways which moved Prussian troops more rapidly to the front than those of her enemies; by the breech-loading rifle which allowed the Prussian infantryman to fire from the safety of a prostrate position; by the telegraph system which allowed the General Staff to communicate with and to co-ordinate their forces, although so much larger than previous armies, simultaneously and instantly. The Industrial Revolution had far more impact on European warfare than the French Revolution.

4. *War and The Industrial Revolution, 1848–1975*

Prussia was the first state to see the military application of certain technological advances. The first and most important innovation of the Industrial Revolution was the steam-engine, perfected in England in the 1760s. In the 1820s it was successfully applied to locomotion, with Stephenson's *Rocket*, and in the 1830s it was successfully applied to navigation with Brunel's *Great Western*. On land, the new invention was almost immediately used for military purposes: the railways of almost every continental state, led by Prussia, were laid out according to the dictates of national defence so that troops could be moved to anticipated fronts in the minimum time. Experiments were carried out to see how long it took to move a body of troops over a given distance. At sea, steamships swiftly took over from sailing ships in navies as in merchant fleets. A second important technological innovation which was immediately used for war was the perfection of steel-founding. Steel was immediately used for armaments and particularly for armour-plating: warships were now clad in steel, making possible dramatic increases in the size of ships (the average European warship in 1800 was only 2,000 tons; the average in 1900 was 20,000 tons). On land, cannon were now made of steel, with improved protection and enhanced fire-power. There was a third important change: the metal cartridge with percussion cap was invented in the 1840s, making it unnecessary to handle powder and shot separately; then in 1862 the cartridges were first placed on a belt and harnessed to a machine-gun capable of rapid fire (the Gatling gun). These technological advances – unlike those of the seventeenth and eighteenth centuries – were of lasting importance. Machine-guns continue to play a central role in all conventional fighting, using metal cartridges very similar to those designed over a century ago; the steamship remained central to naval strategy until after the Second World War; and as late as 1941 the railway could win wars: without the transportation of highly trained forces from Manchuria to Moscow, across the Trans-Siberian railway, Stalin's capital would have fallen to the Germans and with it, perhaps, the structure of Soviet power would have collapsed.

Unlike the technological improvements of the Renaissance, the advances associated with the Industrial Revolution created a new and highly significant preoccupation among military planners: the need to avoid technical backwardness. Numerous disasters over the years illustrated the consequences of failing to keep abreast of the latest developments: at sea, in 1853, one of the last fleets of wooden ships, belonging to Turkey, was completely destroyed by Russian ironclads at the battle of Sinope; in 1905 the ironclad Russian fleet itself was totally destroyed by the superior armament of the Japanese navy at the battle of Tsushima. On land, the lesson of the Prussian victories of 1864–71 was clear, and France hastened to copy the rifles, cannon and telegraph system which had been used to defeat her.

Nevertheless, we must not overestimate the speed or the eagerness with which each technological advance was implemented in the nineteenth century. The forces of conservatism were strong and even a country which made an invention might fail to develop it, as France failed to develop the submarine after the successful prototypes built by Goubet and Zédé in the 1880s (using electrical power). One of the strangest stories concerned the breech-loading Dreyse rifle which did so much to bring about Germany's victory over France in 1870–1. In 1840 the Prussian government ordered 60,000 of the new 'needle-guns', but they proved unpopular with the army: the troops objected that the bolt action did not *look* like the traditional hammer, and moreover the gun overheated and smelled obnoxious when fired. The High Command objected that the 'needle-gun' was less accurate than the French alternative (the Minié rifle, which did have the traditional hammer) and that the Dreyse cartridges were so heavy that a soldier could only carry sixty of them at a time. The crucial advantage of the weapon – that it could fire five rounds a minute to the Minié's one-and-a-half – was seen as a drawback by the High Command because it merely encouraged the infantryman to waste his ammunition faster! In the end it would seem that the Prussian government retained the needle-gun mainly to avoid admitting that it had made a mistake which would be costly to put right.[1]

The Prussian victory in 1871, achieved by superior armaments and greatest numbers, set the stage for a new phase of military history. Governments in Europe now became fearful of two military developments: that their enemies might develop a 'secret weapon'; and that they might use their power to assemble an army which in numbers and equipment was far superior to any possible opposition. Thus began the cripplingly expensive 'arms race' which is still with us today. Governments now had the financial and economic capacity first to devise new and better armaments and then to produce them on a scale which, if used, would overcome

[1] Information from D. E. Schowalter, 'Infantry weapons, infantry tactics and the armies of Germany, 1849–64', *European Studies Review*, IV (1974), pp. 119–40.

Table 5. *European army sizes, 1870–1944*

Date	Germany	France	Great Britain	Russia
1870	1,200,000	454,000	345,000	716,000
1900	524,000	715,000	624,000	1,162,000
1914	3,400,000	1,000,000	650,000	2,000,000
1929	115,000	666,000	443,000	570,000
1937	766,000	825,000	645,000	1,324,000
1944	9,125,000	—	4,500,000	5,500,000

SOURCE: P. Q. Wright, *A study of war*, II (Chicago, 1942), pp. 670–1; M. Howard, *War in European history* (Oxford, 1976).

any enemy. At sea, this meant producing more and more 'Dreadnought' and 'Super-Dreadnought' class battleships: at the Spithead review of 1897, for Queen Victoria's Golden Jubilee, 165 modern fighting ships of all kinds were on display to the world. On land, more and more heavy guns and rifles were manufactured, and stockpiled, in the belief that numerical superiority in artillery and small arms would prove decisive in the next war. France in particular, having lost a large quantity of munitions as well as her military prestige in 1870–1, began a programme of massive rearmament. Government expenditure on war materials in 1875–84 averaged 70 million francs a year, ten times the annual average for the decade 1855–64. The total stock of steel artillery rose from 1,229 pieces in 1887 to 12,664 pieces in 1886; 3.8 million Gras rifles (using a metal instead of a paper cartridge for the first time in France) were manufactured between 1874 and 1886, and then a similarly ambitious production programme was undertaken for the Lebel rifle. Expenditure on armaments represented 2 per cent of the French budget from 1820 to 1870, rising to 3.5 per cent in the 1880s, 5 per cent in the 1900s and 5.5 per cent in 1913.[1]

At the same time as this increase in the stock of war materials, there were efforts to enlarge the number of troops at the disposal of each state after 1850. The increases shown in Table 5 were fuelled by conscription (even in Britain between 1916 and 1918 and between 1939 and 1945) and, where national service already existed, by increasing its duration. Everything was done to prepare for a war because it was believed that – like the wars of 1864–71 and the Russo-Japanese war of 1904–5 – any major conflict would be short and decisive. A state which was not ready when hostilities began would be destroyed almost immediately. Curiously enough, even the First World War, which lasted for more than four years, failed to discredit the 'over by Christmas' view of modern war. Even in

[1] Figures from F. Crouzet, 'Recherches sur la production d'armements en France, 1815–1913' in *Conjoncture économique, structures sociales. Hommage à Ernest Labrousse*, ed. F Braudel (Paris, 1974), pp. 287–318.

1939 the Axis powers anticipated a short and decisive conflict. Until January 1942 the German economy was organised to support a short war in which 'armament in width' was required, not 'armament in depth'. For the *blitzkrieg* against England, planes and landing craft were produced *en masse*; for the *blitzkrieg* against Russia, production was switched to tanks and armoured cars. Moreover, this system worked very well: spectacular victories were won and there was no undue pressure on the German economy – consumer expenditure in 1942 was more or less the same, allowing for inflation, as it had been in 1937. Only when the Russians recaptured Rostov in December 1941, proving that the *blitzkrieg* had failed, did the *Rüstung 1942* decree ordain the reorganisation of the German economy to support total war on more than one front for a long period. Guns took over from butter and German armaments production more than tripled between January 1942 and July 1944: tank production rose six-fold; aircraft, weapons and ammunition output rose three-fold.[1]

It was not really until the autumn of 1944 that Germany gave priority to a different method of winning the war: the secret weapon. Until 1914, there was little resort to surprise weapons by the great powers, largely because the leading arms-manufacturers of the main European states supplied several armies with identical equipment. The growing use of steel in gun-founding and ship-building after 1860 had broken the monopoly of the state ordnance factories and allowed private industry to appropriate an increasing share of armaments production. Such firms tended to accept orders wherever they could find them. In 1900 the French Schneider corporation was supplying guns to twenty-three different countries; the German firm of Krupp and the British firm of Vickers supplied only a few less.

After the First World War, however, the rapid advances in scientific knowledge, particularly in physics, led governments to attach a permanent scientific staff to their armed forces in order to apply technological discoveries to military ends. In Germany the 'scientific advisers' produced magnetic mines (which in 1939 almost crippled Britain by destroying hundreds of ships until the 'secret' of de-gaussing was discovered); in Britain the scientists devised radar (which in 1940 foiled the German strategic bombing offensive). As the Second World War dragged on, the search for new weapons naturally accelerated. Germany, conscious that her enemies could always produce a far greater quantity of weapons, aimed at qualitative superiority: the 'Ferdinand' tank, the jet-engined 'zero' fighter, the v1 and v2 rockets. It was, as it happened, not enough: by October 1943 the Russians alone had 5.5 million soldiers, 8,400 tanks (many of them the new su 122 and su 152 models), and 20,770 field guns committed on the eastern front against 2.5 million German soldiers with only 2,304 tanks and 8,037 guns. At this point, it has been observed, the

[1] See A. S. Milward, *The German economy at war* (London, 1965).

Germans were already beaten in the east 'strategically, tactically and numerically'.[1] Only a 'secret weapon' of the destructive force of the atomic bomb could have compensated for such massive inferiority in conventional weapons, and by May 1945 the Germans still did not possess such a weapon (although they were well on the way to doing so). In August 1945 it was the allies who used an atomic bomb, twice, to compel Japan to surrender to them, even though Japanese forces in the field were still far from totally defeated.

The shift to a warfare which is based increasingly on advanced technology has had numerous important effects. First, although the number of fighting men maintained by the great powers has decreased, the cost of war has grown. The cost of the 'secret weapons' in the Second World War was one reason for the delay in using them: one German v2 rocket cost as much as six fighters, and even a fighter cost as much as the basic equipment of an entire infantry regiment. The *per capita* military costs paid by the taxpayers of the major European states rose from an annual 95p in 1870 to £2.30 in 1914, to £12.50 in 1937 and to £100 in 1963. Nor did the costs of war stop here: material destruction caused by armed conflict also increased enormously. It has been estimated that between 1600 and 1945, war was directly responsible for the death of some 54 million military personnel, of whom 16.4 million (30 per cent) died in the two world wars of the twentieth century alone.[2] Even if the exact figures are incorrect, the proportions are plausible. Moreover, the heavy military mortality of the twentieth century has occurred in spite of dramatic improvements in medical care. The pattern of United States war dead is fairly typical:[3]

Table 6. *US army annual war deaths per 100 soldiers*

	Battle	Disease	Total
Mexican War, 1846–8	1.5	11	12.5
Civil War (Union), 1861–5	3.3	6.5	9.8
Spanish War, 1898	0.5	2.6	3.1
First World War, 1917–18	5.3	1.9	7.2

The material costs of war were by no means confined to armies and navies, of course. From the eighteenth century onwards, wars were waged less for the control of towns and provinces and more for the destruction of enemy resources. Harnessing industrial production to military effort intensified the means of destruction, especially with the development of the 'bomber' which could drop high explosives on to strategic targets far away from the

[1] M. Arnold-Foster, *The World at War* (London, 1973), p. 148, citing the *Documentensammlung Jacobsen* of Darmstadt.

[2] L. S. Stavrianos, *The world since 1500: a global history* (3rd edn, Englewood Cliffs, New Jersey, 1975), p. 73, citing *The world population situation in 1970* (United Nations Organisation, 1973).   [3] P. Q. Wright, *A study of war*, I (Chicago, 1942), p. 243, n. 63.

fighting line. The social impact of the bomber is reflected in the fact that, whereas 95 per cent of the casualties in the First World War were military personnel, the figure for the Second World War was only 52 per cent.[1] The rest were civilians.

The increasing reliance on technology to win wars increased civilian involvement in armed conflict in other ways. It is significant that hardly any of the major technical advances – tanks, airplanes, radar and so on – were made by military personnel. After 1918 much important military work was shifted out of the military professions and given to civilian departments, universities and scientific research centres. Even a crucial and permanent activity such as decoding enemy military messages was entrusted to civilians. During the Second World War the British Intelligence Centre at Bletchley was the home of a team of linguists and academics, very few of whom had seen any active service. Nevertheless they intercepted and decoded a formidable volume of communications between the various units of the axis armies, providing the allied ground forces with crucial advance warning of enemy movements and enemy intentions. There can be no doubt that the work of the cryptographers at Bletchley played an important part in allied victory. And yet such civilian involvement in war could bring problems. The Bletchley Centre, for example, discovered in 1941 that some of its intelligence reports, although correct and relevant, were being disregarded by the field commanders: they were simply not believed, because the officers in the front line were unaware of the original source of the information and the situation only improved when senior officers in the field were told that allied intelligence was able to decode almost every message transmitted by the Germans. Since then, civilian control of warfare has grown with every advance in technology, and with it civilian–military friction has become a major problem. The soldier has become more suspicious as he is required to handle weapons of ever greater complexity.

And yet there remains one sphere of military action where the individual fighting man still reigns supreme: guerrilla activities. After the defeat of Napoleon in 1815, the *jäger* or *chasseur* units which had grown up to fight guerrilla actions in the eighteenth century tended to disappear. The wars of the nineteenth century were too fast, those of the early twentieth century too slow for guerrilla groups to thrive. However during the Second World War the existence of extensive occupied territories, both in Europe and in the Far East, permitted the growth of sophisticated 'resistance' groups who were trained to attack the occupying forces, and were equipped by the allied powers. As the war proceeded, both in Europe and Asia these groups became committed to communism and, under the direction of leaders such as Mao Tse Tung and Ho Chi Minh, they used their resources

[1] A. Corvisier, 'La mort du soldat depuis la fin du Moyen Age', *Revue Historique*, 1975, p. 13.

to influence the political settlement which would follow the war. In Asia, the governments which were restored by the allies in South East Asia in 1945 have now almost all been destroyed by the descendants of the 'resistance' groups. Guerrilla warfare also survived at sea in the twentieth century. The classic privateer of the industrial age is the submarine, operating alone below the surface of the sea, destroying enemy vessels in much the same way as John Paul Jones, Jean Bart and the Buccaneers (except that the submarine commanders have no interest in plundering the cargoes or ransoming the crews of their victims).

At a basic level, therefore, the structure of warfare in the twentieth century has not really changed from the traditional tripartite pattern of earlier times. The Industrial Revolution has transformed the means employed in each form of conflict; but the aims of those different forms are scarcely changed. First, at present, comes the enormous nuclear stocks of NATO and the Warsaw Pact. These are essentially a deterrent to would-be aggressors. Nuclear arms play much the same role today as bastions in the sixteenth and seventeenth centuries and the Maginot line in the 1930s: they cannot be used offensively, but they warn potential enemies that any attack would be costly and, ultimately, unsuccessful. Neither bastions nor nuclear weapons can be used to achieve those political aims which, from time to time, states conceive against their neighbours or, perhaps, against groups of their subjects. It was and is therefore necessary to possess armed forces equipped with conventional weapons: pike and sword in the age of the Reformation, musket and bayonet in the age of Enlightenment, tanks and bombers in the nuclear age. The peasant revolts of seventeenth-century France, the Paris commune and the 1956 Hungarian rising were all suppressed by liberal use of these conventional weapons, as if a regular war were being fought. Whether for use against foreign aggression or internal opposition, moreover, the scale of military preparedness is unprecedented. In 1959 the United States, in addition to its formidable domestic forces, maintained over 1,400 foreign military bases, 275 of them major ones, in thirty-one different countries. Finally comes 'irregular warfare'. The roving brigand bands and 'free companies' of the Hundred Years War are the ancestors of the 'Irish Republican Army' and the 'Palestine Liberation Army', drawing their manpower from those who have left regular army service or who cannot thrive in civilian life, and using conventional weapons either supplied by friendly foreign powers or stolen from the occupying forces. Their success depends upon the support of the local population, for without local support they cannot disappear between 'terrorist' acts. War and politics are inseparable both at the top and at the bottom of the military spectrum, throughout the long period surveyed in this essay. This should not surprise us. Industrial power may have transformed the world of man, but it has scarcely changed his nature.

SELECT BIBLIOGRAPHY

The outstanding recent survey of war is Michael Howard, *War in European History* (Oxford, 1976), which may be read with pleasure and profit by anyone. There are also useful general surveys in most volumes of the *New Cambridge Modern History*.

On Renaissance warfare, the recent study of M. E. Mallett, *Mercenaries and their masters: warfare in Renaissance Italy* (London, 1974) is informative and enjoyable, but it does not replace two older works: P. Pieri, *La crisi militare italiana nel rinascimento* (2nd edn, Turin, 1952), and M. Hobohm, *Machiavellis Renaissance der Kriegskunst* (2 vols., Berlin, 1913).

The idea of a military revolution was advanced by M. Roberts, *The 'Military Revolution', 1560–1660* (Belfast, 1956; reprinted in a slightly amended form in M. Roberts, *Essays in Swedish History* (London, 1967), pp. 195–225). It has been challenged by G. Parker, 'The "Military Revolution" – a myth?', *Journal of Modern History*, XLVIII (1976), pp. 195–214. There are a number of studies of individual armies during early modern times, of which the outstanding one is undoubtedly that of Louis XV's armies by A. Corvisier (see note 1, p. 207 above). Others not mentioned in the notes but possessing special merit are: F. Redlich, *The German military enterpriser and his workforce* (2 vols., Wiesbaden, 1964); H. J. Webb, *Elizabethan military science: the books and the practice* (Wisconsin, 1965); and J. W. Wijn, *Het krijgswezen in den tijd van Prins Maurits* (Utrecht, 1934).

On the armies of the revolutionary era, there are many books and articles. Any selection would be invidious. However, particular value may be attached to J. Shy's collection of essays (see note 3, p. 209 above); P. Paret, *Yorck and the era of Prussian Reform, 1807–1815* (Princeton, 1966); R. Glover, *Peninsular preparation: the reform of the British Army, 1795–1809* (Cambridge, 1963); and (on a rather narrower front, but one of exceptional interest), J. Houdaille, 'Pertes de l'armée de terre sous le premier Empire', *Population*, année 1972, pp. 27–50.

The literature on modern war is yet more voluminous, making any selection even more idiosyncratic. However a useful starting-point is S. E. Finer, 'State and nation-building in Europe: the role of the military', in C. Tilly, ed., *The formation of national states in western Europe* (Princeton, 1975), and there is a first-rate bibliography in T. Ropp, *War in the Modern World* (Duke University, 1959).

CHAPTER VIII

REVOLUTION

'REVOLUTION' in its fullest sense should mean a vital transformation of society, something far beyond any ordinary shaking-up, a decisive transfer of power both political and economic. This can happen very seldom. But Europe has known many lesser eruptions, resembling it in some measure. Overt class conflict has been only occasional, disharmony among classes or social groups has been ubiquitous, and in all these collisions its presence can be traced. They have been of many species; and with Europe's always uneven development growing more and more uneven, forms of revolt belonging to distinct stages of history might be going on in different regions at the same time.

Europe's mutability must be traced to fundamental features of its make-up. Underlying them has been its duality, the discordant nature it derived from its Roman-Christian and Germanic-feudal ancestry. Both strands made for close interweaving of state and society, in most of Asia joined by mechanical, external clamps. Both gave rise to a wealth of political or politically relevant institutions of all kinds, which forces of change could work on and through, even if often obstructed by them. In Europe also, unlike most of Asia, many autonomous polities packed close together meant that exterior factors were always liable to intensify internal frictions.

In medieval times movements of revolt included those of peasants against landowners, towns against lords, urban workers against employers in centres of nascent capitalism, peoples against foreign domination. Most strident of all was the example set by the dominant class itself, the feudal lords. It could take opposite forms, one that might be called 'constitutional', the other, in times of ruling-class disintegration, anarchic faction fighting. All these types of rebellion continued into the sixteenth and seventeenth centuries, forming new combinations and sometimes reaching higher levels; this entire era of transition may be termed a single protracted revolution, whose outcome varied from region to region. At the bottom of it was the struggle between the masses, chiefly agricultural, and the upper classes living at their expense and bent on depriving them of what betterment they had gained, a good deal through the lucky accident of the Black Death, by reimposing old burdens or devising fresh ones.

Political and social confusion, before the state could be built up anew, gave opportunity for prolonged though scattered resistance, all the way across Europe. Great peasant revolts broke out in turn, early in the modern epoch before reorganisation of the propertied forces had got too far: in Hungary in 1514, in Germany in 1524–5, in Croatia in 1573. As in China's peasant risings, there was an admixture of other social elements, which served as catalyst and might furnish some guidance. Most rebels were trying to defend their small possessions or rights, as peasants or artisans; among some of the dispossessed, and a few idealists, there might be a primitive socialist idea of goods or poverty shared. They were all defeated. Lack of combination was still more marked among the masses than among their superiors. They were weakened by their own numbers, growing afresh and bringing increased pressure on the land and further stratification among the tillers. In Germany these received some, but inadequate, reinforcement from the urban poor; in Valencia in 1520–2 the *Germania* or Brotherhood of the urban lower classes drew too little backing from a countryside where Christian and Morisco were at odds.

Bloodthirsty and massive repression made for quiescence in subsequent times. So, more permanently, did the rise of new state-forms, holding out at times some small protection to the peasant, though protection he had to pay dearly for, but steadily tilting the balance of power in favour of the privileged classes by improved military organisation. In France even during the civil wars, in Germany during the Thirty Years War, mutiny could flare up again in the villages only rarely and briefly. But although the revolt of the masses was subdued, it was not without some share in the long-term remodelling of Europe, if in the oblique fashion that has most often marked their contribution to history. Their aspirations found expression, so far as they had any distinct ideology, in Anabaptism, which, persecuted and driven underground, still helped to push northern Europe into the Reformation. Cramped and half-hearted though this was by comparison, it was nevertheless a kind of revolution, opening the road – if again in very roundabout style – to all later progress. One consequence of schism was to lend a sanction to rebellion, since a ruler who attacked the true faith could be deemed a tyrant, and forfeited his claim to obedience.

Even the boldest were chary of recognising a right of disobedience in the common people. Althusius was one political theorist who grudgingly admitted it, but he like most others much preferred to leave the right to the 'ephors', the magistrates, spokesmen in other words of solid men of substance.[1] Fear of social upheaval persisted, and hastened the reconstruction of state power. Three main types of monarchical government were developing. One was the Muscovite, a semi-Asiatic despotism based on a new service-nobility; the others corresponded more or less with the Protestant and Catholic territories, though like their churches they had much in common. In the northern area more survived of the old 'Estates monarchy': the propertied classes were represented, with a degree of vitality proportionate to their own, by provincial or national assemblies.

[1] *The Politics of Johannes Althusius*, ed. F. S. Carney (London, 1964), pp. 186–7, 190.

Southward the 'absolute' monarchy was freeing itself in the course of the sixteenth and seventeenth centuries from the restraint of such bodies, and expanding its civil and military machinery far more rapidly. Once established it would prove very difficult to get rid of, or even modify. By contrast the 'northern' state, looser and less heavily equipped, was more prone to change, revolutionary change though this might be. Attempted revolt anywhere might be bedevilled by foreign meddling; on the other hand rebels might receive encouragement and aid from abroad. Moreover the swelling armies and their chronic wars were undisciplined and unpopular, and instead of bolstering order sometimes helped to disrupt it, while their cost was enough to plunge the richest treasury into bankruptcy.

In general, class conflict in its elemental shape of poor against rich was being relegated to the eastern realms where feudal reaction was going furthest and reducing the cultivators to complete serfdom; principally to the Russian borderlands where there was most room to fight it out. Western countries were moving towards more complex crises, social strife inter-mixed with political and ideological issues. One was the Revolt of the Comuneros in 1520-1.[1] Urban patriciates were protesting against official encroachments; dislike of taxation brought in the humbler citizenry, who had little or no share in the management of their towns; and they were joined by a good many noble *frondeurs* and churchmen with one motive or another for dissatisfaction. A way forward was what Castile required, but too little political initiative could be mustered, too many supporters wanted to go backward instead. There was no true capital city, and the disturbance remained bottled up in the north. While the leadership fumbled, the commonalty grew self-assertive and obstreperous. There was a riot of wool-carders and other plebeians at Segovia; at Valladolid a democratic committee wielded power in the streets; unrest spread to some of the feudal estates. Before long the united front against an absentee king was breaking up, the nobility changing sides, the wealthier townsmen losing heart; the movement fizzled out.

Some of the same ingredients could be found in the French broils after 1562, complicated by religious hatreds and regional jealousies. Monarchy and old church kept the upper hand in the capital and its surrounding provinces; the opposition drew most of its strength from frontier areas, less advanced and only half assimilated, with a character and traditions of their own. What should have been the leading social forces were split, because many from the middling or upper-middle strata had been drawn off into government service or a rentier existence, as well as by creed and locality. Once the sword was drawn, the Huguenot urban section was overshadowed by the military, men of the gentry class for whose restless energies and hungry wants the Italian wars had provided a safety-valve until the peace of 1559. It was something like an anticipation of the reliance

[1] See H. L. Seaver, *The Great Revolt in Castile (1520-1)* (London, 1929).

of weak progressive movements in later days on army support, as in Spain.

Also as often later, Catholicism had more success in enlisting popular allegiance, at any rate in some of the towns, Paris above all: the countryside was indifferent, having nothing to gain or lose. Paris however got out of hand, as Valladolid had done, and radical-democratic demands mingled with religious fanaticism. During the long-drawn contest there were stirrings of constitutional theory in both camps, as one or the other faced the prospect of having to live under hostile sway; each in turn was ready to endorse limitations on monarchical power. But the destructiveness of the wars, foreign intervention, fear of the plebs taking the bit between its teeth, compounded by symptoms of rural revolt, made sensible men end by agreeing that order and prosperity could only be looked for under a restored and still more authoritarian crown and bureaucracy. The States general, which had shown occasional signs of reviving and taking the lead, expired.

Even in Muscovy during the Time of Troubles about the close of the sixteenth century it might seem as if the Zemski Sobor was coming to the fore. But it was no more than a recent creation of the tsars, unlike the far older assemblies of central and western Europe, and the most active party in it was the service-gentry whose grand aim was the final enserfment of the refractory peasantry. There were moments when runagate serfs, free Cossacks from the borderlands, disgruntled small fief-holders of the south, and factious boyars, could be found jostling together in the same rebel army; but nothing could keep them together for long.[1] Here as in several other countries the dying out of an old dynasty had been the signal for grievances of every kind to boil over; a new one was found, and within a few decades the autocracy was firmer and more rigid than ever.

By taking advantage of the troubles to invade Russia the Poles had stirred up a fever of patriotism, or xenophobia dyed with religion. National consciousness was awakening in many corners of Europe, in its initial forms, and could borrow from and in turn fortify all other turbulent passions. One of the first, and one of the few successful struggles for independence was the Swedish breakaway from Denmark in the 1520s. This was at least in part the divorce of a relatively egalitarian society from a feudal monarchy, and brought on the scene an authentic nation with much internal development as well as external expansion in store for it. Irish resistance to English conquest was more primitive; Ireland had never been a State, and had no national organs. Much the same can be said of the last Morisco rising of 1568 in southern Spain, likewise fiercely religious.

It was typical of revolts both national and social in being provoked by intensified pressure from above. In the next reign but one Olivares embarked under stress of war on a programme of further central control and stiffer taxation of the non-Castilian provinces of Iberia. Out of this

[1] See P. Avrich, *Russian Rebels 1600–1800* (London, 1973).

came in 1640 the rebellions of Catalonia and Portugal. Both of these had preserved their own institutions, which were unlikely to initiate defiance but, once this was afoot, could give it some leadership, usually poor, and respectability in the eyes of the higher classes and (always important) the church, and seek to keep the people within bounds. In Catalonia, with more commercial stir and bustle than Portugal, and a peasantry which for centuries had shown readiness to fight against oppression, this was less easy; jarring social interests fanned the agitation, but also fostered disagreements.

Sicilian and Neapolitan insurrections in 1647 were aimed more directly against native oppressors than against Spanish rule: Madrid paid the penalty for a colonial policy based on patronage of the aristocracy, but it was able to recover control because the classes were incapable of uniting against it. In the Neapolitan case however there were signs of rural and urban poor joining forces. This was a menace seldom encountered; in the neighbouring Papal States, for example, endemic disorder and brigandage in the countryside never swelled into serious revolt, because Rome, a city of prelates and prostitutes, could supply no inspiration or aid as Naples on occasion could. Altogether the cluster of revolutionary movements about mid-seventeenth century was very much the result of economic decay accompanied by the political and military running down of Spain, which had made itself the policeman of Europe. While the Spanish Habsburgs went downhill the Habsburgs of Vienna were still endeavouring to plant themselves firmly. They had already got the better of their own Austrian subjects and of the Bohemians, whose joint disaffection ended in the fiasco of 1620 because the nobility was disunited and hesitant, the burgher estate enfeebled, and the peasantry, reduced to serfdom by its masters, had nothing to hope for from following them.

In some restricted areas of Europe a more sweeping transformation was being prepared by obscure economic currents and their social and intellectual concomitants. In sum this meant that while the rural masses were being pushed down, some propertied groups were evolving towards a more modern pattern. There are no pure classes in history, any more than pure races, and any 'class' is partly an ideal concept or abstraction. But out of a medley of social fragments, few of them clearly demarcated, there was a gradual drawing apart of two contrasted classes, or congeries: an aristocracy, with the court for rallying-point, 'neo-feudal' by comparison with its forerunners, and a bourgeoisie, still more distinct from the old burgherdom.

This entity, hard to define, was manifestly different from anything that had gone before in Europe, or ever emerged in old Asia. It was a nation-wide body, in place of the mosaic bits of one that the citizenry of scattered towns had represented. Its hallmark was an economic composition shifting in the direction of capital involved in production. Wealth derived from finance, trade, colonial booty, could be fairly well accommodated within the social and political order as reconstituted after the late medieval breakdown. More indigestible, and in the long run far more significant, was industrial capitalism, which in the Middle Ages had made only small sporadic beginnings. Now it was growing from above, as merchant capital for instance connected with maritime trade turned to ship-building or ship-owning, or encouraged investment in them by others; and at the same time from below, among the petty commodity producers, artisan or peasant, as newer conditions favoured the rise of the luckier or more ambitious into small capitalists or labour-employing farmers.[1] Technological innovation was part of the process, and underpinned all the rest.

In Spain and most of the Counter-Reformation lands impulses towards industrial growth were soon damped down. France was the country fullest of ambivalences; there was far more vigorous growth here, but here too the absolutist State which made it possible also piled up obstacles against it. It was in the Netherlands, under foreign, fairly lax tutelage, and in a not over-governed England, that a really congenial setting was to be found. Aided by the printing-press, far the biggest factor of mutation among all the novelties of the age, the classes most nearly concerned were acquiring each an appropriate ideology or ethos, derived from Protestantism and furnishing some common ground to capital and labour. Calvinism was groping towards social and moral integration in an altering world; and whatever its precise relationship with emergent capitalism, the two, wherever they were together, stimulated and helped to mould each other.

Out of this flux was coming the epoch of 'bourgeois revolutions': events very rare, even counting unsuccessful ones, though their influence has always radiated far beyond their own boundaries. They can be seen as broadened, national repetitions of former struggles of town against feudal overlord, but with a much more complex make-up. Their title is misleading.[2] They were not projected, fought, and won by any bourgeoisie, though this class would be their chief heir. Capitalism was as yet embryonic; its presence could give a fresh turn to diverse social strivings and tensions, older or newer; only after these burst out, and transformed the environment, could it fully take shape. There are no revolutionary classes in

---

[1] Marxism has extended the term 'industrial capital' to agriculture; 'productive capital' seems preferable. Marx did not forget that 'feudal' and 'bourgeois' are only useful abstractions, as R. S. Neale points out in his introduction to *Feudalism, Capitalism, and Beyond*, ed. E. Kamenka and R. S. Neale (London edn, 1975), p. 11. For a Marxist analysis of the transition see M. Dobb, *Studies in the Development of Capitalism* (London, 1946). A penetrating review of the literature is given by I. Wallerstein in *The Modern World-System. Capitalist agriculture and the origins of the European world-economy in the sixteenth century* (New York and London, 1974).

[2] See on this M. N. Pokrovsky, *Brief History of Russia* (English edn, London, 1933), vol. I, pp. 143-4; and I. Deutscher, *The Unfinished Revolution – Russia 1917-1967* (London, 1967), pp. 21-2. In a controversy among British Marxist historians in 1947 I wrote: 'Bourgeois revolutions, like "bourgeois art", are made for the more or less reluctant bourgeoisie by the radical petty-bourgeoisie.'

history, none whose intrinsic nature compels revolt. Bourgeoisies have at most manipulated other social forces, and often have been shoved forward by them.

Nor of course were the popular forces which did a great deal of the fighting eager to establish bourgeois rule, or capitalism. The outcome of any such mêlée could not be foreseen or intended by anyone, with any clarity; resulting from a unique historical compound, it was accidental, though also in another sense inevitable. What the masses were doing when they took part was to recommence on new ground their old struggle against exploitation, the weight of an unjust world resting on their backs. They themselves were undergoing a metamorphosis, with the coming up from their ranks of the petty entrepreneur, that mode of formation of capitalism which Marx saw as the 'truly revolutionary' one. This modest pioneer was still close to his workers, and could share many of their feelings; he was not a Manchester mill-owner with swarms of imported hands from Ireland. With such men in the van the people, who had failed in their own battle against the old order, might achieve another kind of vindication.

It was in religious guise that the old spirit had lingered on most tenaciously. Vistas of material progress which the age now dawning could open up were visible at first only to the higher classes, and could only gradually acquire a meaning for the poor. Their aspirations, in harsh unfamiliar conditions, fixed themselves with intense ardour on the hope of a better life in another world. In the Netherlands they were going to the stake by thousands, or fleeing abroad, for many years before the rebellion began. But in this north-western corner of Europe where things were altering most rapidly, Anabaptism was tempered by Calvinism, and fanatical devotion began to be tinged with fresh hopes for the world below as well as the world to come. Together these two urges could inspire a will to fight such as no thought of materials benefit by itself is likely to infuse, except in professional soldiers.

'Bourgeois revolution' may be conceived then not as a simple substitution of one dominant class or economic system for another, but more broadly as a whole social organism outgrowing its skin. Any true revolution must be the response of an entire society, though not of all its members equally, to a novel situation pressing on it; not surprisingly it has always, in one degree or another, had a national as well as a social dimension. This holds good most obviously of the first and lengthiest of the bourgeois revolutions, that of the Netherlands.[1] It began as a defensive reaction against the desire of Philip II's distant government to strengthen

[1] Of expert pronouncements on this subject since the standard work by P. Geyl, *The Revolt of the Netherlands (1559–1609)* (London, 1932), a student has remarked discouragingly: 'we find versions so much at odds with each other that only a dyed-in-the-wool historian can continue to put his faith in the value of history as a serious discipline.'

its hold and increase its exactions; national movements were to be provoked in the same fashion by Charles I in Scotland and George III in America, as well as by Philip IV in Catalonia. But this one was at the same time a convergence of constitutional and religious protest with economic ambitions engendered by growing productive forces in what had long been a focal area of commerce and manufacture, and, along with these, mounting social tensions.

First to come forward were some of the high nobility, resentful of being dislodged from their armchairs in the royal service by the new centralism. Blue blood, more inflammable and readier to run risks, to gamble with life and fortune rather than lose 'face', as well as revenue, made a valuable if paradoxical contribution to this as to all bourgeois revolutions; while the house of Orange provided a rallying-point for the provinces, each too fond of going its own way. For their part the men of money were drawn on by this example, pushed on by pressure from behind. When the fervour of the streets became uncomfortably stormy, and outbursts of religious fury in the south seemed to imperil the social as well as ecclesiastical fabric, rich burghers and landed nobles there equally preferred to retreat to the shelter of the Spanish sceptre. It was the same falling out of classes as had put an end to the Comunero movement half a century before.

In the south all further advance came to an end, as did Protestantism. Failure there could be redeemed by success in the north, not yet too far gone in class antagonisms to be capable of united exertion, but ready to take over the torch of economic growth. Religious zealotry, though only of a minority, did much to sustain the war effort; but in spite of this and the appeal of patriotism, the Dutch like the Huguenots in their civil wars had often to rely for a field army on foreign mercenaries led by the nobles. Towns could defend themselves, and a host of southern refugees reinforced both determination and industrial growth. Another multitude of fugitives was pouring into England and hastening its evolution. Indeed for capitalism to win supremacy some such windfall addition to the ranks of labour, in areas where conditions were propitious, may have been indispensable.

Gradually a new country was revealing itself to Europe, unmistakably different from any predecessor. Its seven free provinces were a disjointed federation, its institutions showed a marked continuity from medieval times. There was no inclination among the wealthy urban groups now in power to sweep them away. Expanding capitalism might require in principle a unified national market; capitalists wanted, on the contrary, maintenance of the jumble of separate authorities which they themselves, as 'Regents', mostly directed. Unsatisfactory as these arrangements might be in many aspects, political and economic both, they were far less an obstacle to progress than the unyielding framework of the monarchies. The republic looked forward instead of backward, outward instead of inward, very unlike the Portugal which regained independence not much later. And some currents from the tempestuous sea of European popular revolt found entry into its national life, and did something there for the common man and his rights. Here was a 'bourgeois revolution' which was also, to the small extent then attainable, a 'bourgeois-democratic' one, inaugurating a capitalist era not in economic terms alone but with the constitutional and cultural values capable of co-existing with it.

In England, of the bigger countries, the state as a distinct entity was least in evidence, yet conflict between it and the more unstable sections of the nation, when it came, was violent. With no hypertrophied bureaucracy to distort class relations as in Spain or France, political dissensions were more free to assert themselves, while moods of dissatisfaction were fomented by lack of openings for a legion of the educated, younger sons and others, who would elsewhere have been functionaries. Tudor rule rested on a more organic unity of government and ruling class, within which the latter remained very much a governing class also. This was the case in particular with the wealthier gentry, or middle grade of landlords. They had a platform in the House of Commons, where their representatives – a practice very exceptional in Europe – sat with and habitually took the lead over those of the boroughs. England thus shared with the Netherlands the two opposites of political continuity from the past and a revolutionary leap from this base into the future.

A shift of agrarian relations was taking place, in the direction of capitalism, or oftener a hybrid variant of this, nowhere to become predominant except in England, in which the landowner was sleeping partner to a farmer who paid rent and employed labour. It gave such landlords an admixture of bourgeois mentality, while only partially detaching them from their feudal antecedents, and leaving intact much of their collective personality at the same time as the apparatus of manorial law. From the amalgam arose a type very incongruous with any bred by ledger and counting-house, and apter for a challenge to government than any bourgeoisie has been. In the civil wars it was to take some appreciable share in the fighting, not content to fight merely by proxy. All the same, its ties with the urban upper strata were multiplying.[1] Everywhere within range of London the squirearchy felt the magnetic pull of Europe's biggest city and its enormous concentration of riches. All such influences work selectively on individuals, families, groups, not on an entire class, and this one itself, with the rapid turnover of landed property, was in a state of flux. Here is a reason why dividing-lines in the civil wars often appear so erratic and unpredictable.

Bigger-scale manufactures were on the increase from Elizabeth's later

[1] See the essays by L. Stone and A. Everitt on 'Social Mobility in England 1500–1700', in *Past and Present* (Oxford), 33 (1966); and L. Stone, *The Causes of the English Revolution, 1529–1642* (London, 1972).

years, profiting by inflation and the influx of refugees and their skills. Cottage industry had been widespread for a very long time, and it helped to extend the climate of capitalist enterprise into the countryside. In early Stuart times difficulties were being encountered, principally of markets, for which the government was likely to be blamed. It, needless to say, did not know what 'capitalism' was, and had no more notion of systematically obstructing it than of promoting it. On any narrow scrutiny of its policies and of capitalist requirements, whether on the land or in industry, it seems impossible to conclude that the former constituted shackles which the latter were compelled to snap.[1] On a wider view it is far easier to agree that without drastic political change the national development would have been impeded more and more by a regime less and less in harmony with it. More immediately this was out of step with an alliance of classes strong and self-confident enough to aim at managing national as well as local affairs, instead of leaving them in the hands of royal councillors. There was too, as in all such cases, pressure of popular unrest which could usefully be diverted against the court, even though it was aroused by things for which the court's opponents, or their backers, had most responsibility. Riots against enclosures of village lands were still occurring on the eve of the civil wars. Against usury there was outcry from all sides; its morbid proliferation was part and parcel of early capitalism, an evil of a time when one social order was crumbling and another stumbling into existence.

As always, the approaching collision was not a straightforward one, but was taking place very much at a tangent, amid a welter of minor or extraneous issues, calculations, and – at least as important – miscalculations. Crown and Commons, hitherto so close-knit, were moving apart, each side preoccupied with its own needs, and each thinking to safeguard itself by undermining the other, while proclaiming, and even believing, that it was only defending itself against the other's trespassing. Above all, as in every parallel case, it was shortage of money, the result of inflation and heavier calls on expenditure, that compelled the government to embark on courses which its opponents would regard as revolutionary, subversive of Magna Carta and that half-real, half-fabulous ancient English constitution on which the parliamentary lawyers took their stand.

Bourgeois revolution headed by semi-capitalist landowners could only be a garbled affair, though an event so momentous, so complex, and to contemporary eyes so enigmatic, could scarcely come about less confusedly. Most readily felt by the men of the times were the religious contentions kindled by and interacting with social change, sensations not to be contained within the artificial walls of the Elizabethan Church. Heavenly problems are easier to sum up in thirty-nine or some other number of theses, convenient for disputation, than the more intricate and

---

[1] For a criticism of this hypothesis, see my review of C. Hill, *The Century of Revolution 1603–1714* (London, 1961), in *New Left Review* (London), 11 (1961).

tenebrous concerns of this earth. Calvinism was seeping from town into country, within the radius of the new economy, and taking on its Puritan complexion, as English as England's agrarian capitalism. Entering the countryside in the wake of this, it had a very specific rural middle class to work on, made up of independent yeomen and tenant-farmers. It forged links between them and the gentry, and between both and the townsmen. Political parties, destined to play so towering a role in the fortunes of western Europe, were in their infancy; the religious sect supplied a model.

Revolution when it came took the form of protracted civil war, because monarchist ideology was still very much alive, like the conservative social strata it appealed to. Social and regional boundaries largely coincided, and whereas in the French 'wars of religion' the capital and its environs were mostly with the crown, here they were against it. London's internal politics were complicated, and it went through a municipal revolution of its own, the displacement of an old patriciate by the merchant groups which had been thrusting their way to the front. Its adhesion to the parliamentary side carried immense weight, in spite of the fact that there were no levers of power by which the whole country could be quickly grasped, and there was no army: each side had to build a force from scratch. Possession of the metropolis, and identification with anti-Catholic feeling, lent the parliamentary cause a national flavour akin to that of the Netherlands revolt; royalists could be suspected of plotting to use the Irish against their own country. 'Populist' language was much in vogue; rebellion spoke in the name of the People, who were also God's chosen.

Popular clamour at the outset, loudest in London, had its familiar effect of polarising the opposition. Some of those who declined to go further with it when it took up arms must have felt that too hazardous a precedent for insubordination was being given to the masses.[1] But in the fields peasant revolt had long since dwindled to no more than haphazard rioting. Landless labourers, such as more and more of the cultivators were becoming, have been surprisingly submissive nearly everywhere, as if the ploughman loses his soul when he loses his patch of land. During the civil wars they remained inert, thereby allowing the fight to go on to a finish. As to the gentry, they had less fear of losing their authority now because they were so long accustomed to laying down the law in their own districts. Yet many of them hung back, as reluctant as their city cousins to fight their own battle for power. Cromwell filled their places by making officers out of plebeian enthusiasts; by so doing he ensured success, but also ensured further strife to follow.

It can be said with some truth that Parliament got a better army because

[1] D. Pennington, in *Past and Present*, 6 (1954), p. 87 – replying to B. Manning – lays stress on the fact that more than two-fifths of the members of the Long Parliament took the king's side. But the fact of a nearly unanimous parliamentary opposition before 1642 is more significant than that of so many changing sides when it came to the gamble of civil war.

it paid better wages; yet in the New Model a militant élite at least among the soldiers was fired by zeal for the cause, and the less alacrity the gentry displayed the more easily these men could make the cause their own. Many of them were yeomen, through whom the peasantry can be seen making its last stand. Like the small entrepreneur in industry, the farmer employing a few hands was still embedded in the mass he was to rise above. He would still, down to Cobbett's younger days, live in patriarchal fashion with his labourers eating at his own table. It might then be said that these men were fighting on the wrong side. Agrarian capitalism would leave most of them servilely dependent on the landowners for their farms. They were groping; their position and destiny were deeply contradictory; it was the measure of the divergence between the real world, or historical process, and their perception of it, that religion was so much the stuff of their thinking. Leaders like Cromwell would make the most of it to hold their followers together until the enemy was routed.

When victory allowed discords to rise to the surface, the army was at once a big trade union and a miniature republic, its 'agitators' the parliament of the common man. In their debates with Cromwell and the senior officers at Putney in November 1647 the revolutionary tide reached its furthest point, in democratic arguments astonishingly modern. But though Levellers, like Chartists in days to come, might formulate principles of political democracy, inarticulate longings for social reform could not so well crystallise into a programme out of the cloudy millenarian dreams of the sects. Meanwhile the Levellers' modern-mindedness put them ahead of their times.[1] Revolution more than anything else can only be carried forward by minorities, vanguards, always liable to find themselves too far in front, and impotent. Within the army the élite was not at one with the bulk of the soldiers, more concerned about arrears of pay than about more ideal goals. In the Commonwealth years the army as a whole drifted out of sympathy with the rustic mass, unpolitical and virtually non-religious.

Left free to enjoy the spoils, the winners too were disoriented, uncertain what polity would suit them best. They did not set about framing capitalist blueprints, nor did the economy burgeon as soon as Charles's head was off. Every class, not Marx's peasantry alone, has two souls, and a bourgeoisie 'arriving' has always exhibited more clearly than any other a duality of lofty purpose and sordid greed, not seldom in the same individuals.[2] A messianic sense of mission to humanity, transcending national frontiers, easily degenerated, as in Dutch precedent, into imperialism and

---

[1] A compendium of their views can be found in D. M. Wolfe, ed., *Leveller Manifestoes of the Puritan Revolution* (New York, 1944).

[2] Cf. Belinsky, in a letter of 1847: 'The middle class is always great in its struggle, in the pursuit and attainment of its aims. In this it is generous and cunning, hero and egoist, for only its chosen act, sacrifice themselves and perish, while the fruits of achievement or victory are reaped by all.' (See V. G. Belinsky, *Selected Philosophical Works* (Moscow, 1948), p. 500.)

slave-trading. In the village, gentry power meant elimination of feudalism so far as this consisted of obligations of landowner to crown, retention of feudal law which he could take advantage of against the cultivator. 'Bourgeois revolution' could thus include a taking over of antiquated property rights into new hands. From the point of view of mankind's devious future all this might be 'progressive'; for the majority of the peasants, now unmistakably to be reduced to helotry, it was very much the reverse.

It is however an error, to which Marxism has too often succumbed, to view all resistance by the common man to new-fangled property demands as a futile obstacle to progress, to be swept aside by 'history'. In this as in many eras it altered the channel of history, and helped to drive it on – not in a straight line, but there are few straight lines in human annals. Fear among the well-to-do of social revolt, once their Protector was off the scene, was one motive for their decision to bring back the Stuarts; their blatant selfishness had pushed the better aspects of the Commonwealth out of sight, and prevented it from winning any general esteem. Charles II received the throne on their terms. Parliament went on vastly strengthened. It spoke for landowners and moneyed men, but with it a system of law and convention continued to evolve which in the town if not in the village included some rights for the common man. To this extent, as in Holland, what had happened was a 'bourgeois-democratic' revolution, and it left the way open for further struggles later on. As token of this there remained a circumscribed freedom of religion. Survival of the nonconformist sects had a positive value: they were not simply blind alleys, but in their way sanctuaries of liberty and civic spirit.

In Scotland in those years, a far poorer and more feudal realm, the swaddling clothes of religion lay more thickly on the vanguard of the commonalty, and kept social consciousness from breaking through as it did up to a point in England. Patriotism, the common man's other incentive, was still little more than the xenophobia of the medieval wars of independence, and hindered any learning of the lessons that contact with English Levellers might have taught. Higher up in the scale there was greater enlightenment; lairds and traders of the more far-sighted kind were bent on securing a more profitable partnership with rich England, not on sealing themselves off from it.[1] Because of this, and of the Cromwellian occupation, there was some shift of power from lord to laird, and to laird now more closely connected with burgher. In this light the epoch had for Scotland too something of the stamp of bourgeois revolution.

A Leveller pamphlet was republished in France in 1652, during the Frondes;[2] and after 1688 philosophers wrestled anew with the conundrum of when it might be legitimate for a people to perform the 'sovereign act',

[1] See D. Stevenson, *The Scottish Revolution 1637-44* (Newton Abbot, 1973), pp. 314-15, etc.

[2] C. Hill, *Society and Puritanism in Pre-Revolutionary England* (London edn, 1966), p. 207.

as Locke called it, of overthrowing its government. None of them wanted to see this happen often, and on foreign opinion revolution and regicide in England must have had on balance, like all such cataclysms later, an influence more deterrent than stimulating. Louis XIV's feat of restoring absolutism on a yet higher level, and the artificial sunshine of Versailles, must have added to this. In France aristocracy and bourgeoisie could seem to be reaching a point of equilibrium. In 1721 Montesquieu depicted their happy mingling in the salons – 'A Paris règne la liberté et l'égalité'. Only Fraternity was still to join them.

Eighteenth-century Enlightenment derived from the more cultivated aristocratic as well as middle-class circles of western Europe; though the economic recovery which it accompanied was bound to follow the capitalist lines pioneered by Holland and England, and the concept of Progress which it fertilised was more appropriate to social *milieux* whose full unfolding was yet to come. As for the People, as an explosive force it was dwindling in this tranquil interval to Mob. Religion's fierier elements were overlaid by the more soporific: when Christianity returned to active life it would be an adjunct of conservatism, as under Catholic skies it had always been. Russia, further dragooned by Peter the Great, was a partial exception: some schismatic Old Believers, arch-conservatives in theology, figured in the mass revolts led by Bulavin in 1707 and Pugachev in 1773, the last on a grand scale before 1905. Both took place, like earlier ones, in the south-eastern marches where state power was still consolidating itself.

In western as in eastern outskirts the demands of the age met with pockets of recalcitrance: the Highlands, Corsica, later Ireland. North America was more remote still, but quite up to date, with a political philosophy stemming from the English-speaking common stock of 1688. Its war of independence was fought by colonies free from feudal fetters and hastening towards capitalism. It was not a 'bourgeois revolution' in the sense of marking a transfer of class power, but it was bourgeois-national, and also democratic in creating more equality of civic rights (for white men) than Europe could yet envisage. Repercussions on Europe were considerable, though they are hard to assess. 'The American Constitutions were to liberty what a grammar is to language', wrote Tom Paine.[2] In the Enlightenment there was a pervasive unease between faith in human nature in the abstract and distrust or fear of human beings in the mass; the spectacle of America encouraged the more optimistic view. By this date also monarchy in most of Europe was losing its gloss. Insurrection flared up in the unwieldy Habsburg Empire, from Belgium to Hungary, against Joseph II's bureaucratic centralising. For this he had some better motives than the Spanish Habsburgs long before, but it aroused similar antipathy; and as then, the privileged sort could divert the ill humour of

[1] *Lettres Persanes*, LXXXIX.
[2] *Rights of Man* (7th edn, London, 1791), p. 93. Cf. *The Impact of the American Revolution Abroad*, a 1975 Library of Congress symposium (Washington, 1976).

the poor, now showing itself once more, away from themselves against the alien ruler. Aristocratic circles took the lead; in Belgium they soon had to face radical middle-class competition.

Smollett travelling through France in 1766 had a shrewd inkling of catastrophe in the offing.[1] Half-heartedly the old regime at its last gasp sought to raise its drooping credit by piecemeal reforms, which can be adduced as proof that revolution was 'unnecessary'. This is to suppose the bureaucracy equal to the task of mobilising enough public support to bear down obstruction from vested interests, its own messmates for ages, without letting public tumult sweep it away with them. When the test came it soon proved that monarchy was no more than a ghost, in which no one really believed. Its dispossession was a revolution pure and simple, only vestigially a civil war like the English.

First in the field, as against Joseph II, was the aristocracy, which for some time had been trying to reassert itself, and make the most of its archaic feudal rights. With the treasury empty it faced for the first time the ugly prospect of having to pay taxes in earnest. Its demagogy stirred up the excitement that soon overwhelmed it. It then displayed the incapacity, the loss of self-reliance born of lack of any serious duties, by running away. A more intelligent set of nobles had been reading the Encyclopaedia, and understood that things could not stay as they were; these men had a good deal to do with launching the Revolution and propping and guiding it in its opening stages.

The bourgeoisie was a conglomerate, as 'middle classes' always are; but its component parts had sufficient in common for the Jacobin clubs to enrol 'a complete cross-section of them', individuals of the most active, stirring sort from each.[2] During a long era of internal peace and economic advance a shift of the centre of gravity had been taking place, from the more State-affiliated sections – official, tax-farming, rentier – towards the more independent and productive. This development must have been retarded by the fate of the Huguenots, by which France lost economically and lost perhaps still more morally or psychologically. Since then the loss had been made good. Financial and mercantile capital increased and multiplied; manufacturing capital had a more obscure growth, still mostly small-scale and in the form of cottage industry. It might well seem time for capitalism from above and from below to merge into a single system, and build a capitalist France. One impediment was the very imperfect record of the monarchy in clearing away the debris of the past and creating the

[1] Tobias Smollett, *Travels through France and Italy* (1766), Letter XXXVI.

[2] C. C. Brinton, *The Jacobins* (New York, 1961), pp. 70–1; cf. chap. III generally, and G. Lefebvre, *Quatre-Vingt-Neuf* (Paris, 1939), Part 2, 'La Révolution bourgeoisie'. A. Cobban, *The Social Interpretation of the French Revolution* (Cambridge, 1964) maintains that there was no such thing as a revolutionary bourgeoisie in a capitalist sense; cf. a commentary by C. Lucas, 'Nobles, Bourgeois and the Origins of the French Revolution', in *Past and Present*, 60 (1973).

uniformity needed for a national market, in place of a maze of provinces, laws, jurisdictions. Such conditions had not hampered the Netherlands too much in their heyday, but they had fallen behind by now, and with the Industrial Revolution under way in Britain from about 1780 there was need of a new dispensation.

Yet modern capitalism has been remarkably versatile, once in motion, in accommodating itself to varying environments. No necessity of capitalism alone would have conjured up a revolution, let alone a 1789, or driven the Assembly to proclaim on the night of 4 August 'the entire abolition of the feudal system'. An event so apocalyptic, in Hazlitt's phrase, could only come from a conflux of angry forces, immense and torrential because it happened so late, when an industrial proletariat had begun to take its place while an old-world peasantry was still in being. Moreover another path to fortune was soon diverging from the harder industrial highroad. On a far bigger scale than in the English revolution, accessions of private wealth came the way of citizens with money to invest through the selling of church lands, a windfall not dissipated long ago as in Protestant countries, and of *émigré* and crown estates.

Every revolution is a 'revolution of the intellectuals', in so far as only they are called on to gather up and codify the press of obscure thoughts, hopes, rancours that such times breed. Those of 1789 were heirs to a long epoch of reforming ideas dammed up. It may not be fanciful to see in the exaggerated devotion of classical French literature and drama to rules of logic, symmetry, regularity, an unconscious protest against the signal lack of these virtues in the national life, and a prologue to the grand endeavour of the Revolution to reorganise and systematise everything, including religion; not merely to standardise weights and measures, but to translate them all into a scientific decimal language. In 1789 the reign of Reason was being inaugurated. It spelled good order, concord, abroad as at home: the Revolution and the applause of watching Europe were, among many other things, a rejection of three centuries of the military follies of kings.

Any prospering class (or nation) and its spokesmen are too ready to assume that what is good for it is good for all, and must therefore be rational and 'natural'. But an intelligentsia always has far wider horizons than those of the social strata out of which it chiefly sprouts; at history's supreme moments they are startlingly widened, and it can feel itself, with less self-deception than in commonplace times, the conscience or guardian of all classes. In the more idealistic participants, not in socialist revolutions alone, awareness of the miseries of the poor, longing to remedy them somehow, has always been at work. To Wordsworth's enthusiastic officer friend the Revolution was a crusade against pauperism.[1] With such sentiments may be associated the optimism of the Industrial Revolution

[1] *The Prelude*, Book Nine.

in its dawn, not yet brooding on satanic mills or iron laws, full of faith in the capacity of science, applied to man's needs, to banish human ills. Tremors of a social earthquake lurked within a revolution dedicated to the sanctity of Property, that anointed successor of monarchy and birth. As Mathiez said, 'the agrarian law which alarmed the Girondins was neither a myth nor a phantom'.[1]

In reply the law of 18 March 1793 pronounced sentence of death on anyone who should tamper with the rights of ownership. Sales of *biens nationaux*, snuggeries in the bureaucracy, buttressed the new regime with material interests, but also enveloped it in a miasma of greed, intrigue, corruption. Between them and any soaring vision of an enslaved world ransomed at last, the gulf was deep. Yet with all its shortcomings this revolution did promote the welfare of at least some humbler folk, notably the better-off peasants, considerably more than its forerunners had done. Hence it had less recourse to other-worldly promises as substitutes for bread and butter, even if it made great use of will-o'-the-wisps like Liberty and Fatherland. Impatience to ring out the old and ring in the new went with the freedom of the men of 1789 from religious habits of mind; intellect as well as capital had been maturing.

Caged up since the advent of the modern state and its armaments, agrarian bitterness was set free by the crisis of 1789 to erupt afresh. It had been envenomed of late by heavier feudal exactions, and grabbing of village commons by landlords. An indiscriminate jacquerie, such as the *Grande Peur* for a while seemed to be turning into, would have alarmed and alienated all good bourgeois. But the *gros paysan* who came to the front was a respectable figure, a kulak, who would be stolidly conservative once he got what he wanted, liberation from feudal dues and tithes and relief from taxation. Long an avid buyer of further scraps of land, he himself belonged to a time of capitalism in the making; bourgeoisie and rural petty-bourgeoisie were growing up together. From 1793 war, for the first time requiring positive mass support, resulted in sales of government lands in small lots. Content with their gains, the better-off peasantry threw up no separate leadership.

There could be no simple panaceas like these for the grudges long accumulating in town slums, and sharpened now by the bad harvests and distress which hung over the threshold of this as of many revolutions. Had there been a massive factory proletariat straining to break out of its prison,[2] the bourgeoisie would have been thrown into panic as much as by a *levée en masse* of the countryside. Most wage-earners however were employed in small workshops, still close, as always in the preliminary

---

[1] A. Mathiez, *The French Revolution* (1922–7; English edn, London, ?1928), p. 206.
[2] The growth of a modern factory working class is overstated by D. Guérin, *La lutte de classes sous la première République 1793–1797* (Paris, 1946). Cf. A. Soboul, *The Parisian Sans-Culottes and the French Revolution 1793–4* (trans. G. Lewis, Oxford, 1964).

stages of industrial capitalism, to the small masters they worked side by side with. Other workers were artisans on their own, who detested the old order which kept them half-starved, but whose instincts like those of the small masters went against the grain of bourgeois revolution because big capitalism was a threat to their autonomy, as large estates, whether bourgeois or feudal, were to the peasantry. No mutual aid of town and village toilers was possible. Food scarcities and profiteering set urban sansculottes and cultivators with surpluses to hoard at loggerheads, while rural labourers and poor, who also suffered, had no organisation and no link with the slums.

Jacobin dictatorship in the 1793–4 climax of revolutionary grandeur and ferocity meant the forcible holding together of class and mass forces and tensions, by a frantic effort, against foes at home and abroad. Even within a single class like the bourgeoisie, when most fully determined on a common purpose, individuals cannot be counted on to sink their private advantage for it. In an emergency it must find men to coerce it and its auxiliaries, and these are likely to be drawn from outside its own ranks, or from their margins. A militant vanguard now stood in the same relation to the run of the mill frequenters of Jacobin clubs as these did to the bulk of the social strata they came from. It was more petty-bourgeois or professional than bourgeois or commercial, and with a stronger infusion of the intellectual and idealistic, without which action beyond the sphere of routine is impossible. To Robespierre it could even appear that the chief stumbling-block in the way of this revolution was precisely the bourgeoisie: 'pour vaincre les bourgeois, il faut rallier le peuple'.[1]

Gramsci said of these Jacobins that their vision went far beyond the immediate wants of any class, and embraced a long stretch of history still to come.[2] They drew their vital essence not from France alone but from the reservoir of all Europe of the Enlightenment: if a revolution is national, it belongs to Europe or the world as well. For their watchword of audacity they owed a debt to the heroic cult of arms of the French nobility of bygone days, with which the endless wars of the monarchy had infected other classes too. A vortex like that of 1793–4 takes on a demonic power, over and above the wills or feelings of those who serve it, and who may well have the sensation of actors treading a giant stage, instead of men obeying their own volition. Rhetoric and ritual, bizarre costume and self-dramatisation, so often remarked on, might descend to the histrionic, but were proper enough to the hour of destiny, the collective fever that chooses certain men to exalt, and before long to exhaust, if it does not physically destroy them.

Jacobin boldness was cemented by close connections with a Paris on

---

[1] P. S.-C. Deville, *La Commune de l'an II* (Paris, 1946), pp. 43–4.
[2] *Selections from the Prison Notebooks of Antonio Gramsci*, ed. Q. Hoare and G. N. Smith (London, 1971), p. 78.

which the kings had conferred a primacy now all the more unquestioned because of the erasure of the old provinces from the map. It was thanks to Paris that revolution once set in motion could stride so far and fast, at the cost of leaving much of France behind. But the voice of Paris was for direct democracy, sovereignty of the people assembled in their Section meetings, and with this the Jacobin concept of revolutionary centralism was, before the end of 1793, incompatible.[1] Government by Terror rose above, not from, the masses, and its axe had a double edge; the Commune of Paris was deprived of the status of a parallel authority, the ultra-left leadership was destroyed. None the less, pressure of hunger and hope in the capital pushed the Committee of Public Safety into measures it would not have turned to of its own accord. Prominent among them was the fixing of maximum prices for food and other commodities. Lloyd George's mind went back to that experiment when he told his Clydeside hecklers, at the height of the First World War, that their demand for price-controls was too 'revolutionary'.[2]

Concentration of purpose such as the Jacobins sought to achieve could be no more than short-lived. It depended too much on the synthetic fraternalism of war; peril of invasion deepened the nationalistic flavour shared by all revolutions, and recognisable already in the anti-English tone of sundry *cahiers* of 1789. With this exigency receding, unity flagged, and with it the better impulses it released. In Robespierre was personified the frustration of anticlimax, and the convulsive search for an escape from it by means of the guillotine. When Thermidor brought the turn of the now isolated Jacobin leaders to furnish victims, the bourgeoisie left to its own devices let its stupid greed run wild. What was coming to the top was the froth of financial speculation, instead of capitalism's more constructive self; a not unfamiliar story. Babœuf's 'Conspiracy of the Equals' in 1796 was a hopeless last stand of revolutionary idealism,[3] though it was also the first milestone along an untravelled road. He saw 1789 simply as a rising of poor against rich, an antithesis of urban and rural masses on one side and the propertied minority, aristocratic or bourgeois, on the other. To enlarge civic into social equality, by curbing exorbitant possessiveness, was an idea that had glimmered before the sansculottes; a more novel, more far-reaching idea of collective ownership glimmered before Babœuf and his associates.

Animosities left festering by the Revolution could find relief only in further warfare beyond the frontiers. France's inner contradictions and the energies stored up by them set French armies marching across Europe,

[1] See A. Soboul, 'Some Problems of the Revolutionary State 1789–1796, in *Past and Present*, 65 (1974).

[2] C. Wrigley, *David Lloyd George and the British Labour Movement* (Hassocks, 1976), p. 120.

[3] See *Babœuf et les problèmes du Babouvisme. Colloque international de Stockholm, 1960* (Paris, 1963).

reforming and plundering at once as the Revolution had done at home. Things were following the same trajectory as in the earlier bourgeois revolutions, with a fidelity that contemporaries could not fail to be struck by, and influenced by. One had ended with Orange aspiring to a populist autocracy; another with Cromwell as would-be founder of a dynasty. Bonaparte fulfilled their ambitions. Under his aegis all the winners at the gambling-table had their gains legitimised and guaranteed. He styled himself heir of the Revolution, and clearly with much justification, though he inherited far less of its ideals than of its material accomplishments. These provided a fairly broad foundation for his regime; he had no need to rule through the army, like Cromwell. But only in the realm of metrics, removed from the social arena, was the grand aim of renovation realised in full; in law, administration, family and all else, it suffered some or much obstruction. Without a new earth there could be no new heaven, and religion had to be brought back to assist in the winding up of the Revolution.

Despite this, France had done nearly all that Reason could propose to equip it for a majestic step forward, and this, it was clear as the whirlwind subsided, should mean a step towards industrial capitalism. There was now a perfected administrative uniformity, more congenial than the 1789 design of local self-government to a bourgeoisie with so strong an imprint of state service in its historic formation. There was a national market, freed of all impediments, and a government eager to see it fructify. Napoleon could even talk of wishing to be remembered as creator of French industry. His kingdom was a chamber swept and garnished for the bridegroom. Yet steam-age industry was tardy in putting in an appearance, whereas in Britain, where it enjoyed far fewer modern conveniences, it was forging ahead. Instead the post-1815 years saw government jobs multiplying by leaps and bounds. Democratic principles enshrined in the law of inheritance hindered accumulation of capital. Peasant proprietorship, given a fresh lease of life by the agrarian revolt of 1789, hindered the flow of labour into industry. Businessmen might well shrink from becoming employers of those dour artisans who had carried the Revolution on their pikes. It may then be argued that doctrines of equal rights, and the intervention of Demos in politics, had impeded economic progress. On the other side it can be said that the peasants' insistence on their share of the spoils imposed a check on the bourgeois estate-buying, the diversion of investment funds into land, which must be counted as one more cause of industrial torpor. But once again, history was not moving in a direct line. As to the gospel of Reason, there is a fallacy in any expectation of its leading straight on to capitalism, a mode of ordering life which may be rational in its daily detailed workings, but as a historical phenomenon, a compartment of human evolution, is not.

A verb *révolutionner* was coined in 1795, and Englished a couple of years later. Blind accident would give place from now on to deliberate planning. But this was a game two could play at. Burke had warned Europe that 1789 would sour the 'easy good nature' of all kings,[1] and now conservatism was forewarned and forearmed. If the coming age was to be one of insurrectionary parties and movements, it would be one of counter-revolution and White Terror also, enlisting popular forces on behalf of reaction. They got their start in Catholic backwaters like the Vendée and Brittany, and Naples with its San Fede; everywhere they owed much to the heavy-handedness with which bourgeois regimes imposed themselves on a countryside of which they had scant comprehension.

As Lenin was to observe, French historians after 1815 like Mignet and Guizot 'were forced to recognise that the class struggle was the key to all French history'.[2] Marx grew up expecting to see the bourgeoisie in other lands emulate their French exemplars. But a revolution is 'glorious' for its middle-class beneficiaries, like that of 1688, in proportion as it gives them power cheaply, without recourse to the aid of Demos, or Caliban. From this point of view 1789 was a far from happy and glorious memory. 'I begin to see they are no great hands at revolutions', Wolfe Tone wrote of the Irish merchantry in 1793.[3] Factories and machines confirmed the primacy of industry within the capitalist family, but economic strength might mean political weakness, for with it went the herding together of multitudes of sullen mill-hands. It may have been illusion that made the new proletariat, that strange race of beings, appear even more menacing than the all too well-known artisans of the Paris faubourgs. At any rate employers were reluctant to quarrel with their government when it meant giving their workmen an opportunity to quarrel with *them*. Their ancestors had clung to the apron-strings of monarchy; now, after the interlude of revolutionary fits and starts, they would soon be turning to another species of autocrat, a Napoleon III or a Bismarck.

In western Europe it was Spain and Portugal that had least industrial growth and most political turmoil; and in a way the meagre proletarian presence made it seem not too risky, until late in the nineteenth century, to resort to armed force as a lever. Here the bourgeoisie was of a watery consistency, largely made up of speculative financiers, money-lenders, land-buyers, lawyers. Ideas came from outside, far more than from any home-spun thinking. Politics meant first and foremost, as to a lesser extent in France, scrambling for government jobs: this made control of the state a vital object, though the ups and downs of faction left its nature little altered. Land was the other big prize, and seizure of clerical and royal estates bulked far larger among the gains of the moneyed classes than it had done in France, because here there was no question of sharing

---

[1] *Reflections on the French Revolution* (Everyman edn, 1910), p. 36.

[2] 'Karl Marx' (1915), in Lenin, *Collected Works*, vol. 21 (Moscow, 1964).

[3] F. MacDermot, *Theobald Wolfe Tone and his Times* (1939; Tralee edn, 1968), p. 99.

with the peasantry: on the contrary the village commons were added to the takings. Landlordism was only imperfectly defeudalised. Repression and spiritual blinkers kept the miserable peasantry quiet; its failure to rebel in any strength is, all the same, remarkable.

In the towns artisans and cognate groups were ready enough to work off their restless radicalism in bouts of action, but singularly slow to learn any lessons from experience. They tailed behind Liberal leadership; this however relied more willingly on the army, that is on an officer corps mainly middle class, with professional grievances and ambitions which could for a while attach themselves to the Liberal cause. On this footing the long and murderous Carlist war of 1833-9 performed, clumsily and bunglingly, something of the function of a bourgeois revolution: it crippled the church and turned a decrepit absolutism into a quasi-constitutional monarchy, with a less rusty administration. Liberals had no desire to mobilise the peasants, except as conscripts, and left many of them to be drawn into the reactionary blind alley of Carlism. Economy and political life continued to limp. It might well seem to onlookers that the more brawling, the less progress, and that Spain offered a salutory object-lesson in the futility of revolution.

In England the bourgeoisie played on working-class discontent to simulate revolution and get what it wanted in 1832, with an adroitness that Ernest Jones was to warn the workers against later on.[1] In 1848 the old bourgeois radical Brougham was staggered by Europe's abrupt plunge into real anarchy – 'Revolutions made with the magic wand of an enchanter, – Monarchies destroyed at a blow, – Republics founded in a trice, – Constitutions made extempore...'[2] Bourgeois revolution was having its ultimate flare-up. Half Europe was drawn into a whirlpool of contending passions, whose origins lay in diverse epochs of history. Paris underwent in February a self-conscious repetition of the prelude to 1789, of only languid interest now, especially to famished workmen. Their rising in June followed this stage lightning like a real thunderclap; it showed the significance of a living revolutionary tradition, such as England had lost, but in France could be taken over from the middle classes by the proletariat.

Many years later Engels was to declare that British conservatism was saved by the June days in Paris, which frightened the petty-bourgeoisie and confused the workers.[3] More obviously on the Continent middle-class radicals were thrown into alarm, and this was redoubled by tumults

---

[1] 'The middle classes will *speak* ultrademocracy...will be glad to see – nay, as they did in 1830 – will incite you to commit violence, from a twofold reason: 1. It will intimidate their rivals into submission; 2. It will afford them an excuse for not giving you what they promised...' (J. Saville, *Ernest Jones, Chartist* (London, 1952), p. 170; the words belong to 1851.)

[2] *Letter...on the Late Revolution in France* (3rd edn, London, 1848), p. 30.

[3] Engels in *London Commonweal*, 1 March 1885, cited by J. Bryne in *Rebellion 1857*, ed. P. C. Joshi (Delhi, 1957), pp. 300-1.

nearer home, Luddite attacks on mills in western Germany for instance. Of Jacobin resolution there was little display anywhere. In Russia nothing happened; widespread revolt by the peasants on their own had been brought to an end, and no other class was ready to come forward. In middle Europe villagers seized the chance to strike a blow at what remained of feudalism, as in France in 1789, and they came off better than the townsmen because from now on the old order was obliged to reckon the value of a contented peasantry as social ballast.

A contented upper-middle class would be even better. Despite the fiasco of 1848–9, Europe had reached a point where change was self-sustaining, not to be halted by any conscious will. With machinery for multiplier, capitalist production took on a qualitatively new momentum. Formerly it might be useful to rulers, but was not essential, and could be allowed to decay. Now it was indispensable to any state ambitious of great-power rank. More and more at the same time, capital dominated and overshadowed the capitalist, whose hesitant political claims might well be disarmed if the monster he served was given a free run. Compromise could be reached, in other words, on terms amounting to a peaceful transition to capitalism. Germany was the classic illustration. Its bourgeoisie, Treitschke was to complain, was too timid and convention-bound for any revolutionary deeds: an aristocrat, a Bismarck, was called for.[1] Every bourgeoisie, or other class, has its own local character; social conditioning and psychology, besides more measurable economic attributes, determine its behaviour. Bismarck learned from Napoleon III to abandon Metternich's strategy of peace and collective security against revolution, for one of war to divert bad humours outward and identify reaction with patriotism. Engels might exert himself to interpret the unification of Germany as a 'revolution' forced on the Junkers,[2] and so in a certain sense it was, but it bore only too much resemblance to Liberal subservience to the army in Spain. Yet at their own task of industry-building the German chimney-barons, politically spineless, quickly proved themselves the most efficient in Europe.

Since the French Revolution, Europe has been highly charged with nationalist fluids, in addition to class antagonisms, and for these too 1848–9 was a climactic turning-point, and a dismal failure. National and Liberal risings sometimes fell foul of each other, and the Habsburgs were able to get some nationalities on their side, much as the Carlists profited by Basque and Catalan regionalism. The besetting weakness of nationalist movements at all times was that, glowingly romantic as they looked from a distance, they were riddled with sordid ill-will of class against class.[3]

[1] G. A. Craig, Introduction to Treitschke's *History of Germany in the Nineteenth Century* (selections; Chicago, 1975), p. xx.

[2] Engels, *The Role of Force in History* (1887–8; English edn, London, 1968).

[3] See my essay on 'Nationalist Movements and Social Classes', in *Nationalist Movements*, ed. A. D. Smith (London, 1976).

Only very slowly and reluctantly did most of them begin to contemplate any social reconstruction. No doubt idealists looked forward to a happier future for their poorer fellow-countrymen, taking it too much for granted that the mere fact of independence would ensure this. A social programme capable of rousing the masses would be only too likely to alienate those called on for sacrifices. Parnell showed rare insight and courage when he broadened Irish Home Rule by merging it with the land war, but this was easier in Ireland because so many landlords were aliens as well as absentees.

Poland embarked twice over on a war of independence, but was a glaring case of refusal by the *haves* to give up anything to the *have-nots*. Foremost in the fight were the gentry, ardent for Polish freedom but with no intention of granting freedom to Polish ploughmen. When industry and its reflexes gained ground, as in Poland later in the century, mill-owning and landowning sectors would be hard to harmonise, capital and labour still harder. In northern Italy a bourgeoisie entering on life rather earlier was desirous of national union and independence, but did not relish the flurry of little plots and risings which were Mazzini's method; still less did it wish to see workers and peasants roused to action. It put itself behind Cavour, and achieved its ends by means chiefly of French intervention. It was satisfied with an Italy which was an enlarged kingdom of Piedmont, conservative and undemocratic, very much as Germans were satisfied with a fatherland made in the image of Prussia. No people in fact (except the Norwegians, who did not have to take up arms) won liberty without foreign help, direct as in the case of Belgium in 1830, indirect as in that of Hungary, with Austria's humbling by Prussia. Like Italy these other countries were spared the need to invoke, and then recompense, the masses. After the Polish defeat of 1863 there was no similar attempt in Europe before the First World War, except in Balkan irredentas.

Meanwhile the revolt of the masses of which respectable Europe lived in chronic fear had evolved little by little from sansculotte to Bolshevik. There was a long twilight when alarmists talked of 'Red Republicanism', loudest in 1848 and at the time of the Paris Commune in 1871; in 1936 the phantom Red Republic, like a Flying Dutchman's vessel, was sighted again through conservative telescopes in Spain. In the background of all this was the rise of socialism, ushered in by the prodigious upheaval of 1789–1815 and the parallel phenomenon of the Industrial Revolution. Between them they constituted one of those rare junctures when men are able to look over the ramparts, outside the three dimensions, of their world of use and wont.

Like Anabaptism three centuries before, socialism could put on either a pacific or a warlike guise. Utopians such as Weitling hailed the speedy approach of a harmonious communist society, installed by general agreement. Proudhon, summoning property and government to vanish simultaneously, was the prophet of another persistent evangel. Against both of these Marx pitted his thesis of socialism to be set up and maintained, as the bourgeois order had been, by organised force. In the factory proletariat he saw the instrument of destiny. Only a class altogether outside the society built on private ownership could undertake, and would have no choice but to undertake, its root-and-branch abolition.

Marx himself designed no revolutionary party, and the workers' parties committed to his teachings which sprang up before his death were apt to stifle revolution under the wrappings of organisation, or reduce it to a lifeless fetish. Numerous other movements were in the field, to say nothing of those individuals already often to be met with by the 1850s, 'ultra-revolutionaries for whom nothing was radical enough', nine-tenths of them 'heroes only in words'.[1] After the fall of the Commune its survivors in exile were torn by recriminations among a dozen sects. Anarchism in varying shapes continued the chief rival of Marxism, with the countervailing defect of leaving the winds of revolution to their own spontaneous devices, unharnessed to any mill-wheel. Blanqui was a man apart, one of those paladins for whom 'the act of revolution was almost an end in itself'.[2] He strove for the social, not merely political emancipation of the toilers, but relied on chosen groups, in Mazzini's style, for his battering-ram, instead of rallying the toilers to emancipate themselves. Nihilism in tsarist Russia was an extreme version of the same trust in violence exercised on behalf of the many by a few.

In London after the disasters of 1849 the émigrés – not Marx, in his citadel of the British Museum – 'made plans for the overthrow of the world and day after day and evening after evening intoxicated themselves with the hashish draught of thinking that "tomorrow it will begin"'.[3] It is on the whole striking that the century of industrialisation passed off with so little of the working-class mutiny so vividly longed for or dreaded. An occasional whiff of grapeshot was one corrective, as musketry had been for mutiny in the fields. What mattered more, the proletariat and the idea of socialism never coalesced so completely, so explosively, as Marx anticipated. They came nearest it at times when, as in 1848 and 1917, big industry, though dominant elsewhere and striding towards world domination, was at an early stage in the centres concerned. 'It is the revolutionizing of all established conditions by industry *as it develops* that also revolutionizes people's minds', Engels wrote near the end of his life;[4] scarcely taking account of how much this told against any picture of a proletariat steadily

---

[1] F. Lessner, in *Reminiscences of Marx and Engels* (Institute of Marxism-Leninism, Moscow, n.d.), p. 168.

[2] J. Joll, *The Anarchists* (1964; London, edn, 1969), p. 139.

[3] Wilhelm Liebknecht, 'Reminiscences of Marx', in *Selected Works* of Karl Marx, ed. V. Adoratsky (Moscow, 1935), vol. I, p. 109.

[4] Letter to F. A. Sorge, 31 Dec. 1892; Marx and Engels, *Selected Correspondence* (Moscow, 1953), p. 535.

tempered and fortified in revolutionary consciousness by experience. Rather, as it grew accustomed to the modern scheme of things, it moved towards acceptance, seeking a place in it, like the German bourgeoisie, instead of trying to fashion a better one. With this went the fact that industry was adding rapidly to the stock of wealth, and out of their superfluity the rich could be induced or compelled, slowly and painfully, to part with a modicum to the poor. Facility of emigration to North America was an important sedative, not of working-class disgusts alone.

European institutions, from police to parliament, tested by long weathering of storm and stress, proved as a rule resilient enough to contain the situation. Russia was far less well equipped, and socialism transplanted there could be more disruptive. But Marxists in so backward a country faced an extremely complex task, which was to be the source of interminable controversy. It was the paradoxical one of pushing on a bourgeois revolution, as the indispensable preliminary to a socialist one, but with more democratic goals than any hitherto, and with socialist-led workers supplying the want of grit among the middle classes and their leaders. All this was what Lenin had in view in the thick of the chaotic revolution of 1905; but the Russian bourgeoisie, the least Jacobin in Europe, was predestined to stray into the 'Prussian' path of accommodation with autocracy. When this collapsed in 1917[1] the revolutionary spark failed to leap from Russia to the west, too heavily conditioned against it, and left him in something like the isolation of Cromwell and the army after 1649. His gamble did more in the West to benefit conservatism, as the Commune had done, by giving it a target for anti-socialist propaganda, and so assisting the rise of fascism, twentieth-century Europe's pseudo-revolutionary substitute for the overtly counter-revolutionary movements of the nineteenth.

Russia had remained a reservoir of agrarian revolt[2] because, in the absence of any real challenge from a bourgeoisie, tsarism was not compelled to conciliate the peasantry more than very meagrely. Socialist revolution could hitch itself on to this force, as bourgeois revolution had drawn vitality from the struggle of the small producers against feudalism. In both cases things turned out for the masses far otherwise than they expected. Capitalism levied its tolls from smallholders as greedily as feudalism, if more stealthily; socialism would drive or shepherd them into collective agriculture. A second and related similarity is that socialist revolution also has been closely associated with nationalism. This by itself has seldom or never resorted to force with success; on the other hand class bitterness by itself seems too negative or rejective to raise emotion to the necessary temperature.

[1] L. Trotsky, *The History of the Russian Revolution* (trans. M. Eastman, London, 1932), is unique as an account of a revolution by a leading participant.

[2] This factor, in Russia and a number of regions outside Europe, is discussed in E. R. Wolf, *Peasant Wars of the Twentieth Century* (London, 1971).

Lenin looked to Asia to reinforce or reinvigorate the European spirit of rebellion. Historians may look to the innumerable revolutionary movements of the 'Third World', all making their own use of ideas and methods borrowed from Europe, for some fresh light on the mechanics of change in Europe's own record. Revolutions of all sorts everywhere, like all wars, must share some attributes. They have regularly seen generations as well as classes confronting each other. China has proved afresh how much intellectuals can count for when times are out of joint and classes in disarray.

Edmund Wilson has described the metamorphoses undergone by the French Revolution in the historical writing of the following century, and the emergence from them of the Marxist and Leninist concepts of revolution.[1] Soon after 1917 a sensible scholar could declare that 'the study of revolutionary theories is an essential part of social philosophy'.[2] Social science was slow to grapple with this task, as one of its exponents complained in 1964.[3] Most of them preferred to study 'normal' conditions, as economists have been attracted by equilibrium rather than slumps. Gustave le Bon was content to dismiss revolutionism as a psychological disorder, 'an envious hatred of every kind of superiority...Cain, in the Old Testament, had the mind of a Bolshevik'.[4] In recent years the question has been faced more seriously, even if answers have not seldom looked highly academic.[5] An intelligent survey of much of the debate can be found in Wertheim's book,[6] over such issues for example as whether revolutions have been the consequence of spells of exceptional economic hardship, and whether they are likelier to come when governments are harshest or when they have begun to make concessions.

In a remarkable survey of social violence of all types in modern France, Italy and Germany,[7] the Tillys find much reason to doubt two hypotheses which have had wide currency: that revolt is a chaotic symptom of breakdown of authority, and that it is engendered by rapid social change, such as a shift from rural to urban life. They show that, on the contrary, any serious resistance requires forms of organisation, not anarchy, and long-held convictions of right and wrong, rather than simple disorienta-

---

[1] E. Wilson, *To the Finland Station* (London, 1941).

[2] C. Delisle Burns, *The Principles of Revolution* (London, 1920), p. 7.

[3] H. Eckstein, ed., *Internal War. Problems and Approaches* (New York, 1964), p. 1. He adds of this collection: 'there is no use pretending that the essays have achieved the end intended' (p. 5). Cf. P. Schrecker, 'Revolution as a Problem in the Philosophy of History', in C. J. Friedrich, ed., *Revolution* (New York, 1969), p. 35.

[4] G. le Bon, *The World in Revolt. A Psychological Study of Our Times* (trans. B. Miall, London, 1921), p. 179.

[5] E.g. C. Johnson, *Revolution and the Social System* (Stanford University, 1964), p. 10: 'Revolution is the acceptance of violence in order to bring about change.'

[6] W. F. Wertheim, *Evolution and Revolution* (English edn, Harmondsworth, 1974). See also D. W. Brogan, *The Price of Revolution* (London, 1951), and P. Calvert, *A Study of Revolution* (Oxford, 1970).

[7] C., L. and R. Tilly, *The Rebellious Century 1830–1930* (London, 1975).

tion. These conclusions may be extended to the whole history of popular revolt, fuelled by material distress but never simply 'materialistic', always with its own standards, however indistinct, of justice and human brotherhood. These ideals have been enshrined in the perennial myth of Utopia, as naive tradition or in more learned guise. Much Utopian hopefulness has been descried even behind the front of Marx's 'scientific' socialism.[1]

Resentment against exploitation has been the subterranean fire smouldering under the surface of European life. It could break out most effectively in situations where property interests were at odds, not as between individuals or groups merely but between species, historical categories like 'feudal' and 'bourgeois'. Such a rift was more clearly marked in 1789 than in 1642. Moreover the English revolution, very unlike the French, had a long pre-history of parliamentary opposition, and started with a political leadership already well seasoned, while in France guidance had to be improvised. Here is a reason why the common people could be kept under firmer control in England, while in France there was more room and more need for their intervention. The sansculottes who put their shoulders to the wheel of the bourgeois revolution were a very mixed lot, agreed only on what they detested. This included capitalism; and they interposed so forcibly that no bourgeois movement anywhere would ever again feel safe in summoning the 'rabble' to its aid. In future it would be oftenest left to military failure, defeats like those of 1870 or 1918, to perform imperfectly the surgery of revolution by getting rid of regimes which there was no adequate internal energy to dismiss.

Of all interpretations of the revolutionary past, the one bequeathed by the middle class in its post-1789 mood to Marx, and elaborated by a long series of Marxists – of revolutions as victories of class over class and of one economic order over another – remains by far the most convincing. All the same, prolonged and minute scrutiny has revealed to adherents and opponents alike its need for very much further refinement.[2] Explorations in this field enrich our understanding of history as a whole. Revolutionary times bring close together and force into intense interaction all those elements, economic, political, cultural and the rest, which ordinarily straggle along far more loosely linked. None of them by itself is capable of explaining fundamentals; it is such times of fusion that provide the historian with his finest laboratory.

---

[1] See e.g. F. L. Polak, *The Image of the Future* (Leyden, 1961), vol. 1, pp. 268–71.

[2] There is no better way to appreciate this than to go through the relevant contributions to *Past and Present* since it began in 1952. Some of them will be found collected in *Crisis in Europe 1560–1660*, ed. T. Aston (London, 1965), and *French Society and the Revolution*, ed. D. Johnson (Cambridge, 1976). For two recent Marxist works, see F. Marek, *Philosophy of World Revolution* (English edn, London, 1969), and J. Woddis, *New Theories of Revolution* (London, 1972).

CHAPTER IX

THE SCIENTIFIC REVOLUTIONS

I

THE activity of science has dramatically transformed society; since 1850 applied science has become the basis of the means of economic production in Europe. While modern society depends on industrial production based on the application of scientific results, the spectacular achievements of science in the last century have led to a transformation in the nature of science itself. The organisation of scientific activity for the generation of useful, practical knowledge has acquired a new meaning and impulse in the twentieth century, a development which has been described as the emergence of 'industrialised science', science as an industry producing applicable knowledge. An understanding of the dominance of science in contemporary culture and society demands an analysis of the social and intellectual transformations which led to such striking confidence in the value of the investigation and control of nature and the emergence of science as a socially-organised activity.[1]

The profound conceptual changes in physics in the twentieth century, the abandonment of the doctrines of absolute space and time in Einstein's theory of relativity and of causality and determinism in quantum mechanics, has customarily led to a depiction of the development of science by means of a disjunction between 'classical' or 'Newtonian' and 'modern' science. This historiographic framework is unsatisfactory, for the development of science must be seen in a broader perspective, as a social and cultural phenomenon. The attainment by natural science of appropriate methods of enquiry and social institutions, its methods being viewed as trained and organised common sense and its aims customarily regarded as value-free, is a feature of its recent history. Since its emergence in the Renaissance as a seminal feature of European intellectual life, two major periods of scientific change stand out: first, the intellectual revolution of the seventeenth century in which the cognitive basis of modern natural science is traditionally seen to have been established, and second, the emergence of science as a professional activity in the early nineteenth century when the social structures were established which provided the basis for the integration of science into the fabric of social life.

The spectacular intellectual triumphs of sixteenth- and seventeenth-century astronomy and physics have long been characterised as the 'Scientific Revolution'. The depiction of scientific change as a 'revolution' first occurs in the eighteenth century; while this term usefully indicates

[1] J. R. Ravetz, *Scientific Knowledge and its Social Problems* (Oxford, 1971).

that scientific development cannot be represented as a simple cumulative process involving the accretion of scientific facts, the term 'revolution' is ambiguous in that it implicitly denies the continuity of intellectual traditions that is present even in episodes of dramatic conceptual change.[1] Nevertheless, seventeenth-century scholars from Bacon, Galileo and Descartes to Boyle, Newton and Leibniz display in their writings a self-conscious awareness of the significance of the intellectual transformation in the period. This 'Scientific Revolution' has been traditionally characterised as a philosophical revolution in which teleological explanations of natural phenomena were replaced by explanations in terms of mechanical laws, in which the hierarchical closed world of medieval cosmology with its dichotomy between celestial and terrestrial physics was replaced by the concept of an infinite universe with a unified physics and astronomy grounded on the mathematical, mechanical physics of Newton. The new science of the seventeenth century was described by E. J. Dijksterhuis as 'the mechanization of the world picture' which 'meant the introduction of a description of nature with the aid of the mathematical concepts of classical mechanics'. The Scientific Revolution is depicted as culminating in the Newtonian synthesis of mechanics and astronomy, and the metaphysical reorientation fundamental to the establishment of the mechanical philosophy is seen as having provided the conceptual framework for science in the following two centuries. According to this interpretation, the mechanical philosophy conceived nature as a law-governed system in which God's relation to nature was viewed merely as a first cause, and the appeal by scientists to laws of nature established knowledge of nature as independent of divine providence. Associating the intellectual revolution of the seventeenth century with the secularisation of thought, Dijksterhuis concluded that 'the mechanization of the world picture led with irresistible consistency to the conception of God as a retired engineer, and from this to His complete elimination was only a step'.[2]

This traditional account is misleading in its emphasis on the modernity of the seventeenth-century revolution in scientific thought, in its depiction of the process in which this revolution occurred, and in its characterisation of the implications of this intellectual revolution for later developments. Although the shifts in intellectual attitude in seventeenth-century conceptions of nature were profound it is misleading to label this transition 'the Scientific Revolution' if this is meant to carry the implication that later developments can be comprehended in terms of the intellectual categories propounded in this period. While the metaphysical reorientation of seventeenth-century thought can be characterised as the emergence of a new cosmology and the mechanical conception of nature, the view of

[1] T. S. Kuhn, *The Structure of Scientific Revolutions* (Chicago, 1962).
[2] E. J. Dijksterhuis, *The Mechanization of the World Picture* (Oxford, 1961); E. A. Burtt, *The Metaphysical Foundations of Modern Physical Science*, 2nd edition (London, 1932).

nature as regulated by mechanical laws was grounded on theological premisses which aimed to interpret laws of nature as manifestations of the operations of providence. The remarkable efflorescence of science was for some linked to a conception of progress in which human enlightenment and amelioration were viewed in terms of a providential conception of history, in which the revival of learning was seen as a counterpart to the spiritual redemption of man. The seventeenth-century Scientific Revolution was as much a social and cultural phenomenon as a revolution in scientific method and cosmology, and its impact on the cultural life of Europe was profound. To eighteenth-century intellectuals from Voltaire to Priestley science provided a model of rational discourse, and the value of the investigation of nature was rarely (though on occasion violently) questioned.[1]

By the late eighteenth century the activity of science was acquiring a new cognitive and social status, and the period 1780–1850 witnessed another major transformation in which the image of the 'natural philosopher' as the investigator of nature was to be succeeded by the image of the 'scientist', the professional investigator of technical problems. The term 'scientist' was coined by William Whewell at the 1834 meeting of the recently-formed British Association for the Advancement of Science, a body formed with the intention of establishing the professional status and organisation of science. Whewell reported that the members of the Association felt the need of a general term to describe their pursuits, but that the traditional term 'philosopher' was regarded as being 'too wide and lofty a term', so Whewell's neologism 'scientist' was proposed. The activity of science itself was seen to be changing; the generic 'natural philosophy' was yielding to newly-defined and specialised scientific disciplines with distinctive concepts and techniques for research, and the transformation from an avocation to a vocational pursuit led to the emergence of a specialised and trained élite and to the proliferation of institutions concerned with the furtherance of the activities of professional scientists.

II

The recovery of Greek learning in western Europe from the Islamic world, which began in the twelfth century, had led Christian thinkers to interpret Aristotle's physics in the context of an interpretation promulgated by the Islamic philosopher Averroes; in particular, the Aristotelian system was interpreted as asserting that nature was a necessary emanation from God. This and other doctrines which contradicted Christian theology were condemned by the bishop of Paris in 1277, leading many philosophers and theologians to reject Averroistic necessitarianism and to develop a voluntarist theology which stressed divine omnipotence and the autonomy of the divine will. The view of nature as a contingent artefact of divine

[1] P. Gay, *The Enlightenment: An Interpretation* (2 vols, London, 1967–70).

omnipotence led to a weakening of confidence in the physical explanations offered by Aristotle, and in offering alternatives to Aristotle's theories in the fourteenth century Oresme and Buridan sought to demonstrate the uncertainty of natural knowledge; God's creative power was not constrained by principles of necessity or physics, and the stress on divine omnipotence embraced the notion of a divine legislator who concurs with the framework of the law that he has established. Descartes was to draw upon these arguments in formulating a concept of the lawlikeness of nature as grounded upon divine omnipotence. Despite the criticisms of many of Aristotle's arguments by medieval scholars the Aristotelian cosmology was the accepted theory of the universe; a spherical, geocentric cosmos, the planets being embedded in concentric, 'crystalline' celestial spheres, and a dichotomy being supposed between the celestial and terrestrial regions. The attempt by Aquinas to prove the existence of God by an appeal to Aristotelian physics illustrates the assimilation of Christian theology to the physics of Aristotle, the Aristotelian concepts of a first mover of celestial motions and a first efficient cause in nature being used to support the Christian concept of a God who created the universe and maintained its operations.[1]

The Renaissance witnessed new attempts at achieving a harmony between faith and reason. The recovery of the Platonic *corpus* led to a revival of the neoplatonic tradition which emphasised a hierarchical universe descending through levels of perfection from God to the corporeal world. This tradition was linked to syncretistic and magical attitudes to nature. The publication by the Florentine scholar Ficino of the *Corpus hermeticum* and the assimilation of hermetic ideas in the late-fifteenth and sixteenth centuries was of primary importance. Although in reality these texts date from the hellenistic period, comprising a heterogeneous blend of mysticism, Christianity and magic, they were considered at the time as being of Egyptian or even Mosaic origin and as the source of Greek philosophy. Stressing a tradition of *prisca sapientia* (ancient wisdom), the attribution of Greek philosophy to a Hebrew tradition secured the legitimacy of pagan wisdom. The *Corpus hermeticum* stressed an astrological cosmology in which the terrestrial and celestial realms are connected in a web of affinities and correspondences, and in which matter is impregnated with the divine *spiritus* through which stellar influences act. The aim of natural magic was to grasp the hidden powers of nature and the laws of sympathy and antipathy between material things by activating the planet, metal, or gem in which the *spiritus* is stored. The cosmos was a unity manifesting occult influences, a web of active powers. Man is the focal point of the hierarchy between material and spiritual entities; according to the doctrine of correspondences man mirrored the world in

[1] E. Grant, *Physical Science in the Middle Ages* (London, 1971); A. C. Crombie, *Robert Grosseteste and the Origins of Experimental Science* (Oxford, 1953).

microcosm, and could activate spiritual agencies by magic and alchemy. This divinisation of nature is reflected in the Renaissance magical *corpus* which aimed at a restoration of esoteric knowledge. In Ficino's natural magic the sun is envisaged as corresponding to God in the visible world, its rays of light corresponding to the *spiritus*; in Cornelius Agrippa's natural magic cabbalistic doctrines of the powers of names and the occult virtues of talismans are invoked as means of acquiring power over nature; and in the writings of Pomponazzi an attempt is made to provide a systematic account of the agency of divine powers upon matter through the mediation of the planets.[1]

The chief significance of the hermetic tradition for the intellectual revolution of the seventeenth century was its emphasis on the ways in which the powers of the universe could be captured and controlled for human ends. The work of Paracelsus in the first half of the sixteenth century aimed to transform hermetic ideas into a universal science of nature grounded upon the neoplatonic concept of the visible world envisaged as the outward shell of an invisible realm of active power infused into matter by God, and of correspondences and analogies between the macrocosm and the microcosm. Man was regarded as uniting in himself the constituents of the natural world, and knowledge was to be achieved through union with objects in experience and through the correspondence between man and nature, rather than through the categories of Aristotelian philosophy.[2] Paracelsus emphasised that the coming millennium would witness the recovery of knowledge lost at the Fall, providing an eschatological dimension to the hermetic concept of esoteric wisdom. These themes are taken up again in Francis Bacon's scheme for the reformation of learning, in which the belief that Christian civilisation was approaching the final judgement is associated with the belief that the millennium would be accompanied by the advancement of learning and the dominion of man over nature.[3]

Theological arguments were fundamental to the formulation of scientific concepts in the seventeenth century, and were of fundamental importance in the establishment of the mechanical world view. Considering the 'mechanization of the world picture' the cardinal feature of the Scientific Revolution, A. Koyré attributed two characteristics to its enunciation, the mathematisation of nature and the destruction of the hierarchical, finite cosmos of Aristotelian physics. The impact of Copernicus' *De revolutionibus orbium coelestium* (1543) was of crucial significance for both these developments, initiating a transformation in the conception of the universe. The Copernican theory attempted a restructuring and systematisation of the Ptolemaic astronomical system on the basis of the

[1] F. A. Yates, *Giordano Bruno and the Hermetic Tradition* (London, 1964); D. P. Walker, *The Ancient Theology* (London, 1972).　　[2] W. Pagel, *Paracelsus* (New York, 1958).
[3] P. M. Rattansi, 'The social interpretation of science in the seventeenth century', in P. Mathias (ed.), *Science and Society 1600–1900* (Cambridge, 1972).

supposition of heliocentrism. In his use of traditional geometrical models which explained the planetary orbits in terms of complex combinations of circular motions Copernicus seems the reformulator of Ptolemaic astronomy; but while Ptolemy's *Almagest* was a collection of loosely-connected models of the motions of the sun and individual planets as viewed from the earth, in the Copernican system the motions of all the planets are viewed as a unified planetary system in relation to the motion of the earth, so that Copernican astronomy provides a unified and systematic mathematical treatment of planetary motions. Nevertheless, the Copernican theory did not have any decisive computational advantages; and the supposition of heliocentrism was in conflict with Aristotelian physics, a difficulty which Copernicus could only meet by adopting the arguments of the medieval commentators, for example in appealing to optical relativity in support of his contention that the apparent motion of the stars could be explained if the earth were in motion and the heavens were stationary, rather than by supposing the motion of the heavens as viewed from a stationary earth. A key feature of his argument, which probably reveals his basic motivation, was his stress on the centrality of the sun as symbolic of God in the visible world, evoking the symbolism of Ficino's neoplatonism. The aesthetic and theological dimensions of the Copernican system were crucial to its assimilation.

Following the Renaissance neoplatonic belief in the harmony between the celestial and terrestrial realms, of the visible world as a reflection of the divine, Kepler envisaged the structure of planetary orbits as corresponding to the perfections of mathematical relationships. In his *Mysterium Cosmographicum* (1596) he interpreted the order of the planets consequent on the Copernican system in terms of geometrical relationships between the regular solids, emphasising the systematic and unified character of the heliocentric system. The philosophical and theological persuasiveness of the Copernican hypothesis to him appears in his search for physical principles, his belief that the motive power of planetary motion lay in the sun as the centre of the planetary system, drawing the analogy between the physical efficacy of the sun and divine agency. In subsequently abandoning his original speculative cosmology in his later writings his continuing belief in cosmic harmony was manifested in his attempt to relate the mathematical relationships of the planetary orbits to musical harmonies. The culmination of his mathematical 'war' on the planet Mars was the *Astronomia nova* (1609), a new astronomy in which the traditional mathematical astronomy of the Ptolemaic and Copernican systems, the mathematics of circular motion, was abandoned in favour of the supposition of elliptical planetary orbits, the motions of the planets being determined by Kepler's laws.[1]

[1] T. S. Kuhn, *The Copernican Revolution* (Cambridge, Mass., 1957); A. Koyré, *The Astronomical Revolution* (London, 1973).

The publication of *De revolutionibus* initiated a process in which the conception of the cosmos and of man's place in nature was dramatically transformed. By the end of the seventeenth century the hierarchical, geocentric cosmos of Aristotelianism was replaced by a conception of the universe as infinite in extent. Galileo's telescopic observations led him to question the immutability of the heavens, a doctrine fundamental to the terrestrial–celestial dichotomy of Aristotelian physics, and the growing belief in the plurality of worlds in infinite space threatened basic assumptions about the uniqueness of man. The earth was a planet and the heavens were robbed of their immutability and perfection, and the problem of reconciling the theory of a moving earth with biblical texts troubled theologians. The condemnation of the Copernican hypotheses of heliocentrism and the moving earth by the Catholic Church in 1616, and the trial of Galileo; and John Donne's lament in 1611 that the 'new philosophy' called 'all in doubt' and that the intelligibility and stability of the cosmos was 'all in pieces, all coherence gone', attest to the difficulty in assimilating the new ideas. Nevertheless, heliocentrism and the associated doctrines (which had not been propounded by Copernicus) of an infinite cosmos and the plurability of worlds became part of the intellectual baggage of educated men in the seventeenth century. A. O. Lovejoy has stressed the ambiguity of the medieval geocentric cosmos: though man was given a central place in the drama of creation, the centre of the world was the furthest removed from the incorruptible heavens, and 'Copernicanism' was opposed partly because it was viewed as removing man from the humblest part of the world. Yet the acceptance of the idea of the plurality of worlds led to a denial of the doctrine that the cosmos had been created for the utility of man; man's pride was humbled, and the rejection of the anthropocentric doctrine is an important aspect of the shift in sensibility consequent on the acceptance of heliocentrism. The implications of Galileo's conclusion of the untenability of the doctrine that the earth alone was the domain of generation, corruption and mutability was drawn with awesome force in John Wilkins' assertion in 1638 that the inhabitants of other worlds were redeemed 'by the same means as we are, by the death of Christ'.[1]

The full implications of the new cosmology involved the postulation of the infinite cosmos and its incorporation into the mechanistic world view. The intellectual reorientation associated with the introduction of Descartes' mechanical philosophy had a profound effect on European thought. Descartes conceived his physics as a rational system grounded on metaphysical foundations whose truth was guaranteed by divine veracity, a system of philosophy based on the methods of geometry, and which was conceived as a total refutation of Aristotelian physics. Descartes explained

[1] A. O. Lovejoy, *The Great Chain of Being* (Cambridge, Mass., 1936); A. Koyré, *From the Closed World to the Infinite Universe* (Baltimore, 1957).

the characteristics of material entities in terms of geometry and motion; all natural phenomena were held to arise from matter in motion, spatial extension being the defining property of matter and action by contact the only mode of change in nature. Descartes' theory of matter supposed three elements distinguished by the different size and motion of their particles, and his cosmology supposed a rotating fluid forming a series of celestial vortices which carry the planets with them as they rotate, the contact of the particles composing the vortices producing the planetary motions. Descartes argued that the original creation and the continued existence of matter was contingent on God's will; God imposed the laws of motion upon nature and the matter and motion in the world is maintained by divine sustenance. The concept of nature as subject to mechanical laws was grounded on the view that the laws of nature had their source in the efficacy of the divine will, the immutability of the laws of nature being a consequence of divine perfection and immutability. While the first principles of the mechanical philosophy, the principles of matter and motion, establish the possible causes of phenomena in terms of the laws of motion whose certainty is secured by divine veracity, experiments provide crucial tests between possible explanations. Cartesian physics postulated hypotheses in which phenomena were explained in terms of the laws of matter and motion; but Descartes' mechanical models were not envisaged as an account of actual physical mechanisms but were merely illustrative of the possibility of mechanical explanations, though founded on the basic principles of the mechanical laws of matter and motion.[1]

From the publication of Descartes' theory of physics in the 1630s and 1640s Cartesian natural philosophy achieved a remarkable influence, although the 'mechanical philosophy', as a programme of scientific explanation, became detached from specifically Cartesian philosophical doctrines. As Robert Boyle expressed it, writing in the 1660s, the mechanical philosophy purported to trace all natural phenomena to the two principles of matter and motion. The diversity of philosophical outlook of the early members of the Royal Society in the 1660s, in which interests in alchemy and hermeticism coexisted – often in the same individual – with the corpuscularian mechanical philosophy, illustrates the confused intellectual complexion of the period. Although Renaissance neoplatonism may at one time have seemed to be an alternative to Aristotelianism, after 1650 the mechanical philosophy, though transformed from Descartes' original explication, was becoming the dominant intellectual force. English natural philosophers were especially concerned with the theological implications of Descartes' philosophy. The Cambridge philosopher Henry More was initially attracted to Descartes' ideas but came to see Descartes' concept of

---

[1] F. Oakley, 'Christian theology and the Newtonian science', *Church History*, 30 (1961); R. S. Westfall, *The Construction of Modern Science: Mechanisms and Mechanics* (London, 1971).

extension as the defining characteristic of matter as a threat to the immateriality of God and spirits; if all that was extended was material then God would be material, a conclusion which was indeed drawn by Thomas Hobbes. Hobbes' materialist theory of nature in which God was considered corporeal and only as a first efficient cause seemed to express the 'atheistic' implications of Descartes' concept of matter, and in expounding his corpuscularian mechanical philosophy in the 1660s Boyle included qualities such as texture as well as extension among the primary or defining qualities of matter so as to clearly distinguish between matter and spirit. Boyle stressed God's continued causal agency in nature, arguing that the laws of nature were God's decrees imposed by the divine will. Boyle rejected any attempt to substantialise laws of nature or to consider them as immanent in matter; the passivity of the material corpuscles implied that matter was incapable of originating activity and that only God could act causatively. Boyle was concerned to insist on the harmony between the study of nature and the revealed truths of the Bible, emphasising that reason and revelation were complementary.[1]

These philosophical and theological themes are apparent in Newton's development of the mechanical theory of nature, the Newtonian world view being generally considered the epitome of the 'Scientific Revolution'. Newton studied Descartes' works as an undergraduate at Cambridge in the early 1660s and developed many of Descartes' mechanical and mathematical concepts, extending and transforming them in the process, but More's view of the mechanical philosophy exercised a pervasive influence on his intellectual development and he rejected central features of Descartes' philosophy of nature. Newton considered that to suppose with Descartes that extension was the defining quality of body would be to offer a path to atheism, for he argued that space was not created but had existed eternally. While the existence of matter in space is contingent on God's will, space itself is the unconditioned condition for the existence of matter. The concept of absolute, infinite space that was fundamental to the Newtonian cosmology was thus conceived in theological terms as the arena of divine activity. God was present in the infinite space of the Newtonian cosmos and the universe was the 'temple of God', as Newton succinctly expressed it. In his *Principia Mathematica* (1687) Newton developed Descartes' theory of mechanics into his own Newtonian laws of motion, but although he had long continued to accept the Cartesian explanation of planetary motion as arising from the rotation of celestial vortices, by the early 1680s he had abandoned the Cartesian principle of explaining motion by the contact between particles of matter in favour of

[1] J. E. McGuire, 'Boyle's conception of nature', *Journal of the History of Ideas*, 33 (1972); M. Boas, 'The establishment of the mechanical philosophy', *Osiris*, 10 (1952); R. S. Westfall, *Science and Religion in Seventeenth Century England* (New Haven, 1958); R. L. Colie, *Light and Enlightenment* (Cambridge, 1957); S. I. Mintz, *The Hunting of Leviathan* (Cambridge, 1962).

an explanation of planetary motion in terms of a gravitational force of attraction acting across void space. This became the conceptual kernel of his *Principia*, which achieved a synthesis of planetary and terrestrial motions in Newton's laws of motion and in which Kepler's laws of planetary motions were given a secure, mathematical foundation.

The Newtonian world view is a mathematical theory of nature and his scientific achievement is grounded on the revolution in mathematics which occurred in the sixteenth and seventeenth centuries, which was initiated by the analytic programmes of Viète, Fermat and Descartes. The analytic geometry which Newton imbibed from Descartes had led to a shift from the visual to the abstract in mathematics. The properties of curves were characterised by algebraic symbols; visual representation was replaced by equations expressing the relations between geometrical quantities which defined the properties of curves. The calculus methods which were developed independently by Newton and Leibniz extended these methods to the treatment of infinitesimal quantities, and they applied their mathematical methods to the solution of physical problems. In his *Principia* Newton represented the curve traversed by the motion of a planet under the influence of a gravitational force of attraction as a sequence of infinitesimal impulses, the attractive force being considered as a series of discrete impulses of force. The changes in motion of the planet are represented by means of Newton's infinitesimal analysis, and the introduction of the concept of a force of attraction is grounded on his mathematical construction of the motion of planets.[1]

The application of mathematics to the treatment of mechanical problems represents a major achievement of seventeenth-century science; the mathematisation of nature was fundamental to Dijksterhuis' description of the new science of the seventeenth century as the 'mechanization of the world picture'. The analytic geometry and infinitesimal calculus developed in the seventeenth century enabled the physical problems of mechanics, including studies of changes of celestial and terrestrial motion, to be represented mathematically; relations between physical quantities were expressed in terms of relations between geometrical quantities which were represented by algebraic symbols. The separation of analysis from geometry in the eighteenth century led to the development of flexible and direct methods for the mathematical expression of physical quantities in which mathematical physics was stripped of its geometric foundations. The work of continental mathematicians including Johann and Daniel Bernoulli, D'Alembert and Euler extended the range of the mathematical treatment of mechanical problems.[2]

[1] R. S. Westfall, *Force in Newton's Physics* (London, 1971); D. T. Whiteside, 'Before the *Principia*' and 'The mathematical principles underlying Newton's *Principia Mathamatica*', *Journal for the History of Astronomy*, I (1970).
[2] C. Truesdell, *Essays in the History of Mechanics* (Berlin, 1968).

The mathematical façade of his physical arguments enabled Newton to claim that his concept of a gravitational force acting across void space was a mathematical rather than a physical concept like Descartes' theory of vortices, but he vehemently denied that he supposed the 'absurdity' that bodies could act through void space 'without the mediation of any thing else', affirming that 'gravity must be caused by an agent'. Arguing that matter was inert and incapable of originating and sustaining activity, being characterised by 'passive' qualities such as extension and impenetrability, he denied that gravity was an essential property of matter; in denying that gravity could be explained in terms of such passive qualities he rejected the view that gravity could be reduced to the explanation by the Cartesian mechanical philosophy of matter and motion. In Newton's view gravity was to be attributed to the causal agency of 'active principles' conceived as the manifestation of God's causal agency in nature. Functioning as the cause of motion and gravity active principles were regarded as laws of nature rather than as divine abrogations of the laws of nature, for in affirming the voluntarist doctrine of divine omnipotence Newton supposed that God's will was the only causally efficacious agency in nature; while all natural phenomena were constrained by God's will, nevertheless God worked through secondary causes by divine concurrence with the order of nature that He had established. In introducing the concept of active principles Newton was not returning to the enchanted world of hermeticism, though he rejected the intelligibility of Descartes' theory of nature in terms of matter and motion. In the hermetic view of nature active agents were immanent in matter, whereas for Newton matter was inert and passive, God being the cause of its activity. Although the Newtonian cosmology was rendered intelligible by an appeal to theological principles, it was also a theory of natural philosophy which united terrestrial and celestial phenomena in terms of a mathematical mechanics.

Newton considered that the ultimate purpose of natural philosophy was to shed light on the problem of God's relation to nature, to understand the cosmos including God as the creator and sustainer of nature. Newton supported his theory of universal gravitation by an appeal to the hermetic tradition of *prisca sapientia*, arguing that his theory of gravity was a restatement of Pythagorean doctrines which had been hidden in enigmatic phraseology. The task of the natural philosopher was the rediscovery of the true system of the world, the restoration of the Mosaic revelation by experiment and mathematics, and hence the reconstruction of a unified wisdom of creation. Newton's biblical and alchemical studies were complements to his scientific work; both assumed that a true body of knowledge was available to the wise in antiquity and was couched in esoteric form. The penetration of hermetic mysteries was a counterpart to his scientific studies, and Newton sought to demonstrate the conformity between the Mosaic and Newtonian philosophies, the harmony between the natural and the divine, so as to restore man to his pristine state or moral perfection and understanding of nature.[1]

The metaphysical implications of theology were directly relevant to the formulation of scientific theories, and the motivation of seventeenth-century intellectuals towards the study of nature received sanction from theological doctrines. On this issue there has been considerable controversy over R. K. Merton's elaboration of Max Weber's thesis on the relation between Calvinism and capitalism. Merton argued, partly on the basis of statistical evidence, that Puritan values provided a religious motive for the pursuit of science; the Puritan attitude of self-restraint and diligence furthered an interest in the cultivation of science in seventeenth-century England. Attempts to portray the Puritan concern with science in terms of the impact of developing capitalism are unconvincing, in that while economic incentives arising from the expansion of trade might explain an interest in practical mathematics and the use of scientific instruments to further the needs of navigators, surveyors and merchants, the universalist aims of Puritan scientific attitudes demand an explanation in religious terms. Despite the problem of defining the Puritans as a group it is apparent that the cultivation of science was an important social pheno-menon in seventeenth-century England and that in the mid-century period of Puritan dominance Puritan intellectuals encouraged a commitment to the study of God's book of nature as complementary to the study of the book of God's word.[2]

This connection is apparent in the writings of Francis Bacon and ex-plains the impact of the Baconian *corpus* on Puritan intellectuals, demon-strating that theological obligation was a crucial feature of the motiva-tions that led men to study the natural world. In developing his scheme for the reformation of learning in works such as the *Valerius Terminus* (1603), the *Advancement of Learning* (1605) and the *Instauratio Magna* (1620), Bacon criticised the scholastics as spiders spinning philosophical webs and the craftsmen as ants collecting information, urging that the natural philo-sopher should emulate the bee, gathering information and transforming it into a system of knowledge. While he castigated the hermetics for the pretentious deceits of magic, and Paracelsus for attempting to find the truths of nature in the Scriptures, he recognised that the aims of these men

[1] A. Koyré, *Newtonian Studies* (London, 1965); J. E. McGuire, 'Force, active principles and Newton's invisible realm', *Ambix*, 15 (1968); J. E. McGuire and P. M. Rattansi, 'Newton and the "pipes of pan"', *Notes and Records of the Royal Society*, 21 (1966); B. J. T. Dobbs, *The Foundations of Newton's Alchemy* (Cambridge, 1975); F. E. Manuel, *A Portrait of Isaac Newton* (Cambridge, Mass., 1968); F. E. Manuel, *The Religion of Isaac Newton* (Oxford, 1974).

[2] R. K. Merton, *Science, Technology and Society in Seventeenth Century England* (New York, 1970); C. Hill, *Intellectual Origins of the English Revolution* (Oxford, 1965); C. Webster (ed.), *The Intellectual Revolution of the Seventeenth Century* (London, 1974); A. R. Hall, 'Science, technology and utopia in the seventeenth century', in Mathias, *Science and Society*.

were noble, in seeking to control nature, even if their methods were full of error. For Bacon science was to be prosecuted in a disciplined and orga- nised manner by renouncing the intellectual pride of the scholastics and the vanity of the methods of the hermetics; having lost his dominion over nature at the Fall, man must regain it with patient humility through labour and manual operations, as God had ordained. Science was directed towards a religious end, and the restoration of man to his sovereignty and power would lead to the redemption of mankind. The achievements of craftsmen led Bacon to see in the mechanical arts the model for collabora- tive, experimental science. The pristine knowledge of Solomon would be restored in Solomon's House, the brotherhood of scientists in Bacon's *New Atlantis* (1627).[1]

Bacon's concept of the reformation of learning was grounded on mil- lenarian eschatology, and he appealed to the prophetic texts of the book of Daniel in his association of the revival of learning and the return of the dominion of man over nature with the Christian utopia. For Bacon and his Puritan followers, man had lost his dominion at the Fall, but the Bible promised the restoration of knowledge. The ethical and religious orienta- tion of Bacon's philosophical programme was based on the eschatological scheme of biblical prophecy, and the revival of learning came to be seen as providing the means for the realisation of the utopian paradise. To Puritan commentators the technological discoveries of the Renaissance singled out by Bacon as indicating the return of man's dominion over nature – the invention of printing, gunpowder and the compass – seemed to herald an intellectual regeneration based on experimental science, whose ultimate meaning was intelligible in terms of the millenarian texts of the Bible. These ideas, and the millenarian writings of continental reformers such as Comenius, were developed by the group of Puritan intellectuals associated with Samuel Hartlib who fostered programmes of a utopian character during the English Civil War. To these men the Puritan revolution seemed the time appointed for the restitution of man's dominion over nature, and these millenarian ideas led to the elaboration of utopian schemes which aimed at the utilitarian exploitation of scientific knowledge, a humanitarian programme grounded on the belief in its relevance to social amelioration and spiritual enlightenment. The Puritans stressed the importance of the reformation of education and the study of medicine, technology, agri- culture and economic planning, subjects relevant to the humanitarian ends of their scientific programme.

Bacon's experimental method and its adoption after the Restoration by the 'Bacon-faced' Royal Society has frequently been seen as an important feature of the revolution in scientific method in the seventeenth century. The experimental studies of Boyle and Hooke were justified by an appeal to Bacon's philosophical precepts, but reference to Bacon frequently

[1] P. Rossi, *Francis Bacon. From Magic to Science* (London, 1968).

served an apologetic purpose. In his *History of the Royal Society* (1667) Thomas Sprat sought to minimise the connection of the Royal Society with the ideology of the Civil War period, representing the Baconian experimental philosophy of the Society as a reaction to the activities of the Puritans. While Bacon's experimental method exercised a more limited influence than Sprat claimed, the visionary force of Bacon's writings had exercised an important effect on the generation that came to prominence in the Royal Society, and its impact was an enduring legacy of Puritan scientific attitudes. While the concerns of the Puritans may seem at variance with the achievement of a man such as Newton whose scientific work seems more congruent with modern scientific attitudes, the pervasive theological orientation of seventeenth-century science suggests that the endeavours and attitudes of the Puritans had an important impact in motivating men towards the study of nature. Although Puritanism was not a factor relevant to all aspects of the intellectual complexion of the seventeenth century, its impact demonstrates that theological beliefs were an important determinant of the emergence of the new scientific world view.[1]

This transformation in seventeenth-century thought, the triumph of a mechanistic philosophy of nature over Aristotelianism and hermeticism, had a decisive influence upon the intellectual climate, as manifested in the weakening of traditional beliefs in astrology, witchcraft and magical healing. While the assumptions of astrology were consistent with heliocentrism the rejection of the Aristotelian distinction between the terrestrial and celestial realms and of the doctrine of correspondences dealt a mortal blow to the credibility of astrological influence of the stars upon the earth; and the Newtonian cosmology envisaged the universe as a mechanical system of infinite dimensions rather than as a connected hierarchical structure whose operations were determined by celestial influences. While the impact of neoplatonism had fostered the plausibility of magical activities and astrology, the acceptance of a mechanistic world view led to the rejection of the animistic conception of the universe. In representing God as the lawgiver, Boyle argued that the search for scientific laws would enable the natural philosopher to distinguish the ordinary workings of nature from God's true miraculous interventions. Because the animistic view of nature blurred this distinction it was to be rejected, and hence the study of nature by human reason would enable the philosopher, as the priest of nature, to comprehend God's intentions. Although the magical desire for power over nature had contributed to the new attitudes to the natural world in the seventeenth century, the 'Baconian' experimental methodology offered a controlled and disciplined experimentalism congruent with the mechanistic world view which rejected the intelligibility of elaborating a web of influences between the macrocosm and the microcosm.[2]

[1] C. Webster, *The Great Instauration. Science, Medicine and Reform 1626–1660* (London, 1975).   [2] K. Thomas, *Religion and the Decline of Magic* (London, 1971).

III

The mechanistic world view of seventeenth-century science was formulated in the context of theological arguments that served to justify the concept of the lawlikeness of nature. The crucial point at issue in the controversy between Leibniz and Newton's spokesman Samuel Clarke in 1715–16 was over the question of divine interventions in the natural world. While Newton considered that divine interventions in nature were required to repair irregularities in the motions of the planets and demonstrated God's omnipotence, Leibniz contended that God had foreseen the wants of nature and that the laws of nature established by God were sufficient for the operations of nature. He rejected the Newtonian attempt to bridge the gap between the natural and the supernatural, arguing that God's providential control implied perfect foresight. The view that natural laws were sufficient for the explanation of natural processes was to become the dominant view in the eighteenth century. The progress of science itself as much as the critiques of Voltaire, D'Alembert and Hume, seemed to favour the rejection of Newton's distinctive theistic philosophy of nature. By 1800 Laplace was able to explain planetary perturbations in terms of Newtonian celestial physics, enabling him to find the hypothesis of God simply unnecessary. The increasing popularity of deism, the religion of reason, which subsumed divine causality under the concept of laws of nature, conceiving divine action as a first efficient cause and restricting divine agency to the creation of the universe and the establishment of immutable natural laws which maintained the operations of nature independently of divine energy, was a manifestation of the increasing secularisation of thought. Yet most scientists remained Christians, emphasising divine transcendence and activity and rejecting the subsumption of divine activity under the laws of nature; and some continued to insist on the compatibility of biblical theism and the comprehension of nature in terms of scientific laws.[1]

A famous example illustrative of the dominance of a theistic philosophy of nature is the confrontation between the 'uniformitarian' and 'catastrophist' geologists in England in the 1830s. Lyell asserted the absolute uniformity of geological forces both in kind and intensity, and on the basis of the principle of the uniformity of nature he rejected divine interventions in the course of the history of the earth, with the exception of the introduction of man which he retained as a supernatural event; while his opponents pointed to the occurrence of discontinuities in the geological and fossil records, and argued that the occurrence of distinct geological periods and the introduction of new species could not be explained by natural causes, and that their occurrence required divine intervention, albeit via secondary

[1] Paul Hazard, *The European Mind 1680–1715* (London, 1953).

causes. The controversy illustrates the shift in theological sensibility since the seventeenth century, for while both parties could agree that the wisdom of God was manifest in the works of creation, there was unease at schemes of conciliation which grounded theology on geological argument, and an increasing recognition of the futility of harmonising geology and the biblical account of creation. The application of the principle of the uniformity of nature in Darwin's theory of evolution by natural selection in his *Origin of Species* (1859), which explained the introduction of new species (including man) in terms of uniform natural processes, sustained the secularisation of knowledge, though Darwin's theory did not necessarily imply the renunciation of a belief in God as the creator of the universe or in the evolutionary process as the product of design. There was a growing commitment in the nineteenth century to a belief in the uniformity of nature, the restriction of divine action in nature to the creation of the universe, the rejection of the supposition of divine interventions to explain apparent discontinuities in the natural world, the separation of the natural and the supernatural, and the interpretation of science as theologically value-free. Enlightenment secularism had stripped the idea of progress of its eschatological foundations, and the methods and ideology of science were detached from theological implications; the theologically-neutral, progressive and secular optimism of the scientific endeavour was seen as expressing the 'material spirit of the age', as the physicist James Clerk-Maxwell succinctly put it in his inaugural lecture at Cambridge in 1871.[1]

The secularisation of scientific knowledge is one manifestation of the growing autonomy of scientific activity in the period 1780–1850. The professionalisation of science was reinforced by changes in the cognitive content of scientific knowledge, in which the secularisation of scientific thought was accompanied by the emergence and consolidation of newly-defined and specialised scientific disciplines. The 'natural philosophy' and 'natural history' of the eighteenth century were transformed into 'physics', 'chemistry', 'biology' and 'geology', each having its distinct boundaries, subject-matter, conceptual structure, techniques of investigation and trained, specialised practitioners.

In the *Principia* Newton offered the paradigm of a mathematical science of mechanics, and though he expressed the hope that all physical phenomena could be subsumed under analogous mathematical methods, illustrating his intentions by a mathematical treatment of optical refraction, in his *Opticks* (1704) the treatment of the problems of optics and chemistry was based on an experimental methodology and a speculative theoretical structure, an atomistic ontology which became bloated in later

---

[1] C. C. Gillispie, *Genesis and Geology* (Cambridge, Mass., 1951); R. Hooykaas, *The Principle of Uniformity in Geology, Biology and Theology* (Leiden, 1963); W. F. Cannon, 'The problem of miracles in the 1830s', *Victorian Studies*, 4 (1960).

editions of the *Opticks* to include a variety of explanatory agents, forces, active principles and the aether. This disjunction of methods and models was reflected in eighteenth-century natural philosophy. While the mathematical laws of mechanics were formulated on the basis of experiential concepts, and hypothetical entities such as atoms were eschewed, the phenomena of heat, light, electricity, magnetism and chemistry were explained by the supposition of short-range forces between atoms and in terms of relationships between ordinary matter and the imponderable fluids of heat, light, electricity and magnetism which were frequently viewed as different manifestations of the aether. These theories were speculative and largely qualitative, though attempts were made, notably by Laplace and Berthollet in Napoleonic France, to formulate a quantitative theory of the short-range forces of optics and chemistry. Indeed Laplace envisaged a unified natural philosophy in which the phenomena of mechanics would be explained in terms of molecular forces. The abandonment of this programme in Fresnel's wave theory of light and Fourier's *Analytical Theory of Heat* (1822) led to the emergence of a new style of physical explanation. Fresnel's theory of light as the vibrations of a universal fluid and Fourier's rejection of hypothetical entities in the science of heat in favour of a mathematical theory based on the experiential concept of temperature and formulated by analogy with the mathematical theories of mechanics, led to the rejection of the imponderable fluids.

Although Fourier's vehement anti-hypotheticalism was not accepted, his arguments were influential in that the new 'physics' was concerned with the formulation of mathematical, mechanical models, while speculative hypotheses, non-mathematical and non-mechanical, were rejected. Fourier's mathematical method implied the unification of mechanics and the phenomena of heat, light and electricity, the bridging of the traditional conceptual dichotomy in natural philosophy. Thus William Thomson's demonstration in the 1840s of the mathematical equivalence and physical analogy between the laws of heat, the motion of fluids, elasticity and electricity, his attempts to link mechanics and the study of heat, and Maxwell's discussion of the method of physical analogy in which the mathematical form common to the laws of heat and electricity brought the relations between disparate phenomena into prominence, emphasised the unity of the phenomena of 'physics', as the subject came to be called. The principle of the conservation of energy developed in the 1840s stressed the unity of the phenomena of physics, the relation between mechanics and heat, light, magnetism and electricity; and in articulating his formulation of the principle Helmholtz emphasised that the principle of the conservation of energy implied the reducibility of phenomena to mechanical principles. The programme of 'physics' became the programme of mechanical explanation, and the unifying role of the energy concept served to bring the phenomena of physics within the framework of mechanical principles.[1]

The emergence of 'physics' from natural philosophy, as a science with a newly-defined conceptual content and unity, was accompanied by the loosening of the ties between natural philosophy and chemistry. In the seventeenth and eighteenth centuries chemistry was associated educationally and professionally with the practice of medicine and pharmacy, but in the early decades of the eighteenth century Stahl and Boerhaave stressed that chemistry was a branch of natural philosophy rather than a manipulative art associated with alchemy and pharmacy. The Newtonian theory of nature provided an approach to chemical phenomena grounded on physical principles, rendering chemical phenomena intelligible in terms of short-range forces between particles. This programme exerted considerable influence in the eighteenth century, though Stahl resisted the subsumption of chemistry under a physicalist model, arguing for the conceptual autonomy of strictly chemical principles; in his view chemistry alone could penetrate the deepest secrets of nature and provide the key to a universal natural philosophy. Although Stahl's theory of phlogiston, the chemical principle of combustion, was to be rejected in Lavoisier's *Elements of chemistry* (1789), Lavoisier's renunciation of an explanation of chemical phenomena in terms of Newtonian atoms and forces in favour of a system of chemical classification based on narrowly chemical principles reflects the tradition of chemistry to which Stahl's writings had given rise. The Newtonian search for force mechanisms was also rejected in Dalton's *New system of chemical philosophy* (1808) in favour of a system of quantification based on the relative weights of chemical atoms; chemistry was loosed from its physicalist underpinning, the chemical theories of Lavoisier and Dalton providing a viable conceptual structure for chemical analysis and the elucidation of chemical substances. Chemistry had achieved a conceptual autonomy from 'physics', and the focus of debate among chemists in the first half of the nineteenth century on the content and conceptual foundations of their science turned to a discussion of the relationship between organic and inorganic compounds, the problem as to whether organic compounds required explanation in terms of concepts quite distinct from those applicable to the study of inorganic compounds. Only by the middle of the century was the essential unity of organic and inorganic chemistry accepted, chemistry as a subject becom-

[1] P. M. Heimann and J. E. McGuire, 'Newtonian forces and Lockean powers: concepts of matter in eighteenth century thought', *Historical Studies in the Physical Sciences*, 3 (1971); R. Fox, 'The rise and fall of Laplacian physics', *Historical Studies in the Physical Sciences*, 4 (1974); T. S. Kuhn, 'Energy conservation as an example of simultaneous discovery, in M. Clagett (ed.), *Critical Problems in the History of Science* (Madison, 1959); P. M. Heimann, 'Helmholtz and Kant', *Studies in History and Philosophy of Science*, 5 (1974); P. M. Heimann, 'Maxwell and the modes of consistent representation', *Archive for History of Exact Sciences*, 6 (1970); L. P. Williams, *Michael Faraday* (London, 1965).

ing established as a unified, autonomous science, with accepted conceptual boundaries.[1]

Similar conceptual, discipline-oriented transformations can be found in the emergence of 'biology' and 'geology'. The term 'biology' was first used early in the nineteenth century, and contemporary definitions emphasised that the science should be concerned with the vital functions of organisms, with physiology rather than with the concerns of traditional natural history, the classification and description of species including minerals as well as plants and animals. The study of the vital processes of organisms such as respiration, generation and sensibility became the focus of 'biology'; though the relevance of physico-chemical methods to vital processes remained the subject of debate, the subject-matter of the science had been defined as the study of the functional processes of organisms. The term 'geology' was also first used in this period, and agreement was achieved over the main principles and nomenclature of the science. Turning away from a disconnected body of knowledge of fossils and minerals and speculations over cosmogony, geologists regarded field-work as their method and the study of landforms and geological strata became the subject-matter of geology. Despite disagreement over the nature of geological processes there was agreement over the content of the science, and acceptance of geological maps and sections as expressive of its conceptual principles.[2]

The specialisation of scientific activity was accompanied by increasing opportunities for the pursuit of a scientific career and the wider availability of a scientific education in early nineteenth-century Europe. In the eighteenth century science prospered in universities as an appendage to medical education, and was firmly established only in universities such as Edinburgh and Leiden which had important medical faculties. At Oxford and Cambridge university chairs were frequently sinecures, while in German and French universities the emphasis was on teaching and professional training rather than the pursuit of scholarship and science. Opportunities for patronage were few; itinerant lecturers and textbook writers in England, and a few illustrious continental scientists such as Euler, D'Alembert and Maupertuis who were salaried occupants of scientific academies, were able to derive some financial sustenance from the practice of science. A notable feature of the development of science in early nineteenth-century Europe was its emergence into a socially-organised intellectual enterprise providing career opportunities for the new scientific specialist. This process took different forms in different countries, but the nature of this social transformation of scientific activity can be seen from an

[1] A. Thackray, *Atoms and Powers: An Essay on Newtonian Matter – theory and the Development of Chemistry* (Oxford, 1970): H. E. Guerlac, *Lavoisier – the Crucial Year* (Ithaca, 1961); R. P. Multhauf, *The Origins of chemistry* (London, 1966).

[2] W. Coleman, *Biology in the Nineteenth Century* (London, 1971); M. J. S. Rudwick, *The Meaning of Fossils* (London, 1972).

examination of the social integration of science in Germany, France and Britain.

In the early nineteenth century the German universities became transformed into institutions in which a scholar's devotion to research was the fundamental feature of professional ideology. An intellectual development that began in ancient history and classical philology became the model for the pursuit of scientific research. Under the leadership of the mathematician Jacobi and the physicist Neumann at Königsberg and the chemist Liebig at Giessen, by the 1830s independent scientific investigation by the student was coming to be regarded as a basic pedagogical tool. The study of the sciences was prized for its intrinsic intellectual value, and research and the publication of scientific results became the dominant characteristic of a scientific career to be pursued within a research-oriented university. Intellectual and social competition to succeed in scientific research led to an increase in specialisation, the creation of new fields of scientific investigation, and the universities expanded to absorb an increasing number of professors who were establishing themselves in new scientific disciplines. In France, by contrast, institutional conditions did not favour research; oratory was valued and one of the main criteria for academic success was the ability to cultivate large popular audiences for scientific lectures. A career as an academic lecturer or bureaucrat came to be the avenue for public success, and the social integration of science followed the prevailing cultural pattern.

While there was no typical pattern of scientific professionalisation in Britain there were a number of different opportunities for pursuing a scientific career. The paucity of state support for science and the absence of a regular career structure for the scientist led Babbage and Brewster to complain in the early 1830s that science was in decline in Britain, a complaint that illustrates the concern that was felt about the prospects of science as a career in Britain. The dramatic institutional expansion of science in early nineteenth-century Britain illustrates the increasing public recognition of scientific activity. The prevailing cultural mode in Britain emphasised self-help, individualism and libertarianism rather than state intervention or control, and manifested itself in the diversity of the national organisation of science. In the course of the period 1780–1830 the scientific scene in Britain was transformed by a burgeoning of scientific institutions, mainly voluntarily supported and devoted to the cultivation of specific scientific specialisations, which was paralleled by the growth of 'literary and philosophical' societies in the provinces. Between 1780 and 1830 a plethora of specialist societies, devoted to geology, mineralogy, astronomy, zoology and engineering, proliferated and flourished, and the new professional self-awareness led to the foundation of the British Association for the Advancement of Science in 1831, a body which sought to promote and patronise research by its meetings and research grants, and

the adoption of the neologism 'scientist' for the new scientific professional. Although opportunities for scientific education were limited, the
Scottish universities and the new University of London provided courses
of instruction in science, and from the mid-nineteenth century science was
integrated into the curriculum at Oxford and Cambridge. The provincial
scientific societies provided an audience for science; though largely non-
professional, this audience encouraged the belief in the cultural value of
science even as polite knowledge. By the middle of the century scientists
were securing patronage from government and industry in the form of
research grants and employment opportunities as technical experts.[1]

The integration of science into industrial and government activity after
1850 followed the intellectual and social transformations of science of the
preceding half-century. New science-based industries emerged, requiring
trained, specialised scientific manpower. Thus the discovery of aniline
dyes by W. H. Perkin in 1856 led to the establishment of a new dyestuffs
industry, but despite the British origin of this discovery the industry
prospered best in Germany where the value of research and the training of
chemists was appreciated. The development of the science-based electrical
communications industry stimulated physics education; the training of
students in William Thomson's physics laboratory at the University of
Glasgow was intimately related to Thomson's interests, scientific and
financial, in electrical telegraphy, industrial interests that led to his ultimate
elevation to the peerage. Thomson's scientific prowess established him as
the major figure in the laying of the Atlantic telegraph cable in the 1860s,
and his students performed research crucial to the success of the project in
his Glasgow laboratory; in due course the industry provided employment
opportunities for students graduating from his laboratory. In Germany,
Siemens' success in the electrical industry and concern with precision
engineering led him to found the Berlin Physical–Technical Institute, which
was completed in 1887, where research into fundamental physics and
technology was pursued; consequent on Siemens' belief in the technological utility of physics, pure science and technology were to flourish in
the same institution under the direction of Germany's greatest scientist,
Helmholtz. These examples illustrate the growing industrial utility of
science, which was to lead to the emergence of 'industrialised science'.

The historical relations of science, technology and the Industrial Revolution have been the subject of considerable debate. While assertions of the
essential independence of science and technological innovation in the
Industrial Revolution are common, recent research has sought to demon-

[1] D. S. L. Cardwell, *The Organization of Science in England* (London, 1957); G. L'E.
Turner (ed.), *The Patronage of Science in the Nineteenth Century* (Leiden, 1976); J. Ben-
David, *The Scientist's Role in Society* (Englewood Cliffs, New Jersey, 1971); R. S. Turner,
'The growth of professorial research in Prussia', *Historical Studies in the Physical Sciences*,
3 (1971); J. B. Morrell, 'Individualism and the structure of British science in 1830', *Historical
Studies in the Physical Sciences*, 3 (1971); R. M. McLeod, 'Resources of science in Victorian
England', in Mathias, *Science and Society*.

strate the links between science and industry in the Industrial Revolution and to question the assumption that theoretical advances were relevant to industrial development only after 1850. Part of the problem of analysis arises from the gap between intention and achievement in the application of scientific knowledge. A striking example of a link between science and technology in the eighteenth century is in the development of chlorine bleaching; but the fact that a 'correct' understanding of the chemistry involved had to await the work of Davy early in the nineteenth century does not imply that science was irrelevant to bleaching practice, for the earlier chemical work of Scheele and Berthollet was used by industrial bleachers. The creation of a formally coherent theory and its systematic application was not necessary for its industrial use, for more limited applications of fragmentary scientific knowledge could be of value. A significant minority of manufacturers were sensitive to the utility of science and its prospective implications for technological improvement.

The extent and significance of the links between science and industry are of crucial importance. While the Industrial Revolution in the techniques and organisation of manufacture occurred first in Britain, continental governments were more responsive to the need to encourage scientists to apply themselves to the development of technological processes. The French exercised supremacy in the theoretical aspects of power engineering; and various branches of industry, notably in dyestuffs, heavy chemicals, ceramics, mining and metallurgy were stimulated by state patronage in France to draw upon chemical expertise and research for the development of new techniques. Despite the assumption by British geologists of the practical advantages of their science to mining and of the importance of coal deposits to British industrial supremacy, geologists had little personal involvement in the practice of mining, and mining in Britain remained unresponsive to developments in geology; on the Continent, by contrast, mining technology was recognised as important and there was state patronage of mining education. Nevertheless, Britain's industrial development was in advance of that of continental countries, and it may be accepted that the main determinant of industrial change was the development of the economy rather than of technological innovations; growing industrial demand determined the introduction of new technical processes. Urbanisation, the growth of the population, and the development of canals in Britain aided the expansion of trade, and the acquisition of foreign trading privileges and a colonial empire provided a market for the products of manufacturing industry. While economic and social factors were the determinants of industrial development, industrialisation did involve the application of scientific knowledge.[1]

[1] D. Landes, *The Unbound Prometheus* (Cambridge, 1969); P. Mathias, 'Who unbound Prometheus? Science and technical change, 1600–1800', in Mathias, *Science and Society*; A. E. Musson and E. Robinson, *Science and Technology in the Industrial Revolution* (Man-

In addition to the direct impact, however limited in its overall significance, of scientific knowledge upon industry, there are more diffuse connections between scientific activity and the industrial revolution in
Britain. Scientific knowledge was seen as having practical import. The
foundation of the Royal Institution in 1799 illustrates the prevailing belief
in the utility of the scientific enterprise, many of its founders being landlords with an interest in philanthropy and agrarian reform; Davy's work
at the Royal Institution on agricultural chemistry and the scientific basis
of tanning was performed in response to their interest in agricultural
improvement grounded upon scientific understanding and the practical
application of scientific research. Although Davy's agricultural chemistry
had considerably less practical success than his research on tanning, it was
regarded as important in demonstrating the relevance of natural knowledge to practical ends. The emphasis on utility was not confined to
technical ends, but encompassed religious, intellectual and moral edification. The values of improvement, benevolence and utility which were
associated with the scientific enterprise indicate the important cultural
commitments which the cultivation of scientific knowledge was seen to
encompass in the period of the Industrial Revolution.

The importance of scientific knowledge in the new cultural patterns
associated with the Industrial Revolution can be seen in the way in which
Manchester manufacturers supported the foundation of the Manchester
Literary and Philosophical Society in 1781. The association of scientists
and industrialists in the society had little effect in the direct furtherance of
the application of science to industrial invention and innovation; the
significance of the patronage of science by industrialists is that science
came to be seen as the expression of the cultural values of the new manufacturing élite. In contrast to the traditional topics of polite knowledge,
science expressed the values of technological progress, intellectual enlightenment, and moral and spiritual edification. The enlightened values of
the comprehension of divine wisdom and the promotion of human happi-
ness and improvement were associated with the cultivation of natural
knowledge. The application of technology to economic use was viewed as
leading to the improvement of man's lot; and the progressivist values of
utility were seen as congruent to the cultural norms of the scientific enterprise. Although the impact of scientific research on technological innovation was relatively limited prior to 1850, the cultural values associated with
the pursuit of natural knowledge were a significant characteristic of the
society that produced the Industrial Revolution.[1]

chester, 1969); A. E. Musson (ed.), *Science, Technology and Economic Growth in the
Eighteenth Century* (London, 1972).

[1] A. Thackray, 'Natural knowledge in a cultural context: the Manchester model',
American Historical Review, 79 (1974); R. Porter, 'The industrial revolution and the rise of
the science of geology', in M. Teich and R. M. Young, *Changing Perspectives in the History
of Science* (London, 1973); M. Berman, *Social Change and Scientific Organization. The
Royal Institution, 1799–1844* (London, 1977).

CHAPTER X

SOCIAL THOUGHT AND SOCIAL SCIENCE

I

THE history of the social science disciplines as we know them is a fairly recent one. The word 'sociologie' was invented by Auguste Comte in the 1820s; 'political economy' was first used (in French) in 1613 but did not become current until the second half of the eighteenth century. 'Economics' was first popularised in its modern sense by Alfred Marshall in his *Principles of Economics* (1890); in the 1740s the word was still being used as Aristotle had used it, to denote household management, an activity which included the control of slaves and wives among other possessions. The notion of a 'science' as a distinct discipline did not emerge clearly in England until well into the nineteenth century, and nor did the word 'scientist', invented by Whewell in 1840. Even more significantly, perhaps, the words 'society' and 'social' acquire their modern meanings in English and French only in the late seventeenth and early eighteenth centuries.[1] The contrast between society and the state was central to nineteenth-century German thought but rarely made explicit before that time (though it was anticipated by Thomas Paine, who wrote in 1776 that 'society is produced by our wants, and government by our wickedness').

Social thought, in other words, was until recently both intellectually diffuse, in the sense that 'society' or 'societies' had not yet clearly emerged as an object of study, and socially diffuse, in that the occupational role of 'social scientist', like that of 'natural scientist', had not yet emerged. Nor had the various disciplinary specialisms: economics, sociology, social anthropology, political science and so forth. This means that to write the history of social thought in terms of modern disciplines is not only frustrating, as the same books and authors turn up repeatedly under different headings, but historically insensitive or, as Herbert Butterfield put it, 'whiggish'. What one should do, surely, is ask the rather more general questions: How did people in the past think about what we now call 'society'? Did they think about it at all, as something distinct from the rest of reality? What schemes of classification and explanation did they favour? What position in society did the more influential thinkers occupy and how did this influence their views? Only then, presumably, can one begin to ask questions about developmental trends, continuities and discontinuities.

---

[1] For the history of some of these terms, see Raymond Williams, *Keywords* (Glasgow, 1976).

In adopting this approach, however, one should not forget that most of the writers who are included in standard histories of social thought spent a good part of their time in a reflective examination of their own intellectual activity, comparing their own efforts to what others had done or were doing in the same area. Some saw themselves as contributors to an ongoing tradition; others as initiating a new enterprise, as Hobbes did when he claimed that 'Civil philosophy is no older than my own book *De Cive*.' Historians, of course, are rightly sceptical about this sort of claim, but it is an important feature of the social sciences, and sociology in particular, that rival claims about the origins of the discipline attract passionate support from later practitioners and can usually be seen to correspond to different views of the nature of the subject.

One might of course wish to deny any qualitative difference between the social thought of, say, the Greeks and that of later writers – a view which suggests a certain scepticism about the idea of a social science. Or one might, in the case of sociology, take as one's starting-point Comte's invention of the word 'sociology' (which rapidly replaced earlier neo-ogisms such as 'social physics', 'social physiology' or 'social mathematics'). More seriously, one may simply identify sociology with the professional activities of people calling themselves sociologists and emphasise the growth of sociological societies and journals in the 1890s, the establishment of the first professorial chairs, university courses and so on. But were recognisably 'sociological' activities not being carried on much earlier? What about the statisticians of British 'political arithmetic' in the seventeenth century and their German counterparts,[1] or the social thinkers of the eighteenth century – Montesquieu, Rousseau, Adam Smith and his Scottish contemporaries – let alone nineteenth-century figures like Saint-Simon, Comte, de Tocqueville, Marx and J. S. Mill?

If one tries to give a more sociological account of the history of sociology, the problems merely increase. Should it be seen as a response, either hostile or welcoming, to the challenge of the French Revolution or the Industrial Revolution or to the rise of working-class socialism? Does the story begin earlier in the eighteenth century, as the bourgeoisie consolidated its position in England and Scotland and fought its way to a similar prominence in France? Or at the time of the English Civil War – the age of Hobbes, Harrington and Locke? Or earlier still, with the emergence of commercial capitalism in the trading cities of Italy and the Low Countries?

It is often said that sociology involves the 'scientific' study of society, and in fact many social thinkers have identified themselves with this aim. But again, when does it begin: with Hobbes' attempt to generalise the billiard-ball physics of Descartes and Galileo to include social relations, or

[1] See G. N. Clark, *Science & Social Welfare in the Age of Newton* (Oxford, 1937, 1970). Paul Lazarsfeld, 'Notes on the History of Quantification in Sociology', *Isis*, 1961.

with the rather different approach of Condillac, Condorcet and others at the time of the French Revolution? Or with the twentieth-century cult of 'objective', 'value-free' social science?

The later part of this essay deals mainly with sociology, partly because it is the social science which I know best, but also because it is here that, since the end of the nineteenth century at least, the most important conceptual battles about the nature of social science have been fought. I have not been able to do justice to the other social science disciplines, nor to the more general influence on social thought of, for example, Kant, Nietzsche and Freud.

Any history of this kind is governed by a view about the relative importance of the writers discussed (and those omitted for reasons of space) and hence of the subject matter which they dealt with. The importance which I attach to the Marxist tradition should be clear from the selection and characterisation of what I take to be the crucial themes of social science and in my later treatment of the relationship between Marxism and the social sciences from the end of the nineteenth century onwards. Someone less influenced by Marxist themes would probably pay less attention, for example, to early accounts of class conflict and more to such traditions as natural law and civic humanism.

Some of the writers discussed in this essay considered themselves to be founding a science of society; others were merely concerned to advance the work of their predecessors; in either case, their criticisms of earlier theories were in turn intimately bound up with criticism of society itself or, alternatively, with an attempt to preserve the *status quo* from critical challenge. This essay will emphasise five developments which seem crucial to the social sciences as currently conceived:

(1) the emancipation of social thought from the constraints of a religious frame of reference and the associated need to provide an ideological justification of Christian beliefs – this secularisation took place in sixteenth-century Italy and was slowly consolidated elsewhere in Europe in subsequent centuries;

(2) another sort of secularisation – the separation of social analysis from normative political theory, of description from prescription;[1]

(3) associated with this, the ideal of a scientific approach to social analysis;

(4) a sense of long-term social development which in the eighteenth century came to replace the cyclical conceptions of history which were previously dominant;

(5) more specifically, a stress on the social bases of political forms – the idea that these are grounded in more general social relationships (especi-

---

[1] On the contrasting ideals of scientific knowledge of society and the *practical* social knowledge of ordinary members of society, see Jürgen Habermas, *Theory and Practice* (London, 1974), 'The Classical Doctrine of Politics in Relation to Social Philosophy'.

ally property relations) which *may* be linked to different forms or stages of production.

Taken together, these ideas yield a recognisably 'sociological' view of social structure and social change. With the fifth theme, most clearly articulated by Marx, we enter the central preoccupations of twentieth-century social thought, the realtionship between types of society and the political arrangements and systems of ideas which accompany them and help to sustain them.

Finally, the intellectual innovations listed above can be related, if only tentatively, to the main social changes which have taken place in Europe since the end of the Middle Ages – the development of capitalism and of the independent nation-state. It seems to be no accident that the Italian city-states, where a market society[1] was most solidly established, were also the source of major intellectual innovations at the beginning of the modern period, and also that these ideas had to be transferred to the arena of the large nation-states before social thought as we know it could emerge.

II

What resources were available to social and political thinkers in the sixteenth century? There were three broad conceptual frameworks which, in various ways, have remained influential. First, the classical tradition, centred around the Greek *polis* or city-state and the ideal of the politically active citizen; second, the medieval motion of society as a sort of organism, in which God had allocated individuals to their positions in the social division of labour for the common good and for His own greater glory; and thirdly, the countervailing medieval theme of feudal rights (in the sense of privileges) – a complex set of mutual obligations in which a national monarch appeared as a *primus inter pares*.

The relationship between these themes is a matter of considerable dispute,[2] but it seems likely that the medieval combination of an organic view of society with one which tied individual rights to specific social positions was a powerful source of legitimacy for a rigidly stratified estates society. The classical tradition was reincorporated from about the thirteenth century onwards and its influence can be seen in Renaissance humanism and the 'civic humanism' of the seventeenth and eighteenth centuries, and also, perhaps, in the tension between individualistic and

[1] The relationship between such terms as 'market society', 'commercial society' and 'capitalism' is not at all clear, though 'capitalism' tends to indicate the prevalence of wage labour. The word did not come into general use until the early nineteenth century, though 'capital' was used much earlier. See Williams, *Keywords*.

[2] I have drawn heavily on Walter Ullman, *The Individual & Society in the Middle Ages* (London, 1967). Ullman's approach has been strongly criticised by Francis Oakley, 'Celestial Hierarchies Revisited: Walter Ullman's Version of Medieval Politics', *Past & Present*, 60 (1973).

collectivistic emphases in the Natural Law doctrines[1] which remained influential until at least the eighteenth century.

If one looks more closely at the concepts which were available to social thinkers around 1500, one can see, for instance, the word 'state', which at first had only the meaning of 'condition', developing through 'status' to something like its modern political meaning. This seems symptomatic of the emergence, especially with Machiavelli, of the idea of a relatively circumscribed political system which could be set up and to some extent controlled by a technology of 'statecraft'. But the modern antithesis between state and society was not yet current; nor that between state or society and the 'individual', and nor was there anything like the modern concept of 'the economy'.[2]

It was possible nevertheless for writers such as Machiavelli, Guicciardini and Giovanni Botero to provide sophisticated accounts of social conflicts in terms of the relationship between the various social strata and the state.[3] Italian writers, since the fifteenth century at least, tended to see their societies as divided into upper, middle and lower classes on the basis of wealth and influence, whereas elsewhere in Europe people still thought in terms of the three 'estates': clergy, nobility and the rest. The Italian model was however something of a stereotype – there was more agreement on the *existence* of three groups than on their nature – and there was also a tendency to ascribe distinct personality characteristics to members of different classes; this can still be seen in the ambiguity of the word 'noble'. Where the Italians seem furthest from a modern approach, however, is in their static conception of society and history: they were not of course unaware of social change (in fact one of their major innovations was their stress on the differences between historical periods and their development of a new awareness of anachronism)[4] but they saw cycles of growth and decline where modern thinkers tend to see long-term secular trends. This cyclical approach in turn tended to encourage explanations of an anthropomorphic sort in which, for nations as well as for individuals, success breeds complacency, adversity strengthens the will, and so on. This can be seen, for example, at the beginning of chapter 5 of Machiavelli's *Florentine History*:

Nations, as a rule, when making a change in their system of government, pass from order to disorder, and afterwards from disorder to order, because nature permits no stability in human affairs ... states will always be falling from prosperity to adversity, and from adversity they will ascend again to prosperity. Because valour brings peace, peace idleness, idleness disorder, and disorder ruin; once more from ruin arises good order, from order valour, and from valour success and glory.

---

[1] See pp. 280 f. below.

[2] Peter Burke, *Culture and Society in Renaissance Italy 1420–1540* (London, 1972), chapter 8.

[3] Felix Gilbert, *Machiavelli and Guicciardini. Politics and History in 16th Century Florence* (Princeton, 1965). Stanislav Andreski (ed.), *Reflections on Inequality* (London, 1975) contains extracts from Machiavelli and Botero.

[4] Peter Burke, *The Renaissance Sense of the Past* (London, 1969).

III

By the second half of the eighteenth century, these static or cyclical views are giving way to ideas of progress and development; this is not of course the only difference between the social thought of this period and the most advanced examples of sixteenth-century thought, but it is one of the most significant for subsequent developments.

One can find the beginnings of an idea of secular development in Christian thought, which had to see Christ's time on earth as occurring at a determinate point in history, but this view could be held in conjunction with the belief in the decay of the world which would receive its *coup de grâce* with the Second Coming.[1] This vision of decay was gradually eclipsed, however, by a belief that intellectual progress at least was still taking place, especially in the natural sciences as observed by Roger Bacon (1214–94) and his namesake Francis Bacon who argued in his *Novum Organum* (1620) that 'from our age, if it but knew its own strength and chose to essay and exert it, much more might fairly be expected than from the ancient times, in as much as it is a more advanced age of the world, and stored and stocked with infinite experiments and observations'.

The tension between these two ideas came to a head at the end of the seventeenth century in the 'Quarrel of the Ancients and the Moderns' over the relative merits of classical and modern culture. Bernard de Fontenelle, one of the leading 'moderns', broke away from the analogy with physical senescence and argued that 'men will never degenerate, and there will be no end to the growth and development of human wisdom'.[2]

The extension of this view to the social and political sphere took a little longer; there is a tension, for example, in Giambattista Vico's *Scienza Nuova* (1725) between the cyclical theme which most commentators have stressed – the *corsi e ricorsi* – and a more developmental perspective foreshadowing Hegel's *Phenomenology of Mind* (1807).[3] Montesquieu's *Spirit of the Laws* (1748) has an apparently static Aristotelian framework, but it was quickly given a dynamic twist in Adam Ferguson's *Essay on the History of Civil Society* (1766); Ferguson stressed his debt to Montesquieu. A dynamic, historical approach was central to the Scottish Enlightenment; one critic complained that it required that one begin every subject 'a few days before the flood, and come *gradually* down to the reign of George the third'. This approach was however combined with a certain scepticism about the idea of progress; some continental writers were less inhibited. Turgot argued in 1750 that 'the whole human race, through alternate periods of rest and unrest, weal and woe, goes on advancing,

---

[1] Robert Nisbet, *Social Change and History, Aspects of the Western Theory of Development* (New York, 1969). Cf. J. G. A. Pocock, *The Machiavellian Moment* (Princeton, 1975), p. 31.

[2] Paul Hazard, *The European Mind 1680–1715* (London, 1953).

[3] Leon Pompa, *Vico* (Cambridge, 1975). Isaiah Berlin, *Vico & Herder* (London, 1976).

although at a slow pace, towards greater perfection'. Kant 'ventured to assume' the same trend. As Condorcet put it, 'we pass by imperceptible gradations from the brute to the savage and from the savage to Euler and Newton'.

Another difference between eighteenth-century social thought and that of the sixteenth century was the relatively frequent claim to be using the 'experimental' or, as we might say, 'observational' method, or to be giving an objective 'scientific' description of society and social laws in place of the moralistic emphasis of traditional social theory. This was undoubtedly an important part of the self-image of many eighteenth- and for that matter seventeenth-century thinkers, though their invocation of scientific method was cheerfully combined with an *a priori* and dogmatic psychology. The success of the natural sciences was clearly an influence on social thought, but its effects were visible more in the formulation of programmatic statements than in substantive innovation. In the seventeenth century Hobbes had been strongly committed on the mechanical view of the world and sought to apply it to social phenomena but this did not make his work so very different in practice from that of a more traditional thinker like Harrington.

One of the dangers involved in stressing the imitation by social theorists of natural scientific models, whether from Descartes, Galileo or Newton, is that one may be led to neglect the search for social explanations of developments in the natural sciences themselves.[1] It has been argued that as capitalism became more securely established in the sixteenth and seventeenth centuries, the developing market society found ideological expression both in a mechanical view of nature as a whole and in what C. B. Macpherson has called 'the political theory of possessive individualism'. With the development of capitalism individuals enter the market as independent individuals, first to exchange goods and then increasingly to sell their labour or, more accurately, their ability to work (what Marx called their labour-power) to capitalist employers. It is less important, writes Macpherson, to determine which came first in Hobbes' mind – the mechanical view of nature or the individualistic view of society – than to recognise that 'it is only a society as fragmented as a market society that can credibly be treated as a mechanical system of self-moving individuals'. However, even if this is a useful way of interpreting seventeenth-century thought,[2] it is clear that the principal eighteenth-century writers were not really 'individualists' in this sense.

Whatever the role of natural science as a source of methodological prescriptions and substantive hypotheses about society, it was certainly

[1] Two works which attempt this are: Franz Borkenau, *Der Übergang vom feudalen zum bürgerlichen Weltbild* (Paris, 1934; Darmstadt, 1971). E. J. Dijksterhuis, *The Mechanization of the World Picture* (Oxford, 1961).
[2] Macpherson's book *The Political Theory of Possessive Individualism* (Oxford, 1962) has been strongly criticised by, for example, Keith Thomas and John Dunn.

a powerful example of progress. In this role, it should be seen in conjunction with the idea of cultural progress, symbolised most powerfully for eighteenth-century thinkers in the notion of manners or *moeurs*. Hobbes had described the life of man in the state of nature as 'solitary, poor, nasty, brutish and short'; by the following century, life seemed (at least in the more advanced regions of Europe) rather less precarious and rather more gentle. Once one started to think in terms of cultural progress, it was a short step to a full-blooded dynamic view of the development of civility, civilisation, civil society.

The growth of travel contributed to this awareness. There was, first, the 'discovery' of other civilisations, especially in America. Travellers' tales were enthusiastically read and they provided not only comparative material for works such as Jean Bodin's *Six Books of the Commonwealth* (1576) and later Montesquieu's *Spirit of the Laws* but also a framework for utopias – a developing genre – and works of social criticism such as Montesquieu's *Persian Letters* (1721) and Diderot's *Supplément au Voyage de Bougainville* (first published in 1796 but probably written in 1771). A favourite idea of medieval thought was that of the 'chain of being' which linked all creatures from the angels at the top via human beings of various social statuses down to the most insignificant animal. The sixteenth and seventeenth centuries saw a 'temporalisation' of at least the human part of this chain which anticipates later conceptions of social evolution.[1] The discovery of so many radically different civilisations must have had a considerable impact on the rather sheltered thinkers of Christian Europe; it is perhaps not surprising that it frequently produced an ethnocentric reaction which legitimated ruthless exploitation, forcible conversion and genocide.[2]

In the eighteenth century it became increasingly easy for the intelligentsia itself to travel around Europe; Scots in particular travelled to France and brought back the ideas of the Enlightenment. More generally, travel contributed to the growth of a cosmopolitan and well-informed bourgeois public which was a crucial feature of intellectual life in the period.[3] With the growth of newspapers, public opinion took on an importance which it had had in the past only at times of revolutionary ferment. Precensorship was abolished in England by the Licensing Act of 1695, roughly contemporaneously with the creation of the Bank of England and the formation of the first cabinet government. In France too, despite a more onerous censorship, political journalism became a going concern in the second half of the eighteenth century.

It is perhaps not too fanciful to suggest a connection between the

[1] Margaret T. Hodgen, *Early Anthropology in the 16th and 17th Centuries* (Philadelphia, 1964). See also Arthur O. Lovejoy, *The Great Chain of Being* (Harvard, 1942).
[2] R. L. Meek, *Social Science and the Ignoble Savage* (Cambridge, 1976).
[3] Jürgen Habermas, *Strukturwandel der Öffentlichkeit* (Neuwied & Berlin, 1962).

emergence of a self-conscious bourgeois public and the emergence of the modern concept of *society* in the sense of *a* society. Once this notion was firmly established, it was not difficult to move on to assert the social determination of political events. (The word 'economy' seems to reveal a similar development.)

One aspect of seventeenth- and eighteenth-century reflection on 'society' is the controversy over the sociability or unsociability of man. However implausible it now seems, the notion of society as the artefact of a number of isolated individuals coming together as if to found a commercial enterprise was an important assumption of much seventeenth-century thought. Hobbes gave such uncompromising expression to the idea that man is basically unsociable that the following century was littered with attempts by Shaftesbury, Mandeville and others to refute him.[1] These ideas found their way via Francis Hutcheson to Ferguson, John Millar and Adam Smith (who succeeded Hutcheson as Professor of moral philosophy at Glasgow).

The idea of the social nature of man was of course a commonplace to Aristotle, as was the idea that political events could often be explained by the relationship between different social strata.[2] But in classical Greece and Renaissance Italy the emphasis tended to be on what social and ideological preconditions favoured the desired political regime (in particular the 'civic spirit' of the people). By the time of Montesquieu and Rousseau, a more relativistic attitude to political regimes has set in: geographical constraints such as the size of the territory are seen as prior to questions about the best regime. However admirable Rousseau considers the state form proposed in the *Social Contract* (1762), he emphasises that it is impracticable for a large nation.

The English Revolution had impressed on contemporaries the influence of the distribution of property on political arrangements; it had been seen to operate both as a determinant of political allegiances – those with property coming together to defend it against those with none – and as a resource in the class struggle, enabling one to raise armies. Both the Earl of Clarendon and James Harrington gave a considerable place to these phenomena in their interpretations of the Civil War.[3] Linguet's comment on Montesquieu's book that 'le véritable esprit des lois, c'est la propriété' would not have sounded out of place in seventeenth-century England.

This awareness of the importance of property slowly developed into a focus on economic production, with the distribution of property seen as a function of particular types of production and not just the result of some

[1] See Werner Sombart's rather wild article, 'Die Anfänge der Soziologie' in M. Palyi (ed.), *Erinnerungsgabe für Max Weber*, vol. I (Munich & Leipzig, 1923).
[2] See for example his *Politics*, Book IV, chapter 11.
[3] Christopher Hill, *Puritanism & Revolution* (London, 1965).

remote act of conquest. David Hume complained: 'I do not remember a passage in any ancient author where the growth of a city is ascribed to the establishment of a manufacture' and Voltaire criticised Montesquieu (rather unfairly) for having 'no knowledge of the political principles relating to wealth, manufactures, finances and commerce'. R. L. Meek quotes two passages from William Robertson's *History of America* (1777) as the two basic propositions of the Scottish School:

In every inquiry concerning the operations of men when united together in society, the first object of attention should be their mode of subsistence. According as that varies, their laws and policy must be different . . .
Upon discovering in what state property was at any particular period, we may determine with precision what was the degree of power possessed by the king or by the nobility.[1]

Finally, a rather later example from France: Barnave's *Introduction à la Révolution Française* (c. 1790) gives an interesting twist to Montesquieu's claim that laws are relations arising out of the 'nature of things':

The will of man does not create laws: it has no influence, or hardly any, on the form of governments. It is the nature of things – the social stage which the population has reached, the land it lives on, its riches, its needs, its habits, its customs – which governs the distribution of power . . . as soon as commerce and skills begin to penetrate among the people and create a new source of riches for the working population (la classe laborieuse), there are the beginnings of a revolution in the political law: a new distribution of wealth prepares a new distribution of power. Just as the possession of land raised up the aristocracy, industrial property raises the power of the people; they acquire their freedom, their numbers increase and they begin to influence events.

Two important themes which were virtually absent in sixteenth-century Italy, but pervaded social thought elsewhere in Europe are natural law and the analysis of the social structure in terms of 'estates'. The subject of natural law and natural rights is appallingly complex but it can hardly be ignored, if for no other reason than the prominence of these ideas in the American and French Revolutions.[2] Natural law, even in the Middle Ages, had involved a complex mixture of classical and Christian themes and of individualism and collectivism. What Ernst Troeltsch called 'modern profane natural law', the work of Bodin, Grotius, Hobbes, Pufendorf, Althusius and others was similarly ambiguous: it functioned 'partly to explain the absolutist governments which had been produced by the movement of events, and partly (at a later stage) to justify the emancipation of the citizen from such governments and to proceed to the erection of new political ideals upon that basis'.[3] The same ambiguity pervades

---

[1] R. L. Meek, *Economics and Ideology* (London, 1967), 'The Scottish Contribution to Marxist Sociology'.
[2] Habermas, *Theory and Practice* ('Natural Law and Revolution').
[3] Ernst Troeltsch, 'Natural Law and Humanity in World Politics', in Otto Gierke, *Natural Law and the Theory of Society 1500–1800* (ed. E. Barker, Cambridge, 1934). See also Otto Gierke, *The Development of Political Theory* (London, 1939).

social contract theory, which can be used either to sanction obedience to the state or (with the added premise that the state or the ruler had violated the contract) a natural right to armed resistance; here again there was a gradual shift of emphasis towards individualism. Finally of course the notion of rights can be given an economic content as in the right to a 'fair wage'.

The word 'nature' is of course enormously complex: natural law, natural rights, human nature, the nature of things, laws of nature. To call something unnatural is to make a prima facie case for its abolition, on either moral or technical grounds: to call it natural is to suggest that it is either desirable in itself or at least a necessary evil. Rousseau's discussion of natural and social inequality is a good example of this, as is the use of a more scientistic concept of nature as a legitimating principle in much nineteenth-century thought and in particular in 'social Darwinism'.[1] In the eighteenth century the emphasis lay on 'human nature' as an organising principle for an ostensibly empirical but in practice largely *a priori* psychology. The idea of a unified 'human nature' may perhaps have impeded awareness of social change, but it was a powerful ideological weapon in the Enlightenment critique of the 'unnatural' institutions of the *ancien régime*.

Although the idea of society being stratified into orders or estates had been largely abandoned in Renaissance Italy, it remained current in other parts of western Europe for some time. In France, Charles Loyseau's *Traité des Ordres et simples dignitez* (1610) was frequently reprinted during the rest of the century. According to this model, society was made up of (in order of precedence): the clergy, the nobility and the third estate. Each of these orders was itself internally stratified – the first two according to the obvious criterion of formal rank, the third usually into professionals, minor legal officials, merchants, farm workers, artisans, unskilled labourers and beggars. In theory, the relations of precedence were continuous: the humblest priest ought to precede the highest nobleman. In practice, Loyseau commented 'it can nowadays frequently be observed that men possessing a degree of secular rank are unwilling to give way to priests if these do not have some degree of ecclesiastical rank'. Wealth, however, was officially a criterion of only minor importance.[2]

There is considerable controversy among modern historians about whether this is an accurate picture of the social structure of seventeenth-century France. Roland Mousnier argues that these *were* the salient divisions in French society until the development of classes in the eighteenth century; hence, the peasant 'furies' of the period were not class struggles but protests against the tax demands of the central government

[1] Robert Young, 'Man's Place in Nature', in M. Teich and R. Young (eds), *Changing Perspectives in the History of Science. Essays in Honour of Joseph Needham* (London, 1974).
[2] Roland Mousnier, *Social Hierarchies: 1450 to the Present Day* (London, 1973).

(which the landlords joined their peasants in opposing). Against this view, the Soviet historian Boris Porshnev argues that there was a substantial degree of class antagonism in the French countryside; the Absolutist state shielded the dominant feudal aristocracy against the effects of this antagonism.[1] This controversy serves as a reminder that the 'estates' model was not simply the artefact of rather primitive social thinkers: it corresponded at least to the superficial form of real social relations and its gradual abandonment can be explained by changes in those social relations.

In England the 'estates' model does not seem to have been taken very seriously, but nor was there any general agreement on an alternative, though Sir Thomas Smith's division into 'four sortes: gentlemen, citizens, yeomen artificers and labourers' was influential (*De Republica Anglorum*, A Discourse on the Commonwealth of England, published in 1583, but written some eighteen years earlier). A century later, in his *Observations Upon the United Provinces of the Netherlands* (1673), Sir William Temple gave a similar, though more precise account of the social structure of the Netherlands:

The people of Holland may be divided into these several Classes: the Clowns or Boors (as they call them), who cultivate the Land, The Mariners or Schippers, who supply their Ships and Inland-Boats, the Merchants or Traders, who fill their Towns. The Renteneers, or men that live in all their chief Cities upon the Rents or Interest or Estates formerly acquired in their Families: and the Gentlemen and Officers of their Armies.

Temple, the British Ambassador, went on to say that rentiers rather than merchants predominated in the Dutch government.

Gregory King published in 1696 a 'Scheme of the Income, and Expence of the Several Families of England, calculated for the year 1688' with over twenty categories.[2] Finally perhaps one should mention the influential historical myth of the Norman Yoke as a primitive expression both of patriotism and of popular class consciousness. But although class antagonism was clearly visible in the Civil War and reflected in the contemporary accounts of Clarendon and Harrington,[3] the idea that classes are bound up with particular forms of economic production[4] comes a good deal later, in Barnave's rather conservative account of the French Revolution. By the middle of the nineteenth century, the idea of class conflict had taken hold, though of course bourgeois and aristocratic thinkers hoped that it could be contained.

Alexis de Tocqueville, reflecting on the French Revolutions of 1830 and

[1] Boris Porshnev, *Les Soulèvements Populaires en France de 1623 à 1648* (Paris, 1963). See also A. D. Lublinskaya, *French Absolutism: the Crucial Phase* (Cambridge, 1968) and Roland Mousnier (ed.), *Problèmes de Stratification Sociale* (Paris, 1968).

[2] Summarised in Macpherson, *Possessive Individualism*, pp. 279 ff.

[3] Christopher Hill, *Puritanism and Revolution*, chapter 3.

[4] See Marx's letter to Weydemeyer, 5 March, 1852.

1848, gives a fascinating analysis in his *Recollections* of the way contemporary class struggle differed from that in Florence:

Florence at the close of the Middle Ages presents many analogies with our condition now; first the middle class had succeeded the nobility, and then one day the latter were driven out of government in their turn, and a barefoot gonfalonier marched at the head of the people and thus led the republic. But this popular revolution in Florence was the result of transitory and peculiar circumstances, whereas ours was due to very permanent and general causes, which, having thrown France into agitation, might be expected to stir up all the rest of Europe. For it was not just a party that triumphed this time; men aimed at establishing a social science, a philosophy, and I might also say a common religion to be taught to all men and followed by them. Therein lay the really new element in the old picture.

The later eighteenth century, then, can plausibly be seen as a turning-point in the history of social thought. The idea was firmly established that political arrangements are determined by more basic social causes and that these are subject to change. Normative theories of a natural law or contractarian type were still in evidence but were giving place to a more historical approach, and the normative theory which was to be most influential in Britain, Benthamite utilitarianism, appeared with the scientific trappings of the felicific calculus. There were the beginnings of professional specialisation in both natural and social philosophy, and the latter could boast two reasonably distinct sciences: social statistics or 'political arithmetic' which had flourished in England and Germany in the later seventeenth century (and was now rather in decline) and the political economy of the physiocrats in the 1750s[1] and of Adam Smith. Smith's venture into political economy with *The Wealth of Nations* (1776) was an offshoot of more general moral and political preoccupations, but the book quickly became consecrated as the original text of the first, and still the most prestigious social science – economics.

IV

Nineteenth-century social thought was dominated by the ideas of social development and of the importance of economic production which became prominent in France and Scotland in the second half of the eighteenth century. These ideas can be found not only in Marxism but also in French positivism and Herbert Spencer's social evolutionism. Eighteenth-century thinkers were preoccupied with progress, reason, and the nature and tendencies of modern society: in the nineteenth century these concerns were more sharply focussed on *productive* progress and *scientific* reason in an *industrial* society.

The idea of a social science, that 'society must submit to being treated

[1] On the physiocrats, see C. Gide and C. Rist, *A History of Economic Doctrines* (London, 1915); and R. L. Meek, *The Economics of Physiocracy: Essays & Translations* (London, 1962).

like physical reality under investigation...' (Condillac) was well implanted in France before the Revolution but it was not systematically taken up until later. The Revolution induced a general sense of anxiety among intellectuals and it also, unless they saw it as merely the results of an arbitrary outbreak of pure evil, reinforced their awareness of the social determination of political phenomena. Conservative thinkers like Burke stressed the complexity of human societies and the undesirability of trying to change them according to intellectualistic blueprints.[1] Another response was that of the 'idéologues' led by Destutt de Tracy, and the positivists;[2] the latter emphasised the reform of ideas but in a way which would make them appropriate to the scientific requirements of an 'industrial' or productive class which included not just workers but what we still call 'industrialists' – productive entrepreneurs. A part of this programme, for both Saint-Simon and Comte, was the creation of a science of man to which Saint-Simon devoted his *Mémoire sur la Science de l'Homme* (1813).

Karl Marx's early work too, was in part a response to the French Revolution and in particular its failure to produce a society of liberty, equality and fraternity either in France itself or in Germany.[3] There is a tendency to over-emphasise the philosophical character of Marx's concerns (in particular his critique of Hegel) in his early work. Marx's motives for criticising Hegel and the form of his criticisms were political as much as philosophical, and Hegel himself was by no means remote from the concerns of political economy.[4] Marx (who had no time for Comte but was a careful reader of Saint-Simon) gave a more precise expression to the ideas of the social determination of politics, the specific science (political economy) which was most crucial to the understanding of modern society and the social location of the historically progressive class, the proletariat. Political economy, which in its conventional form was used to legitimate capitalist society, could be turned against that society to reveal its basis, its 'anatomy', in the exploitation of the workers and the economic contradictions which resulted from capitalist relations of production (Marxists have argued ever since whether the eventual collapse of capitalism would result mainly from its intrinsic contradictions or mainly from the growth of a revolutionary consciousness within the working class). The development of these ideas is reflected in the character of Marx's works: the isolated political polemics, philosophical critiques and socio-historical sketches give way to the mature system which Marx sketched

[1] Edmund Burke, *Reflections on the Revolution in France* (1790). On the influence of conservative thought on sociology, see Robert Nisbet, *The Sociological Tradition* (New York, 1966). But see also A. Giddens, 'Four Myths in the History of Social Thought', *Economy & Society*, 1972.
[2] Frank Manuel, *Prophets of Paris* (Harvard, 1962); Leszek Kolakowski, *Positivist Philosophy* (Harmondsworth, 1972).
[3] See his essay 'The King of Prussia & Social Reform' in Karl Marx, *Early Writings* (Harmondsworth, 1975).   [4] See Georg Lukács, *The Young Hegel* (London, 1975).

out in the *Grundrisse* and partially completed in *Capital* and the *Theories of Surplus Value*.[1]

The social thinkers of the early nineteenth century can be divided into those, like Saint-Simon, Comte, Marx and the anarchists, who envisaged a radical transformation if not the complete replacement of the state and of conventional political arrangements, and those who recognised the importance of contemporary social transformations such as the replacement of the *ancien régime* and the growth of the industrial proletariat but wished to retain something like the existing political system. The 'prophets of Paris', men like Condorcet, Saint-Simon and Comte, were not really interested in political details, though they often constructed absurdly elaborate plans of other aspects of the future society; Marx, partly in reaction to these schemes, generally took the view that the political institutions appropriate to socialist and communist society could not meaningfully be planned in advance of the basic socio-economic transformation. The more conservative approach is best represented by Alexis de Tocqueville who provided a brilliant description in his *Democracy in America* (1835–40) of what he took to be the salient features of a modern society and which he expected to manifest themselves in his native France. Tocqueville's *Recollections* show him adapting his moderate conservative beliefs to successive upheavals in French political life. In Britain, John Stuart Mill advocated the preservation of the bourgeois constitutional state by gradual and partial extension of the franchise to the working class (*On Representative Government* (1861), chapter 8). In the event, this 'many-headed monster' was incorporated into the political systems of most western European countries without seriously affecting the way in which politics was carried on; in the United States, this incorporation was accomplished without even the inconvenience of a working-class party requiring to be socialised into the norms of the parliamentary game. Those like Marx and Engels who expected universal suffrage to be the prelude to working-class power underestimated the ability of the bourgeoisie to maintain its hegemony[2] in the new circumstances of a mass democracy.

In the second half of the nineteenth century, sociology began to emerge as a distinct subject with concerns that were recognisably different from those of 'economics' and of conventional political thought. The new subject developed very much under positivist auspices, in the wake of the programmatic statements of Comte and J. S. Mill's influential reflections

[1] A pithy expression of Marx's theory which (unusually) does not contain the word 'class' is the *Preface to the Contribution to the Critique of Political Economy* (1859). See also the *Communist Manifesto* (1848). A good introduction to Marx's work is the selection of readings edited by Tom Bottomore and Maximilien Rubel, *Karl Marx. Selected Writings in Sociology & Social Philosophy* (Harmondsworth, 1963).

[2] On the concept of 'hegemony' see Antonio Gramsci, *Selections from the Prison Notebooks* (London, 1971).

on 'the logic of the moral sciences'. Herbert Spencer's evolutionary system was developed independently of Comtean (and incidentally Darwinian) influence, but he and Comte were firmly identified with each other and with the emergent discipline.

This initial positivist formation tended to isolate sociology from detailed political analysis. Sociology was also cut off, especially in England, from any close relationship with the relatively well-established traditions of social statistics and philanthropic reformism; the elaborate syntheses of Spencer could not easily be related to the painstaking work of fact-gathering reformers like Booth and Rowntree.[1] Another division which particularly affected British social thought was that between sociology and social anthropology; the latter flourished first in an evolutionary form and later, with Malinowski and Radcliffe-Brown, in an early variety of 'functionalism', a theoretical approach which stresses the contribution of institutions or practices to the social systems which contain them. Evolutionary anthropology was an important part of the work of L. T. Hobhouse, Professor of Sociology at the London School of Economics from 1907, but otherwise the two subjects developed in relative isolation, a division which France largely escaped.

The history of sociology around the turn of the century is very much a national story. Émile Durkheim and Max Weber, who have come to be seen as the leading figures of the period, were roughly contemporaries but did not even discuss one another's work. Weber did not begin to think of himself as a sociologist until the last ten years of his life; up to 1909, when he was one of the founders of the Deutsche Gesellschaft für Soziologie, his generally disparaging references to the subject show that he still conceived it in the naturalistic and extravagantly systematising form which it had taken in the work of Comte, Spencer and their successors. His earlier work, bisected by the nervous breakdown which followed his father's death in 1897, is best described as social and economic history, plus some social surveys and, from 1903 onwards, a series of articles on the methodology of the 'cultural sciences' (which essentially means history); these articles were written concurrently with those on *The Protestant Ethic and the Spirit of Capitalism*. By 1913, Weber was working on the systematic treatise which was posthumously published as *Economy and Society*, though even this work takes the form of a series of typologies whose data were provided by historical research, rather than a 'theory' of society in general, modelled on some natural science.

Weber's arm's length relationship to sociology for most of his life is partly explained by the subject's low degree of penetration into the German academic establishment. The only chair in sociology until after

[1] Philip Abrams, *The Origins of British Sociology 1834-1914* (Chicago, 1968). See also Stefan Collini, 'Sociology and Idealism in Britain 1880-1920', *Archives Européennes de Sociologie*, XVIII, 1977.

the First World War was held in Cologne by Leopold von Wiese. Ferdinand Tönnies was officially a 'philosopher' from 1881, an 'economist' in 1913 and a 'sociologist' only from 1921 until 1933. The other 'founding fathers' of German sociology were, for one reason or another, 'marginal': Georg Simmel was Jewish, Robert Michels was a socialist, and Weber was a virtual invalid from 1898 until the beginning of the War.

The position of sociology in France did not look, in formal terms, any more secure: in 1914 the only sociological positions in France were Durkheim's chair in Paris in Educational Science and Sociology, the chair in Bordeaux which he had previously occupied and a lectureship in 'économie sociale'. But Durkheim had his journal, the *Année Sociologique*, and he defined the subject in broad enough terms to include a number of cognate disciplines.[1] Durkheim's own work ranged over suicide, the division of labour and primitive religion. Weber subscribed to the *Année* from its inception; had he been French, he might have begun much earlier to call himself a sociologist.

Despite these national differences, there were common features in the work of the sociologists of this generation. They rejected evolutionary naturalism as represented by Spencer and a number of their contemporaries, though the historical framework with which they tended to replace it was hardly less impoverished.[2] It was Tönnies who picked up Sir Henry Maine's distinction between 'status' and 'contract'[3] and, with his dichotomy of *Gemeinschaft* (community) and *Gesellschaft* (society) set the tone of a whole generation's theorising about the specific character of modern society and the way it differed from earlier forms. *Gemeinschaft* was small, intimate and personal: *Gesellschaft* was anonymous and market-dominated. As Tönnies used the terms, they were 'ideal types', both of which might characterise in some degree the same concrete phenomenon, but there was a clear implication that the transition from earlier forms of society to modern industrial capitalism was a transition from *Gemeinschaft* to *Gesellschaft*. Durkheim made a related distinction in his *Division of Labour* (1893) between 'mechanical' and 'organic' solidarity, while the theme of the impersonal calculation which constitutes the capitalist market is central to Simmel's *Philosophy of Money* (1900) and to Weber's discussion of 'rationalisation'.[4]

---

[1] Terry N. Clark, *Prophets & Patrons: The French University and the Emergence of the Social Sciences* (Harvard, 1973). See also Steven Lukes, *Emile Durkheim. His Life and Work* (London, 1973).

[2] Philip Abrams, 'The Sense of the Past and the Origins of Sociology', *Past & Present*, 55 (1972).

[3] This is one of many places where sociology has drawn on an earlier tradition, the comparative history of institutions (Maine, Fustel de Coulanges, Otto Gierke and many others). See for example, John Burrow, *Evolution & Society. A Study in Victorian Social Theory* (Cambridge, 1966).

[4] Ferdinand Tönnies, *Community & Association* (London, 1955). Georg Simmel, *Philosophy of Money* (London, 1978). Max Weber, *Economy and Society*, 3 vols (New York, 1968).

These writers also tended to reject historical materialism as a system, though Michels was at first a Marxist, Tönnies was always sympathetic, and Weber always saw Marxism as a pre-eminent quarry for useful hypotheses although 'completely finished' as a system. Simmel, too, claimed that his *Philosophy of Money* aimed not to refute historical materialism but to provide it with an extra foundation in a sort of social psychology.

Another important aim of Durkheim and Weber was to distinguish sociology from psychology. Durkheim claimed that whenever a psychological explanation is offered of a social phenomenon one can be sure that it is wrong, though his own book *Suicide* came close to doing just that. Weber, too, was concerned to show that his interpretative sociology of 'action' was only peripherally concerned with psychological processes. Rational action as he defined it did not require a psychological explanation any more than a successful mathematical calculation, and psychological considerations became relevant only when the action deviated from a 'rational' course.[1]

This rather anxious attempt to seal the border with psychology is partly explained by the inchoate nature of that discipline at the time. More importantly, perhaps, the sociologists felt compelled to distinguish their work so carefully from psychology because their own emphasis on the way human behaviour is governed by ideas, norms, values and so on came so close to the domain of an empirical psychology. This emphasis on ideas has sometimes been overstated,[2] but it is clear that these writers were concerned to a significant extent with ideological phenomena: Weber and Pareto investigated the logic of rational action (and the latter in particular the determinants of non-rational action); Durkheim was preoccupied with the nature of social solidarity and shared ideas; Weber's political analysis is centred around the way in which a regime successfully obtains legitimacy in the eyes of the subjects; both Durkheim and Weber devoted a large part of their attention to the consequences of religious beliefs for social solidarity and economic activity.[3]

Finally, one should note that these writers adopt a slightly distant attitude to economic phenomena; they do not by any means ignore them, but they tend to focus on them from an oblique angle. Durkheim talks about the division of labour, but as a form of social solidarity in which

---

[1] Max Weber, *Economy & Society*, 3 vols (New York, 1968), vol. 1. Max Weber, *The Theory of Social & Economic Organization* (New York, 1947). This is an earlier translation of the first part of *Economy & Society*. There is no intellectual biography of Weber which is remotely comparable to Lukes' *Durkheim*. See, however, Marianne Weber, *Max Weber. A Biography* (New York, London, 1975); Arthur Mitzman, *The Iron Cage* (New York, 1970).

[2] Talcott Parsons, *The Structure of Social Action* (New York, 1937). There is a similar emphasis in Göran Therborn's *Science, Class & Society* (London 1976) especially chapter 5.

[3] Weber, *Economy & Society*. See also 'The Social Psychology of the World Religions' in H. Gerth and C. Wright Mills (eds), *From Max Weber* (London, 1948). Émile Durkheim, *The Elementary Forms of the Religious Life* (London, 1915).

economic considerations are very much in the background; capitalist rationalisation appears in Tönnies, Simmel and even Weber under the aspect of its social and even psychological concomitants, as a 'sociological category of economic action' (Weber). The desire which dominates Marx's work, to give an account of capitalist society as a socio-economic totality, has been eclipsed by more specialised preoccupations.

One should remember that economics was also becoming narrower and more specialised at this time; in Germany and Austria the 'historical school' had lost its long rearguard action against the proponents of a general, deductive and subjectivistic economic theory which claimed to deal adequately with the 'economic aspect' of any society, thus obviating the need to study the whole socio-economic totality. Weber himself adopted an intermediate position in this dispute: he stressed the interdependence of the economy and the rest of a society but his models of rational action have a close affinity with the approach of the marginalist economist Karl Menger.[1]

From a Marxist point of view however these developments in both sociology and economics represent a failure to attain the level which Marx had already reached: that of the social basis of economic categories and the economic basis of the rest of social life. The force of this analysis is to cast the classical sociologists of the turn of the century as a sort of intellectual counter-revolution, fragmenting Marx's synthesis and diverting attention away from it.[2] The sociologists retort that the 'synthesis' was a failure anyhow. This is the basis of the long-standing antagonism between sociology and Marxism, with only a handful of individuals and groups daring to move between the lines.[3]

The Marxist critique can usefully be contrasted with Robert Nisbet's view that the central concepts and preoccupations of sociology derive from post-Revolutionary conservatism, with its stress on community, authority, status, the sacred and alienation. In concentrating on the origin of these concepts, Nisbet neglects the way in which Durkheim and Weber for instance were trying to integrate sociological ideas in the service of a revitalised liberalism.[4] But from a Marxist perspective the distinction between conservatism and liberalism is less salient; what counts is the defence of the capitalist *status quo* against the new challenge of the socialist movements. Durkheim was sympathetic to socialism but defined it in an idiosyncratic way and was more interested in a sort of guild socialism of

[1] W. J. Cahnman, 'Max Weber and the Methodological Controversy in the Social Sciences' in W. J. Cahnman and A. Boskoff (eds), *Sociology and History* (New York, 1964). Thomas Burger, *Max Weber's Theory of Concept Formation* (Durham, N. Carolina, 1976).

[2] Alvin Gouldner, *The Coming Crisis of Western Sociology* (London, 1971). Martin Shaw, *Marxism and Social Science* (London, 1975). Göran Therborn, *Science, Class & Society*.

[3] Tom Bottomore, *Marxist Sociology* (London, 1975). Tom Bottomore and Patrick Goode (eds), *Austro-Marxism* (Oxford, 1978).

[4] See note 1, p. 284 above.

occupational groups than in the objectives pursued by the French workers. Weber, too, occasionally expressed a degree of sympathy for socialist ideas but the primacy which he accorded the power position of Germany and his anxiety about the growth of rationalisation and bureaucratisation led him to a qualified defence of the capitalist order. Of the sociologists of this period, only Robert Michels was an active socialist, and he later gravitated towards fascism.

V

The question of the 'critical and conservative tasks of sociology' is an extremely difficult one.[1] The divorce between economics and sociology *has* tended, I think, to trivialise the latter by confining it to the realm of values and norms. But recent moves towards reconciliation, whether under the banner of 'interdisciplinarity' or, more seriously, in the rebirth of Marxist approaches within sociology and the call by economists for a revival of political economy,[2] suggest that these divisions are not insurmountable. At a more basic level, one can say that while few of the classical sociologists have been solidly behind the oppressed, few have been unequivocal conservatives. It is sometimes argued that all social research is critical in the sense that the facts it collects will subvert erroneous beliefs, but this view neglects the way in which theoretical and ideological frameworks structure the facts which are collected and their mode of presentation. The notion that scientific theories are abandoned because of their failure to survive crucial empirical tests has been discredited in the case of the natural sciences;[3] the more realistic view that a community of scientists abandons a theory for a complex mixture of 'good' and 'bad' reasons is even more appropriate to the social sciences, where the word 'theory' is little more than a metaphor.[4]

These considerations raise the further question of the ideological and social preconditions of social thought itself. Clearly, the systematic study of some aspect of society (or for that matter nature) as a full-time occupation presupposes a division between mental and manual labour which in turn presupposes a society which generates an economic surplus adequate to support its non-productive members. More specifically, the science done by amateurs with independent means may differ significantly from that done by large teams of research workers in bureaucratically organised institutes. Social thought as a systematic activity has been the work of a bourgeois intelligentsia, beginning with the gentlemen-scholars of the

[1] Habermas, *Theory and Practice.*

[2] Edward Nell, 'Economics: the Revival of Political Economy' in Robin Blackburn (ed.), *Ideology in Social Science* (Glasgow, 1972).

[3] T. S. Kuhn, *The Structure of Scientific Revolutions*, 2nd edition (Chicago, 1970).

[4] On the use of the term 'theory' in social science, see Robert Merton, *Social Theory & Social Structure*, enlarged edition (New York, 1968), part I, chapter 4: 'The Bearing of Sociological Theory on Empirical Research'.

eighteenth century and ending with the salaried professionals who teach in universities today. This suggests a further hypothesis of a Marxist character, that as the bourgeoisie withdraws to a defensive position in the face of the proletariat, its intellectual activity will become increasingly apologetic, ideological and vapid.[1] But one may argue no less plausibly that the desire to preserve the *status quo* from some real or imaginary threat is just as good a stimulus to sociological insight as the desire to change that *status quo*.

What does seem clear, however, is that social change and crises concentrate wonderfully the minds of social thinkers, as does perhaps their own social marginality. For in a society where nothing appears threatened or historically problematic, nothing is intellectually problematic either. It can hardly be a coincidence that social thought flourished in Florence in the wake of its political conflicts in the fifteenth century, or in England in the middle seventeenth century, or in France and Scotland in the second half of the eighteenth.

Since the First World War, and more particularly since the Second, European sociology has 'taken off' both as a research activity and as a subject taught in universities and increasingly also in schools. Social research has been transformed by the refinement of statistical techniques and the handling of data on punched cards and computers. There is now an enormous social research industry, drawing on sociology and social psychology and devoted to a variety of purposes from the sale of commodities to other forms of manipulation of human populations. Empirical research carried out within sociology tends to be theoretically eclectic and casual; 'theory' is generally confined to the opening and closing paragraphs of the research report.

The dominant theoretical paradigm from the forties to the mid-sixties was the 'structural–functional' approach developed in the United States by Talcott Parsons, Robert Merton and others. In Europe, however, functionalism was more a reference-point than a binding allegiance, and on the Continent it had to compete with various traditions inspired by Marxism.[2] In British sociology, 'conflict theory' (itself – ironically – in large part inspired by a German sociologist: Ralf Dahrendorf) to some extent occupied the position held on the Continent by Marxism.[3]

The theoretical achievements of functionalism and system theory now seem rather meagre, but their demise in the 1960s is more easily explained

[1] Marx believed that economics had made no progress since Ricardo; Lukács claims that bourgeois literature declined after 1848. See also C. B. Macpherson, 'The Deceptive Task of Political Theory', *Cambridge Journal*, 1953–4.

[2] In France, Sartre, Merleau-Ponty and to some extent Alain Touraine; in West Germany, the 'Frankfurt School' of critical social theory, to which a useful introduction is Paul Connerton (ed.), *Critical Sociology* (Harmondsworth, 1976).

[3] Ralf Dahrendorf, *Class & Class Conflict in Industrial Society* (London, 1959). John Rex, *Key Problems of Sociological Theory* (London, 1961).

by other factors such as an anxiety about its conservative flavour and in particular its stress on 'consensus'. Sociologists' sensitivity to this dimension was of course itself largely the product of the upsurge in working-class and student militancy in the late sixties. More recently, the growth of women's movements has given rise to rethinking in other areas of the subject – in particular, a critique of empirical research based on unreflectively held theoretical assumptions.[1]

All this suggests that sociology is a rather insubstantial discipline, with little theoretical ballast of its own, tending, as Marx said of philosophy, to share the illusion of the epoch: conservative or radical according to the spirit of the times, sensitive to racism and sexism only when prodded by active social movements. This impression is I think largely correct, though one can easily point to noble exceptions such as C. Wright Mills and Herbert Marcuse in the United States or the British sociologists who painstakingly charted the acute poverty which persisted amid apparent 'affluence' in the 1950s.

American and European sociology are at present floundering in a theoretical free-for-all which alarms those who were trained in the calmer professional ambience of the fifties. The future development of the subject will inevitably be a product of more general social forces. At present it seems that a loose and undogmatic Marxism is taking up, at least in Britain, the reference-point role which used to be filled by functionalism – not just in theoretical sociology but in specialisms like the sociology of the family or of science. These developments in turn have reopened the question whether the present disciplinary boundaries of the social sciences are ultimately beneficial.

I should like to thank Peter Burke for his very considerable help in the conception and preparation of this essay. I am also grateful to Michèle Barrett, Tom Bottomore, John Burrow, Stefan Collini and Donald Winch for commenting on an earlier version and to Maurice Hutt for drawing my attention to Barnave.

---

[1] See, for example, the two volumes edited by Diana Leonard Barker and Sheila Allen, *Sexual Divisions & Society: Process & Change* and *Dependence & Exploitation in Work & Marriage* (London, 1976).

CHAPTER XI

RELIGION AND SECULARISATION

I

AT first sight it all seems quite simple and obvious. Medieval man lived in a predominantly religious culture, but we live in a predominantly secular one, and the process of the secularisation of European culture took place, for the most part, in the period covered by this volume. The Renaissance, the Reformation, the Scientific Revolution, and the Enlightenment were all milestones on the road to a secular culture and society, and the secularisation process accelerated in the nineteenth and twentieth centuries. One theological position after another was made untenable by repeated attacks and was abandoned for another, further behind the lines, in the shrinking territory of the sacred. Belief in the supernatural was gradually replaced by a more rational, scientific outlook, a process summed up by the sociologist Max Weber as 'the disenchantment of the world' (*Die Entzauberung der Welt*). The clergy lost in turn their monopoly of learning, their power to persecute the unorthodox, and their influence on the policy of governments.

The fundamental change of attitude between the sixteenth century and the twentieth may be summed up in two quotations. In his *General History of the Indies* (1552), Francisco López de Gómara described the discovery of America as 'The greatest event since the creation of the world (excluding the incarnation and death of Him who created it).' But in 1969, when men first landed on the moon, Richard Nixon spoke quite simply of 'the greatest week in the history of the world since the creation'.[1]

This secular trend was celebrated in Auguste Comte's *Cours de Philosophie Positive* (1830 onwards), which divided the history of mankind into three ages, 'the theological or fictitious', the metaphysical, and the scientific; in W. E. H. Lecky's *History of the Rise and Influence of the Spirit of Rationalism in Europe* (1865); in J. W. Draper's *History of the Conflict between Religion and Science* (1874), A. D. White's *History of the Warfare of Science with Theology* (1896), and J. M. Robertson's *Short History of Freethought* (1899), epic accounts in which the heroes of the struggle with obscurantism included Copernicus and Montaigne, Bruno and Galileo, Bayle and Voltaire.

Like urbanisation and industrialisation, with which it is often linked, secularisation appears to have been one of the major social processes which have shaped Western society in the last five hundred years. The

---

[1] Gómara quoted in J. H. Elliott, *The Old World and the New* (Cambridge, 1970), p. 10; Nixon quoted in N. Mailer, *A Fire on the Moon* (London, 1970), p. 365.

process was not always obvious to the clergy and laity who participated in it (the term 'secularisation' was first used in its modern sense in the nineteenth century), but then people are not always aware of the long-term social trends through which they have lived. The fact that contemporaries did not see that the changes which we label 'secularisation' were taking place, or gave these changes a different interpretation, needs to be borne in mind, but is not a valid objection to the employment of the term by twentieth-century sociologists and historians.

Other objections cannot be disposed of so easily. It has been suggested that the term 'secularisation' does not refer to any unified 'master-trend', but only to a number of discrete elements, 'loosely put together into an intellectual hold-all'.[1] It may refer to the decline in the wealth, power, or status of the church; to the increasing autonomy of the laity; to the 'shrinkage' or 'dilution' of the sacred; to the 'death of God'; or, more generally, to the replacement of spiritual values by more material ones, which leads to the paradox that the rise in the wealth and power of the church (diagnosed as increasing 'worldliness'), may indicate secularisation as surely as its decline. The 'secular' is something of a residual concept, defined by opposition to the 'religious', and religion is notoriously hard to pin down with a definition. A historian is professionally bound to point out that in western Europe (the area to which this brief essay is confined), people have had very different conceptions of religion at different periods, have drawn more or less sharp distinctions between the sacred and the profane, and have drawn these distinctions in different places. Draper and White and Robertson went wrong, and made Copernicus and Bruno, for example, seem too modern, because they were not sufficiently aware that the war between 'science' and 'religion' was one in which not only the individual combatants but the aims of the two sides (if there were just two sides) changed from generation to generation.

We might seek to avoid these problems by following the example of the French, and talking not of 'secularisation' but 'dechristianisation'; but then Christianity too has meant something different at different times.[2] There is no escape. To understand changes in the attitudes and values of western Europeans between 1500 and the present, we are going to have to use categories which were themselves changing during the period. However, as a simple working definition, I shall consider secularisation primarily as the process of change from the interpretation of reality in essentially supernatural, other-worldly terms to its interpretation in terms which are essentially natural and focussed on this world.[3]

[1] D. Martin, *The Religious and the Secular* (London, 1969). Cf. B. Wilson, *Religion in Secular Society* (London, 1966), H. Lübbe, *Säkularisierung* (Munich, 1965), and H. Blumenberg, *Die Legitimität der Neuzeit* (Frankfurt, 1966), ch. 1.

[2] J. Delumeau, *Catholicism from Luther to Voltaire* (London, 1977), pp. 293–330.

[3] For examples of wider definitions, É. Durkheim, *The Elementary Forms of the Religious Life* (1912: New York, 1961 edition), pp. 37–63; T. Luckmann, *The Invisible Religion* (London, 1967).

There are other problems. The majority of the population of western Europe has left us no record of their attitudes. Their private assumptions about God and nature, the church and the world may not have been clear even to themselves. There are no windows into men's souls through which the historian may peer. What he can do, however, is to look for changes in the public sector, in the culture, or the 'social cosmology', as it is called in chapter XII, below. It has been suggested that 'Men do not act, as members of a group, in accordance with what each feels as an individual; each man feels as a function of the way in which he is permitted or obliged to act.'[1] These cultural permissions and obligations have a history.

The most immediate problem for the would-be historian of secularisation is the problem of the base-line.[2] When was it that the sea of faith was at the full? It will be necessary to take a look at medieval distinctions between spiritual and temporal, clergy and laity, the church and the world. In the Middle Ages, the term 'church' referred at once to the community of believers (dead as well as living), and to the clergy, an identification suggesting that the clergy were the church *par excellence*. The status of cleric was considered higher and holier than that of layman. Indeed, in medieval English the laity, the unlearned, the vulgar and the unchaste were all described by the same term: 'lewd'. This earthly city was far inferior to 'the glorious City of God', this world to the next. Indeed, the 'world' was associated with the flesh and the devil as a source of temptation every Christian must avoid, and from the twelfth century onwards, treatises on 'the contempt of the world', and 'the misery of the human condition' can be found in increasing numbers.[3] The term 'secular' carried pejorative overtones in the Middle Ages. It referred to mere time-bound existence, as opposed to eternal life, or to the world outside the cloister, the idea being that monks were the true 'religious', while parish priests were mere 'secular' clergy.

It may be objected that this view of the church comes from texts written by the clergy. So it does, and we must beware of making the contrast between a religious Middle Ages and a secular modern period too sharp; but the clergy's social dominance and cultural hegemony is confirmed by other evidence. Their privileges included freedom from secular taxation and from lawsuits in secular courts. When the accused pleaded 'benefit of clergy', his clerical status was proved by a reading-test, another example of the identification between the clergy and the learned. Theology was considered 'queen of the sciences', with philosophy as her 'handmaid'. The higher clergy were prominent in politics, with the pope a 'temporal' ruler to be reckoned with, and the bishops leading magnates. The church was also a great landowner.

It is curious to reflect that Innocent III (pope 1198–1216) was the

---

[1] C. Lévi-Strauss, *Totemism* (1962: Eng. trans., Boston, 1963), p. 70.
[2] G. Le Bras, *Études de Sociologie Religieuse*, vol. I (Paris, 1955), pp. 267–301; Delumeau, *Catholicism*, pp. 227–55.
[3] D. Howard, *The Three Temptations* (New York, 1966).

author of a treatise on the need to despise the world and also one of the most powerful men in Christendom. The wealth and power of the church were, as generations of reformers emphasised, a grave threat to spiritual values, but they also represented the dominance of spiritual values, in the sense that the laity's gifts to the church revealed their commitment to a world beyond this one. Hence a history of secularisation can never be free of irony and paradox.

The hold of religion on the life of the laity was also a strong one in the Middle Ages. Baptism, annual confession and communion, and Sunday mass were all compulsory. The clergy dominated education, just as they controlled the hospitals which looked after the sick, the old and the poor. Birth, marriage and death had a religious meaning; it was especially important to make a 'good death', recommending one's soul to God and the saints. Political power was justified, disasters were explained, and hopes and fears were expressed in religious terms. Space and time were given a religious framework. Heaven and Hell were considered actual places – Heaven beyond the stars and Hell at the centre of the earth. History was divided into periods according to the major events recorded in the Bible, such as the Fall, the Flood, and the Incarnation. Since the Bible was the Word of God (although the Word of God was not contained in the Bible alone), the truths 'revealed' in it were considered superior to the truths discovered by mere human reason. Christianity was a 'mysterious' religion in the sense that it contained mysteries, truths which could not be grasped (let alone discovered) by reason unaided. Revelation was superior to reason as the supernatural was superior to the natural. Supernatural interventions in daily life were taken for granted. God and the saints were believed to work miracles, and miracles were defined as breaches of the law of nature. The law of nature depended on God's ordinary power, but could be suspended by virtue of his 'absolute' power. The devil and his attendant demons were also believed to exercise supernatural powers. The French historian Lucien Febvre once summed up this 'supernaturalist' world view by saying that before about 1650, people lacked any sense of the impossible; they simply distinguished the ordinary from the unusual.

These were the official doctrines of the church. Some of them were challenged by medieval heretics like John Wyclif and Jan Hus. Even the orthodox, from 1100 and still more from 1200 onwards, were thinking increasingly in 'naturalist' rather than in 'supernaturalist' terms – the decline of judgement by ordeal and the rise of natural theology are two important steps in this direction.[1] Secularisation did not begin in 1500, or even with the early Renaissance. All the same, the doctrines summarised above offer some kind of base-line from which to assess later changes.

[1] R. W. Southern, 'Medieval Humanism' in his *Medieval Humanism and Other Studies* (Oxford, 1970), pp. 29–60; W. Ullmann, *The Medieval Foundations of Renaissance Humanism* (London, 1977).

II

There can be no doubt that European learned culture has become more secular since the Renaissance, but the process of its secularisation has been neither sudden nor smooth.

The most distinctive feature of the Renaissance, the revival of antiquity, was a revival of secular ideals, the ideals of the educated Greeks and Romans, men who had not exactly rejected their gods but had certainly come to take them less seriously than their ancestors. The Renaissance 'humanists' were so called because they were interested in the 'humanities' (grammar, rhetoric, poetry, history, ethics), rather than the study of God or Nature. They were not irreligious, but their interests implied the dethronement of Queen Theology from her privileged position in the university curriculum. The humanists placed more stress than medieval intellectuals had done on human reason, at the expense of divine revelation; on the potential dignity of man, as opposed to the misery of the human condition; and on worldly experience (*vita activa*) rather than the retreat from the world (*vita contemplativa*). Lorenzo Valla argued that the monastic way of life was not superior to that of the laity. Marsilio Ficino was so devoted to Plato that he was accused of worshipping him. Pietro Pomponazzi was a 'naturalist' in the sense of one who believed that nature operated according to general laws without the intervention of God, angels or demons; so-called miracles were simply unusual events with natural causes. Pomponazzi also held that natural causes governed the rise and decline of religions – Christianity included – and that the immortality of the soul, although an article of faith, could not be demonstrated by human reason. At a more practical level, at much the same time, Machiavelli's *Prince* gave the ruler advice on how to succeed in this world, if necessary by doing wrong, instead of telling him, as was customary in treatises of this kind, what the law of God forbade him to do.

We do not know how many people shared the views of Pomponazzi and Machiavelli; we do know that their books provoked a chorus of denunciation. In any case, it should not be thought that either man was a secret atheist. They were anticlerical Catholics whose religion had less place for the supernatural than was traditional in their culture. As for neo-platonists like Ficino, their devotion to Plato was not incompatible with Christianity, while their stress on contemplation and escape from 'the prison of the body' was, of course, the reverse of worldly. The Renaissance was not a movement which can be described as secular without any qualification.[1]

[1] P. O. Kristeller, *Renaissance Thought* (New York, 1961); E. Rice, *The Renaissance Idea of Wisdom* (Cambridge, Mass., 1958); C. Trinkaus, *In Our Image and Likeness* (2 vols, London, 1970), esp. ch. 14.

It is even harder to give a straight answer to the question whether the Reformation was or was not a secularising movement. It was primarily a religious revival, a protest against the worldliness of the church in general and the Renaissance papacy in particular. The reformers took the Bible more seriously as a guide to life than their predecessors had done. And yet the Reformation did involve secularisation in more than one sense.

Luther's pamphlet *To the Christian Nobility of the German Nation* was an appeal to the laity against the clergy which expounded the famous doctrine of the priesthood of all believers. What Luther says is that every Christian is a priest. What he implies is that no one is a priest, in the sense that the clergy are not superior to the laity. In practice, in Protestant regions, it was the prince who stepped into the place the pope had been forced to vacate and headed the local church. The so-called 'theocracy' of Calvin's Geneva was an exception to this rule, but the Genevan church was administered by lay 'elders' alongside the clergy. In any case, the Protestant clergy, who were allowed to marry, were closer to the laity than medieval priests had been.

The Reformation also involved a lay takeover of much church property, in particular that of the religious orders: indeed, the term 'secularisation' was first used, in the seventeenth century, to refer to this process.[1] The reformers supported this takeover because they believed that monks were idlers and that the true way to serve God was by work in one's own 'vocation' or 'calling', a term once reserved for the priesthood but now, significantly, extended to worldly occupations. One may therefore call the Reformation a secularising movement in the sense that the reformers advocated a more worldly religion than was traditional, a religion purged of what they liked to call 'superstition', in which the faithful were no longer encouraged to spend their money on candles or masses or indulgences. The other-worldly asceticism of monks and hermits was replaced by a new ideal, the 'worldly asceticism', as Max Weber called it, of the diligent thrifty merchant labouring in his calling.[2]

Meanwhile Catholic Europe was experiencing the Counter-Reformation, a movement in defence of traditional Catholic cults and beliefs against the threat of Protestantism. Yet the Counter-Reformation also involved change, including a sharper separation between the sacred and the secular. Dancing and acting in church were now forbidden, to emphasise that a church was a holy place. Priests were forbidden to wear secular clothes, exercise secular occupations or take part in secular festivities, to show that – whatever Luther had said – they were specially holy people. From the later sixteenth century onwards, they were trained in special

---

[1] Lübbe, *Säkularisierung*, pp. 23–5.
[2] M. Weber, *The Protestant Ethic and the Spirit of Capitalism* (1904–5: Eng. trans., London, 1930), ch. 4.

'seminaries', segregated from the laity, to whom the universities were increasingly abandoned. There is a sense in which this reaffirmation of the special position of the clergy had as its unintended consequence the admission by the church of the autonomy of the laity.

Another unintended consequence of Reformation and Counter-Reformation was the rise of scepticism. Whether some educated men now ceased to believe in Christianity or even in God is a question still controversial among specialists in the period. The clergy denounced 'atheists' and 'libertines', but it is not clear what they meant by these terms or whether atheists in the modern sense existed. We are on safer ground in talking about a rise of 'scepticism' in the more technical sense of doubts about the reliability of the evidence for any proposition. The Protestants had cast doubt on the authority of the pope; the Catholics, on that of the Bible. Little wonder then that the doctrines of the ancient Greek sceptics, best known through a treatise by a certain Sextus Empiricus, should have attracted sixteenth-century intellectuals, or that Montaigne should have taken as his motto the question, *Que sais-je?* What do I know? This fundamental scepticism did not stop Montaigne from practising Catholicism, or, in all probability, from accepting its doctrines. He quoted Tacitus with approval that 'it is more reverent to believe in what the gods have done than to investigate it'.[1]

The sceptics were not the only ancient philosophers to be revived in the sixteenth century. The Stoics, notably Seneca, were also influential in this period, one of religious war in which men needed the consolation of philosophy and in which the stoic virtue of 'constancy' (an inner strength of mind proof against both exaltation and depression), was a necessary form of self-defence. The Netherlander Justus Lipsius published the most popular exposition of neo-stoicism, *On Constancy*, in 1583. Thus, ironically enough, religious conflicts indirectly encouraged the revival of secular philosophies.

Stoicism and even scepticism (applied to knowledge attained by reason rather than to truths known by faith) could be, and were made compatible with Christianity. A greater threat was posed by the revival of a third classical philosophy: Epicureanism. Christians were unhappy with its ethics, based on the axiom that pleasure is the highest good; with its denial of immortality; with its doctrine that 'religion' or 'superstition' was simply the result of man's fear of nature, which increasing knowledge would dissipate; and with its materialist cosmology, without room for divine intervention. 'What is the use', complained Calvin, 'of believing in a God like that of the Epicureans, a God who has retired from governing the world and takes pleasure in doing nothing?' These ideas, as popularised by the Roman poet Lucretius, who died about 55 B.C., in his book *On*

[1] R. H. Popkin, *The History of Scepticism from Erasmus to Descartes*, second edition (Assen, 1964), esp. ch. 1.

the Nature of the Universe, were revived in the sixteenth century and seem to have been fashionable in some upper-class circles in the seventeenth. Giordano Bruno, who was burned in Rome in 1600 for his rejection of Christianity, was an admirer of Lucretius. La Fontaine called himself a 'disciple of Epicurus', and he was not the only one; while three complete French translations of Lucretius were published in the second half of the seventeenth century.

Some of the clergy of the time feared that they were surrounded by 'atheists' or 'libertines', who considered religious doctrines mere fables and were as suspect in their morals as in their faith. These clergymen probably misunderstood what was going on. The epicureans did not preach self-indulgence – that was not what they meant by 'pleasure' – and they were not atheists in the modern sense; there was a place for a creator in their system. However, their God was remote, impersonal, difficult to distinguish from nature or reason, while their morals were detached from religion. The revival of Lucretius, like the revival of Seneca, both expressed and encouraged the secularisation of European learned culture.[1]

One reason for the appeal of Epicurus and Lucretius was that their view of the universe fitted in so well with the new 'mechanical philosophy' of Galileo and Descartes, which was part of the Scientific Revolution of the seventeenth century (above, chapter IX). The Scientific Revolution was not an anti-religious movement. Indeed, the desire to reveal 'the wisdom of God manifested in the works of creation' was one of the main drives towards new discoveries. However, these discoveries revealed incompatibilities between what was written in the 'Book of Nature' and what was written in Scripture, and led to clashes between natural philosophers (not yet called 'scientists') and theologians. In his *Letter to the Grand Duchess* (1615), Galileo declared that it was the Bible which must be reinterpreted in the light of his discoveries and those of Copernicus, not the other way round. The Catholic Church reacted by condemning both Copernicus and Galileo. Descartes escaped condemnation; but his vision of a universe like a huge machine set in motion by a remote God had as little place for the supernatural as Galileo's.

One reaction, notably in England, to the incompatibilities between faith and reason, the Bible and the new philosophy, was to try to reconcile them. A common means of reconciliation was to emphasise 'natural theology' or 'natural religion'; in other words, the knowledge of God which can be obtained by using human reason alone. Two favourite pieces of natural theology were the argument from consensus, that God must exist because he is worshipped everywhere, and the argument from design,

[1] L. Forster, 'Lipsius and Renaissance Neostoicism', in A. Stephens *et al.* (eds.), *Festschrift for R. Farrell* (Bern, 1977), pp. 201–20; J. S. Spink, *French Free Thought from Gassendi to Voltaire* (London, 1960); W. J. Bouwsma, 'The Secularisation of Society in the Seventeenth Century', in *Thirteenth International Congress of Historical Sciences, Proceedings* (Moscow, 1970).

that the fabric of the universe implies the existence of a creator just as a watch implies a watchmaker. These arguments were intended to defend Christianity, but the new emphasis on natural theology also involved changing Christianity by playing down its supernatural elements. From John Locke's *Reasonableness of Christianity* (1695), which argued that 'God is economical with miracles', it was only a step to John Toland's *Christianity not Mysterious* (1696), which tried to show that 'there is nothing in the Gospel contrary to reason or above', and another step to Matthew Tindal's *Christianity as old as the Creation* (1730), which declared Christianity a mere 'republication' of the law of nature, provoking some thirty-odd refutations by 1733. Finally, David Hume's *Essay on Miracles* (1748) suggested that it is impossible ever to prove that a miracle has occurred.

The process of change described in the last few paragraphs may be summed up as the rise of 'Deism', in the sense of the belief in an omnipotent and benevolent but distant and impersonal creator, who does not interfere with the laws of nature; 'a lazy monarch lolling on his throne' according to the seventeenth-century poet John Oldham; 'constitutional monarchy in heaven', according to the intellectual historian Paul Hazard. God was deprived of his 'absolute power' to suspend the laws of nature and work miracles. Spinoza went further than most but in the same general direction when, in his anonymous *Tractatus Theologico-Politicus* (1670), he referred to God as a synonym for nature or the structure of the universe.

In the mechanical universe there was no room for magic or witchcraft any more than for miracles. The great European witchcraze came to an end in the late seventeenth century (though isolated trials and even executions continued to take place), because the majority of educated men stopped taking witches seriously. The phenomena previously explained in terms of witchcraft and the work of the devil were now attributed to natural causes, just as apparently accurate prophecies were now dismissed as tricks or coincidences, and comets explained in natural terms instead of being taken as signs of God's anger. In the eyes of most educated western Europeans, the world was no longer enchanted.[1]

Some intellectuals went further still and undermined Deism. An increasing knowledge of the world outside Europe demolished the argument from consensus by revealing the existence of polytheist peoples. Objections to the argument from design were put forward in Diderot's *Letter on the Blind* (1749), Hume's *Dialogues on Natural Religion* (posthumously published in 1779), and Kant's *Critique of Pure Reason* (1781). In the middle of the eighteenth century, the French *philosophes* launched an

---

[1] E. J. Dijksterhuis, *The Mechanisation of the World Picture* (1950: Eng. trans., Oxford, 1961); R. S. Westfall, *Science and Religion in Seventeenth Century England* (New Haven, 1958); P. Hazard, *The European Mind 1680–1715* (1935: Eng. trans., London, 1953), part 2; R. L. Emerson, 'Deism', in P. Wiener (ed.), *Dictionary of the History of Ideas* (4 volumes, New York, 1973); K. V. Thomas, *Religion and the Decline of Magic* (London, 1971).

open attack on *l'infâme*, as Voltaire called it; that is, on organised religion in general and the Catholic Church in particular. Voltaire's attacks are best known, but Holbach went further. His *Christianity Unveiled* (published under a pseudonym, 1767), described religion as 'founded on imposture, ignorance and credulity'. His *System of Nature* (1770: also pseudonymous) was even more of a Lucretian manifesto, declaring that man was a part of nature, the immortality of the soul an illusion, the existence of God 'not even probable', and the 'supernatural' merely a term for referring to what we do not understand.

Whether deist or atheist, the *philosophes* united in calling for a secular system of education and a morality without religion. Secular interpretations of history were offered by Turgot, in two lectures of 1750, by Voltaire in his *Essay on Manners* (1756), and by Condorcet in his *Sketch for a Historical Picture of the Progress of the Human Mind* (1794), in which the Fall, the Flood and the Incarnation were replaced as historical periods by the agricultural, literacy and French Revolutions. The French revolutionaries secularised the calendar, making A.D. 1792 into Year I.[1]

In Year II, the revolutionaries, notably Robespierre, attempted to put the destruction of *l'infâme* into practice in France. Ecclesiastical property was sold, churches were secularised (in the sense of being converted to lay uses), and priests were secularised (in the sense of turning laymen). Despite obvious similarities to the Protestant Reformation, the events of Year II were unique in constituting the first official rejection of Christianity in modern western Europe. Traditional Catholic festivals were replaced by the cult of Reason and the Supreme Being. In the country where Diderot had been sent to the Bastille for his *Letter on the Blind*, where Rousseau's *Emile* (which advocated a 'civil religion') and Holbach's *System* had been burned in public for their impiety, the official culture ceased to be Christian.[2]

Christianity was soon restored in France, but Year I was symbolic of a new era in which the churches of Europe would be forced on to the defensive. Christians were in for a shock, or rather, for a series of shocks delivered by German philologists, English scientists and militant secularists.

The 'Higher Criticism', developed in German universities in the early nineteenth century, treated the Bible as the work of men, as a historical document (or rather, as an anthology of historical documents), which revealed more about the milieu in which it was written than about God himself. David Strauss, in his *Life of Jesus* (1835), wrote about the Gospels

---

[1] P. Hazard, *European Thought in the Eighteenth Century* (1946: Eng. trans., London, 1954), part 1; P. Gay, *The Enlightenment: an Interpretation* (2 volumes, London, 1967–70); N. Hampson, *The Enlightenment* (Harmondsworth, 1968); F. Manuel, *The Prophets of Paris*, second edition (New York, 1965), chs. 1–2.

[2] J. McManners, *The French Revolution and the Church* (London, 1969), esp. pp. 86–95; M. Vovelle, *Religion et Révolution* (Paris, 1976).

as myth. His aim was not destructive; it was to replace 'the antiquated systems of supernaturalism and naturalism' by a third view, the mythical. However, the main consequence of the higher criticism seems to have been to secularise the Bible, in the sense of encouraging people to think of it as a text like any other. The change came slowly: in 1860 Benjamin Jowett caused a stir in England by publishing an essay on Biblical interpretation in which he put forward the precept, 'Interpret the Scripture like any other book'. In 1863, Ernest Renan caused a still greater stir in Catholic Europe with his *Vie de Jésus*, which presented Christ as a charming idealist but unconcerned with theology and lacking supernatural powers. There was nothing here to surprise an eighteenth-century Deist, but the book sold 60,000 copies in five months, and went through thirteen editions in four years. Renan was denounced as an atheist and a blasphemer; his book was described as 'a new crucifixion' and 'a deicide manifesto'. The British Library contains some 150 refutations of Renan published between 1863 and 1865 alone. The author also received a considerable number of insulting letters.

The scientists too were destructive in spite of themselves. Sir Charles Lyell's *Principles of Geology* (1830–3) suggested that the earth was 'millions of ages' old, and implied that the account of the Creation and the Flood given in Genesis could not be taken seriously. Himself an Anglican, Lyell considered the Flood 'a preternatural event far beyond the reach of philosophical enquiry', and hoped his readers would not suffer 'groundless apprehension' about the implications for religion of the new geology – but the damage was done. Charles Darwin believed in God when he was writing the *Origin of Species* (1859), but, as his fellow-scientist Thomas Huxley pointed out, Darwin's idea of evolution by natural selection undermined the argument from design by offering an alternative to the hypothesis of divine creation. A few years later, a new word entered the English language; 'agnosticism', a term coined by Huxley in 1869 to describe the position of men who believed that we could not know anything about God or any alleged reality 'beyond' phenomena. This position may not sound very different from Montaigne's *Que sais-je?*, but in one important respect it is. Montaigne doubted everything; Huxley and other Victorian agnostics trusted phenomena and reserved their scepticism for the supernatural.[1]

Another new word of the mid-nineteenth century was 'secularism', soon followed by the French *laïcité*; a sign that 'infidels', as Christians called them, were organising themselves and developing more constructive and more aggressive attitudes. Auguste Comte, for example, not only expounded his 'positive philosophy', but also organised a positivist move-

---

[1] O. Chadwick, *The Secularisation of the European Mind in the Nineteenth Century* (Cambridge, 1975); C. G. Gillispie, *Genesis and Geology* (Cambridge, Mass., 1951); K. Nielsen, 'Agnosticism', in Wiener, *Dictionary*.

ment to bring mankind more quickly out of the metaphysical age and into the scientific. In Britain, the secularist movement was organised in the 1840s by George Holyoake and the National Secular Society was founded in 1866. Its president, Charles Bradlaugh, became, after a long struggle, the first member of parliament to take his seat without also taking the Christian oath.[1]

In Britain, characteristically, the secularisation of public life was promoted by voluntary associations acting as pressure groups. On the Continent, from Year II onwards, it tended to be enforced by the state whenever secularists came into power. In Catholic countries there were dramatic clashes on this issue between the Church and governments headed by non-Christians like Jules Ferry (an admirer of Condorcet and Comte), who became minister of education in France, in 1879; Francesco Crispi, a deist who became prime minister of Italy in 1887; Emile Combes, a freemason and a deist who became prime minister of France in 1902; and Teofilo Braga, a positivist who became prime minister of Portugal in 1910. The secularists wanted to separate church and state. The 'lay laws' they advocated, and in some countries passed, mainly in the late nineteenth and early twentieth centuries, included the confiscation of church property (especially the property of the religious orders), the ending of clerical control of education (in some cases, religious instruction was abolished and the clergy forbidden to teach), and the introduction of civil marriage, secular funerals and secular oaths. The symbolic victories of the secularists included the removal of the crucifix from French courts, and the erection of a monument to Giordano Bruno in Rome on the spot where he had been burned.[2]

These victories took place, it must be remembered, in a culture which was still largely Christian, and the long-term process of secularisation was still punctuated by religious revivals. In England in the late nineteenth century, churches and chapels were still being built, the nonconformist conscience was still a force to be reckoned with in politics, new sects (like the Salvation Army) were still being founded, and allusions to the Bible were still widely understood. European public life is not completely secular even today. In Italy, for example, Catholicism is the religion of the state and the Concordat with the church is part of the constitution; the clergy take part in civic functions, and a crucifix is displayed in public buildings. The Christian Democrat party has been in power since 1946. Still, the change since 1850 will be obvious enough, let alone the change since 1500.

[1] E. Royle, *Victorian Infidels* (Manchester, 1974); S. Budd, *Varieties of Unbelief* (London, 1977).
[2] E. Acomb, *The French Laic Laws* (New York, 1941); J. McManners, *Church and State in France, 1870-1914* (London, 1972); P. Manzi, *Cronistoria di un Monumento: Giordano Bruno in Campo de'Fiori* (Nola, 1963).

III

We have been concerned so far with public events like the passing of laws and the publication of books. What difference did the secularisation process make to people's lives? When, and to what extent, did their mentality change? As might have been expected, there is no simple answer to this question. Clergy and laity, middle class and working class, Catholics and Protestants did not change their attitudes at the same time or to the same extent. In this section I shall concentrate on the attitudes of ordinary people – craftsmen and shopkeepers and peasants and their wives and children. Ordinary people knew little of the Renaissance, the Scientific Revolution, the Enlightenment; they did not read Darwin or Comte; they did not initiate the Reformation or pass the lay laws. Simplifying a complex process, we may think of cultural changes of this kind as filtering 'down' to them, or as being imposed on them from above. However, it would be a mistake to imagine that the attitude of ordinary people to these changes was necessarily one of passive acceptance. They sometimes responded by passive resistance, sometimes by open rebellion, and more often by a process of adaptation which (seen from above) looks like misunderstanding, but may equally well be described as reinterpretation, or as the perception of the new in terms of traditional categories.[1]

How can we know what ordinary people thought about the supernatural? There are two major types of source. Heresy trials are a good example of the first type; they give us access to the views of individuals, often expressed in their own words, but it is difficult for the historian to decide how typical or untypical these individuals were. A second type of source gives us access to the attitudes of the silent majority, but only indirect access, through 'indicators' and 'indices' (see p. 9 above) like the statistics for attendance at Sunday mass and Easter communion in different places and periods, statistics which are not altogether reliable and which are in any case difficult to interpret. It is not easy to decide what going to mass or communion meant to people in different periods, and even harder to interpret absences and abstentions. A man may be absent from church on Sunday because he prefers to spend the time sleeping, drinking or fishing; because he dislikes the parish priest; because he has quarrelled with his neighbours, who will be there; because he is ashamed to go in ordinary clothes, and has no Sunday best to put on. However, major differences in attendance rates at different periods demand a more general explanation, and bring us closer to the central subject of this essay. We return to the problem of the base-line. From what position around the year 1500 have the attitudes of ordinary western Europeans changed?

[1] N. Z. Davis, 'Some Tasks and Themes in the Study of Popular Religion', in C. Trinkaus and H. Oberman (eds.), *The Pursuit of Holiness* (Leiden, 1974), pp. 307–36.

Recent research on religious behaviour in certain towns of this period suggests two generalisations.

The first is that from the official (clerical) point of view, the laity were irregular in their religious practice. Many of them did not go to mass or communion as often as the church required. They treated the sacred with a familiarity which the clergy were coming to think quite scandalous (dancing in church on feast-days, for example), as if they made no sharp distinction between the secular and the religious. Popular anticlericalism was common, whether directed against the friars for seducing wives and daughters, or the secular clergy, for demanding tithes.

The second point is that many ordinary townspeople, men and women, were devout in their own way, so much so that the years around 1500 have been called an 'Indian summer of late medieval piety'. The laity participated in major religious festivals such as Good Friday and Corpus Christi, they joined religious fraternities, walked in processions, went on pilgrimages, and prayed before the images of their favourite saints.[1]

Much less is known about the religion of country people around 1500. What is known about the sixteenth and seventeenth centuries in general suggests that we should distinguish between corn-growing areas and areas near towns on the one hand, and more remote areas, pastoral areas, woodlands and mountains on the other. In the more remote areas, the clergy often complain that ordinary people have never heard of Christ, or cannot say how many gods there are (a favourite question of Jesuit missionaries from Brittany to Sicily), or are in as much need of instruction as the heathen. Religious instruction was hard to come by for people living off the beaten track, and the pressures to conform were also much less. In the areas near the towns, on the other hand, the religion of the peasants was close to that of the townsmen.[2]

The religion of the majority has often been described – by the clergy – as a religion of habit, or even as paganism. In the context of secularisation, it is the other-worldliness of popular devotions which needs stressing. Wills of the early sixteenth century show the laity leaving considerable sums of money for masses for their souls. Pilgrimages and the cult of the saints presupposed the belief in miracles. So did the persecution of witches for maleficent acts which were equally supernatural; and there is some evidence that the rise of the witchcraze in the late fifteenth century was in part a response to lay pressure.

When and how did this religion of the majority change? While the

---

[1] J. Toussaert, *Le Sentiment Religieux en Flandre à la Fin du Moyen Age* (Paris, 1963); B. Moeller, 'Religious Life in Germany on the Eve of the Reformation', in G. Strauss (ed.), *Pre-Reformation Germany* (London, 1972), pp. 13–42; Delumeau, *Catholicism*, pp. 226–55; N. Galpern, *The Religions of the People in Sixteenth-Century Champagne* (Cambridge, Mass., 1976), chs. 2–3.

[2] Delumeau, *Catholicism*, pp. 237–48; on England, C. Hill, *The World Turned Upside Down* (London, 1972), esp. chs. 3 and 5.

Renaissance was a minority movement which is unlikely to have made much impression on ordinary people, the Reformation did involve some of them. Luther, for example, was very much concerned to reach the 'common man', as he called him. He wrote in German in order to reach a wide audience and some of his pamphlets became best-sellers. The Reformation was in fact introduced into a number of German cities as a result of pressure on the town council from below. The German peasants who rebelled in 1525 put forward some religious demands, such as the right to elect parish priests, and justified other demands in religious terms, calling for the abolition of serfdom because the whole of mankind had been redeemed by Christ. Luther did not recognise his ideas in the mouths of the peasants, and he denounced the rebellion, but it is possible that the common man had been adapting Luther to his own needs. However, there was no religious revolution. In those parts of Germany where the local prince adopted the Lutheran Reformation, we know from the records of official 'visitations' that the habits and beliefs of the laity had not changed all that much by the later sixteenth century. Most villagers did not attend church regularly; there were communities where no one could be found who could recite the Ten Commandments; the peasants continued to consult soothsayers and to make use of charms and spells invoking the Virgin and the saints, just as if Luther had never existed.[1]

To trace what happened after the late sixteenth century, it will be convenient to concentrate on two relatively well-documented and well-studied areas, one Catholic and one Protestant: France and England.

In France, it is likely that religious practice, as defined by the clergy, was at its height from about 1650 (when missionaries began to penetrate the more remote rural areas of Brittany and elsewhere), to the French Revolution. In most parishes almost all Catholics made their 'Easter duties' of confession and communion; and after the revocation of the Edict of Nantes in 1685, there remained only 200,000 Protestants in a population of nearly 20 million. It is true that a third of the population missed Easter communion in the diocese of Châlons in the 1750s; that two-thirds missed it in the town of Bordeaux; that innkeepers, servants, old soldiers and wine-growers were notoriously difficult to bring to church; but these non-conforming regions and occupations were the exceptions.[2]

It is naturally hard to decide to what extent ordinary people conformed because they were genuinely devout Christians, to what extent out of habit or fear of the consequences if they did not. A parish priest in the Sologne, not far from Orléans, in the early eighteenth century, painted a vivid

[1] A. G. Dickens, *The German Nation and Martin Luther* (London, 1974), chs. 7–8; G. Strauss, 'Success and Failure in the German Reformation', in *Past and Present*, 67, 1975, 30–63.
[2] Le Bras, *Études*, I, pp. 267–301; for a case-study, L. Pérouas, *Le Diocèse de La Rochelle de 1648 à 1724* (Paris, 1964).

picture of the religion of his flock; they were enthusiastic participants in pilgrimages, processions and fraternities, but, in his terms, 'more superstitious than devout', believing in spells and charms and unlucky days and more devoted to the Virgin Mary and the saints than to God himself. We also know that French craftsmen and peasants who read anything at all often read pious books. Of a sample of 450 chapbooks printed at Troyes in the seventeenth and eighteenth centuries and carried round the countryside by pedlars, 120 were religious, and half of these were lives of the saints. The inventory of the stock of a Paris printer who died in 1698 suggests that his best-selling work was the *Pensez-y-bien*, a little book concerned with the art of dying well and with the 'four last things' – death, judgement, hell, and heaven. The most obvious conclusion to be drawn from these scraps of evidence is that the religious attitudes of ordinary people were little different in the eighteenth century from what they had been in the late Middle Ages. Meanwhile the educated laity were becoming more worldly in their attitudes. In Provence, in the course of the eighteenth century, the wills of the local notables reveal progressively fewer invocations to the Virgin Mary and less money spent on funerals and masses for the dead. There was also a decline in vocations to the priesthood at about this time. This new evidence fits in well with the traditional picture of the religion of the eighteenth-century French bourgeoisie, a this-worldly religion not all that different from Deism, in which the ideas of God, sin and death were growing ever more remote.[1]

After 1789, when the pressures to conform were relaxed, there was a sharp decline of religious practice in some areas (around Paris, for example); a rise in the practice of contraception, forbidden by the church (it rose, for instance, in Normandy and in the Hérault region of Languedoc); and a strong reaction in some places in favour of the revolutionary 'dechristianisation' movement, suggesting that it was what the local inhabitants wanted (in the Gard, for instance, 66 per cent of communes established a Temple of Reason). By 1830, half the population of some parishes in Hérault were missing their Easter communion, and in the diocese of Orléans, about 80 per cent of the people were missing it by 1852, provoking the new bishop, Dupanloup, to speak of a 'society without Christ' (*société déchristianisée*). There were now (as there still are) two Frances, the conformist (Brittany, Alsace-Lorraine, Massif Central), and the nonconformist in matters of religion. In general, women went to church more than men, but in some areas, such as Orléans, husbands often forbade their wives to go to confession because they resented clerical interference in their private lives, in their sex lives in particular, and priests

[1] G. Bouchard, *Le Village Immobile: Sennely-en-Sologne au XVIIIe Siècle* (Paris, 1972); R. Mandrou, *De la Culture Populaire aux XVIIe et XVIIIe Siècles: la Bibliothèque Bleue de Troyes* (Paris, 1964); M. Vovelle, *Piété Baroque et Déchristianisation en Provence* (Paris, 1973); B. Groethuysen, *The Bourgeois* (1927–30: abridged Eng. trans., London, 1968).

were bound to ask questions about contraception. However, it must not be thought that the nonconforming peasants of the Orléans area and elsewhere held secular attitudes in the modern sense. They were anticlerical and they may have rejected the church as an institution, but they continued to take the saints seriously and to practice rituals which the modern reader is likely to consider 'magical'. Indeed, it is possible that in some rural areas the people turned against the church precisely because the clergy were trying to root out these 'superstitions'.

It was only in the period after 1870 that the spread of literacy – and perhaps, as it has recently been suggested, that of chemical fertilisers – brought fundamental changes in the attitudes of the French peasants. A good many men stopped going to mass between 1880 and 1900; and whether they continued going to church or not, people no longer took the supernatural as seriously as before. The social cosmology was becoming scientific, in the sense that peasants drove tractors, spread fertilisers, practised family planning and generally lived their lives as if the world were subject to scientific laws rather than subject to supernatural forces which needed to be propitiated. They no longer felt helpless in the face of nature. In the towns, this fundamental change of attitude probably occurred earlier; among women, it probably occurred later, partly because women were less involved in the new world of technology.[1]

In England about 1600, attendance at the Anglican service on Sunday was compulsory, on pain of a fine of one shilling. Easter communion was also compulsory, but local studies suggest that the level of conformity was lower in England than in France at this time. Only 75 per cent of those eligible went to Easter communion in the diocese of Lincoln in 1603; about 50 per cent in the villages of Cogenhoe (Northamptonshire) and Clayworth (Nottinghamshire) in 1676. Pressures to conform were relaxed in England much earlier than in France. In the 1650s, and again after the Toleration Act of 1689, people were excused attendance at their parish church provided that they went to some place of worship, such as a dissenting meeting-house. This condition was obviously unenforceable, as the dean of Norwich, Humphrey Prideaux, wryly commented in 1692:

as to the Toleration Act, unless there be some regulation made in it, in a short time it will turn half the nation into downright atheism . . . no churchwarden will present any for not going to church, though they go nowhere else but to the alehouse.

Some pressure to conform probably remained in villages dominated by a resident squire and parson; it is surely significant that rural dissent was strongest in forest areas with a weak manorial structure, such as the Weald of Kent or Macclesfield Forest in Cheshire. However, when the bishop of Oxford enquired, in 1738, about church attendance in his diocese, a sub-

---

[1] Vovelle, *Religion*; C. Marcilhacy, *Le Diocèse d'Orléans au Milieu du XIXe Siècle* (Paris, 1964); F. Boulard, *An Introduction to Religious Sociology* (Eng. trans., London, 1960); E. Weber, *Peasants into Frenchmen* (Stanford, 1976), chs. 19–20.

stantial minority of vicars reported a substantial minority of absentees, especially among those of the 'lowest rank', suggesting that the reason was 'laziness', or possibly the 'want of decent apparel to appear in amongst their neighbours'. It is also possible that the renting of pews by the well-to-do gave the poor the impression that the church was not for them.[1]

What did ordinary churchgoers believe? And, more important still in the context of secularisation, what were the beliefs of those who stayed away? In the mid-seventeenth century, when it was safer than usual to express unorthodox views in public, it was possible to hear ordinary people, especially in London, saying that the Bible was not the word of God but just 'the conceits of men', 'no more than a ballad'; that there was no heaven or hell; that the soul dies with the body; that Christ was not God; that 'God was never angry nor displeased with man' (in other words, that he was remote and impersonal like the God of the Deists); that God 'does not exist outside the creatures' (a declaration of pantheism); that God is Nature or Reason (the view that Spinoza would express in print in more sophisticated form a few years later).[2]

How widespread these views were is quite another matter, and unfortunately one about which the evidence does not allow anyone to speak with confidence. However, there can be little doubt that millenarian doctrines appealed to ordinary people in seventeenth-century England. The Fifth Monarchy Men, for example, drew much of their support from London shoemakers, tailors, silk-workers, shipwrights and labourers. Millenarianism may be defined as the belief in imminent collective salvation; secular in the sense that what is imminent is the transformation of life on earth, but not at all secular in its means – a battle of supernatural forces, Christ versus Antichrist. Again, the impression left after reading a recent study of the decline of magic in Tudor and Stuart England is that the belief in magic only declined among the upper classes. Popular culture was not becoming more secular in the seventeenth century – or at least, not at the same speed as learned culture.[3]

In England as in France, educated men were, for this very reason, very much aware of popular 'paganism' as they considered it. In the House of Commons in 1628, Sir Benjamin Rudyerd declared that the prayers of the common people in Wales and the North were 'more like spells and charms

[1] A. D. Gilbert, *Religion and Society in Industrial England* (London, 1976), pp. 4–12; P. Laslett, *The World We have Lost*, second edition (London, 1971), pp. 74–6; G. V. Bennett, 'Conflict in the Church', in G. Holmes (ed.), *Britain after the Glorious Revolution* (London, 1969), pp. 155–74; A. Everitt, 'Nonconformity in Country Parishes', in *Agricultural History Review*, 18, 1970, *Supplement*, 178–99; T. Secker, Articles of Enquiry, ed. H. A. Lloyd Jukes, in *Oxfordshire Record Society*, 38, 1957, 6–182.

[2] C. Hill, 'Plebeian Irreligion in Seventeenth-Century England', in M. Kossok (ed.), *Studien über die Revolution*, second edition (Berlin, 1971), pp. 46–61; T. Edwards, *Gangraena* (London, 1646), is, though hostile to the unorthodox, the best single source.

[3] B. S. Capp, *The Fifth Monarchy Men* (London, 1972); N. Cohn, *The Pursuit of the Millennium*, third edition (London, 1970), p. 13; Thomas, *Religion*, especially chs. 18 and 22.

than devotions', and that 'there were some places in England which were scarce in Christendom, where God was little better known than amongst the Indians'. In 1650, Parliament set up Commissioners for the Propagation of the Gospel in these 'dark corners of the land', although missionary activity of this kind seems to have been less intense than in seventeenth-century France.[1]

In Britain, the real change came with the religious revival of the mid-eighteenth century, with John Wesley and his followers. The Methodists did make a serious attempt to convert ordinary people; textile workers in Yorkshire, farm hands in Lincolnshire, tin-miners in Cornwall, and so on. Unlike the parson, the Methodist missionary had the advantage of not being associated with landowning and tithes. The Methodists offered almost unprecedented opportunities for participation in religious rituals and organisations; ordinary men and women too could become class leaders and sometimes even preachers. The fact that Easter communions were down to 10 per cent by 1800 is an indicator of the crisis of the Church of England in the face of Methodist competition rather than an indicator of secularisation.[2]

To take stock of the general religious situation in England and Wales it is convenient to move forward to 1851, the year of the first (and last) religious census. About 7 million people attended public worship in church or chapel on the Sunday of the census; about 11 million did not. After allowance has been made for small children and for people who wanted to attend but were unable, the impression remains of a society more or less equally divided between the churchgoers and the rest. There is reason to believe that this division followed class lines, that more middle-class people went to church than workers. There was as much reason for talking of a 'society without Christ' in Birmingham or Manchester (where the census revealed that attendance at public worship was particularly low), as in the diocese of Orléans; and the urban artisans were described by the census compiler, Horace Mann, in tones like Rudyerd's some two hundred years before; 'like the people of a heathen country'. It is possible that working in factories and workshops encouraged more secular attitudes than working the land, but it should also be pointed out that the inhabitants of large towns escaped the remaining pressures to conform of the more deferential village communities. As for the countryside, the fact that church attendance was lower in 'open' parishes without a squire than in 'closed' ones tells its own story.[3]

[1] C. Hill, 'Puritans and the Dark Corners of the Land' in his *Change and Continuity in Seventeenth-Century England* (London, 1974), pp. 3–47.

[2] R. F. Wearmouth, *Methodism and the Common People of the Eighteenth Century* (London, 1945), especially section 3; Gilbert, *Religion*, pp. 60–8. A major work on the social history of Methodism is to be expected from Dr J. Walsh.

[3] K. S. Inglis, 'Patterns of Religious Worship in 1851' in *Journal of Ecclesiastical History*, 11, 1960; K. S. Inglis, *Churches and the Working Classes in Victorian England* (London,

There was no investigation of beliefs, as opposed to practice, in the 1851 census and one is left wondering whether or not the majority of English people still lived, like the French peasants, in an enchanted world. A recent study of part of Lincolnshire suggests that people still took the supernatural seriously, but that in the later nineteenth century belief in the devil, witches, ghosts and the powers of wise men was on the decline.[1] Here as in France secularisation may have spread with chemical fertilisers.

In England, unlike France, half the population lived in towns by 1851. Some of the urban working class were certainly secular in attitude, indeed militantly so. Some read Tom Paine's *Age of Reason*, published in 1792 and frequently reprinted in the nineteenth century, despite attempts to suppress it; a popularisation of Deism which rejected all churches ('my own mind is my own church'), and presented Christ as nothing but 'a virtuous and an amiable man'. Some working men in the early nineteenth century were atheists, and the mid-nineteenth-century secularist movement received some working-class support. However, secularists were a minority, perhaps 100,000 people altogether in the 1850s.[2] About the beliefs of other absentees from public worship we can do little more than guess: agnosticism? anticlericalism? indifference? It is only relatively recently that public opinion pollsters have turned their attention to religion, and we may end this section with the Speedsearch Spiritual Attitudes Survey of 1974, which reported that 29 per cent of British people believed in a personal God; 35 per cent in a 'life force'; 36 per cent did not believe in God at all.[3] A pity that the survey did not take in other attitudes to the supernatural, including the survival (and revival) of astrology; but it is clear that in Britain the process of secularisation is far from complete. And of course there are parts of western Europe where the level of religious practice is still high; among them Brittany, the Veneto, Navarre and Minho, in northern Portugal.

IV

As religion has come to seem less plausible than it once did, as its hold on daily life has weakened, our psychological and social needs have not grown less. To fill the social and psychological vacuum, some, at least, of the roles of the clergy and the functions of the churches have been taken over by other groups and institutions.

1963); D. M. Thompson, 'The 1851 Religious Census', in *Victorian Studies*, 11, 1967–8; D. M. Thompson, 'The Churches and Society in Nineteenth-Century England', in G. J. Cumings and D. Baker (eds.), *Popular Belief and Practice* (Cambridge, 1972); H. McLeod, *Class and Religion in the late Victorian City* (London, 1974).

[1] J. Obelkevich, *Religion in a Rural Society* (Oxford, 1977).

[2] G. A. Williams, *Rowland Detrosier, a Working-Class Infidel* (York, 1965); Budd, *Varieties*; Royle, *Infidels*.

[3] Discussed in B. Wilson, *Contemporary Transformations of Religion* (London, 1976), pp. 14–15.

This process is most obvious in the deliberate attempts to create a surrogate religion for a disenchanted world, with science, or humanity, or
progress taking the place of God. When Voltaire wrote of the *philosophes*
and their supporters as *l'Eglise des Sages*, he was simply taking an opportunity to be ironically witty. The French revolutionaries took the idea
more seriously and set up a Festival of Reason. Indeed, they made
Voltaire himself into a kind of revolutionary saint, escorting his remains –
not to say relics – to the Pantheon. Voltaire's comments on this episode
would have been well worth hearing. Again, Saint-Simon spoke of the
'religion of Newton' with its 'new priesthood', the scientists; his followers
went further and tried to put his proposal into practice. 'We are going to
found a new religion', one of them, Enfantin, announced in 1831; 'we are
now apostles'. Auguste Comte, once a follower (or perhaps one should
say, a 'disciple') of Saint-Simon, went furthest of all and founded the
'Religion of Humanity' with himself as high priest (he signed himself,
Grand Prêtre de l'Humanité). The new religion had temples, hymns, a
catechism, and even a surrogate Virgin Mary in Comte's dead mistress,
Clotilde de Vaux.[1]

The French were not alone in their wish to replace religion with something positive. Carl Scholl founded a 'church of humanity' in Germany;
British secularists discussed a secular hymn-book and experimented with
ritual; a Temple of Humanity was opened in Liverpool. Ironically enough,
the process of secularisation has not spared these movements, and the
temples of humanity are now empty like the churches.

Yet the psychological and social needs once satisfied by religion and the
churches remain. If there has been no successful total or direct substitute
for religion, there have been many partial or indirect substitutes. Indeed,
the history of Western culture in the nineteenth and twentieth centuries is
largely the history of these substitutes, although the tradition of appropri-
ating religious imagery, language, and ritual for secular use is of course
much older.

In a famous essay, Carl Gustav Jung once compared the 'cure of souls'
practised by the modern psychotherapist with that of the clergy; and it has
been pointed out that as the numbers of clergy in England (for example)
have declined since 1900, so the numbers of the medical profession have
risen.[2] Psychoanalysis can be seen as a substitute for confession; and so
can letters to the advice columns of magazines. To describe the psychoanalytic movement in its early days as a 'sect' would be accurate as well as
malicious. It has, of course, since become a church. The pastoral function
of the clergy has now been taken over by the professional social worker

---

[1] Manuel, *Prophets*, especially pp. 7, 112, 115, 164, 267; D. G. Charlton, *Secular Religions in France 1815–1870* (Oxford, 1963): Williams, *Detrosier*, appendix, prints a secularist form of public worship.

[2] C. G. Jung, 'Psychotherapists or the Clergy' in his *Modern Man in Search of a Soul* (London, 1933), pp. 255–82; Wilson, *Religion in a Secular Society*, p. 72 n.

and, to some extent, by the schoolmaster. There was, surely, a strong element of rivalry in the conflict between the village priest and the village *instituteur* in France under the Third Republic.

'School seems eminently suited to be the World Church of our decaying culture', says Ivan Illich, himself a former priest and now, like a secular Luther, a critic of the 'institutionalisation of values' in general. As for the theologian, the possessor of knowledge which is at once important and unintelligible to the majority, in this age of the division of labour his role has been split among a number of professionals from the physicist to the sociologist (over 25 per cent of a sample of American sociologists surveyed in 1964 had considered becoming clergymen).[1] Who has taken over the traditional clerical role of the moralist? The novelist – or the literary critic? D. H. Lawrence (who once called himself 'the priest of love') or F. R. Leavis?

The appropriation of religious language and religious imagery for secular purposes is most obvious in the arts, just as the process of secularisation itself is most obvious in the arts. In medieval Europe, the major buildings were mainly cathedrals and monasteries; most painting and sculpture, poetry and drama was religious; most music (folksongs apart, a major qualification) was church music. From the Renaissance on, secular buildings (palaces, villas, townhalls), secular paintings (portraits, landscapes, still-life), secular plays (tragedies and comedies), and secular music (suites, concertos, operas, symphonies) became increasingly important.

The new forms were not completely independent of the old. A still-life painting of the seventeenth century may carry a religious message about the vanity of this world; its meticulous naturalism may be in the service of a transcendental view of reality. Compositional schemata and emotional associations may be taken into secular paintings from the christian tradition. Thus Jacques-Louis David's painting of the death of Marat and Benjamin West's *Death of General Wolfe* draw, in their different ways, on the tradition of paintings of the dead Christ, while Joseph Wright's *Blacksmith's Shop* recalls a traditional *Nativity*.[2] In literature we find something similar. Defoe's *Moll Flanders* and his *Robinson Crusoe* have each been described as a secularised pilgrim's progress – a progress to wealth and high social status rather than towards salvation. Borrowings like these may illustrate nothing more than the difficulty of making a completely fresh start, but they may be responses to emotional needs in the author (Defoe had once intended to become a minister), or in his audience.

---

[1] I. Illich, *Deschooling Society* (London, 1971); A. Gouldner, *The Coming Crisis of Western Sociology* (London, 1971), p. 24.

[2] On the arts in general, Martin, *The Religious and the Secular*, pp. 79–99. I. Bergström, *Dutch Still-Life Painting in the Seventeenth Century* (London, 1956), pp. 154–90; J. R. Martin, *Baroque* (London, 1977), ch. 4; R. Paulson, *Emblem and Expression* (London, 1975).

When one looks at the arts in Europe after 1800, it becomes even harder to deny their function as substitutes for religion. Hegel's term 'the religion of art' (*Kunstreligion*), which he applied to the Greeks, is even more appropriate for his own day. Artists, writers and composers, so often treated with contempt in the past, now acquired a priestly aura if not a divine one. Beethoven was detached enough to make ironic remarks about his cult; Wagner, who saw Beethoven as a saint, and even as a redeemer, was not. Concert halls, museums and art galleries of the nineteenth century were not unlike churches or temples; the style of their architecture, the Sunday visits, and the atmosphere of hushed devotion all combine to suggest the comparison. If this corresponds to traditional 'superstition', it is not difficult to find an artistic equivalent for 'enthusiasm' in the nineteenth and twentieth centuries. Goethe's character Werther inspired imitation as if he were a saint. His blue coat and yellow trousers could be seen all over Germany, and some admirers even followed him into suicide. Again, 'Lisztomania', as it was called at the time, gave that composer's concerts the atmosphere of a revivalist meeting, with faintings and convulsions nothing extraordinary. Liszt's 'fans' (and that word is of course abbreviated from the religious term 'fanatic') even preserved his hairs and his cigar-stubs as relics. If we smile at this, the smile must be a somewhat wry one, in an age when the cult of the film star has given place within middle-aged memory to the cult of the pop-singer, while all the symptoms of mania survive.[1]

Such enthusiasm is relatively harmless. It is difficult to say the same for another surrogate religion – politics. The phenomenon is not new of course. Between the thirteenth and the seventeenth centuries, secular monarchs appropriated more and more of the attributes of the clergy and even of God. Just as a bishop was traditionally described as wedded to his diocese, so now was a king described as wedded to his kingdom: 'I am the husband', said James I, 'and all the whole isle is my lawful wife.' 'I am the head', he added, 'and it is my body', a secular version of the doctrine that the church is the mystical body of Christ. The term 'absolute power' was transferred from God to the prince; as God could suspend the laws of nature, so the prince could suspend the laws of his kingdom. There is a sense in which the Virgin Queen, whose portrait hung in the houses of many of her subjects, replaced the Virgin Mary, whose cult had been outlawed in England only a generation before. Lights burned before the image of Louis XIV in Place des Victoires in Paris; blasphemy, according to some contemporaries, for others it was no more than proper reverence for God's viceroy on earth. In any case, Christians had taken the custom

---

[1] A. Schmitz, 'Die Beethoven-Apotheose als Beispiel eines Säkularisierungsvorgangs', in K. Weinmann (ed.), *Festschrift P. Wagner* (Leipzig, 1926), pp. 181-9; H. G. Koenigsberger, 'Music and Religion in Modern European History', in J. Elliott and H. G. Koenigsberger (eds.), *The Diversity of History* (London, 1970), pp. 37-78; E. Morin, *The Stars* (New York, 1961).

of placing lights before images from the cult of the Roman emperors in the first place.[1]

The political appropriation of religious language, ritual and imagery has continued into the nineteenth and twentieth centuries, changing its meaning as belief in the other-worldly has declined. The French Revolution was, as Tocqueville put it, a political revolution which functioned like a religious one. It was presented, as we have seen, as a secular millennium; Year I marked the beginning of the new order. Hegel defined the state as 'the divine idea as it exists on earth': and it may make the violent clashes between Church and state in France, Italy, Spain and elsewhere more intelligible to see them as a kind of religious war. Examples of state- and nation-worship from our own time are not difficult to find. In Italy in the 1930s, for example, there was an official cult of Fascist martyrs, and a chapel was dedicated to them in Palazzo Littorio in Rome. Hitler was seen by his supporters as a prophet, a messiah, a redeemer; as one Nazi put it, 'My belief is that our leader Adolf Hitler was given by fate to the German nation as our saviour, bringing light into darkness.' The phraseology would not have surprised Max Weber, who knew that the charismatic leader would survive the disenchantment of the world. The idea that Marxism is a substitute religion is a commonplace. Marx writes on occasion like an Old Testament prophet, treats the proletariat as a kind of chosen people, sees the coming crisis in apocalyptic terms, and is the object of a cult – the iconodules are still in the ascendant in Russia. In England there was a 'religion of socialism' at the end of the nineteenth century. 'Conversions' took place, and meetings were held in a revivalist atmosphere.[2]

Plus ça change, plus c'est la même chose; or is it? There is a danger of being carried away by metaphor, and of sliding imperceptibly from saying that music (say) is like a religion in some respects, to saying that music *is* a religion. Some people would say that religion is indispensable and exists in one form or another in every society; but it may make for clearer thinking to define 'religion' more narrowly in terms of belief in some sort of supernatural power, and to say that the many functions performed in the past by religion have also been performed by non-religious beliefs and institutions.

To sum up. The simple picture with which we started was not radically wrong but lacking in nuances. Belief in the other-worldly has indeed

---

[1] E. H. Kantorowicz, *The King's Two Bodies* (Princeton, 1957); James I quoted in D. H. Willson, *King James VI and I* (London, 1956), p. 251; F. Oakley, 'Jacobean Political Theology: the Absolute and Ordinary Powers of the King', in *Journal of the History of Ideas*, 29, 1968, 323–46; E. C. Wilson, *England's Eliza* (Cambridge, Mass., 1939), pp. 215–22.

[2] A. de Tocqueville, *L'Ancien Régime et la Révolution Français* (1856), Book I, ch. 3; *Enciclopedia Italiana*, 22 (Milan, 1934), s.v. *Martirio*; J. P. Stern, *Hitler: the Führer and the People* (London, 1975), p. 194; on Marx, K. Löwith, *Meaning in History* (Chicago, 1949), ch. 2; E. B. Bax, *The Religion of Socialism* (London, 1887); S. Yeo, 'A New Life: the Religion of Socialism in Britain 1883–1896', in *History Workshop Journal*, 4, 1977, 5–56.

declined in western European culture over the last five hundred years or so, and the importance of the churches and the clergy (not to mention magicians and witches) has declined with it. At the Renaissance the signs of a secular counter-culture were already visible in the sense that a small group of people wanted religion to emphasise this world more than the next. The mechanisation of the world picture and the rise of a techno-logical culture have proved incompatible with the supernatural elements in Christianity. Hence the middle of the seventeenth century marked an important shift for intellectuals, while the later nineteenth century was the decisive turning-point for many ordinary people in western Europe. There is a connection with the Industrial Revolution in both cases, but the con-nection is indirect. The change in the world-picture of seventeenth-century intellectuals was one of the preconditions of the Industrial Revolution; while the change in the beliefs of workers and peasants in the nineteenth century was one of its unintended consequences.

Of course, the new world-view has its difficulties, like the one it re-placed. If terms like 'grace' and 'salvation' sound increasingly old-fashioned (if not unintelligible), the problems of determinism and the meaning of life have not gone away. We have exchanged a 'closed' predica-ment, in which people were generally unaware of alternatives to the beliefs embedded in their cultural tradition, for an 'open' predicament in which it is possible to choose one's beliefs but in which many people have a sense of 'cultural dislocation', a sense of the absurd.[1] Although it cannot perform the functions of a religion – or even a quasi-religion – there has never been a greater need for cultural history.

[1] R. Horton, 'African Traditional Thought and Western Science', in M. Marwick (ed.), *Witchcraft and Sorcery* (Harmondsworth, 1970), pp. 342–67; R. J. Lifton, 'Protean Man' in B. B. Wolan (ed.), *The Psychoanalytic Interpretation of History* (New York and London, 1971), pp. 33–49.

CHAPTER XII

ON THE LAST 2,500 YEARS IN WESTERN HISTORY
And some remarks on the coming 500[1]

1. *Introduction*

IT may be an indiscreet question, but it is nevertheless a highly legitimate one: 'What actually happened during the last 2,500 years in Western history?' – given that the answer should be a chapter rather than a book, one lecture rather than a series. There is nothing more illegitimate in this question than to ask for a description of what happens at street level as seen from a helicopter circling above, with a macro-view of the situation. This view would necessarily lack insight into the micro-perspective possessed by drivers and pedestrians, their anguish and delight or sheer boredom in trying to match their intentions to get ahead with their capabilities, against the intentions and capabilities of others in the traffic throng. It is legitimate to give answers in terms of traffic flows and charts, of periods of movement and periods of standstill, of the traffic being most rapid in the centre of the lanes and very slow towards the edges (as in hydrodynamics); an analysis of traffic does not have to be through the eyes and minds of those involved although that helps understanding. The question is not illegitimate, it is only indiscreet because of the difficulty of answering; itself a good reason why the question is usually rejected. And yet the question tends to appear and reappear: it is unnecessary to invoke a curious Martian on a quick visit wanting to get some information about 'this thing called Western history'. It is sufficient to note that a sizeable proportion of the Western population – secondary school youth trying to come to grips with history at the actor-level so often seem to want more comprehensive views, until in the end they have been sufficiently discouraged by lack of answers and points of view. To be sure, the textbooks for schools generally deal with the larger processes and periodisations of history, but *one* of the reasons why these textbooks very often prove unsatisfactory is precisely the lack of historical research directed towards these levels of synthesis.

Today there is another reason why this type of enterprise seems not

[1] This article is an outcome of the study Trends in Western Civilization at the Chair in Conflict and Peace Research, University of Oslo. For the sake of brevity a number of notes are omitted in this version. For more evidence and further discussion, see J. Galtung, T. Heiestad, and E. Rudeng, *Macro-History and Western Civilization*, Ejlers, Copenhagen (forthcoming). The TWC Program has been supported by the Berghof Stiftung, The Federal Republic of Germany, and the Norwegian Scientific Research Council.

only important, but mandatory. The point is not so much the idea of a shrinking and increasingly interdependent world, as the circumstance that the West as such during our generation seems to be the target of a more forceful challenge than ever before in recent centuries.[1] The challenge comes partly from outside, from the West's periphery; and partly from inside, from the inner periphery and centre. There is a confrontation between systems, there are blocks on the road, preventing a flow of unimpeded expansion. If expansionism is seen as an essential part of the West, then one implication would be that the West itself is challenged at its heart, which should lead to some self-criticism as well as other reactions, and to some reflections from and by others. In short, not only 'what actually happened during these two-and-a-half millennia?', but 'what is the real nature of the Western enterprise?'[2]

Then there is a third reason arising from the quests for description and theory just mentioned: the need for some image of the *future*. Is it possible – from a historical point of view – to suggest some consequences of the closing of Western expansion in the world?

When things are happening *to* the West, and not only *in* the West, the interest in understanding what the West is about will increase. The oil embargo of 1973–4 was, in a very limited scale, a turning-point in this experience. Less dramatic are Arab examples of economic 'counter-penetration' – the buying of industrial plants in West Germany, of country houses and hotels in Great Britain. Considerable imagination is required to see the effects of such developments and corresponding strategies of *cultural* counter-penetration, of Third World agencies and media introducing Islamic and other non-Western traditions in the Western world.[3]

If the West is in a crisis (the point will be made later that this statement is a tautology, crisis being seen as a part of the definition of the West), and the crisis this time is of a fundamental nature because of the challenge from both outside and inside, then it might be worth trying to look over the fence, across the present into the future. According to empiricist doctrines we cannot know the future, but a less empiricist position would point out that there are many senses in which we do not know the past either, making past and future less different. There is probably no *wie es eigentlich wird* that can be added as a dictum to Ranke's *wie es eigentlich gewesen*. But when it comes to imputing meaning to history, past and

---

[1] A classical account is given by Geoffrey Barraclough in his remarkable *An Introduction to Contemporary History* (London, 1964), especially ch. VI: 'The revolt against the West'.

[2] The globalisation of communication and conflict implies a growing need to spell out similarities and differences between civilisations, cf. Roger Garaudy, *Pour un dialogue des civilisations* (Paris, 1977) and the UNESCO project 'At the crossroads of culture', of which *Cultures and time* (Paris, 1976) is an outcome.

[3] A part of this picture is the new cultural critique of Western social science, cf. T. Asad (ed.), *Anthropology and the Colonial Encounter* (London, 1973) and Y. Atal (ed.) *Social Sciences in Asia* (New Delhi, 1974).

future are not that different, if for no other reason because one of the methods of testing theories is through confrontation with data, and postdiction and prediction are similar as methods.[1] A sense of history implies a sense of the future.

2. Western history: a bird's-eye view

Some limitation in time and space of the subject matter to be discussed is necessary.[2] *As to time:* roughly speaking the 2,500 years between the Greek city-state and the present Western attempts to establish systems of regional states (the United States of America, the European Community, the Soviet Union), but still very far from establishing a World State.[3] *As to space:* roughly speaking what today is known as Europe, and the parts of the world made similar to Europe through a process of 'Westernisation', perhaps also including the westernised élites found in most parts of the world. In fact, there is no difficulty envisaging a continuation of the process of westernisation so as to reach all areas of the world and all parts of the population, ultimately ending in a World State, but for reasons to be spelt out this will not be among the likely images of the future.

There is a further need for sub-division in time and space, so as to make this vast time–space region in world history analytically more manageable.

As to time: we shall stick to the standard sub-division of time into periods, using as reference points for the dividing intervals the traditional dates for the fall of the western Roman Empire (A.D. 476) and the eastern Roman Empire (A.D. 1453). The first period, lasting about one thousand years, will be referred to as Antiquity; the second period also lasting about one thousand years, will be referred to as the Middle Ages; and the third period – so far about five hundred years duration – as the Modern Period, Early Modern 14/1500–1800, and Late Modern thereafter. Thus, there will be no challenge of the conventional wisdom that these are important dividing lines and periods in Western history.

[1] For an excellent discussion of 'The Historian and His Facts', see E. H. Carr, *What is History?* (New York, 1961), ch. I. A general theory of social science methodology avoiding sharp borderlines between past and future is presented in J. Galtung, *Methodology and Ideology* (Copenhagen, 1977), pp. 230–46. For a view not too dissimilar from ours where the interface of history and futurology is concerned, see David Landes, 'Where is Prometheus Bound?', *Proceedings, XIV International Congress of the Historical Sciences* (New York, 1976), pp. 122–49.

[2] The following exposition is based on the concept of 'civilisation', which in itself implies very large space and time perspectives, cf. P. Beneton, *Histoire de mots: Culture et Civilisation* (Paris, 1975). For an account of the rise of macro-history and discussions of modern concepts of civilisation as part of societal analysis, see E. Schulin's magisterial introduction to *Universalgeschichte* (Cologne, 1974).

[3] The typical Western 'peace plan', from the early 1200s till the United Nations, is an alliance/federation/union with a front against the outsiders, the barbarians/pagans/Turks/Russians/yellow peril; the alliance etc. being hegemonical or more federation like. For an analysis, see S. J. Hemleben, *Plans for World Peace through Six Centuries* (Chicago, 1945).

As to space: another tripartite distinction will be made, between Inner-West, Outer-West and Outside. Roughly speaking these concepts correspond to Centre, Periphery and the Rest. Really, it is a dynamic concept: the Centre has moved throughout Western history,[1] the Periphery has expanded, the Rest has shrunk with the expansion of the Periphery and expanded with discovery. Moreover, the Centre has its own centre and periphery, just as the Periphery can be seen as having its own centre and its own periphery.[2] The sub-divisions, however, are not so much geographical as social concepts: cc being the élites in Inner-West, pc being the inner-peripheries and the masses, cp being the élites in Outer-West and pp being the outer-peripheries and the masses in the Periphery. The Rest is largely untouched by all of this; some of it may survive as pockets in the western-penetrated land mass.

So much for time and space: the next problem is the question of what to look for. In very broad terms: *structures* – patterns of millions, billions of human transactions with a certain constancy over time – and *processes*, or the change of structures through time, whether goal-directed or not, whether slow (evolutionary) or quick (revolutionary); in the latter case we shall use the expression 'transformation'.

The enterprise now boils down to an effort to characterise Western history for the whole period, and for the sub-periods in terms of structures and processes. The question then becomes which structures and processes to focus on. There are many candidates; some selection has to be made.

As to structures: as an absolute minimum something must be said about micro-structures and macro-structures, i.e. the type of social structure found respectively inside societies and in the relations between societies. Of course, they may be strongly related to each other and may even be expressions of the same basic social form, but the terms used to describe intranational and international relations are usually different, and should be different, for clarity.

We then turn to *processes* where *time* is a component. One way of classifying processes would be by looking at form rather than content, and simply ask: what is the shape of the process, what is the form of the process as a function of time? Is it rising? or falling? or rising first, then falling (or falling first, then rising)? Or – is it simply constant, no variation at all? The latter is hard to conceive of in social affairs – when pressed for examples the researcher is most likely to resort to nature and laws of

---

[1] For interpretations of the role of shifting centres in Western history, see S. Rokkan, 'Dimensions of State Formation and Nation-Building...', in C. Tilly (ed.), *The Formation of National States in Western Europe* (Princeton, 1975) and W. H. McNeill, *The Shape of European History* (New York, 1974).

[2] For one usage of these terms, see J. Galtung, 'A Structural Theory of Imperialism', *Peace and World Structure, Essays in Peace Research*, vol. IV, ch. 13 (Copenhagen, 1979). The terms refer to the double stratification, by a relation of exploitation, among and within countries.

nature as something that seems reasonably invariant throughout the period of 2,500 years. This is actually important: the size of the world and the shape of the continents, not to mention the number and kinds of atoms in the world remain by and large constant, setting an upper limit for what humans can do as they explore more, but exploit even more.

Given the scarcity of constancy, let us divide the processes into two kinds: those that either rise *or* fall, and those that rise *and* fall. To find a process of the first kind for the entire period cf 2,500 years is difficult, though, but it may not be so difficult for the sub-periods. Processes are not that regular; typically there are ups and downs, even in the sub-periods – processes are rise-*and*-fall processes.

To this should then be added the obvious possibility of discontinuous processes, of sudden jumps or transformations. One thesis would be that there are two such transitions or transformations in the period of history considered: the transition from Antiquity to the Middle Ages and the transition from the Middle Ages to the Modern Period.

Let us then try a quick characterisation of dominant features, not the many exceptions and variations – comparing periods in relative terms.

We see the social structure of Antiquity as predominantly vertical, with tremendous differences in power and privilege, highly exploitative, but also as highly individualistic – and not only for the citizens. The individual is seen as the basic social unit. On the top individual mobility, geographically and socially, is seen as natural and correct; verticality and individuality combining into competitiveness. As a result the period projects on the social stage a very high number of extremely colourful personalities, many of them still with us as fundamental pillars in Western civilisation. They may be found in all fields, politics, arts, sports, religious matters; they may have followers, but it is the individual as such who is seen as the carrier of innovations, ideas, initiatives.

In the Middle Ages this changes. The verticality remains, but individualism is subdued, groups of people are – so to speak – enclosed into a cocoon of collectivities, the leading idea being that of serving the collectivity or the lord on top of it (or the Lord), rather than individual success. Extremely impressive and relatively stable social structures (the church, feudal systems) are built, works of art are produced, but with a certain anonymity, invariant of the concrete individuals participating in it; the period does not hand over the stage to so distinct personalities. Where Antiquity produced actors, the Middle Ages produced structures – or more correctly expressed; where Antiquity had a structure at the top giving much freedom of individual expression to strong and capable actors, the Middle Ages produced actors devoting themselves more to building structures with a certain permanence, less vulnerable to individual idiosyncrasies.

In the Modern Period this changes again, and in a sense back to the structure of Antiquity – the famous rebirth or *Renaissance* being a redis-covery of the culture of Antiquity and releasing the individuals from the ties of collectivism, at the same time exposing him and her to the vulner-ability of being isolated individuals. Being ourselves a part of the period, we would be inclined to see it as more creative, more light than the 'dark' Middle Ages because human individuals play roles that we more easily identify with. Again the number of 'colourful personalities' shoots upward and the individual is once more seen as the carrier of social action.

A similar set of characterisations can now be given for the macro-structure, for relations between societies.

In Antiquity the dominant structure was highly centrifugal: from Inner-West in the eastern and central parts of the Mediterranean increasing areas were incorporated in the Outer-West through bridgehead formation, small replications of the Inner-West in the Outer-West. Together the Inner-Wests ruled over an inner and outer proletariat, surrounded by 'barbarians', pushing the borders of the West relentlessly outward, incorporating barbarians in increasing numbers.

In the Middle Ages this changes. The structure becomes centripetal, apart from the Crusades (seen by some as precursors of the next period, in a sense incorrectly placed in time). The period is used for inner-work in Inner-West, for consolidation.[1]

In the Modern Period this changes again: through the Great Discoveries the centre-periphery model of Antiquity can be replicated on a larger scale, even on an ever-expanding scale into our days. Competitive individualism and expansion of the Outer-West combine into the figure of one particular person: the Discoverer, a lasting hero of the period; ultimately establishing fame through landings on the moon. The image of the discoverer or adventurer is certainly one of the truly classical themes of Western literature since the Homeric epic.[2] It seems that in China com-parable traditions were linked to a fascination with *exotica*,[3] but not to any significant use of Western ideas before the nineteenth century; whereas in the West it can be discerned a more consistent interest in probing and absorbing Chinese and other Eastern traditions.[4]

In the Modern Period Inner-West moves North, and West goes to war

[1] Cf. F. Braudel's apt expression, 'internal Americas'. But this kind of internal expansion also reaches its limits, see A. R. Lewis, 'The Closing of the Medieval Frontier', *Speculum*, xxxiii (1958). Of the two present-day superpowers only the USSR still enjoys the advantage of 'open frontier' in this respect. For an assessment of Siberian potential, see V. Conolly, *Siberia Today and Tomorrow. A Study of Economic Resources, Problems and Achievements* (London, 1974). The very rapid and enforced industrialisation of the USSR is a prime example of internal expansion.　　[2] P. Zweig, *The Adventurer* (London, 1974).

[3] See e.g. W. Blunt, *The Golden Road to Samarkand. Experiences of Explorers and Con-querors of Central Asia* (London, 1973).

[4] Cf. R. Drews, *The Greek Accounts of Eastern History* (Cambridge, Mass., 1973); M. L. West, *Early Greek philosophy and the Orient* (Oxford, 1971); D. Sinar (ed.), *Orientalism and History* (Cambridge, 1954); O. Impey, *Western Interpretation of Oriental Styles* (Oxford, 1977); P. Jullian, *The Orientalists* (London, 1977).

against itself, but from a *global* point of view the result is the same: the Roman Empire writ large, even very large.[1]

Let us then turn to processes, starting with the most conspicuous rise-*and*-fall process for the entire period. These are usually referred to as 'growth' processes, for a reason to be explored later. They can all be seen as variations over one theme: *Man's conquest of Nature.* Nature is driven back (deforestation), cultivated, urbanisation processes take place, transport and communication networks grow and are filled with increasing volumes of goods, people and information, economic cycles are established capable of handling increasing quantities of economic factors, producing ever more goods and services, expanding so as to cover more and more people and ever larger territories with ever-growing speeds of movement.[2] As a consequence of this conquest the human population starts growing, slowly at first, then more quickly. In short, given the constancy of matter there is more man and man-made environment ('rise'), less nature ('fall') – and man also lives longer than before.

Three social processes are involved in this conquest of nature. They can be seen as decreasing from a high level during the apogee of the Roman Empire, and as picking up with increasing speed throughout the Modern Period into our days. There is the growing size of the unit of administration, from villages, towns, cities and city-states roughly encompassing 100 to 100,000 individuals to larger units such as nation-states with as many as 1 million, 10 million and ultimately 100 million individuals. Together with this phenomenon comes the emergence and rapid growth of the administrators of such units, the bureaucrats as a power group.

The growth of bureaucrats in France can serve as an example:[3]

Year	Number of state bureaucrats, in thousands	Population, in millions
1550	10	15
1665	46	20
1789	300	25
1950	1000	50

[1] For the emergence of capitalism the basic fact is precisely the opposite: that the unicentric structure of the Roman Empire was *not* revived in Renaissance Europe. This point is developed in Immanuel Wallerstein's important *The Modern World-System* (New York, 1974), e.g. pp. 127 and 348. The new multi-centric system of nation-states was not only productive of capitalism, but also of European wars, which became increasingly devastating, cf. P. Sorokin, *Social and Cultural Dynamics*, One vol. ed. (Boston, 1957), p. 550.

[2] Such familiar growth-trends are recorded in e.g. W. S. and E. S. Woytinsky, *World Population and Production* (New York, 1953); C. M. Cipolla, *The Economic History fo World Population* (Harmondsworth, 1962), and his *Before the Industrial Revolution. European Society and Economy, 1100–1700* (London, 1976); B. R. Mitchell, *European Historical Statistics: 1750–1970* (New York, 1975); P. Flora, *Indikatoren der Modernisierung* (*Wiesbaden*, 1975).

[3] See Wolfram Fischer and Peter Lundgren, 'The Recruitment and Training of Administrative and Technical Personnel', in C. Tilly (ed.), *The Formation of National States in*

There is also the corresponding growth of economic cycles, meaning networks of transaction with recognisable nodes that can be referred to as Nature, Production and Consumption – raw materials being extracted from Nature, processed in Production, distributed to Consumption in return for labour, money or other forms of value; with various kinds of waste flowing back into nature from production and consumption. Under capitalism as the dominant mode of organising the economic cycle the basic question to be asked of economic cycles is whether they – at least in the long-term – lead to an accumulation of capital. As the cycles expand, the processes become more encompassing and quicker and as capital accumulates, the owners of capital, the capitalists, emerge and grow as a dominant class.

The third phenomenon we would like to point to is the emergence and growth of intellectuals as a power group. The first mass-production of intellectuals in world history appears to have taken place in western Europe in the late sixteenth and early seventeenth centuries.[1] Intellectuals are indispensable in order to make the bigger units comprehensible to those who rule them, since they can no longer be ruled in terms of direct man-to-man relations. They have to be governed according to abstract principles, 'laws', and as the units grow in size, so do the laws. For several reasons the expanding category of 'citizen' as a status common to all living in the same polity grows in importance, and rules are needed to define the rights and duties of citizens. Similarly, for the economic cycles to expand, forms of understanding have to be established whereby consensus can be obtained as to what constitutes equivalent raw materials, equivalent labour, equivalent capital – and equivalent goods and services.

For all such standards to be worked out intellectuals (chemists, physicists, biologists, psychologists and educators, economists and so on) are indispensable. And the same applies to the production process itself in so far as production is processing, i.e. the imprint of some form on nature: it is the task of the researchers to establish that form. As a result of all this an increasing group in the population does work that is increasingly abstract, consisting of manipulating symbols rather than things.

In order to sustain this growing class of bureaucrats, capitalists and intellectuals, engaging in administration, production of goods and services, production of forms of understanding and professional services of various kinds, agricultural yield has to improve quickly so that one family on the land can support more than one family (itself), yielding an agricul-

---

Western Europe (Princeton, New Jersey, 1975), pp. 456–561. For a general analysis of this process, see H. Jacoby, *The Bureaucratization of the World* (Berkeley, 1973).

[1] R. L. Kagan, *Students & Society in Early Modern Spain* (Baltimore, 1975), and Lawrence Stone, 'The Educational Revolution in England, 1560–1640', *Past & Present*, 28 (1964), pp. 41–80. For an interesting comparison, see his 'Education and Modernization in Japan and England', *Comparative Studies in Society and History*, vol. IX (1966–67), pp. 208–32.

tural surplus sufficient to sustain an ever-increasing proportion of the population. After some time there is also the need to support industrial workers, another growing portion of the population, and in order for this to happen industry has to deliver something back to agriculture to increase the yield (tractors and other machines, fertilisers). The result is a complex process characterised, in general, by a decreasing primary sector, increase (but later on decrease) of the secondary sector, and a steady increase of the tertiary sector.

Most of the processes described so far – and many more could be added – have something in common: there have always been ups and downs, particularly from a micro-historical point of view, but macro-historically speaking many of these variables (such as speed of transportation and communication) were relatively constant till a couple of centuries into the modern period. Then they started growing with remarkable turning points in the period 1750–1850, afterwards shooting quickly upward. Thus, looking at these variables alone one would probably draw the conclusion that Western history divides into two periods: before and after what is conveniently referred to as 'the Industrial Revolution'. This is not the view that will be taken here, however: rather, the early part of the Modern Period will be seen as preparing a framework within which the explosive quantitative growth that took place later became possible.

Another major rise-*and*-fall variable for the total period would focus on exploitation: how much surplus value the élites were able to get out of the masses. There was a minimum at the end of the Middle Ages, at a time which should be characterised by a poor landed aristocracy, relatively speaking.[1] This process reached a turning point around the Renaissance after which there has been an increase in the rate of exploitation. The unit in which this has to be studied, is, of course, neither the city-state nor the nation-state but the unit in which the economic cycles have been operating, i.e. increasingly the whole world – the point being that the rich become richer and the poor stay the same or even become more poor. *Impoverishment of the masses was increasingly exported to the Outer-West.*

Let us then focus on the sub-periods, and by the same logic start with the rise-*or*-fall variables. Actually, there is only one we shall focus on in

[1] To postulate a falling population and production in Europe between 1350 and 1500 seems best in accordance with the facts. See Robert-Henri Bautier, *The Economic Development of Medieval Europe* (London, 1971), M. M. Postan, *The Medieval Economy and Society* (Harmondsworth, 1975), and also Robert Lopez, 'Hard Times and Investment in Culture' in: Erwin Panofsky *et al.*, *The Renaissance* (New York and Evanston, 1962). Real wages seem to have risen, as is indicated by Phelps Brown and Sheila Hopkins in 'Seven Centuries of the Prices of Consumables Compared with Builder's Wage-rate' in: Peter H. Ramsey (ed.), *The Price Revolution in Sixteenth Century England* (London, 1971); and B. H. Slicher van Bath, *The Agrarian History of Western Europe, A.D. 500–1850* (London, 1971), p. 327. Markets contracted; there occurred, as Marc Bloch saw it, a 'momentary impoverishment of the seigneurial class' (*Les caractères originaux de l'histoire rural français*, vol. 1 (Paris, 1964), p. 122), at the same time as wages increased. Immanuel Wallerstein considers the seigneurial class as hit by an economic 'squeeze' in this period (*The Modern World System*, pp. 24–6).

this connection: the variable used by Sorokin, ideational versus sensate orientation; a complex variable with a number of attitudinal, behavioural and even structural components.[1] Broadly speaking the proposition would be that each period starts with a high level of idealism, orientated towards being rather than having, towards conquest of self rather than conquest of nature, towards transcendence into the other world rather than transformation of this world. But throughout the period there is deterioration of ideational energy and orientation, and increasingly sensate patterns set in, ultimately leading to not only sensate but sensuous forms of existence. In other words, Sorokin sees a see-saw pattern to history: from high down to low, then up to high again and so on, in an unending pattern. The great periods according to him are the early parts of the three sub-periods, the latter parts being highly sub-standard.

The leading rise-*and*-fall theorist within the sub-periods is, of course, Marx; but it should be added that for him it is probably the period around the Industrial Revolution rather than the Renaissance which is the decisive turning point. Following Hegel with his famous *Stufengang* (Primitivism, Greek antiquity, Roman Christian, German Christian) Marx introduces his own theory of stages – primitivism, slavery (the Greek and Roman periods combined), feudalism (the first part of German Christian) and capitalism (the second part of German Christian).[2] As the theory relates to basic material needs (the misery of the exploited classes) and to concrete social actors attempting, at least potentially, to preserve or to transform structures, the theory became itself an important part of the historical process, because it was related so directly to interests. The theory defines sub-periods by using characteristics of the economic process, and one way of conceiving of Marxism might be to say that a basic point is how many and which production factors are controlled by the ruling class. Under slavery (roughly equivalent to Antiquity) the ruling class controlled both nature, labour (as slaves) and the capital goods; under feudalism it may perhaps be said that some of the grip on nature and labour was relaxed through the complex set of rights and duties regulating the serf–vassal–lord relationship (roughly speaking surplus value in return for 'protection'). Under capitalism capital goods became crucial in the production processes and the hold on nature and labour was relaxed further in the sense that nature in the form of land was distributed more than before (but nature as a source of raw materials less) and in the sense that labour as persons were permitted more mobility than before (but given less power over what to produce and what to do with the surplus after the reproduction of labour itself was secured).

[1] P. A. Sorokin, *Social and Cultural Dynamics*, vol. I (New York, 1962), pp. 66–101.
[2] For a critical analysis of highly ethnocentric perspectives in Marxism, see M. Molnár, *Marx, Engels et la politique internationale* (Paris, 1975). The Western four-stages theory in its modern Scottish origins is the main theme of R. L. Meek, *Social Science and the Ignoble Savage* (Cambridge, 1976).

Against this background the relationship between the means of production and the mode of production unfolds itself, roughly speaking the equivalents of the techniques of production in a broad sense, and the social structure within which production takes place, including control patterns. The basic point here would be relations of compatibility or incompatibility (contradictions) between the two, the postulate being that the mode of production sets a limit for the full development and application of the means of production. The system expands and matures as the means of production make full use of the possibilities given by the mode, but as the means of production then develop further the mode of production becomes more and more like a strait-jacket, and as the contradictions between the actual and the potential mature the system comes to a grinding halt; carrying in its womb the roots of a new social formation.

And that brings us to the last type of process: the discontinuous jump, the structural transformation. We have postulated two such transformations in the total period, well knowing that 'discontinuity' is a misleading metaphor since so much of the new was present in the old, at least in embryonic form, and since so much of the old will survive into the new. Moreover, the transformation period was certainly not a point in time, nor a short interval – but possibly a sub-period of the same order of magnitude where duration is concerned as the sub-periods already mentioned, particularly if the transformation is defined as the period between peak performance of the old and of the new social orders. And the transformation did not take place at the same time throughout the West – the centuries indicated are usually the transformation periods for Inner-West, assuming that Outer-West is lagging behind, or not even participating in the transformation.[1] Even in Inner-West the Renaissance as a 'wave' came to Italy before the Netherlands, to France before England, from which it does not follow that the explanation has to be diffusionist. It would have been much stranger if the process leading to this transformation were perfectly synchronised.

As Western history has been portrayed here the picture is no doubt stereotyped, exaggerating within-period homogeneity and between-period heterogeneity. But we shall stand by that perspective, to the point of maintaining that these fundamental transformations may even have pendular characteristics in the sense that the Modern Period has basic similarities with Antiquity,[2] and it does not seem totally unreasonable to assume that it could be followed by a fourth period bearing some similarities with the Middle Ages. This pendular, or oscillating movement,

---

[1] The problem of 'lags' between élites and masses, between centre and periphery, is termed 'cultural polyglotism' in Lotman et al., 'Theses on the semiotic study of cultures', in Thomas A. Sebeok (ed.), *The Tell-tale Sign. A Survey of Semiotics* (Lisse, 1975).

[2] This point is made by John Hicks in his *A Theory of Economic History* (London, 1969), where he develops his idea of the spiral growth of a market economy in the West.

would then be seen as a characteristic feature of Western civilisation. For a deeper understanding of that feature another conceptual tool is necessary.

3. *On Western social cosmology*

To try to penetrate more deeply into Western history, and particularly to try to conceptualise, if not necessarily explain, some of the basic changes that took place in Western history from Antiquity to the Middle Ages and from the Middle Ages to the Modern Period, the concept of 'social cosmology' might be useful.[1] It is conceived of here as 'deep ideology', a set of usually unquestioned assumptions about all kinds of social things and how they relate to each other; implicit rather than explicit. The metaphor of *social grammar* may be useful here: the idea that there are some basic rules defining elements, their relations and transformation. Thus, it would be difficult to fail to discover some similarities between the street map of Paris, the road map of France and the international map of the relationship between France and her former and present colonies and overseas territories. One might say that these are three concrete manifestations of centre-periphery relations in space, and that they are isomorphic to each other because they express the same structure. It is that structure, then, that becomes a part of the social cosmology of Western civilisation – at least in a certain period. The following three concepts will serve to regulate the usage of the term 'social cosmology'.

First, the idea of *isomorphism* defining what is natural, normal as that which has the same structure (including the same structure over time, or process). Example: the isomorphism between map and terrain, whereby a point in one corresponds to a point in the other, 'above' in one to 'to the north of' in the other, 'between' in one to 'between' in the other, etc. It should be pointed out that in this there is no assumption that social cosmology is an idea: rather, social cosmology is what arrangements of concrete things (like the examples given) and arrangements of abstract things (like the way propositions are related in an axiomatic theory) have in common. Thus, there is no assumption that material arrangements, or the arrangement of ideas, have priority in any sense. The idea of cosmology belongs neither to one nor the other side of this hen–egg pair, but would help define the rules according to which material arrangements are reflected in ideas, and ideas are projected into material arrangements. There are the three very concrete and structurally similar French arrangements in the example above and certain conceptions in the minds of many French (and others) – the two reinforce each other as expressions of the same cosmology.

[1] A parallel concept is found in A. Ja. Gurevitch, *Kategorii srednekovoj kultury* (The categories of medieval culture) (Moscow, 1972). Social cosmology as distinguished from conscious, conceptualised ideology is here called 'social-psychological climate'. Kristian Gerner, University of Lund, has kindly drawn our attention to the work of Gurevitch as well as other references to Russian and Soviet history.

Second, there is the idea of comprehensiveness, completeness, – *holism*. Social cosmology seen as deep ideology, for instance, would reflect some of the obvious similarities between such apparently disparate doctrines as latter-day Christianity, liberalism and Marxism, including serving to define one or the other of them as incomplete ideology because some significant elements are missing. A social cosmology properly constructed would define a complete social grammar, a set of rules for how man should relate to man, man to nature, how man should conceive of how nature relates to nature, and so on; much like the grammar for a language has a certain job to do, including that of defining deficiencies in the language. Needless to say, social cosmology is a construct and its usefulness depends on to what extent it can permit us to formulate insights and even concrete postdictions and predictions about empirical reality. It is more than a list of rules, much like a building is more than a heap of tiles and sacks of cement.

Third, we shall postulate a *yin–yang aspect* to social cosmology. Joseph Needham summarises much of his insight into this important part of Chinese (and hence human) civilisation:[1]

These two great forces (the Yang and Yin) of the universe were always thought of in terms of prototypic wave-theory, the Yang reaching its maximum when the Yin was at its minimum, but neither force was ever absolutely dominant for more than a moment, for immediately its power began to fail it was slowly but surely replaced by its partner, and so the whole thing happened over and over again (p. 29).

But he also goes on to say:

Of course for the Chinese the greater perfection always consisted in the most perfect balance of the Yin and Yang, the female and male forces in the universe. These great opposites were always seen as relational not contradictory; complementary, not antagonistic. This was far different from the Persian dualism with which the Yin–Yang doctrine has often been confused. Indeed, the Yin–Yang balance might be a good pattern for that equilibrium between the forms of experience which we need so much, that harmony between compassion and knowledge power (p. 34).

Thus, we shall not assume that the Western social cosmology is a clear-cut thing, invariant in social and geographical space and in time. It obviously is not, for if it were then there would not be these fundamental changes in what was considered normal and natural, nor the variations in social and geographical space within each sub-period, so far not touched upon at all. So we shall assume that there is something like a dominant/ manifest social cosmology, always accompanied by a recessive/latent social cosmology, like its *alter ego*; and further postulate that whereas the dominant cosmology by definition is that of the centre in the Centre, the alternative cosmology may be particularly pronounced elsewhere – in the inner proletariat or in Outer-West – not to mention in the Outside. Thus,

[1] Joseph Needham, 'History and Human Values: A Chinese Perspective for World Science and Technology', *The Centennial Review* (1976), pp. 1–35.

although one of our points will be that dominant Western cosmology has a tendency to be antidialectical, contradiction-free, our image of that cosmology does not have to share these two Western characteristics, but could be non-Western (Taoist) inspired.

To summarise: social cosmology is seen as something located inside the only concrete social actors there are, individual human beings. One might postulate that human beings have an inborn capacity for a number of social grammars, and that their experiences with the outside world activate and build up one such grammar, partially activating and building some others (the less dominant, the less manifest ones). Each impression from the outside of how things, concrete or abstract, are organised will serve as raw material building up the social grammar. Identical patterns (isomorphisms) are recognised, sedimented unto the deeper recesses of human consciousness, then gradually serving as a cognitive filter rejecting patterns that are different as 'unnatural', 'abnormal', thereby sliding into a more normative concept. The more consistent the environment the more clear and crystallised the social cosmology imprinted on/in the human mind; and the more crystallised the social cosmology, the more consistently (one might hypothesise) will people try to construct that environment: the more 'perfect' and contradiction-free will it appear.

Thus, social cosmology becomes like a program, not unlike the program of a computer; accepting inputs in some forms, rejecting or changing other forms, capable of carrying out some routines and delivering some kinds of output, to the exclusion or partial exclusion of other possibilities. But then there is the basic dissimilarity between human beings and computers: it is given to man to arrive at a certain level of consciousness about how he is programmed, including biological programming, and it is even given to man, probably under very special circumstances, to make changes in his program. This capacity of self-transcendence for the individual, and even Self-transcendence for a collectivity (using capital S for collectivities) may perhaps be seen as one formulation of whatever it is that distinguishes man from other animals, thus giving to man as an individual and as a collectivity the capacity of historicity, meaning by that something different from routine implementation of built-in programs, even if these programs are highly complex. Obviously this may be seen as related to the structural transformations that occasionally do take place in the course of human history, but they can also be found in individual histories, as conversion processes whereby 'he/she becomes a new human being'. But these moments are the exceptions, under normal circumstances people implement their programs, rather unconsciously, individually and collectively, also in completely new life situations – e.g. as settlers on virgin territory.

How, then, should one try to characterise a social cosmology/deep ideology/social grammar? Or, more precisely formulated: how would one write the program of Western civilisation? What are the basic assumptions, the basic routines? And above all, given the hypothetical nature of this construct, what kind of methodology would one make use of? As to the latter the only honest answer seems to be the 'methodology of as if': Western history should be seen 'as if' its actors were enacting a built-in program, choosing the program formulations that seem to render a minimum axiomatic basis for the understanding of a maximum of structures and processes. In so doing one could of course make use of the writings selected by those persons elected by later generations into the various halls of fame, seeing them as exponents of the Western consciousness (or even unconsciousness). But this would be a highly élitist methodology, giving much too much weight to specific individuals and relying much too much on the selection process than took place afterwards. Much better would have been systematic efforts, in the tradition of deep social science investigations, of the deeper-lying assumptions behind peoples' attitudes and behaviour.[1] If this is a question of philosophy one would like to know that of the peoples, not only the philosophy of selected individuals.

Granting that the methodological criterion for stipulating what Western social cosmology might be, is essentially indirect, in terms of whether it produces insights consistent with some basic aspects of Western history, the next question would be: which would be the major dimensions of a social cosmology? In a sense this could be answered by referring to the problem of identifying categories for the description of Western history in the three periods: it is a question of what constitutes natural/normal structures and processes. And essentially this is what we should try to do, but some other categories will be used, more from the field of ideas, less from social theory: the categories of Space, Time, Knowledge, Man–Man relations, and Man–Nature relations. The assumption would be that any social cosmology, as a bare minimum, would have to say something about the nature of social space, social time, what constitutes socially acceptable knowledge, correct man–man relations and correct man–nature relations. If any one of these is omitted, one definitely should say that something basic would be missing; without for that reason claiming that the above list is exhaustive.

Before proceeding along this list it should only be added that for each one of these five dimensions it is not sufficient to try to spell out the dominant Western cosmology. Negations of that cosmology should also be

---

[1] Cf. the French idea of *mentalités collectives*. See Jacques Le Goff, 'Mentalities: a new field for historians', *Social Science Information*, XIII (1974), pp. 81–97. From a methodological point of view experiences of 'first contact' between peoples of different cultures are particularly illuminating, cf. Nathan Wachtel, *The Vision of the Vanquished: The Spanish Conquest of Peru seen through Indian Eyes* (Hassocks, Sussex, 1976); J. Lockhart and E. Otte (eds.), *Letters and Peoples of the Spanish Indies* (Cambridge, 1976); Fredi Chiappelli (ed.), *First Images of America. The Impact of the New World on the Old*, vols. I–II (Berkeley, 1976); N. Cameron, *Barbarians and Mandarins. Thirteen Centuries of Western Travelers in China* (Chicago, 1976); Z. Freeth and V. Winstone, *Explorers of Arabia* (London, 1978).

indicated, not only in order to show what the precise hypothesis about the dominant Western view is (and that can best be done by seeing more clearly what the view is a rejection of); but also to open for images of the non-West in the West, for latent cosmologies. The basic assumption, then, would be that these are cosmologies held by peripheral groups, whether in the Western Centre or the Western Periphery, in other words that the non-West at any given time is carried by segments of the periphery in the West, and – perhaps – also as doubts, as counter-points, in the very centre. In general, this is to say that what we are going to describe will be the cosmology of men more than of women, of the middle-aged more than of the very young and the very old; of the peoples in cities and the centre of a country rather than those in the countryside and in the geographical periphery; and people on top of the social structure rather than those lower down (in contemporary societies meaning those with high income and education, and with high positions in the secondary and tertiary sectors of the economy).[1]

As a matter of fact, throughout Western history women and children, ordinary peasants and labourers have been described as less rational, more 'emotional' – in short, more like the standard descriptions of non-Westerners.[2]

To start with *space*: our assumption is that Western social cosmology sees space as roughly circular or spherical, with a centre located in the West from which everything of importance emanates and radiates to a Periphery waiting for the message. In the West is the cause, in non-West the effect; that West is conditioning the non-West is the normal state of affairs, the converse being abnormal, against the natural order of things, like water running up-hill.

To make this more clear two aspects of this centre-periphery image of the world should be emphasised: it takes in the whole world, to the most remote corner, every part is potentially a part of Outer-West; and it affects the innermost part of human beings, to their attitudes and convictions – in other words it includes the idea of conversion. This is important, for world history has many examples of centre-periphery formations of one kind or the other, but not with that universality and that claim on other peoples' souls. In other words, the Western social cosmology includes the idea of changing the cosmology of others. Nowhere is this so clearly expressed as in Matthew 28: 19–20, 'Go ye therefore and teach all nations...to observe all things whatever I have commanded you.'

There is no twenty-first verse added encouraging the disciples to learn from other cultures and civilisations (from those with other cosmologies),

[1] For a systematic use of these variables to analyse the social cosmology of the people in a number of countries, see J. Galtung, *Peace and Social Structure, Essays in Peace Research*, vol. III (Copenhagen, 1978).

[2] A brilliant study of an aspect of this élitist view is Keith Thomas, 'The place of laughter in Tudor and Stuart England', *The Times Literary Supplement*, 21 Jan. 1977. Cf. P. Burke, *Popular Culture in Early Modern Europe* (London, 1978), e.g. pp. 17–18.

and to engage in dialogues with them. To see oneself as a part of a family of equal civilisations in an equitable relationship was not the Western message.

'What is Western is universal, or at least potentially universal' seems to be another way of expressing the same message. Throughout history this principle has been applied to Christianity, to Western science, to Western economic systems including patterns of industrialisation and commercialisation, to Western social and political institutions, Western languages[1] and other aspects of Western culture, and developmental models in general. There is an interesting doubleness here: a sense of sharing, of not wanting to keep all these good things for oneself alone (as it is expressed in the Letter to the Romans 10: 12–13, 'there is no distinction between Jew and Greek; for the same Lord is Lord of all'; and then on the other hand the sure conviction that the centre generating all these products for universal distribution is the Inner-West (again one could imagine a hypothetical verse, this time added to the Letter to the Romans, to the effect that the headquarters of all this will be in Rome).

Several alternative conceptions could be imagined along this dimension. Thus, there is the possibility of regarding the world as politically flat, as equipped with many and equally important centres, as seeing oneself as one among several equals. There is the Chinese idea of contracting the world till it includes only one's own group, defining all outsiders as 'barbarians' – which in our terminology would be tantamount to a world image consisting only of Inner-West and the Outside, no periphery any longer. The outside would not count, it is merely a context like stellar space – at most something to be on guard against because it could be potentially dangerous. China approached the outer world with much such aloofness. The Chinese had four words for foreigners in addition to the idea of foreigners: 'north barbarians', 'east barbarians', 'south barbarians', 'west barbarians'. Barbarians were interesting in so far they had to be prevented from overrunning China. Some trading had to be performed with the foreigners, imperial princesses sent to marry their rulers and tribute exacted to prove their submissiveness to the emperor, but – they were *a priori* inimical to advanced culture. While exacting tribute the Empire took no interest in how the barbarians ran their country, and thought of themselves superior in a cultural way rather than in economic and military terms.

And then there is the possibility of conceiving of oneself as being in the periphery, in other words of changing the roles in the cosmology – a conception which actually would be Western because there would be a steep centre-periphery gradient, only inverted. It was a part of Western political/military colonisation and economic/cultural imperialism that

[1] See J. Galtung and Fumiko Nishimura, 'Social structure, thought structure, and language', in Galtung *et al.*, *Macro-history and Western Civilization* (forthcoming).

those who formerly belonged to the outside started perceiving themselves as belonging to the Outer-West Periphery, internalising the image Inner-West had of those parts of the world; thereby colonising themselves.[1]

One important factor associated with this centre-periphery outside gradient would be the degree of alienation relative to the outer circles. The Outer-West may be seen with contempt, but it is nevertheless useful; the Outside is an implacable enemy to be crushed. Peoples not wanting or not wanted for incorporation (like American Indians or European Jews), and too weak to resist the onslaught from the Inner-West, will be threatened by extinction, in direct violence; others that are incorporated into the Outer-West (which geographically may be next door to the Inner-West like the use of Africans as slaves) may be similarly exposed to structural violence.[2]

Thus the historical importance of the centre-periphery gradient with which the world is equipped in Western social cosmology is its compati-bility with patterns of attitudes and behaviour that can best be charac-terised as Fascist. A social cosmology equipping the world with a flatter social gradient would be compatible with warfare and robbery, conquest, subjugation, extortion (taxation!), but not with coercion into Western attitudes and beliefs, and practices and institutions. There is a difference between conquering India in order to exact taxes, ruling over the Indians but letting them do pretty much as they always did – the Mughal way, and the Western way: conquering them, converting them to adopt all kinds of non-Indian routines down to the smallest post office in the villages.

Let us then turn to the dimension of *time*, just as for space above in the sense of *social* time.[3] There are at least three different aspects of the way in which Western social cosmology, perhaps, may be said to conceive of time: linearity, the idea of progress, and the idea of purification. Although related to each other they should also be kept analytically separate. The obvious case for keeping these time aspects separate is that whereas the Christian concept of time is strictly linear it has not necessarily in all periods been associated with any idea of (social) progress.

Through linearity time is seen as an arrow moving from past to present into future, the three being distinct intervals/points in time, never to be revisited. Circular time concepts can be seen as a reflection of the many cycles found in nature (such as the annual seasons) and in human life (which has family cycles): there are intervals or points on what from a

---

[1] A remarkable study of Western textbooks, including colonial editions, is Roy Preiswerk and Dominique Perrot, *Ethnocentrisme et Histoire* (Paris, 1975).

[2] For the concept of 'structural violence', see J. Galtung, 'Violence, Peace and Peace Research', *Essays in Peace Research*, Vol. 1 (Copenhagen, 1976).

[3] An abstract, but highly rewarding study of social time is Niklas Luhmann, 'Weltzeit und Systemgeschichte, Über Beziehungen zwischen Zeithorizonten und sozialen Strukturen gesellschaftlicher Systeme', in P. C. Ludz (ed.), *Soziologie und Sozialgeschichte* (Opladen, 1972).

Western point of view would be linear time sufficiently similar to be seen as identical, thus leading to the notion of time as something running around in a circle. The notion of spiralling time combines the two, giving to time a linear and a circular component and the possibility of discussing the relative strength of these two components. Thus, the Chinese calendar works with cycles of twelve lunar years, adding to this a linear counting of years in the Western manner.

From the point of view of social cosmology the environment would be important here: some environments are rich in cyclical experience, especially environments with biological/organic ecosystems; other environments are richer in linear processes, for instance environments equipped with industrial processes (more based on inorganic materials, or non-degradable organic materials). However, the point here would not be that Western social cosmology has developed time concepts with much stronger linear than cyclical components because the West is so industrialised. It is rather vice versa: that industrialisation and its consequence, the non-cyclical accumulation of products *and* of waste, was seen as natural/normal because it fitted with linear time concepts that for some other reasons for a long time had been prominent in the West.

The second aspect, the idea of progress, equips time with value: from bad to good, or at least from worse to better. During most of the early Modern Period a revival of ancient cyclical views coexisted with Christian linearity. It was only in the eighteenth century that the expansion-oriented, Western Idea of Progress was firmly established, but even this before the Industrial Revolution. It should be noted that this idea is not the same as linearity, which in and by itself is a more neutral concept. The assumption is not, however, that the Western time concept simply looks like the upward turning exponential curve, e.g. of the compound interest so important under capitalism as an economic system, bent on capital accumulation. This may have been important, however, in making the idea of compound interest look natural/normal. The curve shape fits.

Progress may be the condition of the present, but there is a qualitatively different past and also a qualitatively different future in more refined versions of Western time cosmology. Thus, the past is often equipped with ideas of Original Bliss, some kind of paradise; Original Sin or some kind of fall; and then Enlightenment. Correspondingly, the future can be seen as equipped with Crisis, Struggle which may end once more in a Fall, but also in a Catharsis – what in German is known as an *Endzustand*.[1] It is a

[1] The idea of an *Endzustand* is particularly clear in the Western utopian tradition. The utopia tends to be a small, static, isolated and well-organised society, taken out of any geographical and historical context, equipped neither with inter-societal relations, nor with a dialectic that will drive society through processes and transformations into an uncertain future. The quest for the final, the perfect, receives its compelling expression, but on paper only. For an analysis of this phenomenon, see Ralf Dahrendorf, 'Out of Utopia: Toward a Reorientation of Sociological Analysis', *American Journal of Sociology*, Vol. 64 (1958–9),

dynamic, highly dramatic time concept; and it becomes even more dramatic if it is assumed that at any particular time the moment Now is placed
just in front of Crisis. Hence, just as what has been said above about
space gives to the point Here, as long as it belongs to Inner-West, the
character of being central in space, the time cosmology gives to the
point Now in time the character of being central in time; a watershed in
human history (as will be seen the present essay on Western history is no
exception from this rule, thus being in itself a clear example of Western
thinking).

A concept such as this would also exercise a normative function on art
that uses time as a medium, such as music and drama: there would be a
build-up, a crisis and a struggle, a tension release and *finale*, as in a sonata
from the Vienna classics, or a traditionally well composed drama. Correspondingly, one would expect the social cosmology of space to be reflected
in spatial art, such as painting, sculpture, architecture: there should
be a relatively clear subdivision of space into centre and periphery,
as expressed, for instance, in the role of perspective in Renaissance
art.[1]

Then there is the idea of purification which gives more substance to the
idea of progress. This is related to Western non-dialectical thinking:
things are not good *and* bad, but good *or* bad. The good and the bad may,
however, be mixed together, meaning that progress is the task of sorting
the good from the bad, the pure from the impure. Sometimes this process
takes place inside the individual, exorcising evil spirits or whatever else
that might be evil from body and soul. Then it may take the form of
sorting good individuals from bad individuals; in the legal processes the
guilty from the non-guilty; in the medical processes the healthy from the
non-healthy and in the educational processes the bright from the dull.
Those who are sorted out may then be placed in special institutions
(prisons, hospitals, special schools or even be exterminated, seen as
belonging to the outside rather than to the periphery – leaving possible
centre belongingness out of serious consideration. And it may be seen as a
pattern applying to the way Western man relates to nature: the quest for
purification in chemistry and physics, for pure material that can enter the
industrial processes defining the impurities as waste using the entire
process to divide between the two as one more expression of the idea of

---

pp. 115–27. The conflict-free and abstract nature of the utopian elements in dominant
Marxism are analysed in Daniel Tarschys, *Beyond the State: The Future Polity in Classical
and Soviet Marxism* (Stockholm, 1972), especially pp. 48–86 and 88–134.

[1] For one discussion of the role of the perspective, see S. Y. Edgerton, Jr., 'Linear
Perspective and the Western Mind: The Origins of Objective Representation in Art and
Science', *Cultures*, vol. III (1976), pp. 77–104, or his *The Renaissance Rediscovery of Linear
Perspective* (New York, 1975). Differences between the Renaissance perspective in painting
and the inner-directedness of East-European *icons* are pointed out in B. A. Uspenskij,
'"left" and "right" in icon painting', *Semiotica*, vol. 13 (The Hague, 1975).

progress through sorting. The idea of nation-state building should also be seen in this perspective, as a process of ethnic purification.)[1]

In the most important Western eschatology, the Christian one, all these figures of thought are found with some clarity: paradise, the fall, enlightenment, progress (assuming that more and more people become devout Christians), the crisis as purgatory approaches, and the *Endzustand* in the paradise regained, except for those who lose the battle and end in the opposite extreme. A human life consisting of many such cycles built into the total life cycle, which again is built into the life cycle of a society or a civilisation seen in these terms, cannot fail to become dramatic.

Again, alternative time cosmologies would be flatter, less dramatic. Time could run around in a circle, revisiting the same points, not being equipped with any particular ups or downs. It could also be linear, but similarly flat. Or it could have many ups and downs, from infinity to infinity, never assuming anything to be perfectly good or perfectly bad, hence no struggle to be *the* decisive struggle. Processes would be seen in a dialectical, not in a progress-through-purification perspective. There are many alternatives, but it seems difficult to conceive of a time cosmology more dramatic than the Western one.

Let us then turn to *knowledge* as a third aspect of social cosmology. Essentially it is a question of epistemology: what is the nature of knowledge, how does it come about, how is it composed? One model of the Western image of knowledge might be as follows.

In order to understand anything it has to be subdivided, fragmented into its smallest parts or units (such as atoms and then further on into the various particles), and units have to be characterised by a set of variables (at the very least in the form of dichotomies). The process is analytic, not synthetic; knowledge is built on the basis of units and variables, not holistically.[2]

As a second step variables are then related to each other, predominantly in a linear fashion, and usually bilaterally, two at the time, referred to as cause and effect, or condition and consequence (but there may be sets of variables on either side of this relationship). The relation is binary and linear; there may be relevant conditions effecting the relationship, but these are either thought away, or removed by creating artificial circumstances, e.g. laboratory conditions. These conditions are then reified and seen as more real, as more *essence* than what is nature given. The pure

---

[1] For an analysis of the Western concept of territory, see Jean Gottmann, 'The Evolution of the Concept of Territory', *Social Science Information*, XIV (1975), pp. 29–47. A critical, historical perspective on nation-states as large political units is presented in L. Kohr, *The Breakdown of Nations* (London, 1957).

[2] For discussions of the strongly mechanistic and quantifying trends in Western culture, see Lynn White, *Machina ex Deo. Essays in the Dynamism of Western Culture* (Cambridge, Mass. and London, 1968) and R. Guénon, *The Reign of Quantity as the Signs of the Times* (London, 1953).

relationship is seen as an automaton: a button is pushed and something happens: universally operational.

The third part of the knowledge production consists in an effort to tie these bilateral relations, *propositions*, deductively in a *theory*. The theory has the same structure, it is also binary and linear, but between propositions (or sets of propositions) called premises and conclusions rather than between variables, and the relation is one of inference/deduction rather than causality/conditioning. When built by those who master the craft the system can be constructed with considerable elegance, as in mathematics. At this point a certain reification also sets in: the construct may become more real than reality, the deductive, logical relations may be seen as causal relations and intellectual mastery of something through theory formation as the equivalent of political mastery or social control. In this sense mathematics becomes a part, or a tool, of the Western cosmology, not only because it is deductive, but because it is contradiction-free. The assumption, of course, is not that non-Westerners could not develop mathematics, but that they would not put it to such uses.

Alternative ways of conceiving of knowledge can be imagined. Thus, more holistic images of reality, in the West usually conceived of as 'intuitive' may attain status as basic knowledge. Further, much more complicated ways of relating variables can be imagined, including patterns of circular causation, feed-back cycles, and so on. And as to theory formation: its role may be downgraded to something less important, preferring knowledge in the form of disconnected propositions rather than very well integrated, deductive pyramids. As a matter of fact, in the latter the centrism referred to under space and time above re-enters: knowledge is organised from a hard core of central propositions (axioms), then there is a periphery of less basic propositions and there is an outside of irrelevance. Mastery of that hard core, here and now, becomes essential for anyone who wants to command the universe, meaning wanting to command man and nature;[1] the fourth and fifth aspects of Western social cosmology respectively.

Any social cosmology will have to have something to say about relations between human beings, and the basic assumption here would be that the dominant Western choice is in favour of seeing vertical relations as natural/normal, and the individual as the basic social actor. These two elements actually combine into one: the idea of struggle between individuals, in the regulated, even institutionalised form called 'competition' or in the open form referred to as 'fight'. Another way of expressing this perspective is in the idea of 'social Darwinism', it being understood that when Darwinism was accepted as a perspective on evolutionary biology it was because it fitted into Western social cosmology rather than vice versa.

[1] See J. Galtung, 'Deductive Thinking and Political Practice', *Essays in Methodology*, vol. II (Copenhagen, 1978).

Competition, struggle and fight can be seen as aspects or expressions of conflict, and a basic element in Western social cosmology can perhaps be expressed as follows: conflicts should be accompanied by processes whereby winners and losers can be identified. There are many examples of such processes: wars, battles, duels, verbal duels, legal battles, court processes in general, debates, elections, games (both of strategy and of chance), etc. Each such process serves the purpose of segregating winners from losers, thereby implementing the idea of sorting referred to under time above. It should be noted, though, that these processes can also usually be applied between groups; thereby opening for a general verticality that does not presuppose individualism. In a conflict resolution mechanism such as voting, however, individualism is built in at least in so far as individual votes are counted, defining clearly the winning and the losing parties as majorities and minorities.

Alternative social cosmologies might see the collectivity as the fundamental actor, even if the purpose basically is individual welfare – only that the individual welfare is seen as very much dependent on the situation of the collectivity. By collectivism, as opposed to individualism, however, is meant something more than the emphasis placed on various levels of social organisation: it is also a question of a certain uniformity within the collectivity, of emphasising what members have in common rather than what might distinguish them individually. In this type of social grammar individuals would be less detachable since they would have less meaning dislocated from the group, both as actors and as distinguishable entities in general. Individual mobility, both geographically and socially would be less meaningful – except on behalf of the group, in order to return and enrich the *corpus mysticum* of the group itself through outside experiences.

Then there are the possibilities of more horizontal social grammars, more based on equality and equity between actors, be they individuals or groups. As is well known from studies of political ideology there is no doubt that such social images have played a considerable role throughout Western history. But with the strong emphasis on actors, and particularly on strong actors as opposed to analysis of social structures, images of horizontal social formations are perhaps more characterised by *equality*, an equal distribution of resources on actors than by *equity*, a social structure made in such a way that it is built into the structure that all positions come out about equal in social interaction. Balance of power between countervailing forces and redistribution, out of self-interest and benevolence, rather than structural change, would be within the Western repertory.

Finally some remarks about the relationship between man and nature. In a sense it can be done very quickly because the basic aspect seems to be

---

[1] An analysis of this is found in J. Galtung, 'Institutionalized Conflict Resolution', *Peace, War and Defence, Essays in Peace Research*, vol. II (Copenhagen, 1976).

this: according to Western social cosmology there is very little doubt that man is above nature, and plays some of the same role relative to nature as God plays relative to man.[1] It is a role of *Herrschaft* rather than *Partnerschaft*, it is not a situation of communion. Just as there is an alternative cosmology to conflict resolution through the individual competition identifying winners and losers, viz. the idea of a group discussion arriving at a consensus that can retain the harmony of the group, there is also an alternative cosmology to this image of man's relation to nature: man as a part of nature, blending his economic cycles with nature's ecocycles in such a way that the two become almost indistinguishable. The Western image has, however, emphasised man's rights over nature more than his duties to nature. Perhaps the peak of this development was the view of nature found in Stalin's and Lysenko's USSR.

Not so much has been said explicitly about the last two aspects of Western social cosmology because in a sense it is not needed. They derive much of their character from the combination with the first three. Only in studying these combinations is it possible to arrive at more holistic images of the Western social cosmology, avoiding the danger of analytical sub-divisions into lists of fragmented dimensions and sub-dimensions.

Thus, combining what has been said about space and time the idea emerges that expansion from a centre in the Inner-West represents progress, when adequately purified of non-Western, racial, impurities at least at the dominant levels. The idea that other social formations than the non-Western ones represent archaic stages, so prominent in liberal and Marxist thinking, stands out as a basic rationale, making processes of conquest for westernisation one way or the other look natural/normal to the point of being not only a right, but also a *duty* of the West ('the white man's burden'; '*mission civilisatrice*'). To this should then be added the Western focus on a small number of key characteristics rather than on total configurations, and the tendency to see social transformations as caused by changes in the causal core, as defined through theory-formation. Westernisation has been seen in terms of convergence to the right faith, acculturation through educational processes, investment and economic growth ultimately leading to a transformation from traditional to modern forms, bringing non-Western societies into the Western stages of development (this is perhaps where the Western harmony between liberal and Marxist thinking is most clear), with revolutions bringing

---

[1] A critique of Western attitudes towards nature from an Islamic point of view is Seyyed Hossein Nasr, *The Encounter of Man and Nature* (London, 1968). But in addition to the dominant Western traditions there are also elements of a *Partnerschaft* attitude towards nature, cf. E. A. Armstrong, *Saint Francis: Nature Mystic* (Berkeley, Los Angeles and London, 1973) and C. J. Glacken, *Traces on the Rhodian Shore. Nature and Culture in Western Thought from Ancient Times to the End of the Eighteenth Century* (Berkeley, 1973). Generally, the history of several popular Christian sects reveals a whole record of unorthodox, 'non-Western' cosmologies, see Malcolm Lambert, *Medieval Heresy. Popular Movements from Bogomil to Hus* (London, 1977).

about transitions from capitalism to socialism of a Western type.[1] In all of this there is the same Western faith that through adequate engineering in the causal core a total transformation of society can be brought about. And when it does not happen, the reaction throughout Western history has been quick and consistent: bringing about the transformation through direct violence, exporting Western patterns through settlers and concentrating convergence on local élites, marginalising and/or eradicating those not wanting or not wanted for incorporation. An epistemology based on few variables is not necessarily ineffective, but when it is effective it may be because the instruments used are profoundly violent, cutting a heel here, a toe there, to make it fit.

In Western cosmology space, time and knowledge combine into expansionism based on a few crucial dimensions. Sooner or later this is bound to upset delicate balances in ecosystems and man–man relations, assuming that these systems are more like biological organisms in the sense of having boundaries and relying on homeostatic mechanisms for survival. They are not simple mechanical systems. The contradictions between what a social cosmology defines as not only possible but even necessary and what the systems can take will lead to a crisis, and for a cosmology to survive the crisis will have to be built into it as a basic ingredient, as natural/normal. The roots of these crises are located in the man–man and man–nature systems themselves: basic human needs, material or nonmaterial may be so undersatisfied for the masses that they either revolt or withdraw into apathy – either possibility being destructive of the social order – or the needs may be so over-satisfied for the élites through overindulgence that their time becomes absorbed by patterns of over-consumption and efforts to overcome the effects of over-consumption. Either effort would absorb energies that could be used to counteract a crisis by channelling more of the social surplus downwards to satisfy the needs of the masses (*panem et circenses*), and/or by crushing their revolts. And correspondingly for nature: when the rules of a good household are not followed, nature will exhibit surface symptoms in the form of depletion of non-renewable resources and pollution; the symptoms of destructions of homeostatic mechanisms maintaining eco-balances deeper down. Thus, on the one hand insatiable expansionism, with no built-in stop signal, and on the other hand exploitative, vertical relations to human beings and to nature, seen as normal/natural and as instruments for expansion to take place. Ultimately crises have to be the outcome, themselves seen as natural and incorporated into the social cosmology – all of this adding up to a rather consistent, but also destructive whole: the Western enterprise.

[1] For a useful survey of modernisation theories, see H.-U. Wehler, *Modernisierungstheorie und Geschichte* (Göttingen, 1975).

4. *Structural fatigue and structural transformations*

Let us now combine what has been said in section 2 above as characterisation of the sub-periods of Western history with what has been said in the preceding section about social grammars expressed as social cosmologies into one of the key hypotheses of the present essay: it is the social cosmology that defines a sub-period. It defines the micro- and macro-structures through what it has to say about man–man and man–nature relations and about spatial arrangements in general; in addition it helps defining the processes through what it has to say about time and knowledge. When a period comes to an end the social cosmology has to change; when the social cosmology changes basically, a period is coming to an end. It is the social cosmology that assures continuity, but not for ever: sooner or later major breaks will occur.

More particularly, the assumption will be that the dominant social cosmology described in the preceding section regulates and defines the basic structures and processes of Antiquity and the Modern Period. These are the Western periods *par excellence*; the Middle Ages being a non-Western time-pocket in Western history. Or, to phrase it more carefully: during the Middle Ages all the suppressed parts of the composite Western social cosmology came up to the surface, the parts that had been recessive or latent during Antiquity. There is not only a re-emergence of suppressed structures like smaller units of administration, more 'self-reliant' local economies, etc., but also the addition of new elements, such as Germanic pastoral traditions, creating the basis for a more mixed economy.[1]

Thus our point is not an attempt to state the primacy of ideas. Rather, the breakdown of west Roman culture and economy is seen as the carrier of two closely related preconditions – or necessities – of the medieval cosmology.

Instead of an expansive, outward-directed implementation of the usual Centre-Periphery cosmology with a steep gradient running from the Western top to the non-Western bottom, the opposite cosmology was invoked: inner-directed, much less concerned with transforming the outside world, engaged in work inside the West, inside Western organisations such as the relations between the tiers of the feudal system and the inner workings of the church system, and with the inner-life of human beings.

One objection here could be that if Westerners were less 'centrifugal', more inner-directed, in that period it was because they were, to a large extent, challenged by Islam in its surprisingly rapid expansion after the death of the Prophet (A.D. 632). However, the thesis is not that the West had 'lost their will to live' (see footnote no. 3, p. 358, quoting R. M.

[1] Cf. G. Duby, *The Early Growth of the European Economy*, Eng. trans. (Ithaca, N.Y., 1974), p. 26 and F. Braudel, *Civilisation matérielle et capitalisme* (Paris, 1967), pp. 79 and 88.

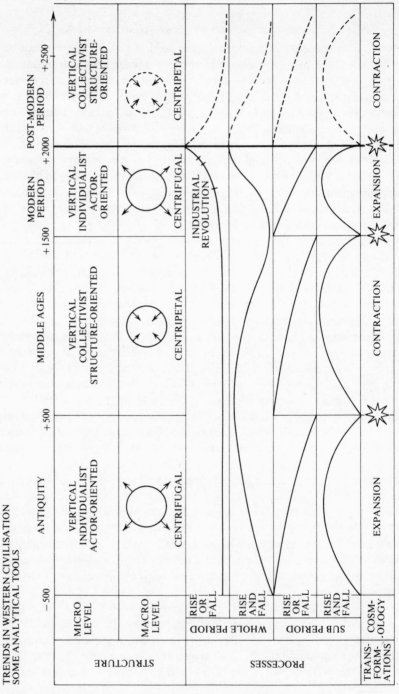

Fig. 15. Trends in Western Civilization: some analytical tools. (*See facing page.*)

Nixon) – they were stemming the tide of Islam at Tours (A.D. 732), ultimately evicting the Arabs from the Iberian Peninsula (A.D. 1492). The
thesis is that they were less bent on expansion, more on self-defence and
'inner-work'; and that seems to be the case also in the parts of Europe not
under Arab influence. It may also be noted that – except for some minor
parts of today's Yugoslavia (and some other places) they preserved their
Christian integrity even after five centuries of Ottoman rule.

The medieval time pattern was less dramatic: instead of expansion
towards the limits, production and reproduction of crises, a more regular
flow of time with more moderate oscillation at least where external events
are concerned, with drama removed from the global (meaning up to the
perimeter of the Roman Empire) macrocosm into the human microcosm.

In short, the social cosmology that was latent, carried by peripheral
forces only during Antiquity became the manifest cosmology of the
Middle Ages, and correspondingly we would assume that the social
cosmology that was latent in the Middle Ages (for instance as the ethos of
the *burghers* in the cities, gradually taking over from the landed aristocracy) became the manifest cosmology of the Modern Period.

So far a sub-period has been identified with a social cosmology and the

---

Fig. 15. In this diagram there are four phases in Western civilisation: the
three traditional historical ones (Antiquity, the Middle Ages, the 'Modern Period'),
and one future period, simply referred to as 'post-modern'. With four phases there
are three transition periods, seen as the high dramas of the history of Western civilisation. The first one is often referred to as the 'fall of the Roman Empire', a value-
loaded term – since it somehow assumes that the Roman Empire was 'good' and
should have lasted. Why not the 'rise of the Middle Ages'? (Incidentally, the
dividing line at A.D. 500 should not be taken too seriously; it should be seen not as
a line but as an interval, and many would draw its mid-point earlier, more towards
A.D. 300.) The second is the Renaissance (the fall of the Middle Ages – which
might also be dated earlier, at the 'Middle Ages Renaissance'), and the third
transition period, repeating much of what happened at the end of the Roman
Empire, is what we are experiencing now. Structurally speaking each period is seen
as dominated by certain themes; centrifugal and individualist in Antiquity
and the Modern Period; collectivist and centripetal (inward-oriented) in the Middle
Ages and the postulated post-modern period. All of this is then seen in the light
of various types of processes that take place. There are long-term processes throughout the span of Western civilisation – such as deforestation. There are oscillating
processes such as the tendency to exploit the small in society. There are processes of decline, a rapid upsurge and decline again – like Sorokin's idea about
the deterioration of morals in any belief system. And there is the Marxian idea
about contradictions that mature and then lead to the death of a certain social
formation and the birth of a new one. All of this should also be read vertically so
as to get a sense of the situation prevailing at a certain period of time, e.g. *now*
(vertical, individualist, expansionist, exploitative on the world level, demoralised,
full of contradictions) with the hypothesis of what comes next (a period with some
formal similarities with the Middle Ages).

transformation from one period into another with the transformation in social cosmology. The question then becomes: why do periods at all come to an end? And after that, the second and much more difficult question: how do transformations take place at all?

We assume that the social cosmology sets the broad definition of the period, defining the basic rules of social transactions, at the micro- and macro-levels. Within these rules an enormous amount of activity then takes place; millions, billions of transactions adding up to structures and processes most of which have to be – in conformity with the predominant social cosmology. As this happens there will be 'problems', here defined as individual, or collective, frustrations or conflicts. Goals are set, individually or collectively, in conformity with the social cosmology. But not all goals are realised; there are blocks on the road. Sometimes these blocks are seen as being due to other individuals or collectivities searching for the satisfaction of their goals, in which case there is conflict; sometimes the blocks are seen as resulting from, for instance, the limitations set by nature, in which case there are frustrations. The question is how to solve all these problems, and the answer would be: in accordance with the rules, with the social cosmology. The social cosmology sets the outer limits, within those limits growth processes may take place, things may rise and increase, including problem accumulation. The task given to the social and cognitive structure is to produce solutions to the problems.

And this is where the concept of 'structural fatigue' may be useful. In metallurgy a structure yields services up to a certain point when the metal becomes, for instance, brittle. Similarly we assume that the social structure, and the cognitive structure, both have a finite capacity for producing solutions: sooner or later that capacity will be exhausted.

One way of expressing this principle of limitation would be through the language of permutations. Any given social grammar has a limited number of combinations to offer, hence a limited number of strategies for solving problems. As the society runs through these strategies and one after the other fails to meet the bill, a more fundamental crisis is building up: that of exhausting the repertory. This in itself would not be so dangerous unless there is a clear awareness of approaching the end of the spectrum of possible solutions, either because the gamut of possibilities has been run through very recently, or because the system has a good memory even of attempts that were made in the distant past. If both the inner periphery and the outer periphery revolt, and nature at the same time shows her limitations as host to the human race, this is all difficult but not in itself dangerous to the systems as long as the élites are convinced that there are still some possible strategies left to be attempted. It is only when these strategies have been exhausted, the problems continue to accumulate unabated and there are no more games left to play that the challenge becomes overpowering. It is at this stage that the élites might abdicate even voluntarily, or let themselves be beaten out of defeatism, or even join the new forces in the search for fundamentally new formulas: the abdication of the Tsar regime in 1917 is a prime example. A more thorough sell-out of ancient customs and beliefs was the voluntary conversion, during a couple of generations, of the Roman upper classes to Christianity.[1]

That all these conditions of exhaustion should hold true at the same points in time and space will appear unlikely, so these periods of profound crisis should be seen as very rare in the history of mankind. But without speculating on their number, how would one imagine that the systems would react to such crises?

In a sense the choice is simple and given by what has been said above: *change program or else perish*. These two possibilities are not so different since the change of program, or social cosmology in other terms, is tantamount to the disappearance of a social order. It means that a period is coming to an end. It does not necessarily mean biological death, extinction, for individuals or groups. The same individuals or groups may continue, but with a new program, thus constituting a new social order. A transformation has taken place.

This leads us to another key hypothesis: the result of inability to solve problems could be extinction or subjugation to conquerors. But Western civilisation has displayed a certain capability of self-transcendence.

For this to happen one necessary condition may be that *the next program was present in the preceding social order in latent form*, in other words that the system had sufficient diversity, pluralism in its apparent unity, to harbour its own negation.[2] One could then imagine several models: that the carriers of the latent cosmology in the preceding order become the rulers in the next because they have a new program to offer, or that the rulers are more or less the same persons or the same strata, only that they learn in time to co-opt ideas and persons from the peripheries of their own creation; and/or from their own nagging doubts, from the deeper recesses of their mind. In this there is some of the same source of strength as in mature ecosystems: the more diversity, the more resilience in times of crisis. The more homogeneous and uniform the deep ideology, the more vulnerable the systems because there would be nowhere to turn for alternative solutions or – to be more precise – paradigms within which solutions can be found or the problems seen as imaginary, as products of weird ways of thinking.

Thus, it is assumed that during the late Middle Ages a more individualistic, more mobile, highly competitive, expansive and dynamic cosmology

---

[1] For the problem of social 'fatigue' in the form of declining republican *virtue*, see J. G. A. Pocock, *The Machiavellian Moment. Florentine Political Thought and the Atlantic Tradition* (Princeton, New Jersey, 1975).

[2] We share Denis de Rougemont's conclusion, after a survey of the way leading Western theorists in history have analysed the nature of Western Civilisation: 'It is noteworthy that all the authors who have contributed to our becoming aware of the unity of culture, conceive it as unity in diversity' (*The Idea of Europe*, Eng. trans. (New York and London, 1966), p. 423). Obviously the way of specifying that diversity may differ.

was present in the successor élites to the landed aristocracy, the *city burghers*. Without that kind of deep ideology much of what they did later would have become meaningless; on the other hand they also needed the concrete accumulation of capital in order to have a power base behind their claims as successor élites. Correspondingly there must have been groups towards the end of Antiquity already carrying the social cosmology that made the Middle Ages meaningful, with the monastic orders as a key expression of that social grammar (and as a reaction to the form Christianity took when it was adjusted to the organisational structure of the Roman Empire in the form of the Catholic Church, and to the structure of contradiction-free, deductive Greek thinking in the form of theology).[1]

To get an image of this process it should be remembered again that social cosmology is not identified with an explicit ideology. As deep ideology it is a set of unquestioned, usually highly implicit assumptions about the nature and relations between material objects and between non-material objects, which means that changes in social cosmology may start at any point. Thus, it would be impossible to accept the Marxist idea that such transformations necessarily have to start somewhere in the productive infrastructure. Essentially it is a question of changes not *in*, but *of* a total configuration, and it may well be that the question 'where does the change start' in itself is a wrong question, a product of Western epistemological linearity, a little bit like asking of a carousel which point started to move first. The Western effort to arrange events along a continuum of linear time is also an effort to establish causal relations, the assumption being that a necessary (but not sufficient) condition for something to be the cause is that it takes place prior to the consequence. After the time order has been established, this distinction between necessary and sufficient conditions is then easily forgotten, as in much historical writing, itself usually linear.

To use another image: if a country goes to war against another country there are usually many acts of war taking place at different points in space and time: this does not mean that the first event is the cause of the others, they are all parts of the same general 'scheme of things'. And it is this configuration the social cosmology is supposed to express; only that we do not presuppose that it can be located in the clear consciousness of some historical super-general.

There may perhaps be one particularly dramatic, even traumatic event that crystallises the issue and sets the tone, thereby becoming a collective

---

[1] This is how the main elements in Christianity is characterised by a leading non-Western philosopher, Radhakrishna: 'The Jews first invented the myth that only one religion could be true. As they, however, conceived themselves to be the "Chosen People", they did not feel a mission to convert the whole world. The Jews gave to Christianity an ethical passion and a sense of superiority; the Greeks gave the vague aspirations and mysteries of the spirit a logical form, a dogmatic setting; the Romans with their practical bent and love of organization helped to institutionalize the religion.' (*Eastern Religions and Western Thought* (Delhi, 1974), p. 10.)

reference point for the entire society. The history of the Jewish people is filled with such events, culminating in the Nazi eradication of European Jews.

Ways of organising things will then crystallise around that nucleus, as they do for a scientist who has experienced a fundamental insight, or for anybody for that matter who has known a moment of Truth and organised his or her life around that experience. After that things are done differently, first in one field (for instance arts, town-planning), then in other fields (for instance science), in still others (economic relations of production and consumption, international relations). The model would not be that one particular of these 'new ways of doing things' causes the other which then, in turn, causes the next, but that the new ways belong to the same family just as the old ways belonged to the same family. This relationship is very well expressed by C. G. Jung: 'synchronicity takes the coincidence of events in space and time as meaning something more than mere chance, namely, a peculiar interdependence of objective events among themselves as well as with the subjective (psychic) states of the observer or observers'.[1] The same type of 'non-Western' thinking is found in the more enlightened traditions of astrology: it is not the position of the celestial bodies, etc., at the moment of birth that conditions personality characteristics (or vice versa); they belong to the same family of things – exposed to the same macro-cosmic influences. Consequently, once a new logic or program is gaining acceptance, changes will have to take place accordingly in all, or almost all, fields.

More particularly it is our hypothesis that among the changes which took place between the Middle Ages and the Modern Period, it was the change in social cosmology that paved the way for modern capitalism. Technology alone did not pave the way. Innovations relating to navigation and seafaring in general, or technology making industrial production possible, eventually could have been made much earlier, in the midst of the Middle Ages, and they would either have passed unnoticed or not have been put to such uses because those uses were meaningless, even repulsive given the social cosmology of the period. The interesting point about Heron's steam-engine in Antiquity is not its technological precocity, but the way it was used: to open temple doors. Later, Byzantium developed a rather sophisticated steam and hydraulic technology – producing roaring mechanical lions, elevating thrones, and performing artificial earthquakes.

Similarly, the Chinese employed their capacity of discovery differently from the Europeans. A supreme example of their early capability is the enormous maritime expeditions – to India and East Africa in the years between 1405 and 1433.[2] These explorations were pursued by the court

[1] C. J. Jung, 'Synchronicity: An Acausal Connecting Principle', preface to *The I Ching – Book of Changes* (Princeton, 1962), p. xxiv.

[2] See J. J. L. Duyvendak, *China's Discovery of Africa* (London, 1949).

eunuchs, opponents to Confucian orthodoxy. Exotica such as giraffes were brought home. A later eunuch project in 1471 was deliberately obstructed by the mandarins. That was the end of these vast expeditions. Overseas expansion seemed less urgent and less meaningful to the Chinese rulers than to the Western ones.

After the Renaissance, when 'man woke up and discovered himself', in other words re-enacted a program of competitive individualism at the micro-level and Centre-Periphery formation (imperialism) at the macro-level, all such innovations in the West could be put to meaningful use, as defined by the cosmology. Competitive individualism could be translated economically into the free market behaviour of entrepreneurs (all the more because of the individualistic emphases in Protestantism), and expansionism, ultimately into the most remote corner of the world, would fit the new social cosmology of space and time, given the rapid accumulation of capital, products, and waste products brought about by industrialism. The knowledge part fitted the new way of treating human beings and nature, in terms of very few, specific aspects and in a universalistic manner (as labour-sellers, and in terms of chemical and physical properties); in short almost everything was prepared cosmologically for the advent of modern capitalism which would then fit like a hand in a glove, being seen as entirely natural and normal. There was only one thing missing: where was the crisis, where was the struggle, where was the catharsis needed to complete the cosmology where time was concerned?

And this is where, to our mind, Karl Marx enters the picture, completing the Western cosmological configuration.[1] Capitalism was too optimistic, its exponential formula of compound interest just shot up into the air in a much too unproblematic manner. What Karl Marx delivered was an image of crisis, thereby giving to capitalism an incentive to be on guard, ever-inventive, not to relax and indulge as capital accumulates unabated. Marx also promised struggle, and he promised catharsis – the communist future society. In this sense liberalism and Marxism not only have similarities, they also complement each other (as in the modern social democratic state) because they are both compatible with, and expressions of, the same dominant Western social cosmology. It should be added though, that there may have been changes and adaptations in the original doctrines so as to conform, with some perfection, with the Western social grammar, and that the overpowering influence of the underlying cosmology is the basic reason why the capitalist and East European societies of today become so similar.

To summarise: there is the general hypothesis that the social cosmology sets the tone for a period; and that the transformation from one social cosmology to another – or from one *ethos* to another, as it is sometimes

[1] For more details, see J. Galtung, 'Two Ways of Being Western: Some Similarities Between Marxism and Liberalism', in *Macro-History and Western Civilization*.

called – *is* the change of period. Such changes come about when the possible solutions to problems compatible with the given social cosmology have been exhausted, and there is awareness that they have been exhausted. Thus, if the élites managing the societies still have some options left, the point is not whether these options are effective or not – that is another problem – the point is that they feel secure in their adaptive capacity within the existing paradigm. We shall revert to the special hypothesis that such transformations in Western history are linked to a certain Western capacity of diversity, pluralism. Not only are there co-existing ideologies, compatible with the same deep ideology (but presenting themselves as if they were profoundly antithetical to each other); there is also a certain presence of anti-paradigmatic deep ideologies on which to build. What is the significance of this phenomenon for the future? Historically, the extreme heterogeneity of cultural models in the West was partly a function of its development at the largest inland sea in the world, the Mediterranean, at the crossroads and fringes of the great Mesopotamian and Egyptian traditions.[1] From the point of view of structural fatigue this is important because 'where multiple cultural models are available, departures from old ways become more and more probable'.[2]

The breakdown of the west Roman Empire added a new element to the Graeco-Roman heritage of diversity – *sectorial differentiation*: the way the Christian Church survived the Roman state and became an autonomous sector of society. Thus the new Church logically entailed the differentiation of the state, and later the separation of *politics* and *economy* from the social–religious control mechanisms of a traditional society.[3] (In the USSR these mechanisms are revived in the form of the Party.) To the diversity of cultural models and sectorial differentiation (segmentation) corresponded the *multiplicity of political units* in Medieval and early modern Europe.[4] The compound pluralism of this structure contained

[1] Cf. Perry Anderson, *Passages from Antiquity to Feudalism* (London, 1974), pp. 20–1; Gordon Childe, *The Prehistory of European* Society (Harmondsworth, 1958), pp. 104, 112–13, 157, 170.

[2] W. H. McNeill, *The Shape of European History* (New York, 1974), p. 34. In McNeill's view this long-term historical structure marks the 'true uniqueness of Western civilization'. (*The Rise of the West* (Chicago, 1963), p. 539.)

[3] As for the role of Machiavelli and the recognition of the relative autonomy of politics, see F. Chabod, *Machiavelli and the Renaissance* (New York, 1965), p. 116 and particularly p. 118: 'The minds of political theorists were no longer trammelled by Catholic dogma.'

For the separation of the economy, see Louis Dumont, *From Mandeville to Marx: Genesis and Triumph of the Economic Ideology* (Chicago, 1977); A. O. Hirschmann, *The Passions and the Interests. Political Arguments for Capitalism before its Triumph* (Princeton, New Jersey, 1977); Jean Baechler, *The Origins of Capitalism*, trans. E. Cooper (Oxford, 1975), ch. 7: 'The Genesis of the Market'; Jon Elster, *Leibniz et la Formation de l'Esprit Capitaliste* (Paris, 1975).

[4] See Perry Anderson, *Lineages of the Absolutist State* (London, 1974), p. 428; cf. also Childe, *The Prehistory of European Society*, p. 172. Or, as Gibbon characterises the advantages of the modern West in contrast to uni-centric Rome: '...the progress of knowledge and industry is accelerated by the emulation of so many active rivals'. (*The History of the Decline and Fall of the Roman Empire*, ed. J. B. Bury (London, 1901), vol. IV, p. 166.)

dynamic potentials for *competition, warfare, innovation*.[1] The multiplicity of political centres and their conflicts implied a continuous learning and diffusion process, very different from the kinds of knowledge monopolies known in for example, Imperial China.

Another feature of the pluralist structures is the Western tradition of mass mobilisation and mass politics, of competing élites basing their legitimacy on alternative traditions and enlisting popular support. Within the cosmology of Christian universalism popular movements in the West have generally been bent on centre-formation rather than withdrawal from the body politic. The unparallelled precocity of Western mass education is an expression of the same trend.[2]

Today there is one special reason why these historical sources of instability, change, and strength no longer are efficient for the West. Through the politics of capitalist dominance and westernisation, Western culture and commercialised technology are acquired and used everywhere, increasingly *also as weapons turned against the West*. This is a process well known from history. After long periods of subjugation (and hence communication) outside the Chinese (or Roman) Walls the 'barbarians' always ended up learning the techniques of power.[3] What has been said so far about structural fatigue applies, *a fortiori*, to Western civilisation because it is programmed to be both expansionist in space and growth-oriented in time. For a civilisation that remains stable, enclosed in the same pocket of space and with each generation fairly much simply repeating the life patterns of their ancestors there will still be problems: nature, and other societies, may present new challenges.

But Western civilisation adds to this by itself generating *new* problems, through its own dynamism – as well as new resources for solving some of those problems. The difficulty comes when the problems arising from using nature and other peoples as resources increase more quickly than the resources – and that is one way of formulating the problem of Western society today.

All societies have their 'soft underbellies' – when a society overstretches or overextends itself, the total problem surface becomes more than the society can handle – without fundamental change. To this can then be added another hypothesis: Transformations in the future will be more fundamental because of all the devices existing for storing collective memory, making it more painfully clear to people that repertories are already being exhausted. Each possible action will already be imprinted

---

[1] Cf. Peter Mathias (ed.), *Science and Society 1600–1900* (Cambridge, 1972), pp. 7–8 and p. 80: 'We may conclude that together both science and technology give evidence of a society increasingly curious, increasingly questing, increasingly on the move, on the make, having a go, increasingly seeking to experiment, wanting to improve.'

[2] See n. 1, p. 325.

[3] Cf. Braudel, *Civilisation matérielle et capitalisme*, p. 69; or Gibbon: 'before they can conquer, they must cease to be barbarous'. (*Decline and Fall*, vol. IV, p. 167.)

with memories of failures from the past. At the same time the traditional mechanism of escape, migrating to another and virgin point in space where each stone – as the Japanese say – does not carry a footprint, trying to enact the old program in a new environment, is also seriously curtailed: the earth being very well discovered by now. Of course, there is the outer space as a possible stage for re-enacting the dominant Western program, but what has come within human reach so far seems to be too little, and too late. Outer space as a possible safety valve – a new 'frontier' – for Western expansionism will probably play some role, however, as it already has done.

5. *After 'The Modern Period' – what?*

From the history of the past let us now enter the history of the future. What kind of harvest can be reaped from our speculations about the past and converted into speculations about the future?

The short formulation would be as follows: we shall assume that 'the Modern Period', characterised by rigorous enactment of the dominant Western cosmology, is coming to an end. The end may be near, it may be more remote – or, as has been the case earlier: it may be a process that only in historical perspective looks as a transformation into a new period, for instance filling the twenty-first century. It is further assumed that – for the West – the successor period in many regards will be antithetical to the present one. This does not mean that it will be identical with the Middle Ages, just as the Modern Period was not identical with Antiquity, but there will be similarities.[1] Finally, it is assumed that dominant Western social cosmology will survive during this period (which may be shorter than preceding periods because of the memory factor mentioned), and break forth again in a period after the next one, in some kind of new Renaissance where Western man once more 'rediscovers' his competitive and imperialistic ego, looking down at the time spiral, identifying himself with the heroes of the Greek and Italian city-states.

The reasoning behind these conclusions is as follows. Westernisation is seen as a wave continuing its expansion outwards, from the Inner-West, incorporating more and more of the outside into the Outer-West. There is resistance on the way such as the emergence of the East European social formations: their incorporation, at least where major features are concerned, was a relatively easy task because the social cosmology was the same. Incorporation of China will prove more difficult, perhaps even be unsuccessful, not because it is socialist, but because it is China and manages to find socialist expressions of a cosmology that is not Western.

---

[1] All the time it must be emphasised that we are speaking of *structural* similarities between the Middle Ages and the post-Modern period – such as is also done in L. S. Stavrianos, *The Promise of the Coming Dark Age* (San Francisco, 1976), pp. 2–13. That is: similarities of the kind Hicks (*A Theory of Economic History*) perceives between the Graeco-Roman and the Modern economies.

Nevertheless the outward expansion is unmistakable: Western type 'growth poles' appear in the Third World (another way of saying 'periphery'), acquire the technologies to enact Western social cosmologies that may have been more latent with them, and establish their own small and big empires. The New International Economic Order (NIEO) could be seen in this perspective as a set of instruments facilitating the diffusion of capitalism in general, and Westernisation in general, from traditional Western centres to new centres – which then would be 'Western' although not necessarily located in the West.[1] Thus, for some time to come it will still look as if the West is expanding rather than stagnating.

But a closer look at Inner-West and the outer periphery, as well as on the impact on nature, will reveal a different picture. The historical fact is that for the last five centuries or so westerners have increasingly been everywhere, other people have not been in the West except to serve Western interests, and in well-regulated numbers. An enormous energy supply has been necessary for this expansion, and the assumption is that part of it stems from the way in which Western time cosmology energises man, making him believe that *now* is particularly important, critical, and makes him unleash accumulated energies into concentrated work on a limited spectrum of reality. All over the world Western man has spun his organisation networks, with centres in the West, radiating towards the peripheries, integrating, bringing countries and people together in the centre and disintegrating, fragmenting, keeping countries and people and individuals apart from each other in the periphery. The division of labour has been clear: the most enriching tasks in the centre, the routine tasks in the periphery, and terms of exchange between labour-sellers and labour-buyers and between raw material exporters and the exporters of industrial products and services always in favour of the latter. The highly asymmetric distribution of material wealth in favour of the Inner-West bears testimony to the success of this strategy – at least in material terms.[2]

But there are also considerable costs in the Inner-West. Some of them are physical, somatic, expressing themselves in new causes of death (from serious stress, from pollution), brought about by this particular type of structure. Others are more non-material, psychological but perhaps much more important: a rapidly increasing incidence of psychological disorders of various types, possibly related to the simultaneous growth of big, impersonal organisations and structures (alpha-structures) at the same time as smaller, tighter, more human units (beta-structures) like the family are dissolving.[3]

[1] See 'Poor Countries vs. Rich, Poor People versus Rich – Whom will NIEO benefit?', *Papers*, Chair in Conflict and Peace Research, University of Oslo, No. 63.
[2] J. Galtung, 'A Structural Theory of Imperialism', *Essays in Peace Research*, vol. IV (Copenhagen, 1979).
[3] For an effort to explore how the logic of the alpha structure relates to Western type technology, see J. Galtung, *Development, Environment, Technology*, UNCTAD, Geneva,

An important aspect of the alpha-structures, emerging more and more clearly as the Modern Period took shape, is segmentation, or the division of society into sectors. Segmentation has implied the letting loose of enormous forces and creativity, of which the sectorialisation of the economy as a market system is the prime example. But this process has at the same time increased the potential for *unintended societal consequences* of the activities of the various sub-systems or sectors. This is to say that each sector is continuously in danger of running away from the others and of producing results which may be detrimental to other sectors, thereby threatening the stability of the whole society. Therefore, the process of segmentation has led to more and more attempts at bridging the incompatibilities between the different sectors through functional integration, that is: through the vast apparatus of modern *bureaucracy*, planning and social research, in public and private service.

A modern state today is run by ministries specialising in aspects of social life; a modern corporation by divisions dividing the tasks among themselves. At the human level this shows up as increasing specialisation, corresponding to increasing division of labour: the tasks becoming increasingly specialised meaning that the number of different types of jobs has increased rapidly throughout the period. From the point of view of social cosmology this can be seen as a social manifestation of the Western approach to knowledge: sub-division into knowledge particles, failure to grasp totalities. Integration becomes mechanical, or administrative from the top of the alpha-pyramids (the president's or prime minister's office; the corporation manager), not in terms of meaning. At the top there is at least an overview, at the bottom neither meaning (due to over-specialisation) nor comprehension of the structure. Related to this growth of alpha-structures at the expense of beta-structures comes increasing difficulties in finding good answers to the perennial questions: what is the meaning of it all, why do we engage in all this?

The decline of a commonly accepted 'meaning' within the modern society is accurately described in the 'Disenchantment of the world' theories of classical sociology. The present revival of various occultist traditions,[1] the exploration of Eastern religious experience, and the general trends towards the withdrawal to 'private life' are examples of a new search for meaning. The fatal consequences of this development for the present political systems in the Western world are obvious.[2] Thus the highly segmented and specialised social structure, which was erected to control and exploit nature, has – itself – become a kind of *second nature*,

---

1978; and 'Culture, Structure, and Mental Disease', *Papers*, Chair in Conflict and Peace Research, University of Oslo, No. 42.

[1] For an interesting discussion, see Mircea Eliade, *Occultism, Witchcraft, and Cultural Fashions* (Chicago, 1976), ch. 4: 'The Occult and the Modern World'.

[2] Cf. Richard Sennett, *The Fall of Public Man* (Cambridge, 1977), and J. A. Camilleri, *Civilization in Crisis. Human Prospects in a Changing World* (Cambridge, 1976).

seemingly unmanageable, producing a sense of political helplessness.[1] The very super-complexity of the modern social structure makes it vulnerable to dysfunctioning in parts of the system. A case in point is the formation of the megalopolis, the emergence of cities or urban conglomerates with more than 10 million inhabitants, such as New York, London, Tokyo – also serving as headquarters of giant alpha-structures. The frustration level of such places was borne out by the black-out in New York 13 July 1977, accompanied by mass rioting, theft and arson. In fact, the only 'positive' consequence was that the amount of murder, normally nine or ten per night dropped to five for the total period of thirty-three hours 'because people were too busy destroying shop windows and stealing goods to take the time to kill each other or murder passers-by'.[2] Such an incidence may be a small-scale prefiguration of things to come if anything like a major techno-catastrophe or an acute energy crisis will take place in the modern megalopolis.

At the same time as there seems to be increasing disintegration at the individual psychological level, and at the same as there is a decreasing sense of purpose, there are increasingly angry and effective voices of protest from the Outer-West. The voices come from the masses in the form of statistics convincingly showing how incorporation in the networks spun by Inner-West prove to be a source of disaster deepening and extending their misery, from the élites in the forms of resolutions and actions to the effect that most of these élites want to enjoy the fruits of this exploitation themselves. From nature there are disturbing signs that the levels of depletion and pollution, although far from reaching the outer limits of nature, are symptoms of homeostatic ecosystem mechanisms no longer working as they should. The real 'limits to growth', however, for the Inner-West are not so much to be found in this factor as in the efforts by the Outer-West to constitute their own economic cycles, processing their own raw materials for their own consumption, even competing with the Inner-West inside the Inner-West. In short, the Inner-West is rapidly becoming the victim of its own success.

The Inner-West, gambling on a limited range of variables usually expressed in economic terms (whether in liberal or Marxist parlance) will probably express this crisis as an imbalance between demand and supply. The supply from the industrial machines in the Inner-West could be matched with the demands from a rapidly increasing world population, but not if there is effective Outer-West competition, with a number of countries following in the wake of the first Outer-West country effectively competing with the West – Japan. In a situation of that kind there are essentially two things to do: to increase the demand, or to decrease the

---

[1] See Thomas Luckmann's lucid analysis 'On the Rationality of Institutions in Modern Life', *Archives Européennes de Sociologie*, XIV (1975), pp. 3–15.

[2] *Tribune de Genève*, 16–17 July 1977, p. 3.

supply. To increase the demand there are three possibilities: to conquer new markets, to launch new products or to launch wars in order to produce demand through destruction, of capital, capital goods and consumer goods. To decrease the supply there are also three possibilities: to lower production through unemployment, to lower production through decreased working time, and to lower production by lowering the productivity. Of these six methods the first five are essentially intra-paradigmatic, entirely consistent with dominant Western social cosmology and it is therefore assumed that they will constitute the bases of the politics of the Inner-West for the better part of the rest of the twentieth century. There will be efforts by various means to conquer or re-conquer markets in the Outer-West and the Outside. New products will be launched, and planned obsolescence, with products rapidly fading in and out of production, will be increasingly important. If this does not work: preparation for war *and* wars may be seen as the lesser of the two evils,[1] preferable to disintegration, with a whimper, not a bang, of the Western world system.

Similarly it is assumed that unemployment will become permanent but will be better distributed, leading to patterns of increased leisure for more and more people, thereby contributing even further to a sense of senselessness. In short, this is the type of limited spectrum of possibilities we had in mind in the preceding sections, and it is assumed that it will be exhausted, and lead to structural fatigue.

What is then left is to decrease productivity, which essentially means a change to another mode of production, more artisanal, less industrial. To repeat: the root of the present crisis is seen here as being related to a social cosmology no longer able to produce solutions, but the Western mind will give to the crisis an economic definition. However, for the West to see itself as changing because of pressure from the periphery would be entirely contrary to all Western assumptions about space. Hence, it is more likely that the West will come across a formula making the change look entirely endogenous, and there is very much in Western history during the Modern Period which can provide material for an alternative social cosmology and a new period. It should be noted, however, that when Western youth, disenchanted with the effects of the Inner-West, on its own people, on the Outer-West and on nature, searched other sources of inspiration in the 1960s, it was towards the East they went, like the 'hippie' trail from Iran through Afghanistan, Pakistan, and India, ending up in Katmandu.

There is no reason to assume that the present period has to end with an all-out war, with the Inner-West on the one side pitted against the Outer-West (the Third World) and the Outside (China and some others), with the position of the Soviet Union (the Middle West) being unclear. A

---

[1] Cf. Bruce Russett, 'Pearl Harbor: Deterrence theory and decision theory', *Journal of Peace Research*, vol. IV (1967), pp. 89–106.

scenario of that type would presuppose a vigorous Inner-West élite, full of faith in itself, full of visions and plans and very far from exhausting its physical and mental energy resources as well as its paradigms. If we rather assume that it is approaching the exhaustion point then no such war is necessary. Or, more precisely: it may be argued that these wars have already taken place or are taking place – the many 'local wars' after the Second World War,[1] with the fall/liberation of Saigon/Ho Chi-Minh-Ville as one event perhaps as symbolic as the fall of Byzantium in an earlier transition period. The change of paradigm will come about at the interface between the search for solutions to the imbalance crisis and the search for new meaning. The forerunners are clearly seen: the hippies, the women, student and youth revolts, the search for intermediate/alternative/human/soft/radical technologies, the quest for decentralisation into smaller, more human-sized units, the many social experiments in the Inner-West with new beta-structures (living communes, production communes, consumption communes), and so on.[2]

In short there is already in our midst material which would permit us to say something about the alternative social cosmology. Thus, as to space: it would be centripetal rather than centrifugal, the West would turn inwards (and for that reason no longer be Inner-West, but simply West). There would be less concern with conquering the world, more with conquering the inner-self and self. Most likely there would be some kind of encapsulation; for the West to engage in active dialogue, openly and admittedly with others might be too much of a change, at least to start with.

As to time: a more relaxed life pattern, a time perspective stretching toward infinity in both directions, but also more cyclical, believing less in progress and more in the contradictory nature of things.[3] Again, dialectic thinking will probably not be imported from the rich Taoist sources in China, but there will be efforts to revive Western traditions of this kind. This may, incidentally, have some bearing on the future of mathematics: in mathematics everything is permitted as long as the total system is

[1] See Istvan Kende, 'Twenty-five Years of Local Wars', *Journal of Peace Research*, VIII (1971), pp. 5–22.
[2] Surveys of these trends are given in G. Boyle and P. Harper (eds.), *Radical Technology* (London, 1976).
[3] For a peculiar kind of foresight and insight – perhaps involuntary – see the speech by former US President Richard M. Nixon, 'The President's Remarks to News Media Executives Attending a Background Briefing on Domestic Policy Initiatives', Kansas City, Missouri, 6 July 1971, in *Weekly Compilation of Presidential Documents*, 12 July 1971:

> I think of what happened to Greece and to Rome, and you see what is left – only the pillars. What has happened, of course, is that great civilizations of the past, as they have become wealthy, as they have lost their will to live, to improve, they then have become subject to the decadence that eventually destroys the civilization. The United States is now reaching that period. I am convinced, however, that we have the vitality, I believe we have the courage, I believe we have the strength out through this heartland and across the Nation that will see to it that America not only is rich and strong, *but that it is healthy in terms of moral and spiritual strength* (p. 1039) [italics ours].

Watergate struck two years later.

contradiction-free – a profoundly Western perspective that makes mathematics look like a Western conspiracy to be challenged. And the same type of reasoning would apply to Western epistemology: a search for more holistic images, less concerned with causation and deduction.[1]

As to Man–Man and Man–Nature relations: the general disenchantment with alpha-structures may lead to a growing interest in ways of life more characterised by closeness, closer to other human beings, closer to nature. For this to happen it is not necessary to re-create the extended family and the village; communes of various types and different ways of breaking down the sharp distinctions between city and countryside presently found in the Inner-West (and also in the Outer-West) could be expressions of these new cosmological traits. Less competitive individualism, more collectivism would probably be a part of this. Whether relations will be more horizontal is another matter: at this point one might perhaps expect two coexisting social ideologies, one more vertical and one more horizontal.

So much for social cosmology, and for social structure – but what about the processes mentioned in section 2? It is assumed that the growth processes particularly characteristic of the last 200 years will have to flatten out in the Inner-West, as they eventually did in the Middle Ages, but probably continue in the Outer-West and on the Outside, among other reasons because of the way in which Inner-West has imprinted the other two with its birthmark through the export of a technology that carries the code of the Inner-West. A new cycle would then start with more emphasis on non-material growth, and with much idealism, ideational energy in the Sorokin sense. There will be a new mode of production associated with this. And here the Marxist mechanism might perhaps be turned upside down: not that new means of production lead to a new mode of production; but rather that the search for a new mode of production forces the innovation of new means of production, such as the alternative technologies referred to above. But when we have some doubts about whether this social order will be horizontal it is because it is hard to believe that Westerners will not start, individually or collectively, to compete in non-material growth: who is more collectivist, more mindful of the needs of future generations in relations to nature, who has reached furthest in transcendental meditation, etc. Thus, it might even be that under the guise of some type of material equality and equity, non-material inequality and exploitation may set in between the true believers and the

---

[1] This search is partly a direct result of the spiritual barrenness of the dominant Western science and rationalist Idea of Progress. Precisely because of the limitations of Western rationalism, there is now an enormous market for all kinds of charlatans in astrology, occultism, transcendental meditation and Eastern religion operating in the West; however, these are suppressed traditions which were once widely cultivated even in the West, see e.g. R. S. Kinsman (ed.), *The Darker Vision of the Renaissance* (Berkeley, 1975) and the impressive contributions by Frances Yates.

followers. In this there may be some seeds of destruction of that social order.

If one now assumes that Western history is characterised by some kind of pendulum oscillating between centrifugal and centripetal poles of a composite social cosmology, then the next transformation leading to more expansion, which might come about the moment man really is ready to enter outer space. This will not only be by the rocket-oriented means and methods developed during the last decades, but perhaps also through the understanding of other types of 'energy' ('cosmic energy', 'psychic energy'). Expansionism presupposes space in which to expand, and space there is, provided some means of penetrating it are available. But the idea developed here would be that the next generations of Westerners will be more concerned with inner than outer space, and more with inner than outer man.

Finally, one question: what would happen if the West did not have the composite cosmology we are postulating, in other words if the dominant cosmology were ruling the ground alone? What would happen if the West were really Western? It might not even have survived the disintegration of Greek and Roman society in Antiquity. Having nothing to fall back upon, no reserve ethos instilling meaning in concerted, deliberate action, a will to survive, the Arab and Ottoman onslaughts might not have been present. To give meaning to alternative social structures and processes, when there is no or little hope that 'soon it is all over and good old days are back again' is not something easily improvised. Walking on two cosmological legs, so to speak, gives strength because of the apparent redundancy, at least as long as there is sufficient tolerance in Western society to keep the other leg, the alternative leg, sufficiently alive. For that reason ours is not a prediction of doom, of end to Western society. Just to the contrary, it is actually a prediction of possible emergence of the West's *alter ego*, less materially affluent, but also less exploitative of itself, others and nature. Arnold Toynbee has to some extent a similar perspective:[1]

natives' and Nature have now worked together to bring the growth of the mechanized countries' GNP to a halt... the terms of trade are turning against the 'developed' countries in favour of the 'developing' countries, how will the peoples of the 'developed' countries react? They are going to find themselves in a permanent stage of siege, in which the material conditions of life will be at least as austere as they were during the last two world wars.

And he goes on to say:

When the peoples of the 'developed' countries are forced, by events, to recognize the inexorability of the new facts, their first impulse will be to kick against the pricks. And, since they will be powerless to assault either 'Natives' or Nature, they will assault one another. Within each of the beleaguered 'developed' countries there will be a bitter struggle for the control of their diminished resources.

[1] Arnold Toynbee, in his article 'After the Age of Affluence...', *The Observer*, 14 April 1974 (on the occasion of his eighty-fifth birthday).

One might add: *between* these countries, for this might also constitute a backdrop against which the East–West conflict (between blocks within the Western civilisation, that is) gets a new meaning. Toynbee sees 'a severely regimented way – imposed by a ruthless authoritarian Government' as the most likely outcome 'under the coming siege conditions', not mentioning the possibility of a change in social cosmology under these circumstances. It is, however, such a change that we are predicting.

6. *Conclusion*

To return to the metaphor of the introduction: one's image of traffic will vary according to the altitude from which one is observing it. Micro-history and macro-history represent two different levels, one is not better or worse than the other, they complement each other, but most resources in recent years have been devoted to micro- rather than to macro-history. There are fewer canons of research available in the latter, fewer rules of the game. No doubt more efforts at the macro-levels will change that situation, thereby enriching the total image of the historical process.

Very much on purpose the presentation has avoided, almost completely, references to names and events just as the observer in a helicopter hovering above the city traffic will make reports without names of drivers, and without any mention of smaller incidents. He would concentrate on the centripetal movements in the morning hours of people driving from home to work and the centrifugal movements seven or eight hours later of people driving from work to home; seeing those as the major wave movements, combined with a number of vehicles of other shapes (he might call them delivery cars) running in all directions throughout the day. At night there is mainly silence. Would anybody dare say that this person understands nothing of traffic?

Without making any similar claims let us only conclude with the shortest statement we could imagine about Western history. It is not expansion, nor introspection that are typically Western (certainly not the latter), but the pendular movement between relatively extreme positions facilitated by the contradictory nature of Western society, a contradiction the West itself does its best to deny and to eliminate. In that contradiction lies some of the vigour of the Western civilisation, in its expansive modes some of its major dangers, to nature, to others and to itself. A deeper understanding of this may lead to more self-control. The alternative may be a night – in which there is mainly silence.

INDEX

abortion laws, and birth rate, 112, 113
administration, *see* bureaucracy
agnosticism, 303
agriculture
  capitalist, 131, 132, 134, 135, 138, 228;
    manors in, 126
  demographic pressure, and progress in
    (1750–1800), 100–1
  development of technology of, 54, 66, and
    science of, 148–51
  intensive, of the Netherlands, 116, 132–3
  new crops in, 31, 33–4, 34–5
  percentage of workforce in (different
    countries, 1900), 110
  pests and diseases in, consequent on mono-
    culture and intensification, 17, 35–6
  productivity of, 133–4, 146, 325–6
  terms of exchange between industrial
    products and products of (France
    1350–1450 and after 1500), 100
Agrippa, Cornelius, 252
agronomy, 138–9, 149
  of the Enlightenment, 127
Albania, 81, 88
Althusius, admits right of common people to
  disobedience, 221
America, Europe and grasslands of, 29, 30,
  31, 35
Anabaptism, 221, 226
anachronism, development of awareness of,
  275
anarchism, 244
antibiotics, 37
Antiquity, in the West (to fall of Western
  Roman Empire, A.D. 476), 320, 345
  relations between societies in, 323
  roughly equivalent to Marx's slavery
    stage, 327
  social cosmology of, 343
  social structure of, 322
Aquinas, Thomas, 251
architecture, change from Gothic to Renaissance, 11
Aristotelianism, 250, 251, 252, 253
  triumph of mechanistic philosophy over,
    261
armaments
  cost of, 216
  production and accumulation of, 213–15
  see also guns
armies
  defeats of, and revolutions, 247

difficulties of equipping and financing
  before Industrial Revolution, 206, 208
  English Parliamentary, 230–1
  growth of, and growth of bureaucracy,
    189, 205
  professionalisation of, 211
  railways and, 212
  size of, as chief factor in victory, 204,
    210
  size of, in different countries: (1475–1760),
    204, 205; (1792–1815), 210; (1870–1944),
    214
artisans: urban, 44–5, and village, 44, 117
arts
  fine, and practical, of medieval urban
    artisans, 44–5
  secularisation of, 54, 314–15
  serial history of, 9
  social cosmology reflected in, 337
assemblies: provincial or national, representing propertied classes, 221–2, 228
astrology, 251, 261, 312, 349
astronomy: mathematisation of, by Copernicus, 252–3, Kepler, 253, Laplace, 262,
  and Newton, 256–9
atom bomb, 216
Australasia, Europe and grasslands of, 29,
  31, 35
Austria, population of: birth rate, 111;
  infant mortality, 107; percentage under
  20, 110; rate of natural growth, 108
Austria-Hungary (Habsburg Empire)
  migration from, 110
  population of, 99, 103
  revolts in, 224, 233
  standing army of (from 1570s), 205
Averroes, 250

Babœuf, F. N., 238
Bacon, Francis, 252, 259–61, 276
Bacon, Roger, 276
balance of power, formulation of concept of
  (16th cent.), 6
Balkans, population of, 95; fertility index,
  105
Baltic
  quasi-colonies along, 34
  raw materials from, 31
baptisms, registers of, 94
barbarians, outside Roman and Chinese
  walls, always ended by learning techniques of power, 352